Lecture Notes in Artificial Intell

Edited by J. G. Carbonell and J. Siekmann

Subseries of Lecture Notes in Computer Science

Iyad Rahwan   Simon Parsons   Chris Reed (Eds.)

Argumentation in Multi-Agent Systems

4th International Workshop, ArgMAS 2007
Honolulu, HI, USA, May 15, 2007
Revised Selected and Invited Papers

 Springer

Series Editors

Jaime G. Carbonell, Carnegie Mellon University, Pittsburgh, PA, USA
Jörg Siekmann, University of Saarland, Saarbrücken, Germany

Volume Editors

Iyad Rahwan
British University in Dubai, Faculty of Informatics
P.O. Box 502216, Dubai, UAE
E-mail: irahwan@acm.org

Simon Parsons
City University of New York, Brooklyn College
Department of Computer and Information Science
2900 Bedford Avenue, Brooklyn, NY 11210, USA
E-mail: parsons@sci.brooklyn.cuny.edu

Chris Reed
University of Dundee, Department of Applied Computing
Dundee DD1 4HN, UK
E-mail: chris.reed@computing.dundee.ac.uk

Library of Congress Control Number: 2008923358

CR Subject Classification (1998): I.2.11, I.2, C.2.4, H.5.2-3

LNCS Sublibrary: SL 7 – Artificial Intelligence

ISSN   0302-9743
ISBN-10   3-540-78914-6 Springer Berlin Heidelberg New York
ISBN-13   978-3-540-78914-7 Springer Berlin Heidelberg New York

Springer is a part of Springer Science+Business Media

springer.com

© Springer-Verlag Berlin Heidelberg 2008

Typesetting: Camera-ready by author, data conversion by Scientific Publishing Services, Chennai, India
Printed on acid-free paper   SPIN: 12249947   06/3180   5 4 3 2 1 0

Preface

This volume presents the latest developments in the growing area of research at the interface of argumentation theory and multiagent systems. This area has grown tremendously with many papers appearing in the recent special issue of the *Artificial Intelligence Journal* on "Argumentation" and the special issue of *IEEE Intelligent Systems* on "Argumentation Technologies."

Over the last few years, argumentation has been gaining increasing importance in multiagent systems, mainly as a vehicle for facilitating rational interaction (i.e., interaction which involves the giving and receiving of reasons). This is because argumentation provides tools for designing, implementing, and analyzing sophisticated forms of interaction among rational agents. Argumentation has made solid contributions to the practice of multiagent dialogues. Application domains include: legal disputes, business negotiation, labor disputes, team formation, scientific inquiry, deliberative democracy, ontology reconciliation, risk analysis, scheduling, and logistics. A single agent may also use argumentation techniques to perform its individual reasoning because it needs to make decisions under complex preferences policies, in a highly dynamic environment.

Most papers in this volume appeared in the proceedings of the 4th International Workshop on Argumentation in Multiagent Systems (ArgMAS 2007), which took place in Honolulu, USA, in conjunction with the International Joint Conference on Autonomous Agents and Multiagent Systems (AAMAS). This continues the success of the ArgMAS workshop series, which took place in tandem with AAMAS in New York in 2004, Utrecht in 2005, and Hakodate in 2006.

Often we have invited papers on the topic of argumentation in multiagent systems from the main AAMAS conference as well as other major conferences for the given year, in order to bring together the very best of the year's work on argumentation in MAS into a single volume. This time, we invited revised papers on argumentation in MAS from both AAMAS 2007 and AAAI 2007. These additional contributions were selected on the basis of their scientific quality and relevance to the topics emphasized here. Our objective has been to offer a comprehensive and up-to-date overview of this rapidly evolving landscape, as we did in the previous volumes of this series which were all published by Springer (LNAI 3366, LNAI 4049, and LNAI 4766).

The book is organized into three parts, each addressing an important problem in argumentation and multiagent systems. Part I focuses on issues pertaining to dialogue. This part opens with an invited paper from AAMAS 2007 by Leila Amgoud, Yannis Dimopoulos, and Pavlos Moraitis. This paper attempts to generalize and unify various models of argument-based negotiation (ABN) found in the literature. The second paper, by Iyad Rahwan, Philippe Pasquier, Liz Sonenberg, and Frank Dignum, formally explores some intuitions behind the usefulness of ABN models. Most work on argumentation addresses two-party dialogues. To address dialogues involving more than two agents, in an agent society, Enrico Oliva, Peter McBurney, and Andrea Omicini present a framework based on the notion of co-argumentation artifact.

The fourth paper in Part I is an invited paper by Simon Parsons, Peter McBurney, Elizabeth Sklar, and Michael Wooldridge, which addresses the question of *relevance* in dialogues. The authors show how relevance can help agents decide which arguments to present (i.e., how to carry out a dialogue according to a given protocol). The following paper, by Laurent Perrussel, Sylvie Doutre, Jean-Marc Thévenin, and Peter McBurney, presents a protocol that allows agents to argue about the right to access information in a given context.

Recently, an argument interchange format (AIF) has been proposed by the "argumentation in AI" community. However, while the AIF is quite mature in its representation of static argument structures, its ability to capture argument-based dialogues is still underdeveloped. Part I concludes with a paper by Sanjay Modgil and Jarred McGinnis that addresses this issue.

Part II focuses on using argumentation to automate or support various single-agent reasoning tasks. This part opens with an invited AAAI 2007 paper by Nicolás D. Rotstein, Alejandro J. García, and Guillermo R. Simari. This paper describes how argumentation can be used to mechanize reasoning in belief desire intention (BDI) agents. In a multiagent system, such BDI agents are faced with possibly conflicting social norms. To address the conflict between norms, beliefs, desires, and intentions, the following paper, by Dorian Gaertner and Francesca Toni, presents a framework grounded in assumption-based argumentation.

In the third paper in this part, Maxime Morge presents a framework for practical reasoning based on argumentation. Part II then closes with a paper, by Cássia Trojahn, Paulo Quaresma, Renata Vieira, on using argumentation as a model for mapping multiple conflicting ontologies.

Part III addresses an exciting new area in argumentation research, namely, the relationship between models of argumentation and models of learning. The section opens with an invited paper from AAMAS 2007, by Leila Amgoud and Mathieu Serrurier, on using argumentation to perform classification tasks normally found in the machine learning literature. This is followed by another AAMAS 2007 invited paper, by Santi Ontañón and Enric Plaza, which explores the use of argumentation to facilitate dialogue among cased-based reasoning agents who want to learn jointly from past cases. This part is wrapped up by two papers by Wataru Makiguchi and Hajime Sawamura on the relationship between symbolic and neural network-based models of argumentation.

We conclude this preface by extending our gratitude to the members of the Steering Committee and members of the Program Committee, who together helped make the ArgMAS workshop a success. We also thank the authors for their enthusiasm to submit papers to the workshop, and for revising their papers on time for inclusion in this book.

December 2007   Iyad Rahwan
                                                                                                         Simon Parsons
                                                                                                            Chris Reed

Organization

Program Chairs

Simon Parsons	City University of New York, USA
Iyad Rahwan	British University in Dubai, UAE
	(Fellow) University of Edinburgh, UK
Chris Reed	University of Dundee, UK

ArgMAS Steering Committee

Antonis Kakas	University of Cyprus, Cyprus
Nicolas Maudet	Université Paris Dauphine, France
Peter McBurney	University of Liverpool, UK
Pavlos Moraitis	Paris Descartes University, France
Simon Parsons	City University of New York, USA
Iyad Rahwan	British University in Dubai, UAE
	(Fellow) University of Edinburgh, UK
Chris Reed	University of Dundee, UK

Program Committee

Leila Amgoud	IRIT, France
Katie Atkinson	University of Liverpool, UK
Jamal Bentahar	Laval University, Canada
Guido Boella	Università di Torino, Italy
Brahim Chaib-draa	Laval University, Canada
Carlos Chesnevar	Universitat de Lleida, Spain
Frank Dignum	Utrecht University, The Netherlands
Rogier van Eijk	Utrecht University, The Netherlands
Frank Guerin	University of Aberdeen, UK
Joris Hulstijn	Utrecht University, The Netherlands
Anthony Hunter	University College, London, UK
Antonis Kakas	University of Cyprus, Cyprus
Nikos Karacapilidis	University of Patras, Greece
Nishan Karunatillake	University of Southampton, UK
Nicolas Maudet	Université Paris Dauphine, France
Peter McBurney	University of Liverpool, UK
Jarred McGinnis	Royal Holloway, University of London, UK
Sanjay Modgil	Cancer Research UK
Pavlos Moraitis	Paris Descartes University, France

Table of Contents

Part III: Argumentation and Learning

A General Framework for Argumentation-Based Negotiation

Leila Amgoud[1], Yannis Dimopoulos[2], and Pavlos Moraitis[3]

[1] IRIT – CNRS, 118, route de Narbonne, 31062 Toulouse, France
amgoud@irit.fr
[2] University of Cyprus, 75 Kallipoleos Str. PO Box 20537, Cyprus
yannis@cs.ucy.ac.cy
[3] Paris-Descartes University, 45 rue des Saints-Peres, 75270 Paris, France
pavlos@math-info.univ-paris5.fr

Abstract. This paper proposes a *unified* and *general* framework for argumentation-based negotiation, in which the role of argumentation is formally analyzed. The framework makes it possible to study the outcomes of an argumentation-based negotiation. It shows what an *agreement* is, how it is related to the theories of the agents, when it is possible, and how this can be attained by the negotiating agents in this case. It defines also the notion of *concession*, and shows in which situation an agent will make one, as well as how it influences the evolution of the dialogue.

Keywords: Argumentation, Negotiation.

1 Introduction

Roughly speaking, negotiation is a process aiming at finding some compromise or consensus between two or several agents about some matters of collective agreement, such as pricing products, allocating resources, or choosing candidates. Negotiation models have been proposed for the design of systems able to bargain in an optimal way with other agents for example, buying or selling products in e-commerce.

Different approaches to automated negotiation have been investigated, including *game-theoretic* approaches (which usually assume complete information and unlimited computation capabilities) [11], *heuristic-based* approaches which try to cope with these limitations [6], and *argumentation-based* approaches [2,3,7,8,9,12,13] which emphasize the importance of exchanging information and explanations between negotiating agents in order to mutually influence their behaviors (e.g. an agent may concede a goal having a small priority), and consequently the outcome of the dialogue. Indeed, the two first types of settings do not allow for the addition of information or for exchanging opinions about offers. Integrating argumentation theory in negotiation provides a good means for supplying additional information and also helps agents to convince each other by adequate arguments during a negotiation dialogue. Indeed, an offer supported

I. Rahwan, S. Parsons, and C. Reed (Eds.): ArgMAS 2007, LNAI 4946, pp. 1–17, 2008.

by a good argument has a better chance to be accepted by an agent, and can also make him reveal his goals or give up some of them. The basic idea behind an argumentation-based approach is that by exchanging arguments, the theories of the agents (i.e. their mental states) may evolve, and consequently, the status of offers may change. For instance, an agent may reject an offer because it is not acceptable for it. However, the agent may change its mind if it receives a strong argument in favor of this offer.

Several proposals have been made in the literature for modeling such an approach. However, the work is still preliminary. Some researchers have mainly focused on relating argumentation with protocols. They have shown how and when arguments in favor of offers can be computed and exchanged. Others have emphasized on the decision making problem. In [3,7], the authors argued that selecting an offer to propose at a given step of the dialogue is a decision making problem. They have thus proposed an argumentation-based decision model, and have shown how such a model can be related to the dialogue protocol.

In most existing works, there is no deep formal analysis of the role of argumentation in negotiation dialogues. It is not clear how argumentation can influence the outcome of the dialogue. Moreover, basic concepts in negotiation such as *agreement* (i.e. *optimal solutions*, or *compromise*) and *concession* are neither defined nor studied.

This paper aims to propose a *unified* and *general* framework for argumentation-based negotiation, in which the role of argumentation is formally analyzed, and where the existing systems can be restated. In this framework, a negotiation dialogue takes place between two agents on a set $\mathcal{O}$ of offers, whose structure is not known. The goal of a negotiation is to find among elements of $\mathcal{O}$, an offer that satisfies more or less the preferences of both agents. Each agent is supposed to have a *theory* represented in an abstract way. A theory consists of a set $\mathcal{A}$ of arguments whose structure and origin are not known, a function specifying for each possible offer in $\mathcal{O}$, the arguments of $\mathcal{A}$ that support it, a non specified conflict relation among the arguments, and finally a preference relation between the arguments. The status of each argument is defined using Dung's acceptability semantics. Consequently, the set of offers is partitioned into four subsets: *acceptable*, *rejected*, *negotiable* and *non-supported* offers. We show how an agent's theory may evolve during a negotiation dialogue. We define formally the notions of concession, compromise, and optimal solution. Then, we propose a protocol that allows agents i) to exchange offers and arguments, and ii) to make concessions when necessary. We show that dialogues generated under such a protocol terminate, and even reach optimal solutions when they exist.

This paper is organized as follows: Section 2 introduces the logical language that is used in the rest of the paper. Section 3 defines the agents as well as their theories. In section 4, we study the properties of these agents' theories. Section 5 defines formally an argumentation-based negotiation, shows how the theories of agents may evolve during a dialogue, and how this evolution may influence the outcome of the dialogue. Two kinds of outcomes: optimal solution and compromise are defined, and we show when such outcomes are reached.

Section 6 illustrates our general framework through some examples. Section 7 compares our formalism with existing ones. Section 8 concludes and presents some perspectives. Due to lack of space, the proofs are not included. These last are in a technical report that we will make available online at some later time.

2   The Logical Language

In what follows, $\mathcal{L}$ will denote a logical language, and $\equiv$ is an equivalence relation associated with it.

From $\mathcal{L}$, a set $\mathcal{O} = \{o_1, \dots, o_n\}$ of n *offers* is identified, such that $\nexists o_i, o_j \in \mathcal{O}$ such that $o_i \equiv o_j$. This means that the offers are different. Offers correspond to the different alternatives that can be exchanged during a negotiation dialogue. For instance, if the agents try to decide the place of their next meeting, then the set $\mathcal{O}$ will contain different towns.

Different *arguments* can be built from $\mathcal{L}$. The set $\text{Args}(\mathcal{L})$ will contain all those arguments. By argument, we mean a *reason* in believing or of doing something.

In [3], it has been argued that the selection of the best offer to propose at a given step of the dialogue is a decision problem. In [4], it has been shown that in an argumentation-based approach for decision making, two kinds of arguments are distinguished: arguments supporting choices (or decisions), and arguments supporting beliefs. Moreover, it has been acknowledged that the two categories of arguments are formally defined in different ways, and they play different roles. Indeed, an argument in favor of a decision, built both on an agent's beliefs and goals, tries to justify the choice; whereas an argument in favor of a belief, built only from beliefs, tries to destroy the decision arguments, in particular the beliefs part of those decision arguments. Consequently, in a negotiation dialogue, those two kinds of arguments are generally exchanged between agents. In what follows, the set $\text{Args}(\mathcal{L})$ is then divided into two subsets: a subset $\text{Args}_o(\mathcal{L})$ of arguments supporting offers, and a subset $\text{Args}_b(\mathcal{L})$ of arguments supporting beliefs. Thus, $\text{Args}(\mathcal{L}) = \text{Args}_o(\mathcal{L}) \cup \text{Args}_b(\mathcal{L})$. As in [5], in what follows, we consider that the structure of the arguments is not known.

Since the knowledge bases from which arguments are built may be inconsistent, the arguments may be conflicting too. In what follows, those conflicts will be captured by the relation $\mathcal{R}_{\mathcal{L}}$, thus $\mathcal{R}_{\mathcal{L}} \subseteq \text{Args}(\mathcal{L}) \times \text{Args}(\mathcal{L})$. Three assumptions are made on this relation: First the arguments supporting different offers are conflicting. The idea behind this assumption is that since offers are exclusive, an agent has to choose only one at a given step of the dialogue. Note that, the relation $\mathcal{R}_{\mathcal{L}}$ is not necessarily symmetric between the arguments of $\text{Args}_b(\mathcal{L})$. The second hypothesis says that arguments supporting the same offer are also conflicting. The idea here is to return the strongest argument among these arguments. The third condition does not allow an argument in favor of an offer to attack an argument supporting a belief. This avoids wishful thinking. Formally:

Definition 1. $\mathcal{R}_{\mathcal{L}} \subseteq \text{Args}(\mathcal{L}) \times \text{Args}(\mathcal{L})$ *is a* conflict relation *among arguments such that:*

- $\forall a, a' \in \mathrm{Args}_o(\mathcal{L})$, s.t. $a \neq a'$, $a\ \mathcal{R}_{\mathcal{L}}\ a'$
- $\nexists\ a \in \mathrm{Args}_o(\mathcal{L})$ and $a' \in \mathrm{Args}_b(\mathcal{L})$ such that $a\ \mathcal{R}_{\mathcal{L}}\ a'$

Note that the relation $\mathcal{R}_{\mathcal{L}}$ is not symmetric. This is due to the fact that arguments of $\mathrm{Args}_b(\mathcal{L})$ may be conflicting but not necessarily in a symmetric way. In what follows, we assume that the set $\mathrm{Args}(\mathcal{L})$ of arguments is finite, and each argument is attacked by a finite number of arguments.

3   Negotiating Agents Theories and Reasoning Models

In this section we define formally the negotiating agents, i.e. their theories, as well as the reasoning model used by those agents in a negotiation dialogue.

3.1   Negotiating Agents Theories

Agents involved in a negotiation dialogue, called negotiating agents, are supposed to have theories. In this paper, the theory of an agent will not refer, as usual, to its mental states (i.e. its beliefs, desires and intentions). However, it will be encoded in a more abstract way in terms of the arguments owned by the agent, a conflict relation among those arguments, a preference relation between the arguments, and a function that specifies which arguments support offers of the set $\mathcal{O}$. We assume that an agent is aware of all the arguments of the set $\mathrm{Args}(\mathcal{L})$. The agent is even able to express a preference between any pair of arguments. This does not mean that the agent will use all the arguments of $\mathrm{Args}(\mathcal{L})$, but it encodes the fact that when an agent receives an argument from another agent, it can interpret it correctly, and it can also compare it with its own arguments. Similarly, each agent is supposed to be aware of the conflicts between arguments. This also allows us to encode the fact that an agent can recognize whether the received argument is in conflict or not with its arguments. However, in its theory, only the conflicts between its own arguments are considered.

Definition 2 (Negotiating agent theory). *Let $\mathcal{O}$ be a set of n offers. A negotiating agent theory is a tuple $\langle \mathcal{A},\ \mathcal{F},\ \succeq,\ \mathcal{R},\ \mathrm{Def} \rangle$ such that:*

- $\mathcal{A} \subseteq \mathrm{Args}(\mathcal{L})$.
- $\mathcal{F} \colon \mathcal{O} \to 2^{\mathcal{A}}$ *s.t* $\forall i, j$ *with* $i \neq j$, $\mathcal{F}(o_i) \cap \mathcal{F}(o_j) = \emptyset$. *Let* $\mathcal{A}_{\mathcal{O}} = \cup \mathcal{F}(o_i)$ *with* $i = 1, \ldots, n$.
- $\succeq\ \subseteq \mathrm{Args}(\mathcal{L}) \times \mathrm{Args}(\mathcal{L})$ *is a partial preorder denoting a preference relation between arguments.*
- $\mathcal{R} \subseteq \mathcal{R}_{\mathcal{L}}$ *such that* $\mathcal{R} \subseteq \mathcal{A} \times \mathcal{A}$
- $\mathrm{Def} \subseteq \mathcal{A} \times \mathcal{A}$ *such that* $\forall\ a, b \in \mathcal{A}$, *a defeats b, denoted a* Def *b iff:*
  - $a\ \mathcal{R}\ b$, *and*
  - *not* $(b \succeq a)$

The function $\mathcal{F}$ returns the arguments supporting offers in $\mathcal{O}$. In [4], it has been argued that any decision may have arguments supporting it, called arguments PRO, and arguments against it, called arguments CONS. Moreover, these two types of arguments are not necessarily conflicting. For simplicity reasons, in this paper we consider only arguments PRO. Moreover, we assume that an argument cannot support two distinct offers. However, it may be the case that an offer is not supported at all by arguments, thus $\mathcal{F}(o_i)$ may be empty.

Example 1. *Let $\mathcal{O} = \{o_1, o_2, o_3\}$ be a set of offers. The following theory is the theory of agent i:*

- $\mathcal{A} = \{a_1, a_2, a_3, a_4\}$
- $\mathcal{F}(o_1) = \{a_1\}$, $\mathcal{F}(o_2) = \{a_2\}$, $\mathcal{F}(o_3) = \emptyset$. *Thus,* $\mathcal{A}_o = \{a_1, a_2\}$
- $\succeq \; = \{(a_1, a_2), (a_2, a_1), (a_3, a_2), (a_4, a_3)\}$
- $\mathcal{R} = \{a_1, a_2), (a_2, a_1), (a_3, a_2), (a_4, a_3)\}$
- $\mathtt{Def} = \{(a_4, a_3), (a_3, a_2)\}$

From the above definition of agent theory, the following hold:

Property 1
- $\mathtt{Def} \subseteq \mathcal{R}$
- $\forall a, a' \in \mathcal{F}(o_i)$, $a \; \mathcal{R} \; a'$.

3.2   The Reasoning Model

From the theory of an agent, one can define the argumentation system used by that agent for reasoning about the offers and the arguments, i.e. for computing the status of the different offers and arguments.

Definition 3 (Argumentation system). *Let $\langle \mathcal{A}, \mathcal{F}, \succeq, \mathcal{R}, \mathtt{Def} \rangle$ be the theory of an agent. The* argumentation system *of that agent is the pair $\langle \mathcal{A}, \mathtt{Def} \rangle$.*

In [5], different acceptability semantics have been introduced for computing the status of arguments. These are based on two basic concepts, *defence* and *conflict-free*, defined as follows:

Definition 4 (Defence/conflict-free). *Let $S \subseteq \mathcal{A}$.*

- *S defends an argument a iff each argument that defeats a is defeated by some argument in S.*
- *S is* conflict-free *iff there exist no a, a' in S such that $a \; \mathtt{Def} \; a'$.*

Definition 5 (Acceptability semantics). *Let S be a conflict-free set of arguments, and let $\mathcal{T}: 2^{\mathcal{A}} \to 2^{\mathcal{A}}$ be a function such that $\mathcal{T}(S) = \{a \mid a$ is defended by $S\}$.*

- *S is a* complete extension *iff $S = \mathcal{T}(S)$.*
- *S is a* preferred extension *iff S is a maximal (w.r.t set $\subseteq$) complete extension.*
- *S is a* grounded extension *iff it is the smallest (w.r.t set $\subseteq$) complete extension.*

Let $\mathcal{E}_1, \ldots, \mathcal{E}_x$ denote the different extensions under a given semantics.

Note that there is only one grounded extension. It contains all the arguments that are not defeated, and those arguments that are defended directly or indirectly by non-defeated arguments.

Theorem 1. *Let $\langle \mathcal{A}, \mathtt{Def} \rangle$ the argumentation system defined as shown above.*

1. *It may have $x \geq 1$ preferred extensions.*
2. *The grounded extensions is $\mathcal{S} = \bigcup^{i \geq 1} \mathcal{T}(\emptyset)$.*

Note that when the grounded extension (or the preferred extension) is empty, this means that there is no acceptable offer for the negotiating agent.

Example 2. *In example 1, there is one preferred extension, $\mathcal{E} = \{a_1, a_2, a_4\}$.*

Now that the acceptability semantics is defined, we are ready to define the status of any argument.

Definition 6 (Argument status). *Let $\langle \mathcal{A}, \mathtt{Def} \rangle$ be an argumentation system, and $\mathcal{E}_1, \ldots, \mathcal{E}_x$ its extensions under a given semantics. Let $a \in \mathcal{A}$.*

1. *a is accepted iff $a \in \mathcal{E}_i$, $\forall \mathcal{E}_i$ with $i = 1, \ldots, x$.*
2. *a is rejected iff $\nexists \mathcal{E}_i$ such that $a \in \mathcal{E}_i$.*
3. *a is undecided iff a is neither accepted nor rejected. This means that a is in some extensions and not in others.*

Note that $\mathcal{A} = \{a | a \text{ is accepted}\} \cup \{a | a \text{ is rejected}\} \cup \{a | a \text{ is undecided}\}$.

Example 3. *In example 1, the arguments a_1, a_2 and a_4 are accepted, whereas the argument a_3 is rejected.*

As said before, agents use argumentation systems for reasoning about offers. In a negotiation dialogue, agents propose and accept offers that are acceptable for them, and reject bad ones. In what follows, we will define the status of an offer. According to the status of arguments, one can define four statuses of the offers as follows:

Definition 7 (Offers status). *Let $o \in \mathcal{O}$.*

- *The offer o is acceptable for the negotiating agent iff $\exists\, a \in \mathcal{F}(o)$ such that a is accepted. $\mathcal{O}_a = \{o_i \in \mathcal{O}, \text{ such that } o_i \text{ is acceptable}\}$.*
- *The offer o is rejected for the negotiating agent iff $\forall\, a \in \mathcal{F}(o)$, a is rejected. $\mathcal{O}_r = \{o_i \in \mathcal{O}, \text{ such that } o_i \text{ is rejected}\}$.*
- *The offer o is negotiable iff $\forall\, a \in \mathcal{F}(o)$, a is undecided. $\mathcal{O}_n = \{o_i \in \mathcal{O}, \text{ such that } o_i \text{ is negotiable}\}$.*
- *The offer o is non-supported iff it is neither acceptable, nor rejected or negotiable. $\mathcal{O}_{ns} = \{o_i \in \mathcal{O}, \text{ such that } o_i \text{ is non-supported offers}\}$.*

Example 4. *In example 1, the two offers o_1 and o_2 are acceptable since they are supported by accepted arguments, whereas the offer o_3 is non-supported since it has no argument in its favor.*

From the above definitions, the following results hold:

Property 2. *Let $o \in \mathcal{O}$.*

- $\mathcal{O} = \mathcal{O}_a \cup \mathcal{O}_r \cup \mathcal{O}_n \cup \mathcal{O}_{ns}$.
- *The set $\mathcal{O}_a$ may contain more than one offer.*

From the above partition of the set $\mathcal{O}$ of offers, a preference relation between offers is defined. Let $\mathcal{O}_x$ and $\mathcal{O}_y$ be two subsets of $\mathcal{O}$. $\mathcal{O}_x \triangleright \mathcal{O}_y$ means that any offer in $\mathcal{O}_x$ is preferred to any offer in the set $\mathcal{O}_y$. We can write also for two offers o_i, o_j, $o_i \triangleright o_j$ iff $o_i \in \mathcal{O}_x$, $o_j \in \mathcal{O}_y$ and $\mathcal{O}_x \triangleright \mathcal{O}_y$.

Definition 8 (Preference between offers). *Let $\mathcal{O}$ be a set of offers, and $\mathcal{O}_a$, $\mathcal{O}_r$, $\mathcal{O}_n$, $\mathcal{O}_{ns}$ its partition. $\mathcal{O}_a \triangleright \mathcal{O}_n \triangleright \mathcal{O}_{ns} \triangleright \mathcal{O}_r$.*

Example 5. *In example 1, we have $o_1 \triangleright o_3$, and $o_2 \triangleright o_3$. However, o_1 and o_2 are indifferent.*

4   The Structure of Negotiation Theories

In this section, we study the properties of the system developed above. We first show that in the particular case where $\mathcal{A} = \mathcal{A}_\mathcal{O}$ (ie. all of the agent's arguments refer to offers), the corresponding argumentation system will return at least one non-empty preferred extension.

Theorem 2. *Let $\langle \mathcal{A}, \mathtt{Def} \rangle$ an argumentation system such that $\mathcal{A} = \mathcal{A}_\mathcal{O}$. Then the system returns at least one extension $\mathcal{E}$, such that $|\mathcal{E}| \geq 1$.*

We now present some results that demonstrate the importance of indifference in negotiating agents, and more specifically its relation to acceptable outcomes. We first show that the set $\mathcal{O}_a$ may contain several offers when their corresponding accepted arguments are indifferent w.r.t the preference relation $\succeq$.

Theorem 3. *Let o_1, $o_2 \in \mathcal{O}$. o_1, $o_2 \in \mathcal{O}_a$ iff $\exists\, a_1 \in \mathcal{F}(o_1)$, $\exists\, a_2 \in \mathcal{F}(o_2)$, such that a_1 and a_2 are accepted and are indifferent w.r.t $\succeq$ (i.e. $a \succeq b$ and $b \succeq a$).*

We now study acyclic preference relations that are defined formally as follows.

Definition 9 (Acyclic relation). *A relation R on a set A is acyclic if there is no sequence $a_1, a_2, \ldots, a_n \in A$, with $n > 1$, such that $(a_i, a_{i+1}) \in R$ and $(a_n, a_1) \in R$, with $1 \leq i < n$.*

Note that acyclicity prohibits pairs of arguments a, b such that $a \succeq b$ and $b \succeq a$, ie., an acyclic preference relation disallows indifference.

Theorem 4. *Let $\mathcal{A}$ be a set of arguments, $\mathcal{R}$ the attacking relation of $\mathcal{A}$ defined as $\mathcal{R} \subseteq \mathcal{A} \times \mathcal{A}$, and $\succeq$ an acyclic relation on $\mathcal{A}$. Then for any pair of arguments $a, b \in \mathcal{A}$, such that $(a, b) \in \mathcal{R}$, either $(a, b) \in \mathtt{Def}$ or $(b, a) \in \mathtt{Def}$ (or both).*

The previous result is used in the proof of the following theorem that states that acyclic preference relations sanction extensions that support exactly one offer.

Theorem 5. *Let $\mathcal{A}$ be a set of arguments, and $\succeq$ an acyclic relation on $\mathcal{A}$. If $\mathcal{E}$ is an extension of $<\mathcal{A}, \text{Def}>$, then $|\mathcal{E} \cap \mathcal{A}_{\mathcal{O}}| = 1$.*

An immediate consequence of the above is the following.

Property 3. *Let $\mathcal{A}$ be a set of arguments such that $\mathcal{A} = \mathcal{A}_{\mathcal{O}}$. If the relation $\succeq$ on $\mathcal{A}$ is acyclic, then each extension $\mathcal{E}_i$ of $<\mathcal{A}, \text{Def}>$, $|\mathcal{E}_i| = 1$.*

Another direct consequence of the above theorem is that in acyclic preference relations, arguments that support offers can participate in only one preferred extension.

Theorem 6. *Let $\mathcal{A}$ be a set of arguments, and $\succeq$ an acyclic relation on $\mathcal{A}$. Then the preferred extensions of $\langle \mathcal{A}, \text{Def} \rangle$ are pairwise disjoint w.r.t arguments of $\mathcal{A}_{\mathcal{O}}$.*

Using the above results we can prove the main theorem of this section that states that negotiating agents with acyclic preference relations do not have acceptable offers.

Theorem 7. *Let $\langle \mathcal{A}, \mathcal{F}, \mathcal{R}, \succeq, \text{Def} \rangle$ be a negotiating agent such that $\mathcal{A} = \mathcal{A}_{\mathcal{O}}$ and $\succeq$ is an acyclic relation. Then the set of accepted arguments w.r.t $\langle \mathcal{A}, \text{Def} \rangle$ is emtpy. Consequently, the set of acceptable offers, $\mathcal{O}_a$ is empty as well.*

5   Argumentation-Based Negotiation

In this section, we define formally a protocol that generates argumentation-based negotiation dialogues between two negotiating agents P and C. The two agents negotiate about an object whose possible values belong to a set $\mathcal{O}$. This set $\mathcal{O}$ is supposed to be known and the same for both agents. For simplicity reasons, we assume that this set does not change during the dialogue. The agents are equipped with theories denoted respectively $\langle \mathcal{A}^P, \mathcal{F}^P, \succeq^P, \mathcal{R}^P, \text{Def}^P \rangle$, and $\langle \mathcal{A}^C, \mathcal{F}^C, \succeq^C, \mathcal{R}^C, \text{Def}^C \rangle$. Note that the two theories may be different in the sense that the agents may have different sets of arguments, and different preference relations. Worst yet, they may have different arguments in favor of the same offers. Moreover, these theories may *evolve* during the dialogue.

5.1   Evolution of the Theories

Before defining formally the evolution of an agent's theory, let us first introduce the notion of dialogue moves, or moves for short.

Definition 10 (Move). *A move is a tuple $m_i = \langle p_i, a_i, o_i, t_i \rangle$ such that:*

- $p_i \in \{P, C\}$
- $a_i \in \text{Args}(\mathcal{L}) \cup \theta$[1]
- $o_i \in \mathcal{O} \cup \theta$
- $t_i \in \mathcal{N}^*$ *is the target of the move, such that $t_i < i$*

---

[1] In what follows θ denotes the fact that no argument, or no offer is given.

The function Player *(resp.* Argument, Offer, Target*) returns the player of the move (i.e. p_i) (resp. the argument of a move, i.e a_i, the offer o_i, and the target of the move, t_i). Let $\mathcal{M}$ denote the set of all the moves that can be built from $\langle \{P, C\}, \mathrm{Arg}(\mathcal{L}), \mathcal{O}\rangle$.*

Note that the set $\mathcal{M}$ is finite since $\mathrm{Arg}(\mathcal{L})$ and $\mathcal{O}$ are assumed to be finite. Let us now see how an agent's theory evolves and why. The idea is that if an agent receives an argument from another agent, it will add the new argument to its theory. Moreover, since an argument may bring new information for the agent, thus new arguments can emerge. Let us take the following example:

Example 6. *Suppose that an agent P has the following propositional knowledge base: $\Sigma_P = \{x, y \rightarrow z\}$. From this base one cannot deduce z. Let's assume that this agent receives the following argument $\{a, a \rightarrow y\}$ that justifies y. It is clear that now P can build an argument, say $\{a, a \rightarrow y, y \rightarrow z\}$ in favor of z.*

In a similar way, if a received argument is in conflict with the arguments of the agent i, then those conflicts are also added to its relation $\mathcal{R}^i$. Note that new conflicts may arise between the original arguments of the agent and the ones that emerge after adding the received arguments to its theory. Those new conflicts should also be considered. As a direct consequence of the evolution of the sets $\mathcal{A}^i$ and $\mathcal{R}^i$, the defeat relation Def^i is also updated.

The initial theory of an agent i, (i.e. its theory before the dialogue starts), is denoted by $\langle \mathcal{A}_0^i, \mathcal{F}_0^i, \succeq_0^i, \mathcal{R}_0^i, \mathrm{Def}_0^i\rangle$, with $i \in \{P, C\}$. Besides, in this paper, we suppose that the preference relation $\succeq^i$ of an agent does not change during the dialogue.

Definition 11 (Theory evolution). *Let $m_1, \ldots, m_t, \ldots, m_j$ be a sequence of moves. The theory of an agent i at a step $t > 0$ is: $\langle \mathcal{A}_t^i, \mathcal{F}_t^i, \succeq_t^i, \mathcal{R}_t^i, \mathrm{Def}_t^i\rangle$ such that:*

- $\mathcal{A}_t^i = \mathcal{A}_0^i \cup \{a_i, i = 1, \ldots, t, a_i = \mathrm{Argument}(m_i)\} \cup \mathcal{A}'$ *with* $\mathcal{A}' \subseteq \mathrm{Args}(\mathcal{L})$
- $\mathcal{F}_t^i = \mathcal{O} \rightarrow 2^{\mathcal{A}_t^i}$
- $\succeq_t^i = \succeq_0^i$
- $\mathcal{R}_t^i = \mathcal{R}_0^i \cup \{(a_i, a_j) \mid a_i = \mathrm{Argument}(m_i),$
  $a_j = \mathrm{Argument}(m_j), i, j \leq t, \text{ and } a_i \, \mathcal{R}_\mathcal{L} \, a_j\} \cup \mathcal{R}'$ *with* $\mathcal{R}' \subseteq \mathcal{R}_\mathcal{L}$
- $\mathrm{Def}_t^i \subseteq \mathcal{A}_t^i \times \mathcal{A}_t^i$

The above definition captures the *monotonic* aspect of an argument. Indeed, an argument cannot be removed. However, its status may change. An argument that is accepted at step t of the dialogue by an agent may become rejected at step $t + i$. Consequently, the status of offers also change. Thus, the sets $\mathcal{O}_a$, $\mathcal{O}_r$, $\mathcal{O}_n$, and $\mathcal{O}_{ns}$ may change from one step of the dialogue to another. That means for example that some offers could move from the set $\mathcal{O}_a$ to the set $\mathcal{O}_r$ and vice-versa. Note that in the definition of $\mathcal{R}_t$, the relation $\mathcal{R}_\mathcal{L}$ is used to denote a conflict between exchanged arguments. The reason is that, such a conflict may not be in the set $\mathcal{R}^i$ of the agent i. Thus, in order to recognize such conflicts, we have supposed that the set $\mathcal{R}_\mathcal{L}$ is known to the agents. This allows us to capture the situation where an agent is able to prove an argument that it was unable to prove before, by incorporating in its beliefs some information conveyed through the exchange of arguments with another agent. This, unknown at the beginning of the dialogue argument, could give to this agent the possibility to defeat an argument that it could not by using its initial arguments. This could even lead to a change of the status of these initial arguments and this change would lead to the one of the associated offers' status.

In what follows, $\mathcal{O}^i_{t,x}$ denotes the set of offers of type x, where $x \in \{a, n, r, ns\}$, of the agent i at step t of the dialogue. In some places, we can use for short the notation $\mathcal{O}^i_t$ to denote the partition of the set $\mathcal{O}$ at step t for agent i. Note that we have: $\text{not}(\mathcal{O}^i_{t,x} \subseteq \mathcal{O}^i_{t+1,x})$.

5.2   The Notion of Agreement

As said in the introduction, negotiation is a process aiming at finding an *agreement* about some matters. By agreement, one means a solution that satisfies to the largest possible extent the preferences of both agents. In case there is no such solution, we say that the negotiation fails. In what follows, we will discuss the different kinds of solutions that may be reached in a negotiation. The first one is the *optimal* solution. An optimal solution is the best offer for both agents. Formally:

Definition 12 (Optimal solution). *Let $\mathcal{O}$ be a set of offers, and $o \in \mathcal{O}$. The offer o is an* optimal *solution at a step $t \geq 0$ iff $o \in \mathcal{O}^P_{t,a} \cap \mathcal{O}^C_{t,a}$*

Such a solution does not always exist since agents may have conflicting preferences. Thus, agents make *concessions* by proposing/accepting less preferred offers.

Definition 13 (Concession). *Let $o \in \mathcal{O}$ be an offer. The offer o is a concession for an agent i iff $o \in \mathcal{O}^i_x$ such that $\exists \mathcal{O}^i_y \neq \emptyset$, and $\mathcal{O}^i_y \vartriangleright \mathcal{O}^i_x$.*

During a negotiation dialogue, agents exchange first their most preferred offers, and if these last are rejected, they make concessions. In this case, we say that their best offers are no longer *defendable*. In an argumentation setting, this means that the agent has already presented all its arguments supporting its best offers, and it has no counter argument against the ones presented by the other agent. Formally:

Definition 14 (Defendable offer). *Let $\langle \mathcal{A}^i_t, \mathcal{F}^i_t, \succeq^i_t, \mathcal{R}^i_t, \text{Def}^i_t \rangle$ be the theory of agent i at a step $t > 0$ of the dialogue. Let $o \in \mathcal{O}$ such that $\exists j \leq t$ with $\text{Player}(m_j) = i$ and $\text{offer}(m_j) = o$. The offer o is defendable by the agent i iff:*

- *$\exists a \in \mathcal{F}^i_t(o)$, and $\nexists k \leq t$ s.t. $\text{Argument}(m_k) = a$, or*
- *$\exists a \in \mathcal{A}^t \backslash \mathcal{F}^i_t(o)$ s.t. a Def^i_t b with*
  - *$\text{Argument}(m_k) = b$, $k \leq t$, and $\text{Player}(m_k) \neq i$*
  - *$\nexists l \leq t$, $\text{Argument}(m_l) = a$*

The offer o is said non-defendable *otherwise and ND^i_t is the set of non-defendable offers of agent i at a step t.*

5.3   Negotiation Dialogue

Now that we have shown how the theories of the agents evolve during a dialogue, we are ready to define formally an argumentation-based negotiation dialogue. For that purpose, we need to define first the notion of a legal continuation.

Definition 15 (Legal move). *A move m is a* legal continuation *of a sequence of moves $m_1, \ldots, m_l$ iff $\nexists j, k < l$, such that:*

- $\texttt{Offer}(m_j) = \texttt{Offer}(m_k)$, *and*
- $\texttt{Player}(m_j) \neq \texttt{Player}(m_k)$

The idea here is that if the two agents present the same offer, then the dialogue should terminate, and there is no longer possible continuation of the dialogue.

Definition 16 (Argumentation-based negotiation). *An* argumentation-based negotiation dialogue d *between two agents P and C is a non-empty sequence of moves $m_1, \ldots, m_l$ such that:*

- $p_i = P$ *iff i is even, and $p_i = C$ iff i is odd*
- $\texttt{Player}(m_1) = P$, $\texttt{Argument}(m_1) = \theta$, $\texttt{Offer}(m_1) \neq \theta$, *and* $\texttt{Target}(m_1) = \theta^2$
- $\forall \; m_i$, *if* $\texttt{Offer}(m_i) \neq \theta$, *then* $\texttt{Offer}(m_i) \rhd o_j$, $\forall \; o_j \in \mathcal{O} \backslash (\mathcal{O}_{i,r}^{\texttt{Player}(m_i)} \cup ND_i^{\texttt{Player}(m_i)})$
- $\forall i = 1, \ldots, l$, m_i *is a legal continuation of $m_1, \ldots, m_{i-1}$*
- $\texttt{Target}(m_i) = m_j$ *such that $j < i$ and $\texttt{Player}(m_i) \neq \texttt{Player}(m_j)$*
- *If* $\texttt{Argument}(m_i) \neq \theta$, *then:*
  - *if* $\texttt{Offer}(m_i) \neq \theta$ *then* $\texttt{Argument}(m_i) \in \mathcal{F}(\texttt{Offer}(m_i))$
  - *if* $\texttt{Offer}(m_i) = \theta$ *then* $\texttt{Argument}(m_i) \; \texttt{Def}_i^{\texttt{Player}(m_i)} \; \texttt{Argument}(\texttt{Target}(m_i))$
- $\nexists \; i, j \leq l$ *such that $m_i = m_j$*
- $\nexists \; m \in \mathcal{M}$ *such that m is a legal continuation of $m_1, \ldots, m_l$*

Let $\mathcal{D}$ be the set of all possible dialogues.

The first condition says that the two agents take turn. The second condition says that agent P starts the negotiation dialogue by presenting an offer. Note that, in the first turn, we suppose that the agent does not present an argument. This assumption is made for strategical purposes. Indeed, arguments are exchanged as soon as a conflict appears. The third condition ensures that agents exchange their best offers, but never the rejected ones. This condition takes also into account the concessions that an agent will have to make if it was established that a concession is the only option for it at the current state of the dialogue. Of course, as we have shown in a previous section, an agent may have several good or acceptable offers. In this case, the agent chooses one of them randomly. The fourth condition ensures that the moves are legal. This condition allows to terminate the dialogue as soon as an offer is presented by both agents. The fifth condition allows agents to backtrack. The sixth condition says that an agent may

---

[2] The first move has no target.

send arguments in favor of offers, and in this case the offer should be stated in the same move. An agent can also send arguments in order to defeat arguments of the other agent. The next condition prevents repeating the same move. This is useful for avoiding loops. The last condition ensures that all the possible legal moves have been presented.

The outcome of a negotiation dialogue is computed as follows:

Definition 17 (Dialogue outcome). *Let* $d = m_1, \ldots, m_l$ *be a argumentation-based negotiation dialogue. The outcome of this dialogue, denoted* Outcome, *is* Outcome(d) = Offer(m_l) *iff* $\exists j < l$ *s.t.* Offer(m_l) = Offer(m_j), *and* Player $(m_l) \neq$ Player(m_j). *Otherwise,* Outcome$(d) = \theta$.

Note that when Outcome$(d) = \theta$, the negotiation fails, and no agreement is reached by the two agents. However, if Outcome$(d) \neq \theta$, the negotiation succeeds, and a solution that is either optimal or a compromise is found.

Theorem 8. $\forall d_i \in \mathcal{D}$, *the argumentation-based negotiation* d_i *terminates.*

The above result is of great importance, since it shows that the proposed protocol avoids loops, and dialogues terminate. Another important result shows that the proposed protocol ensures to reach an optimal solution if it exists. Formally:

Theorem 9 (Completeness). *Let* $d = m_1, \ldots, m_l$ *be a argumentation-based negotiation dialogue. If* $\exists t \leq l$ *such that* $\mathcal{O}_{t,a}^P \cap \mathcal{O}_{t,a}^C \neq \emptyset$, *then* Outcome$(d) \in \mathcal{O}_{t,a}^P \cap \mathcal{O}_{t,a}^C$.

We show also that the proposed dialogue protocol is sound in the sense that, if a dialogue returns a solution, then that solution is for sure a compromise. In other words, that solution is a "common agreement" at a given step of the dialogue. We show also that if the negotiation fails, then there is no possible solution.

Theorem 10 (Soundness). *Let* $d = m_1, \ldots, m_l$ *be a argumentation-based negotiation dialogue.*

1. *If* Outcome$(d) = o$, *(o $\neq \theta$), then* $\exists t \leq l$ *such that* $o \in \mathcal{O}_{t,x}^P \cap \mathcal{O}_{t,y}^C$, *with* $x, y \in \{a, n, ns\}$.
2. *If* Outcome$(d) = \theta$, *then* $\forall t \leq l$, $\mathcal{O}_{t,x}^P \cap \mathcal{O}_{t,y}^C = \emptyset$, $\forall x, y \in \{a, n, ns\}$.

A direct consequence of the above theorem is the following:

Property 4. *Let* $d = m_1, \ldots, m_l$ *be a argumentation-based negotiation dialogue. If* Outcome$(d) = \theta$, *then* $\forall t \leq l$,

- $\mathcal{O}_{t,r}^P = \mathcal{O}_{t,a}^C \cup \mathcal{O}_{t,n}^C \cup \mathcal{O}_{t,ns}^C$, *and*
- $\mathcal{O}_{t,r}^C = \mathcal{O}_{t,a}^P \cup \mathcal{O}_{t,n}^P \cup \mathcal{O}_{t,ns}^P$.

6   Illustrative Examples

In this section we will present some examples in order to illustrate our general framework.

Example 7 (No argumentation). *Let $\mathcal{O} = \{o_1, o_2\}$ be the set of all possible offers. Let P and C be two agents, equipped with the same theory: $\langle \mathcal{A}, \mathcal{F}, \succeq, \mathcal{R}, \text{Def} \rangle$ such that $\mathcal{A} = \emptyset$, $\mathcal{F}(o_1) = \mathcal{F}(o_2) = \emptyset$, $\succeq = \emptyset$, $\mathcal{R} = \emptyset$, $\text{Def} = \emptyset$. In this case, it is clear that the two offers o_1 and o_2 are non-supported. The proposed protocol (see Definition 16) will generate one of the following dialogues:*

P: $m_1 = \langle P, \theta, o_1, 0 \rangle$
C: $m_2 = \langle C, \theta, o_1, 1 \rangle$

This dialogue ends with o_1 as a compromise. Note that this solution is not considered as optimal since it is not an acceptable offer for the agents.

P: $m_1 = \langle P, \theta, o_1, 0 \rangle$
C: $m_2 = \langle C, \theta, o_2, 1 \rangle$
P: $m_3 = \langle P, \theta, o_2, 2 \rangle$

This dialogue ends with o_2 as a compromise.

P: $m_1 = \langle P, \theta, o_2, 0 \rangle$
C: $m_2 = \langle C, \theta, o_2, 1 \rangle$

This dialogue also ends with o_2 as a compromise. The last possible dialgue is the following that ends with o_1 as a compromise.

P: $m_1 = \langle P, \theta, o_2, 0 \rangle$
C: $m_2 = \langle C, \theta, o_1, 1 \rangle$
P: $m_3 = \langle P, \theta, o_1, 2 \rangle$

Note that in the above example, since there is no exchange of arguments, the theories of both agents do not change. Let us now consider the following example.

Example 8 (Static theories). *Let $\mathcal{O} = \{o_1, o_2\}$ be the set of all possible offers. The theory of agent P is $\langle \mathcal{A}^P, \mathcal{F}^P, \succeq^P, \mathcal{R}^P, \text{Def}^P \rangle$ such that: $\mathcal{A}^P = \{a_1, a_2\}$, $\mathcal{F}^P(o_1) = \{a_1\}$, $\mathcal{F}^P(o_2) = \{a_2\}$, $\succeq^P = \{(a_1, a_2)\}$, $\mathcal{R}^P = \{(a_1, a_2), (a_2, a_1)\}$, $\text{Def}^P = \{a_1, a_2\}$. The argumentation system $\langle \mathcal{A}^P, \text{Def}^P \rangle$ of this agent will return a_1 as an accepted argument, and a_2 as a rejected one. Consequently, the offer o_1 is acceptable and o_2 is rejected.*

The theory of agent C is $\langle \mathcal{A}^C, \mathcal{F}^C, \succeq^C, \mathcal{R}^C, \text{Def}^C \rangle$ such that: $\mathcal{A}^C = \{a_1, a_2\}$, $\mathcal{F}^C(o_1) = \{a_1\}$, $\mathcal{F}^C(o_2) = \{a_2\}$, $\succeq^C = \{(a_2, a_1)\}$, $\mathcal{R}^C = \{(a_1, a_2), (a_2, a_1)\}$, $\text{Def}^C = \{a_2, a_1\}$. The argumentation system $\langle \mathcal{A}^C, \text{Def}^C \rangle$ of this agent will return a_2 as an accepted argument, and a_1 as a rejected one. Consequently, the offer o_2 is acceptable and o_1 is rejected.

The only possible dialogues that may take place between the two agents are the following:

P: $m_1 = \langle P, \theta, o_1, 0 \rangle$
C: $m_2 = \langle C, \theta, o_2, 1 \rangle$
P: $m_3 = \langle P, a_1, o_1, 2 \rangle$
C: $m_4 = \langle C, a_2, o_2, 3 \rangle$

The second possible dialogue is the following:

P: $m_1 = \langle P, \theta, o_1, 0 \rangle$
C: $m_2 = \langle C, a_2, o_2, 1 \rangle$
P: $m_3 = \langle P, a_1, o_1, 2 \rangle$
C: $m_4 = \langle C, \theta, o_2, 3 \rangle$

Both dialogues end with failure. Note that in both dialogues, the theories of both agents do not change. The reason is that the exchanged arguments are already known to both agents. The negotiation fails because the agents have conflicting preferences.

Let us now consider an example in which argumentation will allow agents to reach an agreement.

Example 9 (Dynamic theories). *Let $\mathcal{O} = \{o_1, o_2\}$ be the set of all possible offers. The theory of agent P is $\langle \mathcal{A}^P, \mathcal{F}^P, \succeq^P, \mathcal{R}^P, \texttt{Def}^P \rangle$ such that: $\mathcal{A}^P = \{a_1, a_2\}$, $\mathcal{F}^P(o_1) = \{a_1\}$, $\mathcal{F}^P(o_2) = \{a_2\}$, $\succeq^P = \{(a_1, a_2), (a_3, a_1)\}$, $\mathcal{R}^P = \{(a_1, a_2), (a_2, a_1)\}$, $\texttt{Def}^P = \{(a_1, a_2)\}$. The argumentation system $\langle \mathcal{A}^P, \texttt{Def}^P \rangle$ of this agent will return a_1 as an accepted argument, and a_2 as a rejected one. Consequently, the offer o_1 is acceptable and o_2 is rejected.*

The theory of agent C is $\langle \mathcal{A}^C, \mathcal{F}^C, \succeq^C, \mathcal{R}^C, \texttt{Def}^C \rangle$ such that: $\mathcal{A}^C = \{a_1, a_2, a_3\}$, $\mathcal{F}^C(o_1) = \{a_1\}$, $\mathcal{F}^C(o_2) = \{a_2\}$, $\succeq^C = \{(a_1, a_2), (a_3, a_1)\}$, $\mathcal{R}^C = \{(a_1, a_2), (a_2, a_1), (a_3, a_1)\}$, $\texttt{Def}^C = \{(a_1, a_2), (a_3, a_1)\}$. The argumentation system $\langle \mathcal{A}^C, \texttt{Def}^C \rangle$ of this agent will return a_3 and a_2 as accepted arguments, and a_1 as a rejected one. Consequently, the offer o_2 is acceptable and o_1 is rejected.

The following dialogue may take place between the two agents:

P: $m_1 = \langle P, \theta, o_1, 0 \rangle$
C: $m_2 = \langle C, \theta, o_2, 1 \rangle$
P: $m_3 = \langle P, a_1, o_1, 2 \rangle$
C: $m_4 = \langle C, a_3, \theta, 3 \rangle$
C: $m_5 = \langle P, \theta, o_2, 4 \rangle$

At step 4 of the dialogue, the agent P receives the argument a_3 from P. Thus, its theory evolves as follows: $\mathcal{A}^P = \{a_1, a_2, a_3\}$, $\mathcal{R}^P = \{(a_1, a_2), (a_2, a_1), (a_3, a_1)\}$, $\texttt{Def}^P = \{(a_1, a_2), (a_3, a_1)\}$. At this step, the argument a_1 which was accepted will become rejected, and the argument a_2 which was at the beginning of the dialogue rejected will become accepted. Thus, the offer o_2 will be acceptable for the agent, whereas o_1 will become rejected. At this step 4, the offer o_2 is acceptable for both agents, thus it is an optimal solution. The dialogue ends by returning this offer as an outcome.

7   Related Work

Argumentation has been integrated in negotiation dialogues at the early nineties by Sycara [12]. In that work, the author has emphasized the advantages of using argumentation in negotiation dialogues, and a specific framework has been introduced. In [8], the different types of arguments that are used in a negotiation dialogue, such as threats and rewards, have been discussed. Moreover, a particular framework for negotiation have been proposed. In [9,13], different other frameworks have been proposed. Even if all these frameworks are based on different logics, and use different definitions of arguments, they all have at their heart an exchange of offers and arguments. However, none of those proposals explain when arguments can be used within a negotiation, and how they should be dealt with by the agent that receives them. Thus the protocol for handling arguments was missing. Another limitation of the above frameworks is the fact that the argumentation frameworks they use are quite poor, since they use a very simple acceptability semantics. In [2] a negotiation framework that fills the gap has been suggested. A protocol that handles the arguments was proposed. However, the notion of concession is not modeled in that framework, and it is not clear what is the status of the outcome of the dialogue. Moreover, it is not clear how an agent chooses the offer to propose at a given step of the dialogue. In [1,7], the authors have focused mainly on this decision problem. They have proposed an argumentation-based decision framework that is used by agents in order to choose the offer to propose or to accept during the dialogue. In that work, agents are supposed to have a beliefs base and a goals base.

Our framework is more general since it does not impose any specific structure for the arguments, the offers, or the beliefs. The negotiation protocol is general as well. Thus this framework can be instantiated in different ways by creating, in such manner, different specific argumentation-based negotiation frameworks, all of them respecting the same properties. Our framework is also a unified one because frameworks like the ones presented above can be represented within this framework. For example the decision making mechanism proposed in [7] for the evaluation of arguments and therefore of offers, which is based on a priority relation between mutually attacked arguments, can be captured by the relation *defeat* proposed in our framework. This relation takes simultaneously into account the attacking and preference relations that may exist between two arguments.

8   Conclusions and Future Work

In this paper we have presented a unified and general framework for argumentation-based negotiation. Like any other argumentation-based negotiation framework, as it is evoked in (e.g. [10]), our framework has all the advantages that argumentation-based negotiation approaches present when related to the negotiation approaches based either on game theoretic models (see e.g. [11]) or heuristics ([6]). This work is a first attempt to formally define the role of argumentation in the negotiation process. More precisely, for the first time, it formally establishes the link that exists between the status of the arguments and the offers they support, it defines the notion of concession and shows how it influences the evolution of the negotiation, it determines how the theories of agents evolve during the dialogue and performs an analysis of the negotiation outcomes. It is also the first time where a study of the formal properties of the negotiation theories of the agents as well as of an argumentative negotiation dialogue is presented.

Our future work concerns several points. A first point is to relax the assumption that the set of possible offers is the same to both agents. Indeed, it is more natural to assume that agents may have different sets of offers. During a negotiation dialogue, these sets will evolve. Arguments in favor of the new offers may be built from the agent theory. Thus, the set of offers will be part of the agent theory. Another possible extension of this work would be to allow agents to handle both arguments PRO and CONS offers. This is more akin to the way human take decisions. Considering both types of arguments will refine the evaluation of the offers status. In the proposed model, a preference relation between offers is defined on the basis of the partition of the set of offers. This preference relation can be refined. For instance, among the acceptable offers, one may prefer the offer that is supported by the strongest argument. In [4], different criteria have been proposed for comparing decisions. Our framework can thus be extended by integrating those criteria. Another interesting point to investigate is that of considering negotiation dialogues between two agents with different profiles. By profile, we mean the criterion used by an agent to compare its offers.

References

1. Amgoud, L., Belabbes, S., Prade, H.: Towards a formal framework for the search of a consensus between autonomous agents. In: Proceedings of the 4th International Joint Conference on Autonomous Agents and Multi-Agents systems, pp. 537–543 (2005)
2. Amgoud, L., Parsons, S., Maudet, N.: Arguments, dialogue, and negotiation. In: Proceedings of the 14th European Conference on Artificial Intelligence (2000)
3. Amgoud, L., Prade, H.: Reaching agreement through argumentation: A possibilistic approach. In: 9 th International Conference on the Principles of Knowledge Representation and Reasoning, KR 2004 (2004)
4. Amgoud, L., Prade, H.: Explaining qualitative decision under uncertainty by argumentation. In: 21st National Conference on Artificial Intelligence, AAAI 2006, pp. 16–20 (2006)
5. Dung, P.M.: On the acceptability of arguments and its fundamental role in nonmonotonic reasoning, logic programming and n-person games. Artificial Intelligence 77, 321–357 (1995)
6. Jennings, N.R., Faratin, P., Lumuscio, A.R., Parsons, S., Sierra, C.: Automated negotiation: Prospects, methods and challenges. International Journal of Group Decision and Negotiation (2001)
7. Kakas, A., Moraitis, P.: Adaptive agent negotiation via argumentation. In: Proceedings of the 5th International Joint Conference on Autonomous Agents and Multi-Agents systems, pp. 384–391 (2006)
8. Kraus, S., Sycara, K., Evenchik, A.: Reaching agreements through argumentation: A logical model and implementation. Artificial Intelligence 104, 1–69 (1998)
9. Parsons, S., Jennings, N.R.: Negotiation through argumentation—a preliminary report. In: Proceedings of the 2nd International Conference on Multi Agent Systems, pp. 267–274 (1996)

10. Rahwan, I., Ramchurn, S.D., Jennings, N.R., McBurney, P., Parsons, S., Sonenberg, E.: Argumentation-based negotiation. Knowledge Engineering Review 18(4), 343–375 (2003)
11. Rosenschein, J., Zlotkin, G.: Rules of Encounter: Designing Conventions for Automated Negotiation Among Computers. MIT Press, Cambridge (1994)
12. Sycara, K.: Persuasive argumentation in negotiation. Theory and Decision 28, 203–242 (1990)
13. Tohmé, F.: Negotiation and defeasible reasons for choice. In: Proceedings of the Stanford Spring Symposium on Qualitative Preferences in Deliberation and Practical Reasoning, pp. 95–102 (1997)

On the Benefits of Exploiting Hierarchical Goals in Bilateral Automated Negotiation

Iyad Rahwan[1,2], Philippe Pasquier[3], Liz Sonenberg[3], and Frank Dignum[4]

[1] Institute of Informatics, The British University in Dubai,
P.O. Box 502216, Dubai, UAE
[2] (Fellow) School of Informatics, University of Edinburgh
Edinburgh, EH8 9LE, UK
[3] Dept. of Information Systems, University of Melbourne
Parkville, VIC 3010 Australia
[4] Dept. of Information & Computing Sciences
Utrecht University, Utrecht, The Netherlands

Abstract. Interest-based negotiation (IBN) is a form of negotiation in which agents exchange information about their underlying goals, with a view to improving the likelihood and quality of a deal. While this intuition has been stated informally in much previous literature, there is no formal analysis of the types of deals that can be reached through IBN and how they differ from those reachable using (classical) alternating offer bargaining. This paper bridges this gap by providing a formal framework for analysing the outcomes of IBN dialogues, and begins by analysing a specific IBN protocol.

1 Introduction

Negotiation is a form of interaction in which a group of agents, with conflicting interests, try to come to a mutually acceptable agreement on the division of scarce resources. Approaches to automated negotiation can be classified to those based on (1) auctions; (2) bargaining; and (3) argumentation. A common aspect of auction and bilateral bargaining approaches is that they are *proposal-based*. That is, agents exchange proposed agreements –in the form of bids or offers– and when proposed deals are not accepted, the possible response is either a counter-proposal or withdrawal. Argumentation-based negotiation (ABN) approaches, on the other hand, enable agents to exchange additional *meta*-information (i.e. arguments) during negotiation [6]. This paper is concerned with a particular style of argument-based negotiation, namely *interest-based negotiation* (IBN) [7], a form of ABN in which agents explore and discuss their underlying interests. Information about other agents' goals may be used in a variety of ways, such as discovering and exploiting common goals.

Most existing literature supports the claim that ABN is useful by presenting specific examples that show how ABN can lead to agreement where a more basic exchange of proposals cannot (e.g. the mirror/picture example in [5]). The focus is usually on underlying semantics of arguments and argument acceptability.

I. Rahwan, S. Parsons, and C. Reed (Eds.): ArgMAS 2007, LNAI 4946, pp. 18–30, 2008.

However, no formal analysis exists of how agent preferences, and the range of possible negotiation outcomes, change as a result of exchanging arguments.

Our aim here is to explore how exchanging meta-information about the agent's underlying goals can help improve the negotiation process. To this end, we explore situations where agents generate their preferences using a deliberation procedure that results in hierarchies of goals.[1] We abstract away from the underlying argumentation logic. We use this simplified framework to characterise precisely how agent preferences and the set of possible negotiation outcomes change as a result of exchanging information about agents' goals. To our knowledge, this constitutes the first formal analysis of the outcomes of interest-based negotiation, and how they may differ from proposal-based approaches, namely alternating-offer bargaining. We then present a simple IBN protocol and show that under certain conditions (e.g. that agents' goals do not interfere with each other), revealing underlying goals always leads to an expansion of the set of possible deals. As such, the paper bridges the gap between the theory and practice of ABN, and provides a key first step towards understanding the dynamics of more complex IBN dialogues.

2   Preliminaries

Our negotiation framework consists of a set of two *agents* $\mathcal{A}$ and a finite set of *resources* $\mathcal{R}$, which are indivisible and non-sharable. An *allocation of resources* is a partitioning of $\mathcal{R}$ among agents in $\mathcal{A}$ [2].

Definition 1. *(Allocation) An allocation of resources $\mathcal{R}$ to a set of agents $\mathcal{A}$ is a function $\Lambda : \mathcal{A} \to 2^{\mathcal{R}}$ such that $\Lambda(i) \cap \Lambda(j) = \{\}$ for $i \neq j$ and $\bigcup_{i \in \mathcal{A}} \Lambda(i) = \mathcal{R}$*

Agents may have different preferences over sets of resources, defined in the form of utility functions. At this stage, we do not make any assumptions about the properties of preferences/utility functions (e.g. being additive, monotonic, etc.).

Definition 2. *(Utility functions) Every agent $i \in \mathcal{A}$ has a utility function $u_i : 2^{\mathcal{R}} \to \mathbb{R}$.*

Given their preferences, agents may be able to benefit from reallocating (i.e. exchanging) resources. Such reallocation is referred to as a *deal*. A rational self-interested agent should not accept deals that result in loss of utility. However, we will make use of *side payments* in order to enable agents to compensate each other for accepting deals that result in loss of utility [2].

Definition 3. *(Payment) A payment is a function $p : \mathcal{A} \to \mathbb{R}$ such that $\sum_{i \in \mathcal{A}} p(i) = 0$,*

Note that the definition ensures that the total amount of money is constant. If $p(i) > 0$, the agent *pays* the amount $p(i)$, while $p(i) < 0$ means the agent *receives* the amount $-p(i)$. We can now define the notion of 'deal' formally.

---

[1] This abstraction is common and has been used in the context of automated planning [3] and multi-agent coordination [1].

Definition 4. (Deal) *Let Λ be the current resource allocation. A deal with money is a tuple $\delta = (\Lambda, \Lambda', p)$ where Λ' is the suggested allocation, $\Lambda' \neq \Lambda$, and p is a payment.*

Let Δ be the set of all possible deals. By overloading the notion of utility, we will also refer to the utility of a deal (as opposed to the utility of an allocation) defined as follows.

Definition 5. (Utility of a Deal for an Agent) *The utility of deal $\delta = (\Lambda, \Lambda', p)$ for agent i is:*

$$u_i(\delta) = u_i(\Lambda'(i)) - u_i(\Lambda(i)) - p(i)$$

A deal is *rational* for an agent only if it results in positive utility for that agent, since otherwise, the agent would prefer to stick with its initial resources.

Definition 6. (Rational Deals for an Agent) *A deal δ is* rational *for agent i if and only if $u_i(\delta) > 0$*

If a deal is rational for each individual agent given some payment function p, it is called *individual rational*.

Definition 7. (Individual Rational Deals) *A deal δ is* individual rational *if and only if $\forall i \in \mathcal{A}$ we have $u_i(\delta) \geq 0$ and $\exists j \in \mathcal{A}$ such that $u_j(\delta) > 0$.*

In other words, no agent becomes worse off, while at least one agent becomes better off.[2] We denote by $\Delta^* \subseteq \Delta$ the *set of individual rational deals*.

3   Bargaining Protocol

An *offer* (or *proposal*) is a deal presented by one agent which, if accepted by the other agents, would result in a new allocation of resources. In the alternative-offer protocol, agents exchange proposals until one is found acceptable or negotiation terminates (e.g. because a deadline was reached or the set of all possible proposals were exhausted without agreement). In this paper, we will restrict our analysis to two agents. The bargaining protocol initiated by agent i with agent j is shown in Table 1.

Bargaining can be seen as a search through possible allocations of resources. In the brute force method, agents would have to exchange every possible offer before a deal is reached or disagreement is acknowledged. The number of possible allocations of resources to agents is $|\mathcal{A}|^{|\mathcal{R}|}$, which is exponential in the number of resources. The number of possible offers is even larger, since agents would have to consider not only every possible allocation of resources, but also every possible payment. Various computational frameworks for bargaining have been proposed in order to enable agents to reach deals quickly. For example, Faratin

---

[2] This is equivalent to saying that the new allocation *Pareto dominates* the initial allocation, given the payment.

Table 1. Basic bargaining protocol

Bargaining Protocol 1 (BP1):
Agents start with resource allocation Λ^0 at time $t = 0$
At each time $t > 0$:

1. propose(i, δ^t): Agent i proposes to j deal $\delta^t = (\Lambda^0, \Lambda^t, p^t)$ which has not been proposed before;
2. Agent j either:
   (a) accept(j, δ^t): accepts, and negotiation terminates with allocation Λ^t and payment p^t; or
   (b) reject(j, δ^t): rejects, and negotiation terminates with allocation Λ^0 and no payment; or
   (c) makes a counter proposal by going to step 1 at the time step $t + 1$ with the roles of agents i and j swapped.

---

et al [4] use a heuristic for generating counter proposals that are as similar as possible to the previous offer they rejected.

We characterise the set of deals that are *reachable* using *any* given protocol. The set of reachable deals can be conveniently characterised in terms of the history of offers made (thus, omitting, for now, other details of the protocol).[3]

Definition 8. *(Dialogue History) A dialogue history of protocol P between agents i and j is an ordered sequence h of tuples consisting of a proposal and a utility function (over allocations) for each agent*

$$h = \langle (\delta^1, u_i^1, u_j^1), \ldots, (\delta^n, u_i^n, u_j^n) \rangle$$

where $t = 1, \ldots, n$ represents time.

Definition 9. *(Protocol-Reachable Deal) Let P be a protocol. A deal δ^t is P-reachable if and only if there exists two agents i and j which can generate a dialogue history according to P such that δ^t is offered by some agent at time t and δ^t is individual rational given u_i^t, u_j^t.*

4   Underlying Interests

In most existing alternating-offer bargaining negotiation frameworks, agents' utility functions are assumed to be *pre-determined* (e.g. as weighted sums) and *fixed* throughout the interaction. That is, throughout the dialogue history, $u_i^1 = \cdots = u_i^n$ for any agent i.

We now present a framework for capturing the interdependencies between goals at different levels of abstraction.[4]

---

[3] To enable studying changes in the utility function later in the paper, we will superscript utility functions with time-stamps.

[4] Although this framework is simpler than those in the planning literature, its level of abstraction is sufficient for our purpose.

Let $\mathcal{G} = \{g_1, \ldots, g_m\}$ be the set of all possible goals. And let $sub : \mathcal{G} \times 2^{\mathcal{G} \cup \mathcal{R}}$ be a relationship between a goal and the sub-goals or resources needed to achieve it. Intuitively, $sub(g, \{g_1, \ldots, g_n\})$ means that achieving all the goals $g_1, \ldots, g_n$ results in achieving the higher-level goal g. Each sub-goal in the set $\{g_1, \ldots, g_n\}$ may itself be achievable using another set of sub-goals, thus resulting in a goal hierarchy. We assume that this hierarchy takes the form of a tree (called *goal tree* or *plan*). This condition is reasonable since the sub-goal relation captures specialisation of abstract goals into more concrete goals.

Definition 10. (Partial plan) *A* partial plan *for achieving goal g_0 is a tree T such that:*

- *g_0 is the root;*
- *Each non-leaf node is a goal $g \in \mathcal{G}$ with children $x_1, \ldots, x_n \in \mathcal{G} \cup \mathcal{R}$ such that $sub(g, \{x_1, \ldots, x_n\})$;[5]*
- *Each leaf node is $x_i \in (\mathcal{R} \cup \mathcal{G})$;*

A complete plan is a goal tree in which all leaf nodes are resources.

Definition 11. (Complete plan) *A* complete plan *for achieving goal g_0 is a partial plan T in which each leaf node $r_i \in \mathcal{R}$.*

Example 1. Suppose we have goals $\mathcal{G} = \{g_1, \ldots, g_4\}$ and $\mathcal{R} = \{r_1, \ldots, r_6\}$ such that $sub(g_1, \{g_2, g_3\})$, $sub(g_1, \{g_2, g_4\})$, $sub(g_2, \{r_1, r_2\})$, $sub(g_3, \{r_3, r_4\})$, $sub(g_4, \{r_5, r_6\})$. Suppose also that the agent's main goal is g_1. Figure 1 shows three plans that can be generated. Tree T_1 is a partial plan (since goal g_3 is a leaf node), while T_2 and T_3 are (the only possible) complete plans for achieving g_1.

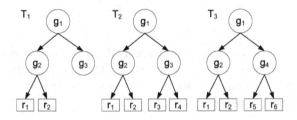

Fig. 1. Partial plans (T_1) and complete plans (T_2, T_3)

Let $gnodes(T) \subseteq \mathcal{G}$ be the set of goal nodes in tree T. And let $leaves(T) \subseteq \mathcal{R} \cup \mathcal{G}$ be the set of leaf nodes in tree T. Let $rleaves(T) = leaves(T) \cap \mathcal{R}$ be the set of resource leaves. And similarly, let $gleaves(T) = leaves(T) \cap \mathcal{G}$ be the set of goal leaves. Note that for a complete plan T, $leaves(T) = rleaves(T)$, that is, leaf nodes contain resources only.

Note that sub is a relation, not a function, to allow us to express goals that have multiple sets of *alternative* sub-goals/resources. Hence, there may be multiple possible plans for achieving a goal.

---

[5] I.e. among alternatives for achieving g, only one is selected.

Let $\mathcal{T}$ be the set of all (partial or complete) plans that can be generated in the system, and let $\mathcal{T}(g)$ be the set of all plans that have g as a root.

Definition 12 (Individual Capability)
An agent $i \in \mathcal{A}$ with resources $\Lambda(i)$ is individually capable of achieving goal $g \in \mathcal{G}$ if and only if there is a complete plan $T \in \mathcal{T}$ such that $leaves(T) \subseteq \Lambda(i)$

We assume that each agent i is assigned a single goal $G(i) \in \mathcal{G}$ that it needs to achieve, and we refer to it as the agent's *main goal*.[6] We further assume that agent i assigns a *worth* to this goal $worth_i(G(i)) \in \mathbb{R}$.

Example 2. Following on Example 1, suppose agent i with goal $G(i) = g_1$ has resources $\Lambda(i) = \{r_1, r_2, r_3, r_4, r_5\}$. Agent i is individually capable of achieving g_1 through complete plan T_2, since $leaves(T_2) \subseteq \Lambda(i)$.

Note that the agent also has the option of retaining its resources and not using it to achieve its goal (e.g. they are worth more than the goal). Here, we say that the agent has selected the *null plan*, denoted $\check{T}$. We can characterise the set of all complete plans that an agent can choose from.

Definition 13. (Individually Achievable Plans) *The set of plans that can be achieved by agent i individually using allocation $\Lambda(i)$ is:*

$$\mathcal{T}_{\Lambda(i)} = \{T \in \mathcal{T} \; : \; leaves(T) \subseteq \Lambda(i)\} \cup \{\check{T}\}$$

We now want to provide a new definition of the utility of an allocation, which takes into account the agent's underlying goal. Therefore, we differentiate between the *intrinsic* value of the resource and its potential contribution to a goal. So, if the agent's resources cannot be used to achieve its goals, then the utility of these resources will be the sum of their intrinsic values, as above. If, on the other hand, the agent is able to achieve its goal using some of its resources, then the utility calculation must take into account the difference between the utility gained by achieving the goal and the utility lost by consuming the resources.

The agent must select the *best* plan, i.e. the plan that minimizes the cost of the resources used. To capture this, let $v_i : \mathcal{R} \to \mathbb{R}$ be a valuation function such that $v_i(r)$ is agent i's private valuation of resource r. Then we can define the cost incurred by agent i in executing plan T as: $cost_i(T) = \sum_{r \in rleaves(T)} v_i(r)$. Then, we can define the *utility of plan* as follows.[7]

Definition 14. (Utility of a Plan) *Let i be an agent with goal $G(i)$ and resources $\Lambda(i)$. And let T_i^* be the set of available alternative plans i can choose from. The utility of plan $T \in T_i^*$ for agent i is a function $\tilde{u}_i \; : \; T_i^* \to \mathbb{R}$ is defined as follows:*

$$\tilde{u}_i(T) = \begin{cases} 0 & \text{if } T = \check{T}, \\ worth_i(G(i)) - cost_i(T) & \text{otherwise} \end{cases}$$

---

[6] Multiple goals can be expressed by a single goal that has one possible decomposition.
[7] Note that so far, we have different notions of utility: the utility of an allocation, the utility of a plan, and the utility of a deal.

Note that for agent i with allocation $\Lambda(i)$ and goal $G(i)$, the set of available alternatives (not considering other agents in the system) is $T_i^* = (T_{\Lambda(i)} \cap T(G(i)))$.

Since the null plan does not achieve a goal and does not incur any cost, the agent retains all its initial resources, and therefore the utility of the null plan is simply the sum of the values of those resources.

Example 3. Following on Example 1, suppose agent i with goal $G(i) = g_1$ has resources $\Lambda(i) = \{r_1, r_2, r_3, r_4, r_5, r_6\}$. Suppose also that $worth_i(g_1) = 85$ and resource valuations $v_i(r_1) = 20$, $v_i(r_2) = 10$, $v_i(r_3) = 6$, $v_i(r_4) = 5$, $v_i(r_5) = 8$, $v_i(r_6) = 7$. Then, we have:
$\tilde{u}_i(T_2) = 85 - (20 + 10 + 6 + 5) = 44$
$\tilde{u}_i(T_3) = 85 - (20 + 10 + 8 + 7) = 40$
$\tilde{u}_i(\check{T}) = 0$

We now define the utility of an allocation for an agent. Note that this is a specialisation of the general utility function in Definition 2. Note also that underlying our framework is the assumption that resources are consumable, at least for the period in question, in the sense that a single resource cannot be used simultaneously in multiple plans. An example of a consumable resource is "fuel" consumed to run an engine.

Definition 15. *(Utility) The* utility *of agent* $i \in A$ *is defined as a function* $u_i : 2^{\mathcal{R}} \to \mathbb{R}$ *such that:*
$$u_i(\Lambda(i)) = \max_{T \in T_i^*} \tilde{u}_i(T)$$

The utility of a deal remains defined as above.

Example 4. Following Example 3, the utility of the resources is $u_i(\Lambda(i)) = 44$, and the best plan is T_2.

5   Mutual Interests

One of the main premises of IBN is that agents may benefit from exploring each other's underlying interests. For example, agents may avoid making irrelevant offers given each others' goals. Knowledge of *common*[8] goals may help agents reach better agreements, since they may discover that they can benefit from goals achieved by one another. In this paper, we focus on the case of common goals.

We first formalise the idea that an agent may benefit from a goal (or subgoal) achieved by another. Suppose an agent j is committed to some plan T_j, written $I_j(T_j)$. Then, another agent i, with $I_i(T_i)$, may benefit from the goals in $gnodes(T_j)$ if one or more of these goals is part of T_i. Note, however, that not every goal in $gnodes(T_j)$ is useful to i, but rather those goals for which j has a complete goal (sub-)tree. Thus, we define the notion of *committed goals*.

---

[8] Note that common goals are different from individual goals of the same kind. Two agents may both want to hang the same picture, or may each want to hang a different picture.

Definition 16. *(Committed Goals) Let $i \in \mathcal{A}$ be an agent with resources $\Lambda(i)$ with $I_i(T_i)$ at time t. The committed goals of i at time t is denoted $cgoals_i^t$ and defined as:*
$$cgoals_i^t = \{g \in gnodes(T_i) \; : \; g \text{ has a plan } T \in \mathcal{T}_{\Lambda(i)} \text{ where } T \text{ is a sub-tree of } T_i\}$$

When there is no ambiguity, we shall drop the superscript t that denotes time.

For the time being, we assume no negative interaction among goals.[9] In other words, the achievement of one goal does not hinder the achievement of another.

Definition 17. *(Achievable Plans) The set of partial plans that can be achieved by agent i using allocation $\Lambda(i)$ given agent j's committed goals $cgoals_i^t$ at time t is:*

$$\mathcal{T}_{\Lambda(i), cgoals_j^t} = \{T \in \mathcal{T} \; : \; leaves(T) \subseteq \Lambda(i) \cup cgoals_j^t\} \cup \check{T}$$

Example 5. Figure 2 shows agent i and j with goals g_1 and g_5 respectively, with all possible plans, the resources owned by every agents and, under every resource, the agent's private valuation. Note that T_2 is possible but not achievable by i with $\Lambda(i)$. Now, suppose plan $I_j(T_4)$. This means that $g_3 \in cgoals_j$. While T_1 is not individually-achievable, it is now a viable alternative for agent i to achieve g_1 since agent j is committed to goal g_3.

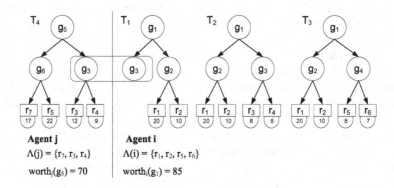

Fig. 2. Agent i can benefit from j's committed goal

The following lemma follows immediately.

Lemma 1. *At any time t, $\mathcal{T}_{\Lambda(i)} \subseteq \mathcal{T}_{\Lambda(i), cgoals_j^t}$*

Proof. Let $T \in \mathcal{T}_{\Lambda(i)}$. By definition 13, $leaves(T) \subseteq \Lambda(i)$, from which it follows that $leaves(T) \subseteq \Lambda(i) \cup cgoals_j^t$. By definition 17, we have $T \in \mathcal{T}_{\Lambda(i), cgoals_j^t}$.

---

[9] In this paper, *negative* interaction among goals is only captured through the overlap of resources needed by two goals. We do not address explicit interference among goals.

From the lemma, it follows that when agents take into account goals committed by other agents, the set of available plans expands, since agents are no longer restricted to considering complete plans. Formally, for agent i with goal $G(i)$ and resources $\Lambda(i)$, the set of available options at time t is now $\mathcal{T}_i^* = (\mathcal{T}_{\Lambda(i),cgoals_j^t} \cap \mathcal{T}(G(i))$. Agents can now consider partial plans, as long as the missing parts of these plans are committed j. From this, it also follows that the utility of an allocation may increase. The example below calculates agent i's utility for partial plan T_1, which was previously not considered.

Example 6. Continuing on Example 5 and Figure 2. We now have $\tilde{u}_i(T_1) = 85 - (20 + 10) = 55$, $\tilde{u}_i(T_3) = 40$ and $\tilde{u}_i(\check{T}) = 0$ (recall that $T_2 \notin \mathcal{T}_i^*$ for now). Therefore, $u_i(\Lambda(i)) = 70$. This contrasts with the calculation that does not take j's goal into account, in which case $u_i(\Lambda(i)) = 40$.

6   Case Study: An IBN Protocol

We showed how agents' utilities of allocations may increase if agents have knowledge of each other's underlying goals. However, full awareness of other agents' goals is rarely achievable, especially when agents are self-interested. Agents may progressively (and selectively) reveal information about their goals using a variety of interaction protocols. For example, agents could reveal their entire goal trees at once, or may do so in a specific order. Moreover, agents may reveal their underling goals symmetrically (e.g. simultaneously) or asymmetrically, etc. We now look at a specific IBN protocol and analyse it using the above concepts.

We assume that agents have no prior knowledge of each other's main goals or preferences; and that prior to negotiation, each agent i considers all individually-achievable plans, for its main goal, using $\Lambda(i)$, as well as potential rational deals. An IBN protocol is presented Table 2. Note that this protocol is asymmetric, since during the IBN sub-dialogue, the agent being questioned is assumed to *fix* its intended plans, while the questioning agent may accept the deal in question by discovering new viable plans that take into account the questionee's goals.

Let us now consider an extension of the previous example.

Example 7. Suppose agent i's initial situation is as described in Figure 3. Here, i begins with two achievable plans: T_3 and $\check{T}$. As shown in Example 6, $u_i(\Lambda^0(i)) = 40$. Suppose i considers acquiring resources $\{r_3, r_4\}$ to enable possible plan T_2. With $\{r_3, r_4\}$, $\tilde{u}_i(T_2) = 85 - (20 + 10 + 6 + 5) = 44$, so i would be willing to pay up to $44 - 40 = 4$ units for $\{r_3, r_4\}$, since he would still be better-off than working solo. Agent j on the other hand only has one possible plan, which is T_4 with utility $\tilde{u}_j(T_4) = 125 - 60 = 65$, but is unable to execute it because it needs r_5. Now, agent i initiates negotiation with j. The following is a possible sequence of proposals:

1. propose($i, (\Lambda^0, \Lambda^1, p^1)$), where $\Lambda^1(i) = \{r_1, r_2, r_3, r_4, r_5, r_6\}$, $\Lambda^1(j) = \{r_7\}$, $p^1(i) = 3$, $p^1(j) = -3$
2. propose($j, (\Lambda^0, \Lambda^2, p^2)$), where $\Lambda^2(i) = \{r_1, r_2, r_6\}$, $\Lambda^2(j) = \{r_3, r_4, r_5, r_7\}$, $p^2(i) = 9$, $p^2(j) = -9$

Table 2. A simple IBN protocol

IBN Protocol 1 (IBNP1):

Agents start with resource allocation Λ^0 at time $t = 0$

At each time $t > 0$

1. propose(i, δ^t): Agent i proposes to j deal $\delta^t = (\Lambda^0, \Lambda^t, p^t)$ which has not been proposed before;
2. Agent j either:
   (a) accept(j, δ^t): accepts, and negotiation terminates with allocation Λ^t and payment p^t; or
   (b) reject(j, δ^t): rejects, and negotiation terminates with allocation Λ^0 and no payment; or
   (c) makes a counter proposal by going to step 1 at the next time step with the roles of agents i and j swapped; or
   (d) switches to interest-based dialogue on δ^t. Let $dgoals^t_i = \emptyset$ for all $i \in \mathcal{A}$ be each agents' declared goals.
      i. why(j, x): j asks i for underlying goal for a resource or declared goal $x \in \Lambda^t(i) \cup dgoals^t_i$;
      ii. i either:
         A. assert$(i, I_i(g))$: i responds by stating a goal, which is added to $dgoals(i)$; or
         B. decline(i): declines giving the information;
      iii. j either:
         A. accept(j, g): j accepts δ^t, if now more favourable; or
         B. seeks more information by going to step 2.d.i; or
         C. pass(j): j skips its turn, moving the protocol to step 2 with i taking the role of deciding what to do next.

At this point, agent i may attempt to know why j needs some resource, say r_3, and the following follows:

4. why(i, r_3)
5. assert$(j, I_i(g_3))$

At this point, i would be willing to give up r_3 and r_4, since plan T_1 now becomes a viable option for i. Moreover, recall that $\tilde{u}_i(T_1) = 55$, so i can now give up resource r_5 for payment 9 in a deal.

8. accept$(i, (\Lambda^0, \Lambda^2, p^2))$

In summary, i gives up r_5 in exchange for getting g_3 and a payment of 5. While j pays 5 for r_5 and achieves its goal (which was not possible before). Both agents gain utility, and the utilities of the deal δ are as follows:

$$u_i(\delta) = u_i(\Lambda^2(i)) - u_i(\Lambda^0(i)) - p^2(i) = (55 - 8) - 40 + 9 = 16$$

$$u_j(\delta) = u_j(\Lambda^2(j)) - u_j(\Lambda^0(j)) - p^2(j) = 65 - 0 - 9 = 56$$

Note that in calculating the utility of i's new allocation, we subtracted 8 since i has given up r_5 in the deal, which it values as 8.

Let us now analyse IBNP1.

Proposition 1. *Every bargaining-reachable deal is also IBN-reachable.*

Proof. If in IBNP1, no agent ever switches to an interest-based dialogues –step (d), then the two algorithms BP1 and IBNP1 become identical. Hence, any deal reachable through bargaining is also reachable through IBN.

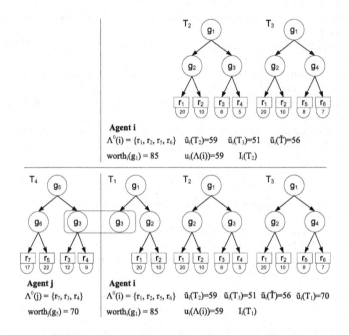

Fig. 3. Different stages of an IBN dialogue

We are mainly interested in how agents' perceptions of the utility of allocations changes over time. Let $dgoals : \mathcal{A} \rightarrow 2^{\mathcal{G}}$ be a function that returns the set of goals declared by an agent. We assume that agents do not lie about their goals, in the sense that they do not declare goals they are not committed to. Formally, $dgoals^t_i \subseteq cgoals^t_i$ for any agent i at any given time t. Let $\mathcal{T}_{\Lambda^t(i), dgoals^t_j} \subseteq \mathcal{T}$ be the set of goal trees that can be achieved by agent i using allocation $\Lambda^t(i)$ given j's declared goals $dgoals^t_j$, i.e.

$$\mathcal{T}_{\Lambda^t(i), dgoals^t_j} = \{T \in \mathcal{T} \ : \ leaves(T) \subseteq \Lambda^t(i) \cup dgoals^t_j\}$$

The below proposition then follows:

Proposition 2. *At any time t, $\mathcal{T}_{\Lambda^t(i)} \subseteq \mathcal{T}_{\Lambda^t(i), dgoals^t_j} \subseteq \mathcal{T}_{\Lambda^t(i), cgoals^t_j}$*

Proof. *Proof of $\mathcal{T}_{\Lambda^t(i)} \subseteq \mathcal{T}_{\Lambda^t(i),dgoals_j^t}$ is similar to proof of Lemma 1. The fact that $\mathcal{T}_{\Lambda^t(i),dgoals_j^t} \subseteq \mathcal{T}_{\Lambda^t(i),cgoals_j^t}$ follows from the assumption that $dgoals_i^t \subseteq cgoals_i^t$.*

This proposition shows that by using protocol IBNP1, the set of available plans for the inquiring agent expands, but never goes beyond the set of plans that take into account all of the counterpart's actual goals. Formally, for agent i with goal $G(i)$ and resources $\Lambda(i)$, the set of available options at time t is now $\mathcal{T}_i^* = \mathcal{T}_{\Lambda(i),dgoals_j^t} \cap \mathcal{T}(G(i))$.

Proposition 3. *Using the protocol IBNP1, at any time t, it is possible for any agent j to obtain complete knowledge of the entire goal structure of the intended plan by the other agent i, provided i does not decline to answer questions.*

Proof. At any given round t, suppose agent i intends arbitrary complete plan $T_i^t \in \mathcal{T}$, and proposes δ^t (Step 1). By definition, leaves$(T_i^t) \subseteq \Lambda^t(i)$, i.e. i must obtain through δ^t every resource needed for achieving T_i^t. After this request (Step 2.d), j could ask why(r) for each $r \in$ leaves(T_i^t). This would be done over $|$leaves$(T_i^t)|$ iterations of Step 2.d. As a result, $dgoals_i^t$ will contain the set of goals that are immediate parents of resources $r \in$ leaves(T_i^t). Similarly, Step 2.d could be repeated to obtain the immediate parents of those goals, until the main goal is revealed. Thus, every intended goal of i will eventually be in $dgoals_i^t$.

The following proposition states that as the negotiation counterpart declares more of its goals, the inquirer's utility of any plan may increase, but can never decline. This is because the inquirer is increasingly able to account for the positive *side effects* of other agents' goals.

Proposition 4. *At any given time t, if the protocol is in stage 2.d initiated by agent i, as the set $dgoals_j^t$ increases, the utility $u_i(\delta^t)$ of the current proposal may only increase.*

Proof. Recall that the set of available alternative plans i can choose from is $\mathcal{T}_i^* = \mathcal{T}_{\Lambda(i),dgoals_j^t} \cap \mathcal{T}(G(i))$, and that $\mathcal{T}_{\Lambda^t(i)} \subseteq \mathcal{T}_{\Lambda^t(i),dgoals_j^t}$. It follows that as $dgoals_j^t$ increases, the set $\mathcal{T}_i^*$ also grows monotonically. Recall that $u_i(\Lambda^t(i)) = \max_{T \in \mathcal{T}_i^*} \tilde{u}_i(T)$. Hence, as $u_i(\Lambda^t(i))$ is applied to maximise over a monotonically increasing set, its value can increase but not decrease. Consequently, $u_i(\delta^t)$ is non-decreasing.

It follows that at any time t where agent j intends plan T_j^t and i is inquiring j's goals, as $dgoals_j^t$ converges towards $cgoals_j^t$, then $u_i(\Lambda^t(i))$ will reach the *objective* utility, that is the utility that reflects the true utility of $\Lambda^t(i)$.

7   Conclusion

While much has been said about the intuitive advantage of argument-based negotiation over other forms of negotiation, very little has been done on making these intuitions precise. We began bridging this gap by characterising exactly how the set of reachable deals expands as agents progressively explore each other's underlying goals. We also presented one specific protocol and showed how it provides one useful way to exchange information about goals.

This paper opens many future possibilities. Although the protocol analysed here is simple, the paper presents a step towards more elaborate analysis of a variety of other IBN protocols (e.g. symmetric ones). Another direction of future research is exploring the case of negative interaction (i.e. interference) among agents' goals. In such cases, agents may not wish to disclose their goals, since this could reduce the likelihood or quality of deals. One would have to explore the trade-off between the potential benefit and potential loss in revealing goals. Finally, the possibility of agents lying about their goals opens up many game-theoretic questions.

It is worth noting that our work differs from multi-agent hierarchical plan merging [1], which assume agents are fully aware of each other's goals. We depart from a position where agents have no knowledge of each other's goals. And while the objective of hierarchical coordination research is on finding optimal ways to maximise positive interaction among the goals of *cooperative* agents, our aim is to explore interaction among self-interested agents who may not be willing to share information about their goals, unless sharing such information benefits them.

Acknowledgement

This work is partially supported by the Australian Research Council, Discovery Grant DP0557487.

References

1. Cox, J.S., Durfee, E.: Discovering and exploiting synergy between hierarchical planning agents. In: Rosenschein, J., Sandholm, T., Wooldridge, M.J., Yokoo, M. (eds.) Proceedings of the 2nd International Joint Conference on Autonomous Agents and Multiagent Systems (AAMAS-2003), pp. 281–288. ACM Press, New York (2003)
2. Endris, U., Maudet, N., Sadri, F., Toni, F.: Negotiating socially optimal allocations of resources. Journal of artificial intelligence research 25, 315–348 (2006)
3. Erol, K., Hendler, J., Nau, D.: Semantics for hierarchical task network planning. Technical Report CS-TR-3239, UMIACS-TR-94-31, Department of Computer Science, University of Maryland (1994)
4. Faratin, P., Sierra, C., Jennings, N.R.: Using similarity criteria to make trade-offs in automated negotiations. Artificial Intelligence 142(2), 205–237 (2002)
5. Parsons, S., Sierra, C., Jennings, N.: Agents that reason and negotiate by arguing. Journal of Logic and Computation 8(3), 261–292 (1998)
6. Rahwan, I., Ramchurn, S.D., Jennings, N.R., McBurney, P., Parsons, S., Sonenberg, L.: Argumentation based negotiation. Knowledge Engineering Review 18(4), 343–375 (2003)
7. Rahwan, I., Sonenberg, L., Dignum, F.: Towards interest-based negotiation. In: Rosenschein, J., Sandholm, T., Wooldridge, M.J., Yokoo, M. (eds.) Proceedings of the 2nd International Joint Conference on Autonomous Agents and Multiagent Systems (AAMAS 2003), pp. 773–780. ACM Press, New York (2003)

Co-argumentation Artifact for Agent Societies

Enrico Oliva[1], Peter McBurney[2], and Andrea Omicini[1]

[1] ALMA MATER STUDIORUM–Università di Bologna, Cesena, Italy
[2] University of Liverpool, Liverpool L69 3BX UK

Abstract. In a social context, people have only partial knowledge about the world and use arguments in order to solve problems, to reduce conflicts, or to exchange information.

Argumentation is a dialogic process, and could occur through direct interaction, or through supports of some sorts—like blackboards, or electronic fora. The same holds for intelligent agents in a multi-agent system (MAS); here, however, it is not clear what could act as a support for argumentation between agents, external to the agents themselves. To this end, this work exploits the agents and artifacts (A&A) meta-model for MAS, exploring the use of artifacts for agent argumentation within a MAS. Along this line, the first aim of this work is to design an argumentation component based on Dung's preferred semantics, combining it with artifact abstraction in order to realise a social support for argumentation in MAS. Using argumentation within the A&A meta-model, we introduce here the notion of Co-Argumentation Artifact (CAA) as an artifact specialised in managing arguments and providing a coordination service for argumentation process in a MAS. In order to give concreteness to our proposal, we also discuss a first CAA deployment based on logic programming and tuple centres exploiting the TuCSoN infrastructure.

1 Introduction

A society mainly evolves through interaction and communication among participating entities. Within a society, people argue in order to solve problems, to reduce conflicts, to exchange information, and to inform each other of some pertinent facts. Argumentation is a useful feature of human intelligence that enables us to deal with incomplete and inconsistent information. People usually have only partial knowledge about the world (they are not omniscient) and often they have to manage conflicting information.

In the same way, the entities that compose an artificial society should be able to deal with partial and conflicting knowledge. Correspondingly, an agent-based model for an artificial society should provide an adequate definition of knowledge with the purpose of providing a realistic reflection of a society. Also, it may be useful to share information in order to successfully deal with partial knowledge.

A novel approach to the design of agent-based artificial societies is based on the notion of coordination artifact [1], which takes inspiration from Activity Theory [2] where any human activity within a society is enabled, constrained or mediated by artifacts.

I. Rahwan, S. Parsons, and C. Reed (Eds.): ArgMAS 2007, LNAI 4946, pp. 31–46, 2008.
© Springer-Verlag Berlin Heidelberg 2008

Coordination artifacts are social constructs shared by agents of a MAS (multi-agent system), and are necessary to mediate interaction among agents, and between agents and their environment. A traffic light, for instance, is a sort of coordination artifact: drivers watching the signal know what they have to do to avoid accidents at an intersection, without any need for direct communication with one another.

Argumentation is an important feature of human intelligence: the ability to understand and manipulate arguments is fundamental to understand a new problem, to reason about actions, and to perform scientific research. An argument is a sequence of inferences leading to a valid conclusion: a set of arguments is managed by an argumentation component that is particularly useful in the case of conflicting information.

In this paper we elaborate on the idea of social support for argumentation in a MAS, by coupling the agents and artifacts (A&A) meta-model for MAS with argumentation theory. In particular, we introduce the notion of Co-Argumentation Artifact (CAA), as a social support based on argumentation theory able to manage conflicting information exchange during the social argumentation processes in a MAS. Agents use a CAA to be guided during the discussion or to find some new information in agreement with their internal goals. A CAA would be useful, for example, to identify subsets of arguments agreeable to all participants in the society.

In this paper, we first introduce our reference notion of Argumentation System (Section 2), then (Section 3) we discuss the properties of an Argumentation Component. In Section 4 the new Co-Argumentation Artifacts abstraction is defined and explained, and a simple example built on top of the TuCSoN coordination infrastructure is discussed.

2   Argumentation System

In this section we introduce the system of argumentation that is the reference for our approach. An argument, in classic logic, is a sequence of inferences that leads to a conclusion. It has three components: beliefs, inference rules and conclusions.

- **beliefs** are facts and rules that represent premises
- **inference rules** are labels that represent inference processes such as deduction or induction
- **conclusions** are facts that represent results of the inference process applied to the beliefs

In our system, we express the argument in predicate logic using the *logic tuple* notation. We take inspiration from Dung's framework [3], and we also define the structure inside the arguments. In [4] an argumentation system formalized in propositional logic is presented. Whereas we follow such an approach, we also try to extend it using predicative logic, which suits a logic programming framework. We assume that Σ contains formulas of a predicate language L distinct in F facts and R rules. The symbol $\vdash$ denotes classical inference process for deduction, induction and abduction, and $\equiv$ denote logical equivalent.

Definition 1. *An argument is a triple* $A = \langle B, I, C \rangle$ *where* $B = b_1, \ldots, b_n, r_1, \ldots, r_n$ *with* $b_i \in F$ *and* $r_i \in R$, $I = \{\vdash_d Deduction, \vdash_i Induction, \vdash_a Abduction\}$ *and* $C = c_1, \ldots, c_n, r_1, \ldots, r_n$ *with* $c_i \in F$ *and* $r_n \in R$ *such that:*

1. *B is consistent*
2. $B \vdash_I C$
3. *B is minimal, so no subset of B satisfying both 1 and 2 exists*

For instance, a classical example of argument like *all men are mortal, Socrates is a man, Socrates is mortal,* in our representation becomes:

- $B = human(Socrates), human(X) \rightarrow mortal(X)$
- $I = \vdash_{MP}$ Modus Ponens
- $C \ni mortal(Socrates)$

Our formalization of the 'Socrates argument' can be easily mapped in a logic tuple. In the process of mapping, we add a the predicate *argument* with the function *name* and other predicates such as *beliefs, infer* and *conclusions* to represent the triple $A = \langle B, I, C \rangle$.

$$argument(name, beliefs([human(Socrates)], [clause(mortal(X), [human(X)])]),$$
$$infer(MP), conclusions([mortal(Socrates)])).$$

A declarative representation of arguments could be useful to store and collect the arguments during the argumentation process. The formula *argument* in our system is the basic unit to represent an argument.

The inference rules we consider for deduction are Modus Ponens (MP), Multi-Modus Ponens (MPP) and Modus Tollens (MT).

$$\frac{B \quad B \rightarrow C}{C} \tag{MP}$$

$$\frac{B_1 \quad B_2 \quad B_3 \quad (B_1 \wedge B_2 \wedge B_3) \rightarrow C}{C} \tag{MPP}$$

The MP is a particular case of MMP with only one premise. Socrates argument is a example of MP deductive argument. Also, MT formula expresses a deductive inference.

$$\frac{\neg A \quad B \rightarrow A}{\neg B} \tag{MT}$$

For example, all human are mortal but Eraclito is not mortal than Eraclito is not human, in tuple form is:

$$argument(name, beliefs([non(mortal(eraclito))], [clause(mortal(X),$$
$$[human(X)])]), infer(MT), conclusions([non(human(eraclito))])).$$

The inference rule that we use for induction is θ-subsumption, as shown in (θ-su).

$$\frac{B}{R} \quad where \ R\theta \subseteq B \tag{θ-su}$$

For example, $mortal(X) \leftarrow human(X)$, θ-subsumes $mortal(socrates) \leftarrow human(socrates)$ with $\theta = \langle X = socrates \rangle$, in tuple form looks like

$$argument(name, beliefs([mortal(socrates), human(socrates)]),$$
$$infer(Su), conclusions([clause(mortal(X), [human(X))])])).$$

This process derives a general rule R from specific beliefs B, but is not a legal inference in a strict sense. Currently, we do not consider a probability value that could be associated to the result of an induction process. Finally the abductive reasoning is expressed with the inference rule shown in (Ab).

$$\frac{B \quad A \to B}{A} \tag{Ab}$$

For example, all humans are mortal, Parmenide is a mortal, then Parmenide is a human, in tuple form looks like

$$argument(name, beliefs([mortal(parmenide)], [clause(mortal(X),$$
$$[human(X)])]), infer(Ab), conclusions([human(parmenide)]).$$

The definition of contrast is not trivial because there are different type of attack well defined in [4]. Following those definitions, two possible types of attack are 'conclusions against conclusions' – called *rebuttals* – and 'conclusions against beliefs'—called *undercuts*.

Definition 2. *Let* $A_1 = \langle B_1, I_1, C_1 \rangle$ *and* $A_2 = \langle B_2, I_2, C_2 \rangle$ *are two distinct arguments,* A_1 *is an* **undercut** *for* A_2 *iff* $\exists h \in C_1$ *such that* $h \equiv \neg b_i$ *where* $b_i \in B_2$

Definition 3. *Let* $A_1 = \langle B_1, I_1, C_1 \rangle$ *and* $A_2 = \langle B_2, I_2, C_2 \rangle$ *are two distinct arguments,* A_1 *is a* **rebuttal** *for* A_2 *iff* $\exists h \in C_1$ *such that* $h \equiv \neg c_i$ *where* $c_i \in C_2$

From the algorithmic point of view it is necessary to identify the opposite predicate: α defeats $\neg\alpha$ in order to find the contrast argument. In our framework we introduce $non/1$ operator that identifies the opposite predicate: $non(mortal(Socrates))$ is opposite to $mortal(Socrates)$. Also we introduce another notion of undercut based on the principle of refutation. To find an attack to the rule, a counterexample is required that disproves its truth. An argument A_1 is attacked through a counterexample contained in the conclusion of another argument. In formula, we consider an implication with only one premise $A \to B \equiv \neg A \lor B$ the contrary is: $A \neg (\neg A \lor B) \equiv A \land \neg B$. An expression with A and the negation of B is a counterexample of the implication. For instance, the following argument undercuts the Socrates example by refuting the implication $mortal(X) \to human(X)$:

$$argument(name, beliefs([human(Eraclito), non(mortal(Eraclito))]),$$
$$infer(T), conclusions([human(Eraclito), non(mortal(Eraclito))]))).$$

This type of attack is possible only with an explicit representation of the rules.

Finally inside the component there are the main algorithms to manipulate the conflict knowledge in order to decide the admissible subset of a set of arguments and to determine whether a new argument is acceptable or not. The definitions of acceptability and admissibility used in our framework are in agreement with [3]. The following definitions are the basic ones in our argumentation system and take inspiration from Dung's framework.

Definition 4. *An argument set S is a* **conflict free** *set iff there exist no $A_i, A_j \in S$ such that A_i attacks A_j.*

Definition 5. *An argument set S* **defends collectively** *all its elements if $\forall$ argument $B \notin S$ where B attacks $A \in S$ $\quad \exists \ C \in S : C$ attacks B.*

Definition 6. *An argument set S is a* **admissible** *set iff S is conflict free and S defends collectively all its elements.*

Definition 7. *An argument set S is a* **preferred extension** *iff S is a maximal set among the admissible set of A.*

We consider also important argument extensions such as acceptability in order to determine whether a new argument is acceptable or not. In the context of preferred semantics the acceptance problem is divided in credulous acceptance or sceptical acceptance, if an argument is in some/all preferred extension.

Definition 8. *An argument A is* **credulous acceptable** *if $A \in$ at least one preferred extension.*

Definition 9. *An argument A is* **sceptical acceptable** *if $A \in$ all preferred extensions.*

3 Argumentation Component

The argumentation component is a system that should be useful in principle in order to control a set of conflicting arguments. An argumentation component is formed by: (1) the concrete representation of arguments and (2) the deployment of algorithms that work over the arguments set. The main functions of this component are to calculate the preferred extensions of a set of arguments and to determine whether a new argument is valid and acceptable. Also, our goals are the deployment of these algorithms within each of the agents of an agent society, and within artifacts embodying the social argumentation processes. This would be useful, for example, to identify subsets of arguments agreeable to all participants in a MAS. We adopt the argumentation system presented in the previous section with a tuple-based notation and the Prolog logic language to implement the algorithms. Prolog is very useful because of the uniform representation of code and data, both represented as first-order logic clauses, which makes writing (meta-)interpreters quite easy [5].

3.1   Computational Model

From a practical point of view computational model is based on predicative
logic and logic programming. Each argument has its own context, where the
argument is true. The context is provided in the argument and is composed
only by the set of beliefs – facts and rules – directly declared in the tuple. The
connection between the premises and the conclusion is expressed in terms of the
corresponding inference process, which is specified in the argument too.

The programs to manage, verify and compare arguments are meta-interpreters
written in Prolog. We have created a library composed of interpreters for each
type of inference rules supported: MP, MT, Su and Ab. When the component
has to evaluates an argument, the program looks for the correct interpreter and
checks if the conclusion is a consequence of the premises.

3.2   Meta-interpreter for Argument Check

The following interpreter for argument check (1) has the argument name as
its input parameter, (2) asserts all of its facts and rules, and (3) verifies its
correctness for the different sorts of inference.

```
check_argument(Name):-
    argument(Name,_,beliefs(facts(F),rules(R)),infer(I),conclusion(C)),
    assert_list(F),
    assert_list(R),
    check_conclusion(I,C).
check_conclusion(mt,[T|C]):-proveMT(T).
check_conclusion(mp,[T|C]):-proveMP(T).
contrary(non(P),P):-!.
contrary(P,non(P)).
```

The contrary term is a support to find opposite predicate. We also add specific relation of opposition like *old vs. young* that in predicate form looks like
contrary(old(X),young(X)) and vice versa; or add the definition of contrary
for the subset like a number.

```
% Meta-interpreter for Modus-Ponens
proveMP([]):-!.
proveMP([Goal1|Goal2]):-
  !,
  proveMP(Goal1),
  proveMP(Goal2).
proveMP(Goal):-
  write('call:'),write(Goal),nl,
  (my_clause(Goal,Body);call(Goal)),!,
  proveMP(Body).

% Meta-interpreter for Modus-Tollens
proveMT([]):-!.
proveMT([Goal1|Goal2]):-
```

```
  !,
  proveMT(Goal1),
  proveMT(Goal2).
proveMT(Goal):-
  write('call:'),write(Goal),nl,
  contrary(Goal,NegGoal),
  my_clause(Head ,[NegGoal|T]),contrary(Head,NegHead),NegHead.
```

Example 1. Check of argument in Modus Ponens and execution trace

```
argument(arg1,1,beliefs(facts([man(john),age(90,john)]),
                 rules([my_clause(old(X),[human(X),age(A,X),A>80]),
                        my_clause(human(X),[man(X)])])),
                 infer(mp),conclusion([old(john)])).
?- check_argument(arg1).
```

```
assert:man(john)
assert:age(90, john)
assert:my_clause(old(_G385), [human(_G385), age(_G395, _G385), _G395>80])
assert:my_clause(human(_G385), [man(_G385)])
prove:old(john)
call:old(john)
call:human(john)
call:man(john)
call:age(_G430, john)
call:90>80
Yes
```

Example 2. Check of argument in Modus Tollens

```
argument(arg3,1,beliefs(facts([non(mortal(eraclito))]),
                 rules([my_clause(mortal(X),[human(X)])])),
                 infer(mt),
                 conclusion([non(human(eraclito))]))).
?- check_argument(arg3).
Yes
```

3.3 Meta-interpreter for Argument Management

Managing the argument set requires in particular an ability to calculate: (1) the relations of undercut and attack between argument; (2) the conflict-free sets; and (3) the preferred extensions. Undercut and attack relations are found by comparing the 'conclusion vs. conclusion' and 'conclusion vs. beliefs' (and vice versa) between two different arguments. The operation of comparison is done in the argumentation component with the check/4 predicate. Each argument has to be compared with the others to find all the relations; if we have to N arguments we have to do $\approx \sum_{i=0}^{N} N^2$ comparisons. At the end of this process, tracing the attack(from,to) and undercut(from,to) we obtain a *defeat graph* where the relations are the arcs and the arguments are the nodes, according to Dung [3].

The core of the argumentation component is represented by the interpreters that manage the arguments in order to find the conflict free sets, the admissible sets, and the preferred extensions.

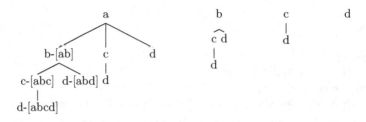

Fig. 1. Search trees generated for 4 arguments

Conflict Free Set. The problem of a conflict free set is already known in graph theory with the name of stable set or independent set. It is in the class of NP-hard problem, for which is very unlikely to find an efficient algorithm. Our idea is to build an algorithm that works incrementally, so to try to avoid the complexity of a growing amount of information—and also, because we foresee a dynamic and distributed scenario where agents share their own arguments at different times.

To solve the conflict free problem, we adopt a constraint-based approach. Our algorithm is based over a standard backtracking strategy. The constraint is the absence of conflicts among arguments (undercut, rebuttal). A solution is consistent if the set of arguments satisfies the constraints. In order to limit the degree of backtracking, consistency is checked before each argument is added to the solution. When the consistency check fails, the algorithm stores partial results, and starts backtracking. Then, it recursively tries to add all the remaining arguments.

In order to limit the size of the search space a branching strategy is used in the phase of set instantiation. The logic program constructs search trees with decreasing depth for all input elements. So, the algorithm tries to find all possible solutions around each argument. After such a search process, the selected argument is removed from the next search space. For example, if we consider a list of four input arguments [a,b,c,d], the resulting search trees are shown in figure 1. There, the possible partial solutions are denoted in square brackets.

The algorithm can also be used in a dynamic context with inputs in succession. To find a new solution, after each update we have to insert new arguments in each existing conflict free set, and run the algorithm again. The following Prolog code has been tested in tuProlog 1.3.0 [6] and shows the main predicates implementing the conflict free set division.

```
selection(X,[X|Rest],Rest).
selection(X,[Head|List],Rest) :-
    selection(X,List,Rest).

turn(ArgumentSet):-
        selection(Name,ArgumentSet,RestArgumentSet),
        argument(Name,_,beliefs(facts(F),rules(R)),_,conclusion(C)),
        newconflictfree(RestArgumentSet,[Name],F,C,[Name]).
```

```
newconflictfree(Arguments,Result,Facts,Conclusions,ConflictFree):-
        selection(Name,Arguments,RestArguments),
        argument(Name,_,beliefs(facts(F),rules(R)),_,conclusion(C)),
        check(Facts,F,Conclusions,C),
        append1(Facts,F,NewFacts),
        append1(Conclusions,C,NewConclusions),
        add2end(Name,ConflictFree,NewConflictFree),
        newconflictfree(RestArguments,NewConflictFree,NewFacts,
                        NewConclusions,NewConflictFree).

check(FL,F,CL,C):-
        not(control(FL,C)),
        not(control(F,CL)),
        not(control(CL,C)).

newconflictfree(_,[],_,_,_):-!,fail.
newconflictfree(_,R,_,_,_):-
        mem(P),
        notsubsetset(R,P),
        retract(mem(P)),
        assert(mem([R|P])),!,
        mem(P1),
        fail.
```

Admissible Set and Preferred Extension. An admissible set of arguments
is a conflict free set that defeats collectively all its elements, referring back to
definition 6. The notion of 'collectively defends' is useful to find a subset of argument that is more consistent than the conflict free set. The Preferred Extension
is the largest set among the admissible sets.

We have to find a conflict free set where if an argument is attacked then there
exists another argument in the same set that attacks the attacker. This is an
indirect form of defense, which we call collective defense.

Our algorithm to resolve the admissible set problem directly uses the conflict
free set calculated in the previous section. Also, the algorithm looks only for
undercut relations because each argument defends itself from a rebuttal attack
but not from an undercut. In a graph representation, the rebuttal relation is a
bidirectional arc; on the contrary the undercut relation is a one-direction arc.

The algorithm basically works by subtracting from each conflict free set the
arguments attacked but not defended by elements of the same set. The remaining
sets represent the solution called admissible sets. The three basic steps that the
algorithm does for each conflict free set are: (1) to find defeat arguments with
respect to the general set, (2) to find defenders from attackers in the general
set, and (3) to remove defeat arguments without defender. Following, the Prolog
code that calculates the admissible sets, again tested in tuProlog 1.3.0.

```
admissible(_,[],[]).
admissible(TotalArguments,[ConflictFreeSet|Rest],Solution):-
        %to find set of attacker to conflict free
```

```
    findundercat(TotalArguments,ConflictFreeSet,Attacker,Defeat),
    %it find the defend argument that block the attack
    findundercat(ConflictFreeSet,Attacker,AttackerFromCF,DefeatOut),
    removelist(DefeatOut,Attacker,AttackerNotDefeat),
    findundercat(AttackerNotDefeat,Defeat,AF,DF),
    removelist(DF,ConflictFreeSet,Sol),
    Solution=[Sol|Result],
    admissible(TotalArguments,Rest,Result).

findundercat([],_,[],[]):-!.
findundercat([H|T],CF,A,D):-
    argument(H,_,beliefs(facts(F),rules(R)),infer(_),conclusion([C])),
    contrary(C,P),!,
 (argument(Element,_,beliefs(facts([P]),rules(_)),infer(_),conclusion(_))->
 (member(Element,CF)->(A=[H|R1],D=[Element|R2]);(A=R1,D=R2));(A=R1,D=R2)),
    findundercat(T,CF,R1,R2).
```

The predicate `findundercut(+General,+Reference,-Attackers,-Defeats)` is used
to find the undercut relation among two sets: (1) general (the set with all arguments) and (2) reference (a conflict free set).

The next step is to find the preferred extensions. We use the previous results,
and find the preferred extensions by looking for the maximal admissible set, in
accordance with the previous definition 7.

4   Co-argumentation Artifact

The main contribution of the paper is the combination of multi-agent argumentation with the A&A meta-model, exploiting agents and artifacts as the two
fundamental abstractions for MAS. In a MAS, argumentation has a central role
that allows agents to argue, to justify positions, and to try to persuade another
agent to endorse some statement. All these features are quite common in a real-
world society, and enable complex global behaviours. Argumentation can be used
to model the communication among agents in a MAS, in particular to model the
dialog between two entities. A set of six primary dialogue types is identified by
[7], that are: persuasion, inquiry, negotiation, information seeking, deliberation
and eristic. All these dialogues can be captured in a argumentation framework
[8], and they are developed strictly among two entities. In [9] an implementation
of information-seeking dialog based on tuple centre architecture is presented.
However, a definition for a dialogue says that a dialogue is a mutual conversation between two or more people. In a society there are forms of communication
among multiple entities that enable humans to work together and achieve their
goals. Following that definition, we can naturally extend the dialogue concept
in MAS from two agents to N agents. For instance, the argumentation-based
dialogues listed above could be transformed in social discussions among agents.

In a social context any action and activity are mediated through *artifacts*, in
accord with Activity Theory (AT) [2]. Mediation is useful to achieve cooperation
between the entities and the coordination of the global system. In particular in

a MAS, mediation among agents has a central role to coordinate activities, to achieve social goals, and to support interaction. Moreover, in a system there are social properties that need to be expressed outside agents. Knowledge too, also according to Distributed Cognition [10], is not bounded inside each individual agent, but is instead distributed across agents and artifacts in the environment.

An artifact is a computational entity used by agents, possibly featuring useful properties such as controllability, malleability, linkability, and situation [11]. The artifact abstraction is introduced in the A&A meta-model for MAS, where agents and artifacts are two basic building block to design the system, more generally to engineering software systems: (1) agents represent task-oriented or goal-oriented components that act pro-actively according to their task or goal; (2) artifacts represent resources or tools that are used by agents during their activities.

In this work, we define a Co-Argumentation Artifact (CAA) as an artifact specialized in managing arguments and providing coordination services for argumentation process in a MAS. The CAA is a mediator of agent interaction and supports a simplified implementation of multi-agent argumentation system. It provides functionality that permits agents to exploit social commitment, enabling them to share, store and exchange arguments.

A simple example of social use of CAA is to fix social acceptance of the arguments: the goal is to determine whether an argument is acceptable with respect to the global knowledge of the community. The CAA applies an argumentation semantics over the shared arguments, which provides for the acceptance criteria. Another interesting example is the use of CAA as a commitment store during the dialog process. Tracing the commitments is fundamental for the next step of the discussion. Also, from the arguments stored during the dialog process the CAA could deduce or induce new knowledge. The introduction of the CAA model provides new support to design communications that involve more entities in a social context.

A similar type of artifact is the co-ordination artifact [1], specialised to provide a coordination service in MAS [12]. A typical use of a co-ordination artifact is enabling the exchange of information among agents in an open and dynamic environment—like a mailbox or a blackboard. Another interesting example is the use of the co-ordination artifact for knowledge mediation where the information can be manipulated by the artifact by either aggregation or induction process.

In this work, we developed a hybrid distributed system combining the argumentation component with a multi-agent co-ordination artifact, which is what we call CAA. Our current implementation of the CAA follows a preferred semantic, providing service to calculate preferred extensions and admissible sets.

The technological support to build co-ordination artifacts is provided here by TuCSoN, a coordination infrastructure for MAS introduced in [13]. TuCSoN provides programmable tuple spaces called tuple centres where agents write, read and consume logic tuples via simple communication operations (out, rd, in, inp, rdp). Tuple centres can play the role of agent coordinators, where coordination rules are expressed in terms of tuples. In particular, coordination in TuCSoN is expressed through the ReSpecT specification language [14]: there, coordination laws are encapsulated in the coordination media, with obvious benefits for the engineering of open and dynamic system like MAS. As a coordination artifact, a tuple centre is also a container of knowledge declaratively represented through logic tuples, and is equipped with Turing-equivalent computational power through the ReSpecT specification language. There, MAS coordination is obtained by governing the exchange of logic tuples through the tuple centres by properly programming their reactive behaviour.

So, in order to realize a CAA, an obvious choice is to exploit a TuCSoN logic tuple centre as a co-ordination artifact. In fact, on the one hand a typical argumentation process is composed of two parts: (1) knowledge representation; and (2) computation over the set of arguments. On the other hand, the tuple centre architecture is also composed of two parts: an ordinary tuple space where the information are stored in form of tuples, and a behaviour specification that defines the computation over the tuple set. Thus, a TuCSoN tuple centre could support the argumentation process by representing knowledge declaratively in terms of logic-tuple arguments, and by specifying the computation over argument set in term of ReSpecT specification tuples. So, our first experimental implementation of a CAA is built as a TuCSoN tuple centre programmed with an argumentation component algorithm (Section 3), and with arguments represented by logic tuples (Section 2). Agents use the CAA and whenever a new argument is added to the tuple centre as a logic tuple the CAA reacts and re-calculates the conflict free sets, the admissible sets, and the preferred extensions, representing them too in terms of logic tuples in the tuple centre.

4.1   Example: Argument Acceptance

We present an application of CAA in a multi-agent context where agents have to decide whether their arguments are socially acceptable. We use the argumentation system presented in Section 2 with preferred semantics, and either credulous or sceptical acceptance. An argument is considered as accepted in the credulous definition if it is contained at least in one preferred extension, and in the sceptical definition if it is contained in every preferred extension. In [15] an algorithm is presented that resolves the credulous and the sceptical decision problems based on an argumentation game formalised with a dialog between two entities. The algorithm could be applied either inside each agent simulating a dialog game, or between two agents. In order to extend the solution to N agents, we propose to use the A&A meta-model by adopting the CAA abstraction.

We foresee a scenario where a group of agents argue about what to do on Saturday night. For instance, the agents are conditioned from the past history of the place where to go, or the possible company. Each agent has its arguments about whether to go or not to go to, say, the El Farol Bar. In order to make a personal evaluation the agents may have some benefit from social information that could retrieve by asking other agents. Besides, when the agents share their arguments, a form of social knowledge is implicitly generated, which provides agents with a social point of view over the Saturday night problem. Also, sharing knowledge and arguments gives the group more chances to take congruent decisions.

More generally, social contexts typically introduce the need to represent and store social knowledge. Since shared, social knowledge belongs in principle to every agent, so to no agent in particular, it should be stored and maintained outside agents: in short, this is what makes it useful to introduce in this scenario the notion of artifact, as an abstraction that agents can use to share, compare and store information.

Here, we consider agents with different knowledge bases composed only of arguments, and an empty CAA only containing the algorithms proposed in the argumentation component. The arguments acceptance is driven generally by a system process divides in three sequential steps. Firstly, the agents share own arguments writing the arguments in the CAA. Secondly, the CAA reacts and calculates the conflict free and preferred extension over the shared arguments. Thirdly and finally, the agents evaluate credulous or sceptical acceptability based on common sets calculated in the CAA. Then, each agent can consult the CAA to undestand the "social acceptability" of its own arguments, but also the other agent's arguments, and possibly deliberate its course of actions based on a shared view of arguments. Also, the CAA keeps track of the overall argumentation process, and could be exploited by an external observe to understand the social behaviour of agents sharing arguments and behaving accordingly.

In particular, in our example the CAA is implemented as a TuCSoN tuple centre called saturdayNight, which processes and combines knowledge expressed by arguments from various agents. In Table 1 the arguments possessed and shared by the three agents are shown. Some arguments are in favor to go out if the conclusion is play(1), or vice versa is play(-1). The support of conclusions should contain the motivation to do the choice, for instance: a favorite kind of music music(rock), a previous nice night result(1) or a good company willgo(susan). Different sets of arguments represent different opinions and motivations that bring an agent to make a decision. The sharing of the arguments enables the composition and completion of the information.

The sets calculated in CAA are expressed with the tuples conflictfreeset, admissibleset and preferredset and calculated using the algorithm explained in section 3. An external observer can look inside the CAA through the Inspector utility provide by TuCSoN, and consult the argument sets. In the following we show the sets computed after the last argument insertion. The sets contains the argument names.

```
conflicfreeset([[argB,argC,argD,musicB,companyB,dayA,dayB,typemusic],
[argB,argC,argD,musicB,companyB,day,dayA,typemusic],
[argB,argC,argD,music,companyB,dayA,dayB],
[argB,argC,argD,music,companyB,day,dayA],
[argA,companyA,day,typemusic],
[argA,music,musicA,companyA,day]])

admissibleset([[argB,argC,argD,companyB,dayA,typemusic],
[argB,argC,argD,companyB,day,dayA,typemusic],
[argB,argC,argD,music,companyB,dayA],
[argB,argC,argD,music,companyB,day,dayA],
```

Table 1. Arguments by Agent1, Agent2, and Agent3

Agent1
`argument(argB,1,beliefs(facts([result(-1)])),infer(t),conclusion([play(-1)])).`
`argument(argC,1,beliefs(facts([result(1)])),infer(t),conclusion([play(-1)])).`
`argument(day,1,beliefs(facts([today(sunday)])),infer(t),conclusion([today(sunday)])).`
`argument(musicB,1,beliefs(facts([non(music(rock))])),infer(t),conclusion([play(-1)])).`
`argument(dayB,1,beliefs(facts([non(today(sunday))])),infer(t),conclusion([play(-1)])).`
...
Agent2
`argument(music,1,beliefs(facts([music(rock)])),infer(t),conclusion([music(rock)])).`
`argument(argD,1,beliefs(facts([result(-1)])),infer(t),conclusion([play(-1)])).`
`argument(companyA,2,beliefs(facts([willgo(susan)])),infer(t),conclusion([play(1)])).`
`argument(companyB,2,beliefs(facts([non(willgo(susan))])),infer(t),conclusion([play(-1)])).`
`argument(musicA,1,beliefs(facts([music(rock)])),infer(t),conclusion([play(1)])).`
...
Agent3
`argument(argA,1,beliefs(facts([result(1)])),infer(t),conclusion([play(1)])).`
`argument(typemusic,1,beliefs(facts([imtired(yes)])),infer(t),conclusion([non(music(rock))])).`
`argument(dayA,1,beliefs(facts([today(sunday)])),infer(t),conclusion([play(-1)])).`
`argument(company,1,beliefs(facts([willgo(susan)])),infer(t),conclusion([willgo(susan)])).`
...

```
[argA,companyA,day,typemusic],
[argA,music,companyA,day]])

preferredset([[argA,music,companyA,day],
[argA,companyA,day,typemusic],
[argB,argC,argD,music,companyB,day,dayA],
[argB,argC,argD,companyB,day,dayA,typemusic]])
```

One should observe that the global preferred sets are different from the ones that each agent could calculate based on its own arguments only. Agents could then read the `preferredset` tuple, and verify in which set its own arguments occur. For instance, `agent1` may want to consider the social acceptability of argument `musicB` that in its own knowledge is accepted, because the argument belong to its own preferred set (`[argB,argC,day,musicB]`). Vice versa, when considering the common preferred extension, the argument is no longer (socially) acceptable because it does not belong to a common set. These sets are calculated from more information than it is available to each individual agent, and in some context they could be considered as more reliable. In any case, agents can autonomously decide what to do with such information—either to use or to ignore it.

In general, the use of a component external to agents to support argumentation within a social agent-based context, like the CAA, easily provides MAS designers with a tool for encapsulating and consistently handling the evolution of social knowledge, and provides agents with an instrument to enhance their ability to deal with their own partial and incomplete knowledge.

Acknowledgments. The authors are grateful for financial assistance received from the EC's Information Society Technologies programme, through the *Argumentation Service Platform with Integrated Components (ASPIC) Project* (IST-FP6-002307); and from the Italian PRIN 2006 through the Project *Extensible Object Systems DUE: Dynamic and Unpredictable Environments (EOS DUE)*. We are also grateful for assistance received from Trevor Bench-Capon, and comments received from the anonymous reviewers and participants at the ArgMAS 2007 Workshop. Some of this work was undertaken while the first author was visiting the Department of Computer Science at the University of Liverpool, UK, and we are grateful to the Department for the support provided.

References

1. Omicini, A., Ricci, A., Viroli, M., Castelfranchi, C., Tummolini, L.: Coordination artifacts: Environment-based coordination for intelligent agents. In: Jennings, N.R., Sierra, C., Sonenberg, L., Tambe, M. (eds.) 3rd International Joint Conference on Autonomous Agents and Multiagent Systems (AAMAS 2004), 19–23 July, 2004, vol. 1, pp. 286–293. ACM, New York (2004)
2. Nardi, B.A.: Context and Consciousness: Activity Theory and Human-Computer Interaction. MIT Press, Cambridge (1996)
3. Dung, P.M.: On the acceptability of arguments and its fundamental role in non-monotonic reasoning, logic programming and n-person games. Artificial Intelligence 77(2), 321–358 (1995)
4. Prakken, H., Vreeswijk, G.: Logical systems for defeasible argumentation. In: Gabbay, D.M., Guenther, F. (eds.) Handbook of Philosophical Logic, 2nd edn., vol. 4, pp. 219–318. Kluwer Academic, Dordrecht (2002)
5. Sterling, L., Shapiro, E.: The art of Prolog: Advanced programming techniques. MIT Press, Cambridge (1994)
6. aliCE Research Group: Tuprolog home page. http://tuprolog.alice.unibo.it/
7. Walton, D.N., Krabbe, E.C.W.: Commitment in Dialogue: Basic Concepts of Interpersonal Reasoning. SUNY Press (1996)
8. Parsons, S., McBurney, P.: Argumentation-based communication between agents. In: Huget, M.-P. (ed.) Communication in Multiagent Systems. LNCS (LNAI), vol. 2650, pp. 164–178. Springer, Heidelberg (2003)
9. Doutre, S., McBurney, P., Wooldridge, M.: Law-governed Linda as a semantics for agent dialogue protocols. In: Dignum, F., Dignum, V., Koenig, S., Kraus, S., Singh, M.P., Wooldridge, M. (eds.) 4rd International Joint Conference on Autonomous Agents and Multiagent Systems (AAMAS 2005), 25–29 July, 2005. pp. 1257–1258. ACM Press, New York
10. Kirsh, D.: Distributed cognition, coordination and environment design. In: European Conference on Cognitive Science, pp. 1–11 (1999)
11. Omicini, A., Ricci, A., Viroli, M.: Agens Faber: Toward a theory of artefacts for MAS. Electronic Notes in Theoretical Computer Sciences 150(3), 21–36 (May 29, 2006); In: Proceedings of 1st International Workshop "Coordination and Organization" (CoOrg 2005), COORDINATION 2005, Namur, Belgium (April 22, 2005)
12. Viroli, M., Omicini, A.: Coordination as a service. Fundamenta Informaticae 73(4), 507–534 (2006) (Special Issue: Best papers of FOCLASA 2002)

13. Omicini, A., Zambonelli, F.: Coordination for Internet application development. Autonomous Agents and Multi-Agent Systems 2(3), 251–269 (1999)
14. Omicini, A., Denti, F.: Formal ReSpecT. Electronic Notes in Theoretical Computer Science 48, 179–196 (2001)
15. Cayrol, C., Doutre, S., Mengin, J.: On decision problems related to the preferred semantics for argumentation frameworks. Journal of Logic and Computation 13(3), 377–403 (2003)

On the Relevance of Utterances in Formal Inter-agent Dialogues*

Simon Parsons[1], Peter McBurney[2], Elizabeth Sklar[1], and Michael Wooldridge[2]

[1] Department of Computer and Information Science, Brooklyn College,
City University of New York, 2900 Bedford Avenue, Brooklyn, NY 11210, USA
{parsons,sklar}@sci.brooklyn.cuny.edu
[2] Department of Computer Science, University of Liverpool,
Ashton Building, Ashton Street, Liverpool L69, 3BX
{mcburney,mjw}@liverpool.ac.uk

Abstract. Work on argumentation-based dialogue has defined frameworks within which dialogues can be carried out, established protocols that govern dialogues, and studied different properties of dialogues. This work has established the space in which agents are permitted to interact through dialogues. Recently, there has been increasing interest in the mechanisms agents might use to choose how to act — the rhetorical maneuvering that they use to navigate through the space defined by the rules of the dialogue. Key in such considerations is the idea of relevance, since a usual requirement is that agents stay focussed on the subject of the dialogue and only make relevant remarks. Here we study several notions of relevance, showing how they can be related to both the rules for carrying out dialogues and to rhetorical maneuvering.

1 Introduction

Finding ways for agents to reach agreements in multiagent systems is an area of active research. One mechanism for achieving agreement is through the use of *argumentation* — where one agent tries to convince another agent of something during the course of some *dialogue*. Early examples of argumentation-based approaches to multiagent agreement include the work of Dignum *et al.* [8], Kraus [15], Parsons and Jennings [17], Reed [26], Schroeder *et al.* [28] and Sycara [29].

The work of Walton and Krabbe [30], popularized in the multiagent systems community by Reed [26], has been particularly influential in the field of argumentation-based dialogue. This work influenced the field in a number of ways, perhaps most deeply in framing multi-agent interactions as *dialogue games* in the tradition of Hamblin [14]. Viewing dialogues in this way, as in [2,24], provides a powerful framework for analyzing the formal properties of dialogues, and for identifying suitable protocols under which dialogues can be conducted [20,22]. The dialogue game view overlaps with work on conversation policies (see, for example, [7,11]), but differs in considering the entire dialogue rather than dialogue segments.

In this paper, we extend the work of [20] by considering the role of *relevance* — the relationship between utterances in a dialogue. Relevance is a topic of increasing interest

---

* This paper is a minor reworking of [18].

I. Rahwan, S. Parsons, and C. Reed (Eds.): ArgMAS 2007, LNAI 4946, pp. 47–62, 2008.

in argumentation-based dialogue because it relates to the scope that an agent has for applying strategic maneuvering to obtain the outcomes that it requires [21,25,27]. Our work identifies the limits on such *rhetorical maneuvering*, showing when it can and cannot have an effect.

The rest of the paper is structured as follows. Section 2 provides the technical background, Section 3 develops a general model of dialogue, Section 4 introduces and compares notions of relevance, and Section 5 shows how relevance impacts dialogues. Finally, Section 6 summarizes and identifies future work.

2   Background

We begin by introducing the formal system of argumentation that underpins our approach, as well as the corresponding terminology and notation, all taken from [2,9,19]. A more complete description may be found in those papers.

A dialogue is a sequence of messages passed between two or more members of a set of agents $\mathbf{A}$. An agent α maintains a knowledge base, Σ_α, containing formulas of a propositional language $\mathcal{L}$ and having no deductive closure. Agent α also maintains the set of its past utterances, called the "commitment store", CS_α. We refer to this as an agent's "public knowledge", since it contains information that is shared with other agents. In contrast, the contents of Σ_α are "private" to α.

Note that in the description that follows, we assume that $\vdash$ is the classical inference relation, that $\equiv$ stands for logical equivalence, and we use Δ to denote all the information available to an agent. Thus in a dialogue between two agents α and β, $\Delta_\alpha = \Sigma_\alpha \cup CS_\alpha \cup CS_\beta$, so the commitment store CS_α can be loosely thought of as a subset of Δ_α consisting of the assertions that have been made public. In some dialogue games, such as those in [20] anything in CS_α is either in Σ_α or can be derived from it. In other dialogue games, such as those in [2], CS_α may contain things that cannot be derived from Σ_α.

Definition 1. *An argument A is a pair (S, p) where p is a formula of $\mathcal{L}$ and S a subset of Δ such that:*

1. *S is consistent;*
2. *$S \vdash p$; and*
3. *S is minimal, so no proper subset of S satisfying both 1. and 2. exists.*

S is called the *support* of A, written $S = \text{Support}(A)$ and p is the *conclusion* of A, written $p = \text{Conclusion}(A)$. Thus we talk of p being *supported* by the argument (S, p).

In general, since Δ may be inconsistent, arguments in $\mathcal{A}(\Delta)$, the set of all arguments which can be made from Δ, may conflict, and we make this idea precise with the notion of *undercutting*:

Definition 2. *Let A_1 and A_2 be arguments in $\mathcal{A}(\Delta)$. A_1 undercuts A_2 iff $\exists \neg p \in Support(A_2)$ such that $p \equiv Conclusion(A_1)$.*

In other words, an argument is undercut if and only if there is another argument which has as its conclusion the negation of an element of the support for the first argument.

To capture the fact that some beliefs are more strongly held than others, we assume that any set of beliefs has a *preference order* over it. We consider all information available to an agent, Δ, to be stratified into non-overlapping subsets $\Delta_1, \ldots, \Delta_n$ such that beliefs in Δ_i are all equally preferred and are preferred over elements in Δ_j where $i > j$. The *preference level* of a nonempty subset $S \subset \Delta$, where different elements $s \in S$ may belong to different layers Δ_i, is valued at the lowest numbered layer which has a member in S and is referred to as $level(S)$. In other words, S is only as strong as its weakest member. Note that the strength of a belief as used in this context is a separate concept from the notion of support discussed earlier.

Definition 3. *Let A_1 and A_2 be arguments in $\mathcal{A}(\Delta)$. A_1 is preferred to A_2 according to Pref, $A_1 \gg^{Pref} A_2$, iff $level(Support(A_1)) > level(Support(A_2))$. If A_1 is preferred to A_2, we say that A_1 is stronger than A_2.*

We can now define the argumentation system we will use:

Definition 4. *An* argumentation system *is a triple:*

$$\langle \mathcal{A}(\Delta), Undercut, Pref \rangle$$

such that:

- *$\mathcal{A}(\Delta)$ is a set of the arguments built from Δ,*
- *Undercut is a binary relation representing the defeat relationship between arguments, $Undercut \subseteq \mathcal{A}(\Delta) \times \mathcal{A}(\Delta)$, and*
- *Pref is a pre-ordering on $\mathcal{A}(\Delta) \times \mathcal{A}(\Delta)$.*

The preference order makes it possible to distinguish different types of relations between arguments:

Definition 5. *Let A_1, A_2 be two arguments of $\mathcal{A}(\Delta)$.*

- *If A_2 undercuts A_1 then A_1 defends itself against A_2 iff $A_1 \gg^{Pref} A_2$. Otherwise, A_1 does not defend itself.*
- *A set of arguments $\mathcal{A}$ defends A_1 iff for every A_2 that undercuts A_1, where A_1 does not defend itself against A_2, then there is some $A_3 \in \mathcal{A}$ such that A_3 undercuts A_2 and A_2 does not defend itself against A_3.*

We write $\mathcal{A}_{Undercut,Pref}$ to denote the set of all non-undercut arguments and arguments defending themselves against all their undercutting arguments. The set $\underline{\mathcal{A}}(\Delta)$ of acceptable arguments of the argumentation system

$$\langle \mathcal{A}(\Delta), Undercut, Pref \rangle$$

is [1] the least fixpoint of a function $\mathcal{F}$:

$$\mathcal{A} \subseteq \mathcal{A}(\Delta)$$
$$\mathcal{F}(\mathcal{A}) = \{(S, p) \in \mathcal{A}(\Delta) \mid (S, p) \text{ is defended by } \mathcal{A}\}$$

Definition 6. *The set of* acceptable *arguments for an argumentation system* $\langle \mathcal{A}(\Delta),$ *Undercut, Pref* $\rangle$ *is recursively defined as:*

$$\underline{\mathcal{A}}(\Delta) = \bigcup \mathcal{F}_{i \geq 0}(\emptyset)$$

$$= A_{Undercut,Pref} \cup \left[\bigcup \mathcal{F}_{i \geq 1}(A_{Undercut,Pref}) \right]$$

An argument is acceptable *if it is a member of the acceptable set, and a proposition is* acceptable *if it is the conclusion of an acceptable argument.*

An acceptable argument is one which is, in some sense, proven since all the arguments that might undermine it are themselves undermined.

Definition 7. *If there is an acceptable argument for a proposition p, then the* status *of p is* accepted, *while if there is not an acceptable argument for p, the status of p is* not accepted.

Argument A is said to *affect the status* of another argument A' if changing the status of A will change the status of A'.

3 Dialogues

Systems like those described in [2,20], lay down sets of *locutions* that agents can make to put forward propositions and the arguments that support them, and *protocols* that define precisely which locutions can be made at which points in the dialogue. We are not concerned with such a level of detail here. Instead we are interested in the interplay between arguments that agents put forth. As a result, we will consider only that agents are allowed to put forward arguments. We do not discuss the detail of the mechanism that is used to put these arguments forward — we just assume that arguments of the form (S, p) are inserted into an agent's commitment store where they are then visible to other agents.

We then have a typical definition of a dialogue:

Definition 8. *A dialogue D is a sequence of* moves:

$$m_1, m_2, \ldots, m_n.$$

A given move m_i is a pair $\langle \alpha, A_i \rangle$ where A_i is an argument that α places into its commitment store CS_α.

Moves in an argumentation-based dialogue typically attack moves that have been made previously. While, in general, a dialogue can include moves that undercut several arguments, in the remainder of this paper, we will only consider dialogues that put forward moves which undercut at most one argument. For now, we place no additional constraints on the moves that make up a dialogue. Later we will see how different restrictions on moves lead to different kinds of dialogue.

The sequence of arguments put forward in the dialogue is determined by the agents that are taking part in the dialogue, but they are usually not completely free to choose what arguments they make. As indicated earlier, their choice is typically limited by a protocol. If we write the sequence of n moves $m_1, m_2, \ldots, m_n$ as $\tilde{m}_n$, and denote the empty sequence as $\tilde{m}_0$, then we can define a protocol in the following way:

Definition 9. *A protocol P is a function on a sequence of moves $\tilde{m}_i$ in a dialogue D that, for all $i \geq 0$, identifies a set of possible moves $\mathbf{M}_{i+1}$ from which the m_{i+1}th move may be drawn:*

$$P : \tilde{m}_i \mapsto \mathbf{M}_{i+1}$$

In other words, for our purposes here, at every point in a dialogue, a protocol determines a set of possible moves that agents may make as part of the dialogue. If a dialogue D always picks its move m_{i+1} from the set $\mathbf{M}_{i+1}$ identified by protocol P given the set of moves $\tilde{m}_i$, then D is said to *conform* to P.

Even if a dialogue conforms to a protocol, it is typically the case that the agent engaging in the dialogue has to make a choice of move — it has to choose which of the moves in $\mathbf{M}$ to make. This exercise of choice is what we refer to as an agent's use of *rhetoric* (in its oratorical sense of "influencing the thought and conduct of an audience"). Some of our results will give a sense of how much scope an agent has to exercise rhetoric under different protocols.

As arguments are placed into commitment stores, and hence become public, agents can determine the relationships between them. In general, after several moves in a dialogue, some arguments will undercut others. We will denote the set of arguments $\{A_1, A_2, \ldots, A_j\}$ asserted after moves $m_1, m_2, \ldots, m_j$ of a dialogue to be $\mathcal{A}_j$ — the relationship of the arguments in $\mathcal{A}_j$ can be described as an argumentation graph, similar to those described in, for example, [3,4,10]:

Definition 10. *An argumentation graph AG over a set of arguments $\mathcal{A}$ is a directed graph (V, E) such that every vertex $v \in V$ denotes one argument $A \in \mathcal{A}$, every argument A is denoted by one vertex v, and every directed edge $e \in E$ from v to $v' \in V$ denotes that v undercuts v'.*

We will use the term *argument graph* as a synonym for "argumentation graph".

Note that we do not require that the argumentation graph is connected. In other words the notion of an argumentation graph allows for the representation of arguments that do not relate, by undercutting or being undercut, to any other arguments (we will come back to this point very shortly).

We adapt some standard graph theoretic notions in order to describe various aspects of the argumentation graph. If there is an edge e from vertex v to vertex v', then v is said to be the *parent* of v' and v' is said to be the child of v. In a reversal of the usual notion, we define a root of an argumentation graph[1] as follows:

Definition 11. *A root of an argumentation graph $AG = (V, E)$ is a node $v \in V$ that has no children.*

Thus a root of a graph is a node to which directed edges may be connected, but from which no directed edges connect to other nodes. Thus a root is a node representing an argument that is undercut, but which itself does no undercutting. Similarly:

Definition 12. *A leaf of an argumentation graph $AG = (V, E)$ is a node $v \in V$ that has no parents.*

---

[1] Note that we talk of "a root" rather than "the root" — as defined, an argumentation graph need not be a tree.

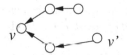

Fig. 1. An example argument graph

Thus a leaf in an argumentation graph represents an argument that undercuts another argument, but is itself not undercut. Thus in Figure 1, v is a root, and v' is a leaf. The reason for the reversal of the usual notions of root and leaf is that, as we shall see, we will consider dialogues to construct argumentation graphs from the roots (in our sense) to the leaves. The reversal of the terminology means that it matches the natural process of tree construction.

Since, as described above, argumentation graphs are allowed to not be connected (in the usual graph theory sense), it is helpful to distinguish nodes that are connected to other nodes, in particular to the root of the tree. We say that node v is *connected* to node v' if and only if there is a path from v to v'. Since edges represent undercut relations, the notion of connectedness between nodes captures the influence that one argument may have on another:

Proposition 1. *Given an argumentation graph $AG = (V, E)$, if there is any argument A, denoted by node $v \in V$ that affects the status of another argument A', denoted by $v' \in V$, then v is connected to v'. The converse does not hold.*

Proof. *Given Definitions 5 and 6, the only ways in which A can affect the status of A' is if A either undercuts A', or if A undercuts some argument A'' that undercuts A', or if A undercuts some A''' that undercuts some A'' that undercuts A', and so on. In all such cases, a sequence of undercut relations relates the two arguments, and if they are both in an argumentation graph, this means that they are connected. This proves the first part of the result.*

Since the notion of path ignores the direction of the directed arcs, nodes v and v' are connected whether the edge between them runs from v to v' or vice versa. Since A only undercuts A' if the edge runs from v to v', we cannot infer that A will affect the status of A' from information about whether or not they are connected. This proves the second part of the result.

The reason that we need the concept of the argumentation graph is that the properties of the argumentation graph tell us something about the set of arguments $\mathcal{A}$ the graph represents. When that set of arguments is constructed through a dialogue, there is a relationship between the structure of the argumentation graph and the protocol that governs the dialogue. It is the extent of the relationship between structure and protocol that is the main subject of this paper. To study this relationship, we need to establish a correspondence between a dialogue and an argumentation graph. Given the definitions we have so far, this is simple:

Definition 13. *A dialogue D, consisting of a sequence of moves $\tilde{m}_n$, and an argument graph $AG = (V, E)$ correspond to one another iff $\forall m \in \tilde{m}_n$, the argument A_i that is advanced at move m_i is represented by exactly one node $v \in V$, and $\forall v \in V$, v represents exactly one argument A_i that has been advanced by a move $m \in \tilde{m}_n$.*

Thus a dialogue corresponds to an argumentation graph if and only if every argument made in the dialogue corresponds to a node in the graph, and every node in the graph corresponds to an argument made in the dialogue. This one-to-one correspondence allows us to consider each node v in the graph to have an index i which is the index of the move in the dialogue that put forward the argument which that node represents. Thus we can, for example, refer to the "third node" in the argumentation graph, meaning the node that represents the argument put forward in the third move of the dialogue.

4 Relevance

Most work on dialogues is concerned with what we might call *coherent* dialogues, that is dialogues in which the participants are, as in the work of Walton and Krabbe [30], focused on resolving some question through the dialogue[2]. To capture this coherence, it seems we need a notion of *relevance* to constrain the statements made by agents. Here we study three notions of relevance:

Definition 14. *Consider a dialogue D, consisting of a sequence of moves $\tilde{m}_i$, with a corresponding argument graph AG. The move m_{i+1}, $i > 1$, is said to be* relevant *if one or more of the following hold:*

R1 Making m_{i+1} will change the status of the argument denoted by the first node of AG.

R2 Making m_{i+1} will add a node v_{i+1} that is connected to the first node of AG.

R3 Making m_{i+1} will add a node v_{i+1} that is connected to the last node to be added to AG.

R2-relevance is the form of relevance defined by Bentahar *et al.* [3] in their study of strategic and tactical reasoning[3], and by Black in her analysis of inquiry dialogues [5]. R1-relevance was suggested by the notion used by Oren *et al.* [16] — though the two notions differ somewhat — and is close to that used by Prakken [21,22,23].

Note that we only define relevance for the second move of the dialogue onwards because the first move is taken to identify the *subject* of the dialogue, that is, the central question that the dialogue is intended to answer, and hence it must be relevant to the dialogue, no matter what it is. In assuming this, we focus our attention on the same kind of dialogues as [20].

We can think of relevance as enforcing a form of parsimony on a dialogue — it prevents agents from making statements that do not bear on the current state of the dialogue. This promotes efficiency, in the sense of limiting the number of moves in the dialogue, and, as in [16], prevents agents revealing information that they might better keep hidden. Another form of parsimony is to insist that agents are not allowed to put forward arguments that will be undercut by arguments that have already been made during the dialogue. We therefore distinguish such arguments.

---

[2] See [12,13] for examples of dialogues where this is not the case.

[3] We consider such reasoning sub-types of rhetoric.

Definition 15. *Consider a dialogue D, consisting of a sequence of moves $\tilde{m}_i$, with a corresponding argument graph AG. The move m_{i+1} and the argument it puts forward, A_{i+1}, are both said to be* pre-empted, *if A_{i+1} is undercut by some $A \in \mathcal{A}_i$.*

We use the term "pre-empted" because if such an argument is put forward, it can seem as though another agent anticipated the argument being made, and already made an argument that would render it useless. In the rest of this paper, we will only deal with protocols that permit moves that are relevant, in any of the senses introduced above, and are not allowed to be pre-empted. We call such protocols *basic* protocols, and we call dialogues carried out under such protocols basic dialogues.

The argument graph of a basic dialogue is somewhat restricted.

Proposition 2. *Consider a basic dialogue D. The argumentation graph AG that corresponds to D is a tree with a single root.*

Proof. Recall that Definition 10 requires only that AG be a directed graph. To show that it is a tree, we have to show that it is acyclic and connected.

That the graph is connected follows from the construction of the graph under a protocol that enforces relevance. If the notion of relevance is R3, each move adds a node that is connected to the previous node. If the notion of relevance is R2, then every move adds a node that is connected to the root, and thus is connected to some node in the graph. If the notion of relevance is R1, then every move has to change the status of the argument denoted by the root. Proposition 1 tells us that to affect the status of an argument A', the node v representing the argument A that is effecting the change has to be connected to v', the node representing A', and so it follows that every new node added as a result of an R1-relevant move will be connected to the argumentation graph. Thus AG is connected.

Since a basic dialogue does not allow moves that are pre-empted, every edge that is added during construction is directed from the node that is added to one already in the graph (thus denoting that the argument A denoted by the added node, v, undercuts the argument A' denoted by the node to which the connection is made, v', rather than the other way around). Since every edge that is added is directed from the new node to the rest of the graph, there can be no cycles. Thus AG is a tree.

To show that AG has a single root, consider its construction from the initial node. After m_1 the graph has one node, v_1 that is both a root and a leaf. After m_2, the graph is two nodes connected by an edge, and v_1 is now a root and not a leaf. v_2 is a leaf and not a root. However the third node is added, the argument earlier in this proof demonstrates that there will be a directed edge from it to some other node, making it a leaf. Thus v_1 will always be the only root. The ruling out of pre-empted moves means that v_1 will never cease to be a root, and so the argumentation graph will always have one root.

Since every argumentation graph constructed by a basic dialogue is a tree with a single root, this means that the first node of every argumentation graph is the root.

Although these results are straightforward to obtain, they allow us to show how the notions of relevance are related.

Proposition 3. *Consider a basic dialogue D, consisting of a sequence of moves $\tilde{m}_i$, with a corresponding argument graph AG.*

1. *Every move m_{i+1} that is R1-relevant is R2-relevant. The converse does not hold.*
2. *Every move m_{i+1} that is R3-relevant is R2-relevant. The converse does not hold.*
3. *Not every move m_{i+1} that is R1-relevant is R3-relevant, and not every move m_{i+1} that is R3-relevant is R1-relevant*

Proof. For 1, consider how move m_{i+1} can satisfy R1. Proposition 1 tells us that if A_{i+1} can change the status of the argument denoted by the root v_1 (which, as observed above, is the first node) of AG, then v_{i+1} must be connected to the root. This is precisely what is required to satisfy R2, and the relationship is proved to hold.

To see that the converse does not hold, we have to consider what it takes to change the status of r (since Proposition 1 tells us that connectedness is not enough to ensure a change of status — if it did, R1 and R2 relevance would coincide). For m_{i+1} to change the status of the root, it will have to (1) make the argument A represented by r either unacceptable, if it were acceptable before the move, or (2) acceptable if it were unacceptable before the move. Given the definition of acceptability, it can achieve (1) either by directly undercutting the argument represented by r, in which case v_{i+1} will be directly connected to r by some edge, or by undercutting some argument A' that is part of the set of non-undercut arguments defending A. In the latter case, v_{i+1} will be directly connected to the node representing A' and by Proposition 2 to r. To achieve (2), v_{i+1} will have to undercut an argument A'' that is either currently undercutting A, or is undercutting an argument that would otherwise defend A. Now, further consider that m_{i+1} puts forward an argument A_{i+1} that undercuts the argument denoted by some node v', but this latter argument defends itself against A_{i+1}. In such a case, the set of acceptable arguments will not change, and so the status of A_r will not change. Thus a move that is R2-relevant need not be R1-relevant.

For 2, consider that m_{i+1} can satisfy R3 simply by adding a node that is connected to v_i, the last node to be added to AG. By Proposition 2, it is connected to r and so is R2-relevant.

To see that the converse does not hold, consider that an R2-relevant move can connect to any node in AG.

The first part of 3 follows by a similar argument to that we just used — an R1-relevant move does not have to connect to v_i, just to some v that is part of the graph — and the second part follows since a move that is R3-relevant may introduce an argument A_{i+1} that undercuts the argument A_i put forward by the previous move (and so v_{i+1} is connected to v_i), but finds that A_i defends itself against A_{i+1}, preventing a change of status at the root.

What is most interesting is not so much the results but why they hold, since this reveals some aspects of the interplay between relevance and the structure of argument graphs. For example, to restate a case from the proof of Proposition 3, a move that is R3-relevant by definition has to add a node to the argument graph that is connected to the last node that was added. Since a move that is R2-relevant can add a node that connects anywhere on an argument graph, any move that is R3-relevant will be R2-relevant, but the converse does not hold.

It turns out that we can exploit the interplay between structure and relevance that Propositions 2 and 3 have started to illuminate to establish relationships between the protocols that govern dialogues and the argument graphs constructed during such dialogues. To do this we need to define protocols in such a way that they refer to the structure of the graph. We have:

Definition 16. *A protocol is* single-path *if all dialogues that conform to it construct argument graphs that have only one branch.*

This gives us the following correspondance:

Proposition 4. *A basic protocol P is single-path if, for all i, the set of permitted moves M_i at move i are all R3-relevant. The converse does not hold.*

Proof. R3-relevance requires that every node added to the argument graph be connected to the previous node. Starting from the first node this recursively constructs a tree with just one branch, and the relationship holds. The converse does not hold because even if one or more moves in the protocol are R1- or R2-relevant, it may be the case that, because of an agent's rhetorical choice or because of its knowledge, every argument that is chosen to be put forward will undercut the previous argument and so the argument graph is a one-branch tree.

Looking for more complex kinds of protocol that construct more complex kinds of argument graph, it is an obvious move to turn to:

Definition 17. *A basic protocol is* multi-path *if all dialogues that conform to it can construct argument graphs that are trees.*

But, on reflection, since any graph with only one branch is also a tree:

Proposition 5. *Any single-path protocol is a multi-path protocol.*

and, furthermore:

Proposition 6. *Any basic protocol P is a multi-path protocol.*

Proof. Immediate from Proposition 2.

So the notion of a multi-path protocol does not have much traction. As a result we distinguish multi-path protocols that permit dialogues that can construct trees that have more than one branch as *bushy* protocols. We then have:

Proposition 7. *A basic protocol P is bushy if, for some i, the set of permitted moves M_i at move i are all R1- or R2-relevant.*

Proof. From Proposition 4 we know that if all moves are R3-relevant then we'll get a tree with one branch, and from Proposition 2 we know that all basic protocols will build an argument graph that is a tree, so providing we exclude R3-relevant moves, we will get protocols that can build multi-branch trees.

Of course, since, by Proposition 3, any move that is R3-relevant is R2-relevant and can quite possibly be R1-relevant (all that Proposition 3 tells us is that there is no guarantee that it will be), all that Proposition 7 tells us is that dialogues that conform to bushy protocols *may* have more than one branch. All we can do is to identify a bound on the number of branches:

Proposition 8. *Consider a basic dialogue D that includes m moves that are not R3-relevant, and has a corresponding argumentation graph AG. The number of branches in AG is less than or equal to $m + 1$.*

Proof. *Since it must connect a node to the last node added to AG, an R3-relevant move can only extend an existing branch. Since they do not have the same restriction, R1 and R2-relevant moves may create a new branch by connecting to a node that is not the last node added. Every such move could create a new branch, and if they do, we will have m branches. If there were R3-relevant moves before any of these new-branch-creating moves, then these m branches are in addition to the initial branch created by the R3-relevant moves, and we have a maximum of $m + 1$ possible branches.*

We distinguish bushy protocols from multi-path protocols, and hence R1- and R2-relevance from R3-relevance, because of the kinds of dialogue that R3-relevance enforces. In a dialogue in which all moves must be R3-relevant, the argumentation graph has a single branch — the dialogue consists of a sequence of arguments each of which undercuts the previous one and the last move to be made is the one that settles the dialogue. This, as we will see next, means that such a dialogue only allows a subset of all the moves that would otherwise be possible.

5   Completeness

The above discussion of the difference between dialogues carried out under single-path and bushy protocols brings us to the consideration of what in [20] we called "predeterminism", but we now prefer to describe using the term "completeness". The idea of predeterminism, as described in [20], captures the notion that, under some circumstances, the result of a dialogue can be established without actually having the dialogue — the agents have sufficiently little room for rhetorical maneuver that were one able to see the contents of all the Σ_i of all the $\alpha_i \in \mathbf{A}$, one would be able to identify the outcome of any dialogue on a given subject[4]. We develop this idea by considering how the argument graphs constructed by dialogues under different protocols compare to benchmark *complete* dialogues. We start by developing ideas of what "complete" might mean. One reasonable definition is that:

Definition 18. *A basic dialogue D between the set of agents $\mathbf{A}$ with a corresponding argumentation graph AG is* topic-complete *if no agent can construct an argument A that undercuts any argument A' represented by a node in AG.*

The argumentation graph constructed by a topic-complete dialogue is called a *topic-complete* argument graph and is denoted $AG(D)_T$.

A dialogue is topic-complete when no agent can add anything that is directly connected to the subject of the dialogue. In other words, every agent has said everything that might change the status of the subject. Some protocols will prevent agents from making moves even though the dialogue is not topic-complete. To distinguish such cases we have:

---

[4] Assuming that the Σ_i do not change during the dialogue, which is the usual assumption in this kind of dialogue.

Definition 19. *A basic dialogue D between the set of agents **A** with a corresponding argumentation graph AG is protocol-complete under a protocol P if no agent can make a move that adds a node to the argumentation graph and which is permitted by P.*

The argument graph constructed by a protocol-complete dialogue is called a *protocol-complete* argumentation graph and is denoted $AG(D)_P$. Clearly:

Proposition 9. *Any dialogue D under a basic protocol P is protocol-complete if it is topic-complete. The converse does not hold in general.*

Proof. If D is topic-complete, no agent can make a move that will extend the argumentation graph. This means that no agent can make a move that is permitted by a basic protocol, and so D is also protocol complete.

The converse does not hold since some basic dialogues (under a protocol that only permits R3-relevant moves, for example) will not permit certain moves (like the addition of a node that connects to the root of the argumentation graph after more than two moves) that would be allowed in a topic-complete dialogue.

which immediately gives us:

Corollary 1. *For a basic dialogue D, $AG(D)_P$ is a sub-graph of $AG(D)_T$.*

Obviously, from the definition of a sub-graph, the converse of Corollary 1 does not hold in general.

The important distinction between topic- and protocol-completeness is that the former is determined purely by the state of the dialogue — as captured by the argumentation graph — and is thus independent of the protocol, while the latter is determined entirely by the protocol. Any time that a dialogue ends in a state of protocol-completeness rather than topic completeness, it is ending when agents still have things to say but can't because the protocol won't allow them to.

With these definitions of completeness, our task is to relate topic-completeness — the property that ensures that agents can say everything that they have to say in a dialogue that is, in some sense, important — to the notions of relevance we have developed — which determine what agents are allowed to say. When we need very specific conditions to make protocol-complete dialogues topic-complete, it means that agents have lots of room for rhetorical maneuver when those conditions are not in force. That is there are many ways they can bring dialogues to a close before everything that can be said has been said. Where few conditions are required, or conditions are absent, then dialogues between agents with the same knowledge will always play out the same way, and rhetoric has no place. We have:

Proposition 10. *A protocol-complete basic dialogue D under a protocol which only allows R3-relevant moves will be topic-complete only when $AG(D)_T$ has a single branch in which the nodes are labelled in increasing order from the root.*

Proof. Given what we know about R3-relevance, the condition on $AG(D)_P$ having a single branch is obvious. This is not a sufficient condition on its own because certain protocols may prevent — through additional restrictions, like strict turn-taking in a multi-party dialogue — all the nodes in $AG(D)_T$, which is not subject to such restrictions, being added to the graph. Only when $AG(D)_T$ includes the nodes in the exact *order that the corresponding arguments are put forward is it necessary that a topic-complete argumentation graph be constructed.*

Given Proposition 9, these are the conditions under which dialogues conducted under the notion of R3-relevance will always be predetermined, and given how restrictive the conditions are, such dialogues seem to have plenty of room for rhetoric to play a part.

To find similar conditions for dialogues composed of R1- and R2-relevant moves, we first need to distinguish between them. We can do this in terms of the structure of the argumentation graph:

Proposition 11. *Consider a basic dialogue D, with argumentation graph AG which has root r denoting an argument A. If argument A', denoted by node v is an R2-relevant move m, m is not R1-relevant if and only if:*

1. *there are two nodes v' and v'' on the path between v and r, and the argument denoted by v' defends itself against the argument denoted by v''; or*
2. *there is an argument A'', denoted by node v'', that affects the status of A, and the path from v'' to r has one or more nodes in common with the path from v to r.*

Proof. For the first condition, consider that since AG is a tree, v is connected to r. Thus there is a series of undercut relations between A and A', and this corresponds to a path through AG. If this path is the only branch in the tree, then A will affect the status of A' unless the chain of "affect" is broken by an undercut that can't change the status of the undercut argument because the latter defends itself.

For the second condition, as for the first, the only way that A' cannot affect the status of A is if something is blocking its influence. If this is not due to "defending against", it must be because there is some node u on the path that represents an argument whose status is fixed somehow, and that must mean that there is another chain of undercut relations, another branch of the tree, that is incident at u. Since this second branch denotes another chain of arguments, and these affect the status of the argument denoted by u, they must also affect the status of A. Any of these are the A'' in the condition.

So an R2-relevant move m is not R1-relevant if either its effect is blocked because an argument upstream is not strong enough, or because there is another line of argument that is currently determining the status of the argument at the root. This, in turn, means that if the effect is not due to "defending against", then there is an alternative move that is R1-relevant — a move that undercuts A'' in the second condition above[5]. With the distinction between R1- and R2-relevance clarified, we can immediately show that:

Proposition 12. *A protocol-complete basic dialogue D will always be topic-complete under a protocol which only includes R2-relevant moves and allows every R2-relevant move to be made.*

The restriction on R2-relevant rules is exactly that for topic-completeness, so a dialogue that has *only* R2-relevant moves will continue until every argument that any agent can make has been put forward. Given this, and what we revealed about R1-relevance in Proposition 11, we can see that:

---

[5] Though whether the agent in question can make such a move is another question.

Proposition 13. *A protocol-complete basic dialogue D under a protocol which only includes R1-relevant moves will be topic-complete if $AG(D)_T$:*

1. *includes no path with adjacent nodes v, denoting A, and v', denoting A', such that A undercuts A' and A' is stronger than A; and*
2. *is such that the nodes in every branch have consecutive indices and no node with degree greater than two is an odd number of arcs from a leaf node.*

Proof. The first condition rules out the first condition in Proposition 11, and the second deals with the situation that leads to the second condition in Proposition 11. The second condition ensures that each branch is constructed in full before any new branch is added, and when a new branch is added, the argument that is undercut as part of the addition will be acceptable, and so the addition will change the status of the argument denoted by that node, and hence the root. With these conditions, every move required to construct $AG(D)_T$ will be permitted and so the dialogue will be topic-complete when every move has been completed.

The second part of this result only identifies one possible way to ensure that the second condition in Proposition 11 is met, so the converse of this result does not hold.

However, what we have is sufficient to answer the question about "predetermination" that we started with. For dialogues to be predetermined, every move that is R2-relevant must be made. In such cases every dialogue is topic complete. If we do not require that all R2-relevant moves are made, then there is some room for rhetoric — the way in which alternative lines of argument are presented becomes an issue. If moves are required to be R3-relevant, then there is considerable room for rhetorical play.

6   Summary

This paper has studied the different ideas of relevance in argumentation-based dialogue, identifying the relationship between these ideas, and showing how they can impact the way that agents choose moves in a dialogue — what some authors have called the strategy and tactics of a dialogue. This extends existing work on relevance, such as [3,16] by showing how different notions of relevance can have an effect on the outcome of a dialogue, in particular when they render the outcome predetermined. This connection extends the work of [20], which considered dialogue outcome, but stopped short of identifying the conditions under which it is predetermined. It also attempts to generalize existing work on the completeness of protocols, such as that in [5,22,23] by obtaining results that are not tied to specific protocols (though they are somewhat weaker than the results that can be obtained when considering specific protocols.)

There are two ways in which we are currently trying to extend this work, both of which will generalize the results and extend its applicability. First, we want to relax the restrictions that we have imposed, the exclusion of moves that attack several arguments (without which the argument graph can be multiply-connected) and the exclusion of pre-empted moves, without which the argument graph can have cycles. Second, we want to extend the ideas of relevance to cope with moves that do not only add undercutting arguments, but also supporting arguments, thus taking account of *bipolar* argumentation frameworks [6].

Acknowledgments

This work was partially supported by the EC, under grant IST-FP6-002307, and by the NSF under grants REC-02-19347 and IIS-0329037. The authors are grateful to Liz Black and Henry Prakken for their comments on the paper, and to Peter Stone for a question, now several years old, which this paper has finally allowed us to answer.

References

1. Amgoud, L., Cayrol, C.: On the acceptability of arguments in preference-based argumentation framework. In: Proceedings of the 14th Conference on Uncertainty in Artificial Intelligence, pp. 1–7 (1998)
2. Amgoud, L., Parsons, S., Maudet, N.: Arguments, dialogue, and negotiation. In: Horn, W. (ed.) Proceedings of the Fourteenth European Conference on Artificial Intelligence, pp. 338–342. IOS Press, Berlin, Germany (2000)
3. Bentahar, J., Mbarki, M., Moulin, B.: Strategic and tactic reasoning for communicating agents. In: Maudet, N., Rahwan, I., Parsons, S. (eds.) Proceedings of the Third Workshop on Argumentation in Muliagent Systems, Berlin, Germany (2007)
4. Besnard, P., Hunter, A.: A logic-based theory of deductive arguments. Artificial Intelligence 128, 203–235 (2001)
5. Black, E.: A generative framework for argumentation-based inquiry dialogues. PhD thesis, University of London (2006)
6. Cayrol, C., Devred, C., Lagasquie-Schiex, M.-C.: Handling controversial arguments in bipolar argumentation frameworks. In: Dunne, P.E., Bench-Capon, T.J.M. (eds.) Computational Models of Argument: Proceedings of COMMA 2006, pp. 261–272. IOS Press, Amsterdam (2006)
7. Chaib-Draa, B., Dignum, F.: Trends in agent communication language. Computational Intelligence 18(2), 89–101 (2002)
8. Dignum, F., Dunin-Kȩplicz, B., Verbrugge, R.: Agent theory for team formation by dialogue. In: Castelfranchi, C., Lespérance, Y. (eds.) Seventh Workshop on Agent Theories, Architectures, and Languages, Boston, USA, pp. 141–156 (2000)
9. Dung, P.M.: On the acceptability of arguments and its fundamental role in nonmonotonic reasoning, logic programming and n-person games. Artificial Intelligence 77, 321–357 (1995)
10. Dung, P.M., Kowalski, R.A., Toni, F.: Dialectic proof procedures for assumption-based, admissable argumentation. Artificial Intelligence 170(2), 114–159 (2006)
11. Flores, R.A., Kremer, R.C.: To commit or not to commit. Computational Intelligence 18(2), 120–173 (2002)
12. Gabbay, D.M., Woods, J.: More on non-cooperation in Dialogue Logic. Logic Journal of the IGPL 9(2), 321–339 (2001)
13. Gabbay, D.M., Woods, J.: Non-cooperation in Dialogue Logic. Synthese 127(1-2), 161–186 (2001)
14. Hamblin, C.L.: Mathematical models of dialogue. Theoria 37, 130–155 (1971)
15. Kraus, S., Sycara, K., Evenchik, A.: Reaching agreements through argumentation: A logical model and implementation. Artificial Intelligence 104(1–2), 1–69 (1998)
16. Oren, N., Norman, T.J., Preece, A.: Loose lips sink ships: A heuristic for argumentation. In: Maudet, N., Rahwan, I., Parsons, S. (eds.) Proceedings of the Third Workshop on Argumentation in Muliagent Systems, Berlin, Germany (2007)
17. Parsons, S., Jennings, N.R.: Negotiation through argumentation — a preliminary report. In: Proceedings of Second International Conference on Multi-Agent Systems, pp. 267–274 (1996)

18. Parsons, S., McBurney, P., Sklar, E., Wooldridge, M.: On the relevance of utterances in formal inter-agent dialogues. In: Durfee, E., Huhns, M., Shehory, O., Yakoo, M. (eds.) 6th International Conference on Autonomous Agents and Multi-Agent Systems. IFAAMAS, Richland, SC (2007)
19. Parsons, S., Wooldridge, M., Amgoud, L.: An analysis of formal inter-agent dialogues. In: Castelfranchi, C., Gini, M., Ishida, T., Johnson, W.L. (eds.) 1st International Conference on Autonomous Agents and Multi-Agent Systems, ACM Press, New York (2002)
20. Parsons, S., Wooldridge, M., Amgoud, L.: On the outcomes of formal inter-agent dialogues. In: Rosenschein, J.S., Sandholm, T., Wooldridge, M., Yakoo, M. (eds.) 2nd International Conference on Autonomous Agents and Multi-Agent Systems, ACM Press, New York (2003)
21. Prakken, H.: On dialogue systems with speech acts, arguments, and counterarguments. In: Proceedings of the Seventh European Workshop on Logic in Artificial Intelligence, Berlin, Germany, Springer, Heidelberg (2000)
22. Prakken, H.: Relating protocols for dynamic dispute with logics for defeasible argumentation. Synthese 127, 187–219 (2001)
23. Prakken, H.: Coherence and flexibility in dialogue games for argumentation. Journal of Logic and Computation 15, 1009–1040 (2005)
24. Prakken, H., Sartor, G.: Modelling reasoning with precedents in a formal dialogue game. Artificial Intelligence and Law 6, 231–287 (1998)
25. Rahwan, I., McBurney, P., Sonenberg, E.: Towards a theory of negotiation strategy. In: Rahwan, I., Moraitis, P., Reed, C. (eds.) Proceedings of the 1st International Workshop on Argumentation in Multiagent Systems, Berlin, Germany, Springer, Heidelberg (2004)
26. Reed, C.: Dialogue frames in agent communications. In: Demazeau, Y. (ed.) Proceedings of the Third International Conference on Multi-Agent Systems, pp. 246–253. IEEE Press, Los Alamitos (1998)
27. Rovatsos, M., Rahwan, I., Fisher, F., Weiss, G.: Adaptive strategies for practical argument-based negotiation. In: Parsons, S., Rahwan, I., Moraitis, P., Reed, C. (eds.) Proceedings of the 2nd International Workshop on Argumentation in Multiagent Systems, Berlin, Germany, Springer, Heidelberg (2006)
28. Schroeder, M., Plewe, D.A., Raab, A.: Ultima ratio: Should Hamlet kill Claudius. In: Proceedings of the 2nd International Conference on Autonomous Agents, pp. 467–468 (1998)
29. Sycara, K.: Argumentation: Planning other agents' plans. In: Proceedings of the Eleventh Joint Conference on Artificial Intelligence, pp. 517–523 (1989)
30. Walton, D.N., Krabbe, E.C.W.: Commitment in Dialogue: Basic Concepts of Interpersonal Reasoning. State University of New York Press, Albany, NY, USA (1995)

A Persuasion Dialog for Gaining Access to Information

Laurent Perrussel[1], Sylvie Doutre[1], Jean-Marc Thévenin[1], and Peter McBurney[2]

[1] IRIT - Université Toulouse I
2 rue du doyen Gabriel Marty
F-31042 - Toulouse Cedex 9 - France
{laurent.perrussel,sylvie.doutre,
jean-marc.thevenin}@univ-tlse1.fr
[2] Dpt. of Computer Science - University of Liverpool
Liverpool L69 3BX - United Kingdom
p.j.mcburney@csc.liv.ac.uk

Abstract. This paper presents a formal protocol for agents engaged in argumentation over access to information sources. Obtaining relevant information is essential for agents engaged in autonomous, goal-directed behavior, but access to such information is usually controlled by other autonomous agents having their own goals. Because these various goals may be in conflict with one another, rational interactions between the two agents may take the form of a dialog, in which requests for information are successively issued, considered, justified and criticized. Even when the agents involved in such discussions agree on all the arguments for and the arguments against granting access to some information source, they may still disagree on their preferences between these arguments.

To represent such situations, we design a protocol for dialogs between two autonomous agents for seeking and granting authorization to access some information source. This protocol is based on an argumentation dialog where agents handle specific preferences and acceptability over arguments. We show how this argumentation framework provides a semantics to the protocol dedicated to the exchange of arguments, and we illustrate the proposed framework with an example in medicine.

1 Introduction

This paper presents a formal protocol for agents engaged in argumentation over access to information sources. We show how two agents, a client and a server, may dialog so that the client tries to get access to information held by the server while the server tries to convince the client that it cannot give it the access. In that context, gaining access to information can be viewed as an argumentation dialog [20,19,18] where agents exchange arguments and counter-arguments in order to set common agreements about authorizations. Agents present arguments which represent their own point of view, i.e. arguments they consider as the more persuasive. Multi-agent dialog based on argumentation [18,17,22,16] for information-seeking [5,23] as well as preference-based argumentation systems [3,2,1,6] have already been studied. These preferences over arguments help agents to characterize their own acceptable arguments which represent the foundation on which agents accept or not to change authorizations: that is, agents controlling

I. Rahwan, S. Parsons, and C. Reed (Eds.): ArgMAS 2007, LNAI 4946, pp. 63–79, 2008.
© Springer-Verlag Berlin Heidelberg 2008

access to information consider to be persuaded as long as their acceptable arguments against giving permission have not been sufficient to persuade their opponent.

There are very few papers dealing with the problem of how agents may control the access [8,9,11] in the context of an argument-based persuasion framework. None of them describe this process in the context of an explicit link between permissions and arguments for and against these permissions. This explicit link enables agents to justify why they provide or do not provide information and thus gives an explicit semantics of the persuasion dialog in terms of arguments about permissions. In [13,12], we present in an informal way a persuasion protocol that embeds this explicit link between arguments and permissions. This paper formalizes this informal protocol.

In this paper, we propose a *persuasion* protocol based on FIPA-ACL oriented performatives [15] which are widely accepted for describing agents dialogs. This protocol is defined in a formal way. A key issue is that the client and the server select and evaluate the received arguments according to their own notion of acceptability: for instance if the server handles preferences over arguments, it evaluates if the received argument is more convincing than the arguments that backed the refusal of access. The contribution brought by this formalization is twofold: a formal description of the different steps that may occur in the persuasion dialog and a semantics of the protocol in terms of multiple preference-based argumentation systems.

The paper is organized as follows. In section 2 we present a motivating example. In section 3 we present the formal framework for representing argumentation-based dialog. In section 4 we describe the protocol that rules the dialog, its characteristics and properties. In section 5 we revisit the initial motivating example and express it in a formal way. We conclude the paper in section 6.

2   A Motivating Example

Robert is a British businessman visiting Brussels for a meeting. During his visit he becomes ill and is taken unconscious into hospital. The staff of the hospital suspect Robert has had a heart attack and seek to prescribe appropriate drugs for his condition. Unfortunately the safe choice of drugs depends upon various factors, including prior medical conditions that Robert might have and other drugs he may be taking. The hospital's agent is given the goal of finding out the required information about Robert, from the agent representing his London doctor.

In order to gain access to information about Robert, the agent of Brussels Hospital establishes the following dialog with the London agent:

Agent of Brussels Hospital: I would like to dialog with the agent of Robert's British doctor; I request Robert's health record.

London agent: I cannot provide you Robert's health record because Robert has only given his British doctor limited consent to pass on his personal information (argument A_1).

Brussels agent: This record could possibly include information that could affect the treatment of Robert's heart failure. I request it, Robert's life may be at stake (argument A_2)!

London agent: I cannot divulge this information, because British law prohibits passing on information without the consent of the provider of the information (argument A_3).

Brussels agent: EC law takes precedence over British law when it would be in the interests of the owner to divulge the information (argument A_4). You should allow me to access the record.

London agent: Only Robert could decide what would be in his interests (argument A_5).

Brussels agent: Robert's doctor owes a duty of care to Robert and, should he die, the doctor might be sued by his family, or the Brussels hospital, or both (argument A_6).

London agent: OK. I provide you the requested record: Robert's history of diabetes is...

As we can see, there are numerous key issues in this dialog. First the Brussels and London agents set an agreement about information that is considered: setting/getting access to some information. Second, London agent interacts with Brussels agent because it *controls* information about Robert's health record. Next London agent presents an argument A_1 which attacks the Brussels agent's request: argument A_1 is an argument against giving permission to Brussels agent; in other words *permissions are argued*. Then Brussels and London agents exchange counter-arguments (A_2...). It follows that they both *share* the same set of arguments (they understand each other) and they also share the notion of attack. Indeed they agree in an implicit way that the proposed argument by the opponent attacks the previously proposed argument. At the end of the dialog, London agent accepts the final Brussels' argument A_6. It follows that in an implicit way, London agent agrees that argument A_6 is an acceptable argument which supports the permission in favor of Brussels. Consequently, London agent *changes the permission* and *provides* the requested information to Brussels agent.

In the following we describe a formal system that embed this kind of dialog.

3 Formal Framework

In this section we describe in a formal way the main concepts that have been previously introduced: access rights, primitives of dialogs and arguments which help us to specify the persuasion process.

First we give some preliminaries. Let Ag be the set of agent identifiers (id). In the following an agent id is represented by a lower case Roman letter (x, y, ...). We assume the information requested is identified by lower case Greek letters (ϕ, ψ...). Let Inf be the set of all possible information ids. This information may be any of: a data record (e.g., one patient's record); a database (e.g., records of many patients); or even the protocol for another dialog (e.g., a client may first request a server to enter into a second dialog, which requires authorization to engage in). The actual content corresponding to information ϕ is denoted by $\langle$content $\phi\rangle$.

3.1 Access to Information

The permission a participant x has to access the content of information ϕ is denoted by a function perm(y, x, ϕ): perm$(y, x, \phi) = 1$ (respectively 0) stands for agent y can give (respectively cannot give) to agent x the content of information ϕ. Formally,

$$\text{perm} : \text{Ag} \times \text{Ag} \times \text{Inf} \mapsto \{0, 1\}$$

Permission is closely linked to the notion of control. An agent can define permissions about information ϕ only if it actually controls the access to ϕ. In the following we represent this notion of control through a function control which associates agents and pieces of information:

$$\text{control} : \text{Ag} \mapsto 2^{\text{Inf}}$$

By splitting control and permission we avoid the problem that an agent gives itself permissions to all pieces of information. For instance, if we consider the motivating example, the agent of Brussels Hospital should not give itself a permission for accessing Robert's file; the permission should be given by the agent of Robert's London Doctor since it is this agent that control the access to the file.

Example 1. Let us consider the initial intuitive example. Let $\text{Ag} = \{b, l\}$ s.t. b is Brussels agent id and l is London agent id; let ρ stands for "Robert's health record" and thus $\text{Inf} = \{\rho\}$. London's control and permission are defined as follows:

$$\rho \in \text{control}(l) \qquad \text{perm}(l, b, \rho) = 0$$

3.2   Primitives of Dialogs

This is the syntax of a persuasion dialog system for information-seeking which requires permission to access the information.

Participants.   There are two participants, a *Client* (requesting information), and a *Server* (controlling access to some information, which it may or may not agree to provide).

Dialog goal.   The Client has the following goal prior to the start of the interaction: to obtain from the Server all the information it needs, using persuasion if necessary. The Server has the following goal prior to the start of the interaction: To provide information to the Client according to the level of access permission the Client has.

Context.   Client and Server may have disjoint knowledge bases. The knowledge base of the Server includes information about the access permissions which each Client has, which may differ by the information concerned.

Arguments.   We assume the arguments exchanged by agents are represented by upper Roman letters $(A, B,...)$. The internal structure of an argument is left abstract.

Communication language.   The primitives of the dialogs presented hereafter are mainly based on [15]. The minimum locutions needed for a dialog between Client x and Server y are:

OpenDialogue(x, y). Client x indicates to Server y that it wants to enter into a dialog.

Ask(x, y, ϕ). Client x asks Server y to provide it with some information ϕ.

Tell$(y, x, \langle\text{content } \phi\rangle)$ Server y provides Client x with the actual content of information ϕ.

DontTell(y, x, ϕ). Server y indicates to Client y that it cannot provide x with information ϕ.

EndDialogue(x, y). Agent x indicates to Agent y that it wants to leave the dialog.

In case Client x would not have the permission to access information ϕ, an argumentation dialog about the addition of this permission in Server y's knowledge base is engaged. In this case, a locution for arguing about the permission related to requested information ϕ may be uttered:

Argue(z, t, ι, A, ϕ). Agent z gives to agent t an argument A stating why the permission should be equal to value ι. In the following, **Argue**$(x, y, 1, A, \phi)$ stands for Client x gives an argument A to Server y as to why it should have the permission (to access ϕ) while **Argue**$(y, x, 0, A, \phi)$ stands for Server y gives to Client x an argument A as to why x cannot have access (to information ϕ).

3.3 Argumentation Framework

In our proposal we require an argumentation framework that enables agents to share the same set of arguments and the same defeat relation between arguments. In addition, each agent should be able to determine its own set of acceptable arguments. It means that even if each agent is able to determine if an argument or a counter-argument is acceptable, it has to share with its opponent the same notion of counter-argument; that is they share the same notion of defeat. Arguments and defeat relation can be represented using the system proposed by [14]. Handling preferences over arguments is one of the simplest way for representing different points of view over the same set of arguments. [1] has presented an extension of [14] that takes into account a unique preference relation. [6] has presented another extension where values are associated to arguments and each agent defines its own set of preferences over these values, and thus over arguments. At this stage, we do not need to enforce the usage of a specific notion of acceptability. Hence each agent evaluates the set of arguments with respect to its own notion of acceptability and its own set of preferences. Formally, we obtain the following definition:

Definition 1 (MPAF). *A Multiple preference-based argumentation framework (MPAF) is a tuple*

$$\langle \mathsf{Arg}, \Re, \bigcup_{x \in \mathsf{Ag}} \geqslant_x, \text{acceptable} \rangle$$

where:

- Arg *is a set of arguments,*
- $\Re$ *is a defeat relation:* $\Re \subseteq \mathsf{Arg} \times \mathsf{Arg}$,
- $\bigcup_{x \in \mathsf{Ag}} \geqslant_x$ *is a set of preference relations s.t.* $\geqslant_x$ *stands for the preference relation over arguments associated with agent x and each relation $\geqslant_x$ is a partial pre-order.*
- acceptable *is a function which maps agent ids to a subset of* Arg *which characterizes acceptability,* acceptable : $\mathsf{Ag} \mapsto 2^{\mathsf{Arg}}$. acceptable$(x)$ *stands for the acceptable set of arguments associated to agent x. Each set* acceptable(x) *is a subset of* Arg *defined w.r.t. the defeat relation $\Re$ and preference relation $\geqslant_x$.*

The strict order associated with $\geqslant_x$ is denoted by $>_x$. $A >_x B$ means that agent x strictly prefers argument A to B. The sets of acceptable arguments may be defined by using semantics which characterize the policy of the access control. For instance, in a context where information is sensitive the notion of acceptability will be restrictive, whereas a standard notion of acceptability such as the semantics of [14] or [1] may be considered in a context where information has not a high level of confidentiality.

In this paper, we focus on a usage of an acceptability based on the sets of arguments which are conflict-free [14,1]. Let us stress that the usage of some specific notion of acceptability does not prevent the general aspect of the framework.

We rephrase the notion of *defence* and *admissible* arguments in the context of multiple preferences. An argument A is x-defended by a set of arguments S w.r.t. a preference relation $\geqslant_x$ iff (i) A defends itself (it is preferred to all its counter-argument) or (ii) for every counter-argument B, there exists an argument C which belongs to S such that C defeats B and B is not preferred to C:

Definition 2 (x-defense). *Let* S $\subseteq$ Arg *be a set of arguments and* $A \in$ Arg *be an argument. A is x-defended by* S *iff* $\forall B \in$ Arg *s.t.* $(B, A) \in \Re$ *then:* (i) $A >_x B$ *or* (ii) $\exists C \in$ S *s.t.* $(C, B) \in \Re$ *and* $B \not>_x C$.

The next step is to rephrase the notion of *conflict-free* set of arguments: all the arguments belonging to an x-conflict-free set of arguments are preferred to their counter arguments w.r.t. a preference relation $\geqslant_x$:

Definition 3 (x-conflict-free). *A set* S *is said to be x-conflict-free iff* $\forall A, B \in S$, *if* $(B, A) \in \Re$ *then* $A \geqslant_x B$.

The next step is to characterize the admissible arguments.

Definition 4 (x-admissible). *A set* S *of arguments is said to be x-admissible iff* S *is x-conflict-free and* S *x-defends all its elements.*

The set of acceptable arguments for an agent x is calculated w.r.t. the set of x-admissible arguments. In a classical way we have the skeptical and the credulous methods for characterizing the set of acceptable argument.

Definition 5 (Credulous and Skeptical acceptability). *Let* Arg *be a set of arguments, $\Re$ be a defeat relation and $\geqslant_x$ be a preference relation. The* credulous *set of acceptable arguments* Cr(x) *defined w.r.t. x is:*

$$Cr(x) = \{A \in \text{Arg} | \exists S \text{ s.t. } S \text{ is } x\text{-admissible and } A \in S\}$$

and the skeptical *set of acceptable arguments* Sk(x) *defined w.r.t. x is equal to:*

$$Sk(x) = \{A \in \text{Arg} | \forall S \text{ s.t. } S \text{ is } x\text{-admissible and maximal w.r.t. } \subseteq, A \in S\}$$

Example 2. Let us pursue our review of the intuitive example. The associated MPAF is defined as:

- set Arg is equal to $\{A_1, A_2, A_3, A_4, A_5, A_6\}$;
- relation $\Re$ is defined as shown on figure 1.
  An arrow between two arguments represents a defeat. That is, argument A_1 is defeated by arguments A_2 and A_6; argument A_2 is defeated by argument A_3. All these defeats are defined in the two directions. Finally argument A_3 is defeated by argument A_4 and argument A_5 defeats A_4.

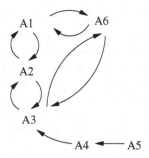

Fig. 1. Defeat Relation over arguments set Arg

- Preference relations for Brussels and London agents are defined as follows (respectively $\geqslant_b$ and $\geqslant_l$):

$$\geqslant_b := A_2 >_b A_1, A_2 >_b A_3, A_6 >_b A_1, A_6 >_b A_3$$
$$\geqslant_l := A_3 >_l A_2, A_1 >_l A_2$$

- Function acceptable is defined as follows. We suppose that both London and Brussels agents use a credulous acceptability. In order to define what arguments are acceptable for each of them, we first calculate the maximal sets which are b-admissible and l-admissible:

$$b\text{-admissible set} = \{A_2, A_5, A_6\}$$
$$l\text{-admissible sets} = \{A_1, A_3, A_5\} \text{ and } \{A_5, A_6\}$$

Second, we associate acceptable arguments to each agent

$$\text{acceptable}(b) := \mathsf{Cr}(b) = \{A_2, A_5, A_6\}$$
$$\text{acceptable}(l) := \mathsf{Cr}(l) = \{A_1, A_3, A_5, A_6\}$$

3.4 Linking Arguments and Permissions

As shown in the intuitive example, arguments proposed by the Client and the Server are closely connected to their goals. The goal of the Client is to obtain information ϕ while the Server aims at not telling ϕ. In our framework, goals can be rewritten as changing the permission or not. It leads us to the idea that we have to connect permissions and arguments; we represent this link by introducing a relation between permissions and arguments which characterizes the notion of *argued permission*. The argued permissions are defined in the knowledge base of the Server and characterize its attitude toward the clients.

Definition 6 (argued permission). *An argued permission is a tuple* $\langle A, y, x, \phi, \iota \rangle$ *s.t. A is an argument, y and x are Server and Client agent ids, ϕ is an information and ι is the value of the permission ($\iota \in \{0, 1\}$). $\langle A, y, x, \phi, \iota \rangle$ stands for: Server y has the argument A in favor ($\iota = 1$) or against ($\iota = 0$) giving permission to Client x to obtain information ϕ.*

In fact, it is possible for Server y to consider arguments in favor of giving permission to x about ϕ and at the same time arguments against the same permission. For instance, an agent should not give access to its password for security reason (argument against the permission) and at the same time it may provide it in emergency (argument in favor of the permission). It follows that there is no redundancy to consider a function that describes permissions and arguments in favor or against permissions. However we have to enforce some constraints on permissions by introducing the notion of *consistent* permission. Let us consider Client x, Server y and information ϕ. We claim that a permission defined by y about x and ϕ is *consistent* with a set of argued permissions if (i) y has the control of ϕ (ii) arguments for and against permissions respect the defeat relation and (iii) this permission is "supported" by at least one argument that is acceptable w.r.t. acceptable(y).

Definition 7 (Consistent permission). *Let* AP *be a set of argued permissions and let* $P = \{\langle A, y, x, \phi, \iota \rangle\}$ *be the set of argued permission supporting permission* perm(y, x, ϕ) $= \iota$ *and* $C = \{\langle A, y, x, \phi, 1-\iota \rangle\}$ *be the set of argued permissions against* perm(y,x, ϕ) $= \iota$. *Permission* perm(y, x, ϕ) $= \iota$ *is said to be* consistent *iff:*

1. *$\phi \in$ control(y);*
2. *argued permissions are constrained by the defeat relation:* $\forall \langle A, y, x, \phi, \iota \rangle \in P$ *such that for any y-admissible set* S *where $A \in$ S, if $C \neq \emptyset$ then $\nexists \langle B, y, x, \phi, 1-\iota \rangle \in C$, $B \in$ S;*
3. *the following constraint holds between the permission and acceptable arguments:*

$$\text{perm}(y, x, \phi) = \iota \iff \exists \langle A, y, x, \phi, \iota \rangle \in \text{AP s.t. } A \in \text{acceptable}(y)$$

The main consequence is that if Server y has adopted a skeptical acceptability relation, then there are no two arguments that belong to the set acceptable(y) which support opposite permissions.

Proposition 1. *Let* perm(y, x, ϕ) $= \iota$ *be a permission. Let* $C = \{\langle A, y, x, \phi, 1 - \iota \rangle\}$ *be the set of argued permissions against* perm(y, x, ϕ) $= \iota$. *Let* Sk(y) *be the set of acceptable arguments. No element of* C *belongs to* Sk(y): $C \cap$ Sk(y) $= \emptyset$.

Notice that the credulous notion of acceptability may entail that acceptable arguments can be in favor and or against a permission at the same time and thus the previous proposition does not hold.

Example 3. Let us pursue our intuitive example. London agent informs that it cannot provide information about Robert because Robert has only given a limited consent (argument A_1). It follows that A_1 is an argument against the request of Brussels agent and that tuple $\langle A_1, l, b, \rho, 0 \rangle$ is an argued permission. However, this argument is not the only one against giving access to Brussels agent. Argument A_3 is also against the authorization while arguments A_2 and A_6 are in favor of the authorization. We get the following set of argued permissions:

$$\text{AP} = \{\langle A_1, l, b, \rho, 0 \rangle, \langle A_3, l, b, \rho, 0 \rangle, \langle A_2, l, b, \rho, 1 \rangle, \langle A_6, l, b, \rho, 1 \rangle\}$$

Notice that permission perm(l, b, ρ) $= 0$ is consistent: first agent l has control of ρ (see example 1); second, all arguments in favor of permission do not appear at the same time in a same l-admissible set (e.g. $A_1 \in \{A_1, A_3, A_5\}$ but A_2 and A_6 do not belong to $\{A_1, A_3, A_5\}$ and third, there exists an argument involved in an argued permission that is acceptable (e.g. $A_3 \in$ acceptable(l)).

4 The Protocol of Persuasion

In this section, we present a protocol of dialog for information-seeking dialog with permissions. The protocol specifies which locutions may be uttered at different points in a dialog, and so defines the rules governing the use of the locutions previously presented. Now we formally define the concept of dialog. A dialog is a structure that combines access authorizations, a multiple preferences argumentation framework, a set of argued permissions, and a sequence of locution utterances.

Definition 8 (Dialog). *Let* $D = \langle$control, perm, MPAF, AP, $\sigma \rangle$ *be a dialog such that* control *is a function associating agents and information,* perm *is an authorization function,* MPAF *is a multiple preferences argumentation framework,* AP *is a set of argued permissions and* σ *is a sequence of locutions.*

Let *length* be a function characterizing the number of elements of a finite sequence of locutions σ and $\sigma[i]$ (s.t. $1 \leqslant i \leqslant length(\sigma)$) represents one element of σ. Now we can express in a formal way the protocol: how the permissions and the arguments are interwoven in order to rule the dialog.

4.1 Requesting Information

First we specify that Client x and Server y have to initiate the dialog. Let $D = \langle$control, perm, MPAF, AP, $\sigma\rangle$ be a dialog s.t. σ is a finite sequence: $\exists n$ s.t. $n = length(\sigma)$. In all the following formulas, logical connectors are used w.r.t. their usual meaning. After opening the dialog, the Client requests some information ϕ (formula (R1)):

$$\sigma[1] = \mathbf{OpenDialogue}(x, y) \implies \sigma[2] = \mathbf{Ask}(x, y, \phi) \qquad \text{(R1)}$$

Formula (R2) states that the Server should provide ϕ if the Server control ϕ and the Client has the authorization to access information ϕ:

$$\sigma[2] = \mathbf{Ask}(x, y, \phi) \wedge \phi \in \text{control}(y) \wedge \text{perm}(y, x, \phi) = 1 \implies$$
$$\sigma[3] = \mathbf{Tell}(y, x, \langle \text{content } \phi \rangle) \quad \text{(R2)}$$

Formula (R3) states that if the Server has no control over ϕ then it should close the dialog:

$$\sigma[2] = \mathbf{Ask}(x, y, \phi) \wedge \phi \notin \text{control}(y) \implies \sigma[3] = \mathbf{EndDialogue}(y, x) \qquad \text{(R3)}$$

Formula (R4) specifies that if the Server has actually provided information ϕ then the dialog is closed by the Server:

$$\sigma[i] = \mathbf{Tell}(y, x, \langle \text{content } \phi \rangle) \implies \sigma[i+1] = \mathbf{EndDialogue}(y, x) \qquad \text{(R4)}$$

Now let us focus on the case which will lead us to the argumentation part of the dialog; that is, where the Server cannot provide information ϕ to the Client. Formula (R5) formally specifies the condition where a **DontTell** locution can be uttered.

$$\sigma[2] = \mathbf{Ask}(x, y, \phi) \wedge \phi \in \text{control}(y) \wedge \text{perm}(y, x, \phi) = 0 \Longleftrightarrow$$
$$\sigma[3] = \mathbf{DontTell}(y, x, \phi) \quad \text{(R5)}$$

4.2   Arguing for Getting Permission

In this section we describe the rules that characterize the persuasion stage. Formula (G1) states that argumentation occurs only if the Server does not want to provide information to the Client:

$$\forall i > 3 \; (\sigma[i] = \mathbf{Argue}(y, x, 0, A, \phi) \vee \sigma[i] = \mathbf{Argue}(x, y, 1, A, \phi)$$
$$\Longrightarrow \sigma[3] = \mathbf{DontTell}(y, x, \phi)) \quad \text{(G1)}$$

If the Server refuses to answer the Client the argumentation stage is initiated. In this paper, for the sake of conciseness we assume that this stage is initiated by the Server. Formula (G2) specifies that the Server has to motivate its refusal.

$$\sigma[3] = \mathbf{DontTell}(y, x, \phi) \wedge \exists A \text{ s.t. } \langle A, y, x, \phi, 0 \rangle \in \text{AP} \Longrightarrow$$
$$\sigma[4] = \mathbf{Argue}(y, x, 0, A, \phi) \quad \text{(G2)}$$

As the Server has given a rationale to the Client, the Client should reply to the Server. Formulas (G3) state that both agents should present acceptable arguments:

$$\sigma[i] = \mathbf{Argue}(y, x, 0, A, \phi) \Longrightarrow A \in \text{acceptable}(y)$$
$$\sigma[i] = \mathbf{Argue}(x, y, 1, A, \phi) \Longrightarrow A \in \text{acceptable}(x) \quad \text{(G3)}$$

Agents are thoughtful according to [18]'s assertion attitudes. Now both Client and Server should present arguments in order to counter the opponent. Let us first focus on the Client. When Client x evaluates the argument proposed by Server y it may face two cases whether it can reply or not to the Server:

The client can reply. Whether the received argument is acceptable or not, Client x argues as long as it can. In such a configuration, Client x considers all of its *acceptable* arguments that defeat the received argument and presents them to the Server. Formula (G4) specifies this counter-argumentation as follows:

$$\sigma[i] = \mathbf{Argue}(y, x, 0, A, \phi) \wedge A \notin \text{acceptable}(x) \Longrightarrow$$
$$\left(\exists B \in \text{acceptable}(x) \wedge (B, A) \in \Re \right) \left((\nexists j < i(\sigma[j] = \mathbf{Argue}(x, y, 1, B, \phi))) \right)$$
$$\Longrightarrow \left(\exists k > i(\sigma[k] = \mathbf{Argue}(x, y, 1, B, \phi)) \right) \right) \quad \text{(G4)}$$

Notice that client x may optimize the counter-argumentation stage by selecting only a subset of counter-arguments among all the possible ones and present them to the server. In this paper, we do not explore this opportunity since it is out of the scope of this paper to evaluate the rationales that support the selection process.

The client cannot reply. The dialog is over if Client x can no longer present a counter-argument to Server y, counter-argument which is acceptable for x. Formula (G5) specifies in a formal way the closure of the dialog: the first line states that Client x has received an argument and second, third and fourth lines of formula (G5) state that x has presented all counter-arguments to y; more precisely the second line states for every argument presented against the permission sent by the Server, Client x has presented (line 4) all the possible counter-arguments (line 3).

$$\sigma[i] = \mathbf{Argue}(y, x, 0, A, \phi) \wedge$$
$$(\forall B, \exists j \leqslant i\,(\sigma[j] = \mathbf{Argue}(y, x, 0, B, \phi) \implies$$
$$\forall C \in \text{acceptable}(x) \text{ s.t. } (C, B) \in \Re$$
$$\exists k < i\,(\sigma[k] = \mathbf{Argue}(x, y, 1, C, \phi)))$$
$$\implies \sigma[i+1] = \mathbf{EndDialogue}(x, y) \quad (G5)$$

Now, let us focus on the Server side. The formulas are similar to formulas (G5) and (G4): as long as the Server can present arguments to the Client to persuade it to not change the authorization, the Server presents the counter-arguments to the Client. In order to write formulas (G5) and (G7) which specify the structure of the dialog, we first characterize the condition $\Psi(i)$ which holds if at time i all arguments which appear in argued permissions have been sent (lines 1 and 2) and all arguments presented by x have been countered (lines 3, 4 and 5).

$$\forall \langle A, y, x, \phi, 0 \rangle \in \mathsf{AP}$$
$$\exists j((j < i) \wedge (\sigma[j] = \mathbf{Argue}(y, x, 0, A, \phi))) \wedge$$
$$\forall B, \exists k\,(k < i) \wedge (\sigma[k] = \mathbf{Argue}(x, y, 1, B, \phi) \implies$$
$$\forall C \in \text{acceptable}(y) \text{ s.t. } (C, B) \in \Re$$
$$\exists l((l < i) \wedge (\sigma[l] = \mathbf{Argue}(y, x, 0, C, \phi)))) \quad (\Psi(i))$$

The Server can reply. Formula (G6) is similar to formula (G4) and specifies that Server y presents all possible counter-argument to an argument presented by x:

$$\sigma[i] = \mathbf{Argue}(x, y, 1, A, \phi) \wedge \neg\Psi(i) \implies$$
$$\left(\exists B \in \text{acceptable}(y) \wedge (B, A) \in \Re\right)\left(\left(\nexists j < i(\sigma[j] = \mathbf{Argue}(y, x, 0, B, \phi))\right) \wedge\right.$$
$$\left.\left(\exists k > i(\sigma[k] = \mathbf{Argue}(y, x, 0, B, \phi))\right)\right) \quad (G6)$$

The Server cannot reply. Server y has received an argument and condition $\Psi(i)$ holds (line 1), it entails that Server y should evaluate the whole set of arguments sent by x so that it may change the permission and provide information ϕ, otherwise the dialog is closed:

$$\sigma[i] = \mathbf{Argue}(x, y, 1, A, \phi) \wedge \Psi(i) \implies$$
$$(\sigma[i+1] = \mathbf{Tell}(y, x, \langle \text{content } \phi \rangle) \vee$$
$$\sigma[i+1] = \mathbf{EndDialogue}(y, x)) \quad (G7)$$

All these constraints enable to characterize the persuasion dialogs about permissions.

Definition 9 (Permission Persuasion-Dialog). *Let* $D = \langle$control, perm, MPAF, AP, $\sigma \rangle$ *be a dialog. D is a* permission persuasion-dialog *iff (i) all permissions are consistent, (ii)* σ *is finite and (iii) all formulas (R1)–(R5) and (G1)–(G7) hold.*

A permission persuasion-dialog does not specify how the Server may change the permission, it just specifies how arguments may be exchanged and how information may be provided. The key characteristic is that the dialog is finite (definition of D) and "well-defined", i.e. the constraints ensures that at the end of the dialog all possible relevant arguments have been exchanged:

Proposition 2. *For any dialog* $D = \langle$control, perm, MPAF, AP, $\sigma \rangle$ *s.t. be a permission persuasion-dialog,* $\Psi(length(\sigma)) = 1$

The final step is the evaluation of the Client's arguments by the Server in order to determine if permission has to be changed.

4.3 Changing the Permission

Server y changes permission related to x and ϕ with respect to a set of rules which characterize principles of *cautiousness* (the server still has a reason not to change the permission) or *trustfulness* (the server has at least one reason to change the permission):

cautiousness. One of the argument presented by the Server has not been defeated by the Client. In other words, the Server has at least one reason for not changing permission. Let **(C-Caut)** be a formula which represents this condition. **(C-Caut)** specifies that the Server has send an argument (line 1) so that the Client has no reply to this argument (lines 2 and 3) with an argument involved in an argued permission that prevents to give permission (line 3):

$$\exists A, \exists i (\sigma[i] = \mathbf{Argue}(y, x, 0, A, \phi) \wedge$$
$$\nexists B \in acceptable(y) \text{ s.t.} (B, A) \in \Re \wedge$$
$$\exists j (\sigma[j] = \mathbf{Argue}(x, y, 1, B, \phi) \wedge \langle B, y, x, \phi, 0 \rangle \notin AP)) \quad \textbf{(C-Caut)}$$

Formula (C1) specifies that if all arguments have been exchanged (represented by condition $(\Psi(length(\sigma) - 1))$) and if condition **(C-Caut)** does not holds (i.e. Client x has countered all the arguments presented by Server y), then server y has to provide ϕ:

$$\Psi(length(\sigma) - 1)) \wedge \neg\textbf{(C-Caut)} \Longrightarrow$$
$$(\sigma[length(\sigma - 1)] = \mathbf{Tell}(y, x, \langle content \ \phi \rangle)) \quad \textbf{(C1)}$$

Once ϕ has been provided, the dialog is closed (see formula (R4)). It follows that permission has to be updated so that it reflects that Client x can access ϕ. Formula (C2) states that if ϕ has been provided w.r.t. the cautiousness principle then the permission is updated (perm' represents the new permission):

$$\text{perm}'(y, x, \phi) := 1 \iff \Psi(length(\sigma) - 1) \wedge \neg\textbf{(C-Caut)} \quad \textbf{(C2)}$$

trustfulness. One of the argument presented by the Client is acceptable for Server y. In other words, the Server has at least one reason to change permission. Formula (**C-Trust**) specifies the condition corresponding to this attitude as follows: lines 1 and 2 state that there exists at least one acceptable argument that is not against permission (according to Server point of view):

$$\exists A, i(\sigma[i] = \mathbf{Argue}(x, y, 1, A, \phi) \wedge$$
$$A \in \text{acceptable}(y) \wedge \langle A, y, x, 0, \phi \rangle \notin \mathsf{AP}))) \quad \text{(\textbf{C-Trust})}$$

Formula (C3) specifies that if condition (**C-Trust**) holds then information ϕ is provided.

$$(\mathbf{\Psi}(length(\sigma)) - 1) \wedge (\textbf{C-Trust}) \Longrightarrow$$
$$(\sigma[length(\sigma - 1)] = \mathbf{Tell}(y, x, \langle \text{content } \phi \rangle) \quad \text{(C3)}$$

As previously, we now state permission change in a trustfulness context:

$$\text{perm}'(y, x, \phi) := 1 \iff (\mathbf{\Psi}(length(\sigma)) - 1) \wedge (\textbf{C-Trust}) \quad \text{(C4)}$$

Since the permission has changed, the set of argued permissions has also to be changed so that the new permission is consistent. That is every argument sent by the Client that is acceptable from the point of view of the Server has to be added to the list of argued permissions AP. Formula (C5) states that all argument received by y and acceptable by y extend the initial list of argued permissions.

$$\mathsf{AP}' := \begin{cases} \mathsf{AP} \text{ if } \nexists i(\sigma[i] = \mathbf{Tell}(y, x, \langle \text{content } \phi \rangle)) \\ \mathsf{AP} \cup \{ \langle A, y, x, \phi, 1 \rangle \mid \\ \quad \exists i(\sigma[i] = \mathbf{Argue}(x, y, 1, A, \phi) \wedge \\ \quad A \in \text{acceptable}(y)) \} \text{ otherwise} \end{cases} \quad \text{(C5)}$$

The first consequence entails by formulas (C1)–(C5) is that the updated permission is still consistent.

Proposition 3. *Let D be a permission persuasion-dialog. Let* perm$'(y, x, \phi)$ *and* AP' *be the updated set of permissions defined w.r.t. formulas* (C1) *and* (C2), *or formulas* (C3) *and* (C4); *let* AP' *be the updated set of argued permissions calculated w.r.t. formula* (C5). perm$'(y, x, \phi)$ *is consistent with respect to the set* AP'.

The second consequence is an entailment relation between the two policies: a permission that has been given w.r.t. the cautiousness principle entails that the permission should also have been given w.r.t. the trustfulness principle (but not vice-versa). This is due to the fact that whenever condition (**C-Caut**) does not hold, condition (**C-Trust**) holds.

Proposition 4. $\neg(\textbf{C-Caut}) \Longrightarrow (\textbf{C-Trust})$

Notice that trustfulness corresponds to the skeptical acceptance attitude of [18]; cautiousness is an acceptance attitude not taken into account by [18].

We conclude the section by assessing the principle of cautiousness and trustfulness whether Server y uses a skeptical or credulous notion of acceptability. As long as Server y uses a credulous acceptability permissions may change:

Proposition 5. *For all permission persuasion-dialog D s.t.* acceptable$(y) = $ Cr(y), *it holds that*

$$\neg((\phi \in \text{control}(y) \wedge \text{perm}(y, x, \phi) = 0) \implies \nexists i(\sigma[i] = \textbf{Tell}(y, x, \langle \text{content } \phi \rangle)))$$

As long as Server y uses a skeptical notion of acceptability, Server y never changes its initial permissions and thus will never provide information when initial permission is equal to 0.

Proposition 6. *For all permission persuasion-dialog D such that* acceptable$(y) = $ Sk(y), *it holds that:*

$$(\phi \in \text{control}(y) \wedge \text{perm}(y, x, \phi) = 0) \implies \nexists i(\sigma[i] = \textbf{Tell}(y, x, \langle \text{content } \phi \rangle)$$

It follows from the previous propositions that an agent which gives to the other agents the ability to persuade itself about permissions should not adopt a too restrictive notion of acceptability. That is, acceptability should be credulous based.

5   Revisiting the Initial Example

In this section we reformulate the dialog between the agent of Brussels Hospital and the London agent as a permission persuasion-dialog $D = \langle$control, perm, MPAF, AP, $\sigma \rangle$ such that control and perm are defined as in example 1, MPAF is defined as in example 2 and AP is defined as shown in example 3. Server y may change permissions w.r.t. trustfulness principle. We have the following sequence σ of locutions (relevant constraints that hold are mentioned on the right part of the locution):

Agent of Brussels Hospital: I would like to dialog with the agent of Robert's British doctor; I request Robert's health record (information ρ).

$$\sigma[1] = \textbf{OpenDialogue}(b, l)$$
$$\sigma[2] = \textbf{Ask}(b, l, \rho) \tag{R1}$$

London agent: I cannot provide you Robert's health record because Robert has only given his British doctor limited consent to pass on his personal information (argument A_1).

$$\sigma[3] = \textbf{DontTell}(l, b, \rho) \tag{R5}$$
$$\sigma[4] = \textbf{Argue}(l, b, 0, A_1, \rho) \tag{G2}$$

Brussels agent: This record could possibly include information that could affect the treatment of Robert's heart failure. I request it, Robert's life may be at stake (argument A_2)!

$$\sigma[5] = \textbf{Argue}(b, l, 1, A_2, \rho) \tag{G1, G3, G4}$$

London agent: I cannot divulge this information, because British law prohibits passing on information without the consent of the provider of the information (argument A_3).

$$\sigma[6] = \textbf{Argue}(l, b, 0, A_3, \rho) \tag{G3, G6}$$

Brussels agent: EC law takes precedence over British law when it would be in the interests of the owner to divulge the information (argument A_4). You should allow me to access the record.

$$\sigma[7] = \mathbf{Argue}(b, l, 1, A_4, \rho) \qquad \text{(G1, G3, G4)}$$

London agent: Only Robert could decide what would be in his interests (argument A_5).

$$\sigma[8] = \mathbf{Argue}(l, b, 0, A_5, \rho) \qquad \text{(G1, G3, G6)}$$

Brussels agent: Robert's doctor owes a duty of care to Robert and, should he die, the doctor might be sued by his family, or the Brussels hospital, or both (argument A_6).

$$\sigma[9] = \mathbf{Argue}(b, l, 1, A_6, \rho) \qquad \text{(G3, G4, G7)}$$

London agent: OK. I will provide you with the requested record: Robert's history of diabetes is...

$$\sigma[10] = \mathbf{Tell}(l, b, \langle \text{content } \rho \rangle) \qquad \text{(C3, G7)}$$

$$\sigma[11] = \mathbf{EndDialogue}(b, l) \qquad \text{(C3)}$$

According to the trustfulness principle (formula (C4)), London agent changes the permission, $\text{perm}'(l, b, \rho) = 1$, because there is an l-acceptable argument A_6 that makes condition (**C-Trust**) true. The set of argued permissions is also updated:

$$AP' = AP \cup \{\langle A_2, l, b, \rho, 1 \rangle, \langle A_6, l, b, \rho, 1 \rangle\} = AP$$

6   Conclusion

In this paper, we have presented a formal framework for handling persuasion dialogs about permissions. Our contribution is two fold: first we represent through an explicit link between arguments and permissions why agents accept or refuse to provide information. The agents can thus justify their behavior. Second, we exhibit a specific class of dialogs, *permission persuasion-dialog*, which helps to characterize two policies for handling permission change (cautiousness and trustfulness). We have shown that enabling permission change entails the evaluation of arguments in a credulous way. The proposed protocol has been shown in the context of multiple preferences argumentation framework; however this protocol of persuasion is sufficiently general so that it can be used with other argumentation frameworks.

Our work is closely related to [11] which proposes in a semi-formal way a general framework for persuasion and negotiation dialog for gaining access to sensitive information. A drawback of this work is that permissions are not considered as first-class objects but are rather viewed with the help of the notion of interest. But interest and permission are different notions and thus it could not be established in a clear way why agents propose arguments in the persuasion dialog. Moreover, even if our work is less general than the proposed in [11], we have been able to exhibit interesting characteristics by focusing on a more specific problem: we have shown that persuasion is closely linked to the acceptability notion and we propose a clear definition of persuasion dialog about permission. G. Boella et al. show in [8] how access control can be handled by using plan argument and an argumentation game. A plan argument is close to our notion of argued permission and an argument game describes the protocol of interaction between the Client and the Server. The main drawback is that the protocol is a one shot protocol: it is not shown how the Client and the Server change their initial set of plan arguments so that they exploit the result of the interaction. In [7] J. Bentahar *et al.* show a persuasion dialog framework where trust aspects have been integrated in a persuasion dialog. The main difference with our proposal is the underlying concept of persuasion. In our proposal, the Server is convinced by the Client as long as the Client has proposed some convincing arguments. The persuasion is a two agent process. In [7], persuasion is based on a preliminary step which helps to evaluate the reputation of the Client. We believe that this approach is not suitable for our context. Indeed, even if trust aspects have to be handled in this kind of problem, we believe that the dialog between the Server and the Client has to be self-contained and thus trust aspects have to be handle by means other than reputation systems.

As future work, we plan to extend the protocol to a family of protocols. That is, in this paper we focus on specific acceptability definitions; our aim is to consider the notions of conflict and acceptability at a more general level and to evaluate the impact on the proposed persuasion protocol. The work made by K. Atkinson *et al* [4] on dialog game for evaluating actions has shown numerous kind of attacks on action proposal. An first work should consist on the rewritten of these different kinds of attacks in our context: that is does the counter-argumentation stage for the Client has the same meaning for the Server? We plan to explore the interest of bipolar argumentation systems [10]. In those systems, a dual relation of the defeat relation is represented which helps to characterize the notion of support in an explicit way. This framework is close to our proposal for representing argued permissions. Our aim is to compare similarities and differences between these two frameworks. We also plan to refine the protocol in order to handled trust issues. That is if a Client has been able to persuade a Server to get permission to access some information, then this result may play the role of an argument in favor of the Client for gaining access to some other information, i.e. the persuasion dialog may be viewed as a trust proof.

Acknowledgments. Peter McBurney is grateful for support from the EC project *Argumentation Service Platform with Integrated Components (ASPIC)* (IST-FP6-002307). Laurent Perrussel is grateful for support from the ANR project *Social trust analysis and formalization (ForTrust)*. Thanks to the anonymous reviewers for their helpful comments.

References

1. Amgoud, L., Cayrol, C.: Inferring from inconsistency in preference-based argumentation frameworks. International Journal of Automated Reasoning 29(2), 125–169 (2002)
2. Amgoud, L., Parsons, S., Perrussel, L.: An Argumentation Framework based on contextual Preferences. In: Proc. of FAPR 2000, London, pp. 59–67 (January 2000)

3. Andreka, H., Ryan, M., Schobbens, P.: Operators and Laws for Combining Preference Relations. In: Wieringa, R., Feenstra, R. (eds.) Information Systems: Correctness and Reusability (Selected Papers), World Scientific Publishing Co, Singapore (1995)
4. Atkinson, K., Bench-Capon, T.J.M., McBurney, P.: A dialogue game protocol for multi-agent argument over proposals for action. In: Rahwan, et al. (eds.), [21], pp. 149–161
5. Bench-Capon, T.: Specifying the interaction between information sources. In: Quirchmayr, G., Bench-Capon, T.J.M., Schweighofer, E. (eds.) DEXA 1998. LNCS, vol. 1460, pp. 425–434. Springer, Heidelberg (1998)
6. Bench-Capon, T.: Persuasion in practical argument using value-based argumentation frameworks. J. Log. Comput. 13(3), 429–448 (2003)
7. Bentahar, J., Moulin, B., Chaib-draa, B.: Specifying and implementing a persuasion dialogue game using commitments and arguments. In: Rahwan, et al. (eds.), [21], pp. 130–148.
8. Boella, G., Hulstijn, J., van der Torre, L.: Argument games for interactive access control. In: Proc. of WI 2005, pp. 751–754. IEEE CS, Los Alamitos (2005)
9. Boella, G., Hulstijn, J., van der Torre, L.: Argumentation for access control. In: Proc. AIIA 2005, pp. 86–97 (2005)
10. Cayrol, C., Lagasquie-Schiex, M.C.: On the acceptability of arguments in bipolar argumentation frameworks. In: Godo, L. (ed.) ECSQARU 2005. LNCS (LNAI), vol. 3571, pp. 378–389. Springer, Heidelberg (2005)
11. Dijkstra, P., Bex, F., Prakken, H., de Vey Mestdagh, K.: Towards a multi-agent system for regulated information exchange in crime investigations. In: Artificial Intelligence and Law, pp. 133–151 (2005)
12. Doutre, S., McBurney, P., Perrussel, L., Thévenin, J.M.: Arguing for gaining access to information. In: Proc. of AAMAS 2007, ACM, New York (2007)
13. Doutre, S., McBurney, P., Wooldridge, M., Barden, W.: Information-seeking agent dialogs with permissionsand arguments. Technical Report ULCS-05-010, Department of Computer Science, University of Liverpool, Liverpool, UK (2005)
14. Dung, P.: On the Acceptability of Arguments and its Fundamental Role in Nonmonotonic Reasoning, Logic Programming, and N-Person games. Artificial Intelligence 77(32), 321–357 (1995)
15. FIPA.: Communicative Act Library Specification. Standard SC00037J, Foundation for Intelligent Physical Agents, 3 (December 2002)
16. Kakas, A., Moraitis, P.: Adaptative agent negotiation via argumentation. In: Proc. of AAMAS 2006 (2006)
17. Parsons, S., McBurney, P., Wooldridge, M.: The mechanics of some formal inter-agent dialogues. In: Dignum, F. (ed.) ACL 2003. LNCS (LNAI), vol. 2922, pp. 329–348. Springer, Heidelberg (2004)
18. Parsons, S., Wooldridge, M., Amgoud, L.: Properties and complexity of some formal inter-agent dialogues. J. Log. Comput. 13(3), 347–376 (2003)
19. Prakken, H.: On dialogue systems with speech acts, arguments, and counterarguments. In: Brewka, G., Moniz Pereira, L., Ojeda-Aciego, M., de Guzmán, I.P. (eds.) JELIA 2000. LNCS (LNAI), vol. 1919, pp. 224–238. Springer, Heidelberg (2000)
20. Prakken, H., Sartor, G.: A dialectical model of assessing conflicting arguments in legal reasoning. Artificial Intelligence and Law 4, 331–368 (1996)
21. Rahwan, I., Moraitis, P., Reed, C. (eds.): ArgMAS 2004. LNCS (LNAI), vol. 3366. Springer, Heidelberg (2005)
22. Rahwan, I., Ramchurn, S., Jennings, N., McBurney, P., Parsons, S., Sonenberg, L.: Argumentation-based negotiation. The Knowledge Engineering Review 18, 343–375 (2003)
23. Walton, D., Krabbe, E.: Commitments in Dialogue: Basic Concepts of Interpersonal Reasoning. SUNY Press (1995)

Towards Characterising Argumentation Based Dialogue in the Argument Interchange Format

Sanjay Modgil[1] and Jarred McGinnis[2]

[1] Advanced Computation Lab, Cancer Research UK, London
[2] Department of Computer Science Royal Holloway, University of London

Abstract. To facilitate development and practical deployment of argumentation systems, a recent shared notation, or *Argument Interchange Format* (AIF), has been proposed for representation and communication of argumentation knowledge amongst agents. The AIF is described as an abstract model, or "ontology", characterising the core concepts and their relationships. Concrete reifications or syntaxes instantiating these concepts have also been described. Thus far the focus has been on representation of argument entities and networks, i.e., arguments and sub-arguments and relations of inference, preference and attack amongst these entities. Requirements were envisaged for a separate core ontology for items relating to the interchange of arguments, such as locutions and protocols. In this paper we propose that the core argument entity and network ontology can be extended to characterise communication in argumentation based dialogues between agents. We also propose a declarative specification of these communicative concepts that is of sufficient generality to serve as an operational semantics. Specifically, we propose use of the Lightweight Coordination Calculus (LCC). We then illustrate our proposal with a use case multi-agent scenario. In presenting this work, our aim is to stimulate further discussion and work on development of the AIF in order to characterise communication in multi-agent dialogues.

1 Introduction

Significant progress has been made in establishing theoretical foundations for argumentation based reasoning and dialogue, and development of these models for agent reasoning and communication. More recently, progress has been made on development of software implementations of these models. In particular, the ASPIC project (Argumentation Services Platform with Integrated Components - www.argumentation.org) is currently developing components implementing state of the art theoretical models for argumentation based inference, decision making and dialogue. The objective is to make these components available for deployment in agent and multi-agent applications in both the commercial and research sectors. An example of the latter is the recently started ARGUGRID project (www.argugrid.org) that aims at associating argumentation enabled agents with service/resource requestors and service/resource providers on the Grid. Argumentation technology will be used to support rational decision making, internal to agents, as well as negotiation, amongst agents.

To facilitate deployment of argumentation technology in multi-agent systems, a recent shared notation, or *Argument Interchange Format* (AIF) [4], has been proposed for

I. Rahwan, S. Parsons, and C. Reed (Eds.): ArgMAS 2007, LNAI 4946, pp. 80–93, 2008.

representation, and communication of argumentation knowledge amongst agents. The aim has been to provide an ontology that can be populated to provide an operational semantics, which, in contrast with existing argumentation mark up languages (e.g., [13]), would enable exchange and sophisticated automated processing of argumentation knowledge in open multi-agent systems. The AIF is described as an abstract model, or "ontology", characterising the core concepts and their relationships. Concrete XML and RDF reifications or syntaxes instantiating these concepts have also been described and are currently being utilised for representation of arguments and their interactions [4,11]. Thus far the focus has been on representation of argument entities and networks, i.e., arguments and sub-arguments and relations of inference, preference and attack amongst these entities. In section 2 we summarise the current state of the AIF as detailed in [4]. This work envisages requirements for a separate core ontology for items relating to the communication of argumentation knowledge, such as locutions and protocols. In section 3 we propose that the core argument entity and network ontology can be extended to model communication between agents engaged in argumentation based dialogues. In particular, we motivate representation of declarative specifications of interaction protocols that are of sufficient generality to serve as an operational semantics. In section 4 we describe how these representational requirements can be met by the Lightweight Coordination Calculus [12]. In section 5 we then illustrate our proposal by referring to multi-agent dialogue scenarios being developed as part of the ASPIC project. In presenting this work, our aim is to stimulate further discussion and work on development of the AIF in order to characterise communication in multi-agent dialogues.

2   The Argument Interchange Format

The AIF is currently specified as a core ontology that can be specialised to capture the representational requirements of a variety of argumentation formalisms. Argument entities are represented as nodes in a directed graph, informally called an argument network (AN). There are two types of nodes, namely *Information nodes* (*I-nodes*) and *scheme application nodes* (*S-nodes*). I-nodes relate to declarative content specific to the domain of discourse, such as claims, propositions, data e.t.c. S-nodes relate to domain independent patterns of reasoning. The present ontology deals with three different types of schemes nodes, namely rule application (RA) nodes, preference application (PA) nodes and conflict application (CA) nodes. RA-nodes can be seen as applications of (possibly non-deductive) rules of inference. For example, in fig.1 *RA-node 1* represents application of defeasible modus ponens to the premises in its child I-nodes, resulting in the inference $flies(opus)$ in *RA-node 1*'s parent I-node. CA nodes can be seen as applications of criteria (declarative specifications) defining conflict, which may be logical or non-logical. In fig.1 the argument for $flies(opus)$ mutually conflicts with (bi-directionally attacks) the argument for $\sim flies(opus)$ since the arguments' conclusions logically contradict as specified in *CA-node 1*. PA-nodes are applications of (possibly abstract) criteria of preference among evaluated nodes. In fig.1 the argument for $\sim flies(opus)$ is preferred to the argument for $flies(opus)$ since the former has a greater degree of support as specified in *PA-node 1*. Note that nodes may possess

Table 1. Semantics of support for node-to-node relationships in an argument network

	to *I-node*	to *RA-node*	to *PA-node*	to *CA-node*
from *I-node*		I-node data used in applying an inference	I-node data used in applying a preference	I-node data in conflict with information in node supported by CA-node
from *RA-node*	inferring a conclusion in the form of a claim	inferring a conclusion in the form of an inference application	inferring a conclusion in the form of a preference application	inferring a conclusion in the form of a conflict definition application
from *PA-node*	applying a preference over data in I-node	applying a preference over inference application in RA-node	meta-preferences: applying a preference over preference application in supported PA-node	preference application in supporting PA-node in conflict with preference application in PA-node supported by CA-node
from *CA-node*	applying conflict definition to data in I-node	applying conflict definition to inference application in RA-node	applying conflict definition to preference application in PA-node	showing a conflict holds between a conflict definition and some other piece of information

different attributes such as title, text, type (e.g. decision, action, goal, belief. . .), creation date, strength (e.g., degree of support), acceptability, e.t.c. These attributes may vary and are not part of the core ontology.

In the context of an argument network, a node A is said to support node B if and only if there is an edge running from A to B. Edge types can be inferred from the nodes they connect. Basically there are two types of edges, namely scheme edges and data edges. Scheme edges emanate from S-nodes and are meant to support conclusions that follow from the S-node. These conclusions may either be I-nodes or S-nodes. Data edges emanating from I-nodes, on the other hand, necessarily end in S-nodes, and are meant to supply data, or information to scheme applications. Table 1 summarises the relations associated with the semantics of support. Notice that I-to-I edges are forbidden, because I-nodes cannot be connected without an explanation for why that connection is being made.

Thus far, the AIF concepts populating argument networks facilitate representation of arguments their constitutive structure, and interactions between arguments. Syntactic XML and RDF instantiations of the AIF's semantic concepts are currently in use [4,11]. For example, the ASPIC project has developed an argument inference engine that implements algorithms [15] for computing the acceptability of arguments under Dung's grounded and admissible semantics [5]. The engine outputs a machine consumable XML document that represents the constructed arguments and their attack and preference relations that define the dialectical proof graph for the acceptability of an argument. In [4], a second group of concepts is envisaged for communication in the context of argumentation. Three main subgroups are identified:

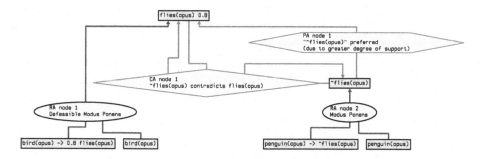

Fig. 1. A concrete example of an argument network

1. *Locutions*: Individual words, phrases or expressions uttered by an agent.
2. *Interaction Protocols*: Rules governing the legality of moves at each point in a dialogue, the effects of locutions on the participants' commitments, and outcome rules defining the outcome of a dialogue.
3. *Communication Context*: Including the communication language defining the set of possible speech acts, the topic language defining the set of possible wff exchanged in locutions, the *ids* of the dialogue participants, their roles in the dialogue, the dialogue topic and type (e.g., persuasion, negotiation etc), background theory rules, commitment stores, and so on.

In the following section we motivate and discuss how locutions and interaction protocols can be characterised in the AIF's existing argument network ontology. The basic idea is that locutions can be represented as content in I-nodes and interaction protocols can be represented by an additional scheme node type, viz. a. vie: *protocol interaction application (PIA) nodes.*

3   Characterising Locutions and Interaction Protocols in the Argument Interchange Format

The current AIF provides an abstract model, or semantics, that allows for multiple syntactic reifications. In particular, specific instances of S-nodes provide a kind of operational semantics that distinguishes the AIF from argument mark up languages: the AIF not only provides for visualisation and inspection of argument structures, but also a semantic model enabling automatic processing of argument structures by software agents. For example, consider the ASPIC inference engine's AIF export of a graph of attacking arguments. A receiving agent can submit an additional attacking argument for linking into the graph, provided that it complies with a conflict application node's declarative specification of what constitutes a valid attack. The scheme nodes thus both 'describe' and 'prescribe' the rationale relating the incoming I-nodes to the supported I-nodes. Similarly, consider the output of a 'dialogue manager' that regulates an argumentation based dialogue between participating agents P and Q. The locutions can be represented as the content of I-nodes. P submits a locution l_1 represented in I-node 1 (see fig.2).

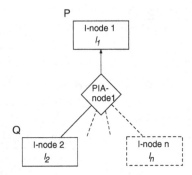

Fig. 2. Protocol Interaction Application node linking I-nodes containing locutions

The interaction protocol that licenses valid replies by Q can be represented by a protocol interaction application (PIA) node - PIA-node 1 - linking Q's incoming replies to I-node 1.

In the context of communication, I-node attributes will, amongst others, include:

- The locution consisting of the speech act and its content (*speech_act(content)*), e.g., *claim(ϕ)*, *argue(A)*, *why(ϕ)*, *concede(ϕ)*, *offer(ϕ)*, *reject(ϕ)*, e.t.c.
- The 'dialogical status' of a locution [10].
- The *ids* of the sending and recipient agents.
- The language for the locution's content, and ontologies which define elements of the content.
- Message management elements such as the message-identifier.

From hereon, we may refer to locutions submitted by agents in a dialogue as 'moves'. In order that a protocol interaction application node encode the rationale for relating Q's replying move(s) to P's move, it may specify:

1. The protocol's legal move function indicating the range of possible speech acts that Q can select from in its reply. For example, in conflict resolution and persuasion dialogues, legal replies to *claim(ϕ)* include *why(ϕ)* and *concede(ϕ)* [10].
2. For each possible speech act, the preconditions that must be satisfied for a locution to contain the speech act. The preconditions may refer exclusively (if the protocol has a social semantics) to Q's commitment store, or additionally to Q's internal reasoning state. The preconditions can also encode strategic considerations that determine the choice of a particular speech act from amongst those licensed by the legal move function, and for any given speech act, the choice of content. For example, if the move being replied to is *offer(O)* in a negotiation dialogue, then the preconditions for a replying move of the form *accept(O)* can be that there is no O' preferred to O according to the decision making mechanism of the replying agent Q [1].
3. For each locution, the post-conditions that must be effected. For example, the effects of a locution on the commitment store of agents Q and P.

4. Whether Q can make a single replying move (*unique move* protocols) or more than one move (*multiple move* protocols) to a move by agent P, and whether Q can reply to a move by P that Q has already replied to (*multi-reply* protocols) or whether Q can reply only once to each of P's moves (*single-reply* protocols).

The majority of existing implementations of argumentation based dialogue systems (see [2] for a review) deploy dialogue managers that enforce the rules of a protocol so as to: 1) constrain participating agents to submitting legal moves, and; 2) define the outcome of a dialogue. In a multi-agent context, one can envisage a mediator agent playing the same role by communicating an AIF representation of the dialogue to participating agents P and Q, in order that P and Q can apply their own constraint solvers to what are effectively semantic constraints encoded in the PIA nodes. Consider figure 3 in which a mediator agent (MA) mediates a persuasion dialogue between P and Q. Each agent submits a move in accordance with the constraints encoded in the PIA-nodes that the MA 'attaches' to the growing dialogue graph. Note that pre and postconditions for locutions are not shown. Their representation will be discussed in sections 4 and 5. Note also that I-nodes may have an attribute indicating the move's 'dialogical status' (*in* or *out*). This allows for an 'any time' definition of the outcome of a dialogue, whereby the status of the initial move indicates that the proponent of the move is currently winning (*in*) or losing (*out*) [10].

1. P moves $claim(c)$ in I-node I1.
2. MA attaches PIA node 1 that has attributes indicating that Q can make multiple moves in response to $claim(c)$ ($n > 1$) since the protocol is a *multi-move* protocol. PIA node 1 also specifies Q's legal replies: $why(c)$ and $concede(c)$.
3. Q moves $why(c)$. Note that MA maintains the 'reply status' attribute of PIA node 1 as $<open>$, so specifying that Q may backtrack and submit an alternative reply to P's first move, i.e., the protocol is a *multi-reply* protocol.
4. MA attaches PIA node 2, specifying the legal replies $argue(A)$ where A's conclusion is c, or $retract(c)$
5. P moves $argue(A)$ in I-node I3. Note that I3 could be linked to the corresponding argument represented as an argument network as described in section 2. This would then expose the A's premises for inspection and challenge by Q.
6. MA attaches PIA node 3, specifying that Q can reply with $why(\phi)$ where ϕ is a premise in the argument A, or $concede(\phi)$ where ϕ is a premise in A or the conclusion of A, or an argument B that defeats A. Again, one could also explicitly represent relations between arguments submitted in locutions. For example, if Q submits B, then the linked argument network representations of A and B could be bi-directionally linked by a conflict application node, and unidirectionally linked from B to A by a preference application node (B defeats A is then a derived relation). Finally, note that Q can submit a move specified by PIA node 3, or backtrack to PIA node 1 and move $concede(c)$. If PIA node 1's 'reply status' was $<closed>$ (indicating a *unique-reply* protocol) then Q would not be able to backtrack. Note that once the dialogue is terminated, any PIA nodes without incoming I-nodes will be removed.

We can now augment table 2 to include a row and column for PIA nodes. So, it may be that a protocol interaction specification may itself be derived by applying rules,

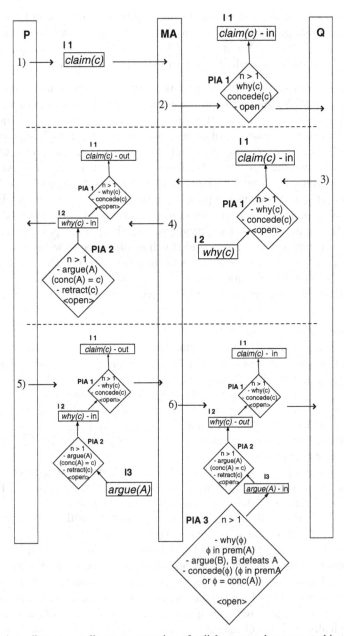

Fig. 3. A mediator agent directs construction of a dialogue graph represented in the AIF

and be in conflict with, or preferred to, other protocol interaction specifications. This is consistent with the view that these specifications can exist independently of a given dialogue instance, and recent works in which the protocol rules that apply during communicative interactions may themselves be part of the domain of discourse and subject to debate. This has been done using the Lightweight Coordination Calculus (LCC) [12], dialogue games and adjacency pairs to create run-time protocol synthesis [7]. This work builds a synthesis engine on top of a traditional LCC expansion engine. Another approach, $\mathcal{RASA}$, is a language specifically designed for the inspection, validation, composition and execution of agent interaction protocols [8]

Thus far we have informally described the role of protocol interaction nodes in effectively specifying semantic constraints that relate replying locutions in a dialogue. In the following section we propose the use of a lightweight coordination calculus that provides an abstract declarative protocol language with a representation of constraints that does not commit users to a particular logic or constraint satisfaction mechanism. The operational semantics of the protocol language are common for the coordination of distributed processes and are defined more fully in [12].

4 The Lightweight Coordination Calculus - A Declarative Operational Semantics

Figure 4 defines the syntax of a protocol language. For those readers unfamiliar with the LCC, it may be helpful to note that the LCC is a declarative logic programming language in the style of Prolog, augmented with CCS (a process calculus for communicating systems). The protocol consists of a set of agent clauses, $A^{\{n\}}$. The protocol will contain a set of at least two clauses because LCC protocols are defined locally (i.e. from the perspective of the participating agent roles). An agent clause is the series of communicative actions expected to be performed by an agent adopting the role defined by the agent definition. This agent definition consists of a role (R) and unique identifier (Id). A role is defined in a similar way as Electronic Institutions [6]: a way of defining communicative activity for a group of agents rather than individuals. The roles act as a bounding box for a set of states and transitions. LCC is based on a process calculus and is therefore well suited to express the concurrency found in multiagent systems.

$$
\begin{array}{llll}
\mathcal{P} \in \text{Protocol} & ::= \langle S, A^{\{n\}}, K \rangle & \\
A \in \text{Agent Clause} & ::= \theta :: op. & \\
\theta \in \text{Agent Definition} & ::= \mathbf{agent}(R, Id) & \\
op \in \text{Operation} & ::= \text{no op} & \\
& \mid \theta & \\
& \mid (op) & (\text{Precedence}) \\
& \mid M \Rightarrow \theta & (\text{Send}) \\
& \mid M \Leftarrow \theta & (\text{Receive}) \\
& \mid op1 \ \mathbf{then} \ op2 & (\text{Sequence}) \\
& \mid op1 \ \mathbf{par} \ op2 & (\text{Parallelization}) \\
& \mid op1 \ \mathbf{or} \ op2 & (\text{Choice}) \\
& \mid (M \Rightarrow \theta) \leftarrow \psi & (\text{Prerequisite}) \\
& \mid \psi \leftarrow (M \Leftarrow \theta) & (\text{Consequence}) \\
M \in \text{message} & ::= \langle m, \mathcal{P} \rangle &
\end{array}
$$

Fig. 4. An Abstract Syntax of the Protocol Language

The agent definition is expanded by a number of operations. Operations can be classified in three ways: actions, control flow, and conditionals. Actions are the sending or receiving of messages, a no op, or the adoption of a role. Control flow operations temporally order the individual actions. Actions can be sequentially ordered, performed simultaneously without regard to order, or given a choice point. The definition of the double arrows, '⇒' and '⇐', denote messages M being sent and received. On the left-hand side of the double arrow is the message and on the right-hand side is the other agent involved in the interaction.

Constraints can fortify or clarify semantics of the protocols. Those occurring on the left of the '←' are post-conditions and those occurring on the right are preconditions. The symbol ψ represents a first order proposition. For example, an agent receiving a protocol with the constraint to believe a proposition s upon being informed of s can infer that the agent sending the protocol has a particular semantic interpretation of the act of informing other agents of propositions. The operation $(M \Rightarrow \theta) \leftarrow \psi$ is understood to mean that message M is being sent to the agent defined as θ on the condition that ψ is satisfiable. The operation $\psi \leftarrow (M \Leftarrow \theta)$ means that once M is received from agent θ, ψ holds.

For example, in figure 3, the first move made is $claim(c)$. The mediator agent could prompt agent P to make this move by sending the following LCC protocol:

$$a(\_, p) ::=$$
$$claim(\phi) \Rightarrow a(\_, q).$$

This is read as: "agent p with any role (represented by the underscore) can send $claim(\phi)$ to the agent q. Depending on the scenario, there are a number of ways this protocol can be modified. If the mediating agent wanted to allow the agent more freedom to choose, subject to satisfaction of a constraint, a protocol such as the following can be imagined:

$$a(\_, p) ::=$$
$$claim(T) \Rightarrow a(\_, OtherAgent)$$
$$\leftarrow findpartner(OtherAgent) \textbf{ and } findtopic(T).$$

This constraint states that if p can find some $OtherAgent$ and topic T then it can send $claim(T)$ to that $OtherAgent$. How and by what means the constraint is satisfied is left to the discretion of the individual agent.

5   A Use Case Scenario: Argumentation Based Dialogues in Medical Multi-agent Systems

In this section we describe an ASPIC use case scenario and outline the use of LCC protocols in this scenario. ASPIC has proposed a general model for argumentation based deliberative reasoning amongst agents deployed in a medical multi-agent system. This involves the use of argumentation to resolve conflicts of opinion as to what is the case (e.g., diagnosis) and what to do (e.g., treatment planning). Agents equipped with the ASPIC inference component for constructing acceptable arguments will engage in dialogues mediated by a mediator agent, as illustrated in fig.3. Two of the key requirements informing the general model were:

1. The need to accommodate heterogenous agents (e.g. human and automated agents) with different knowledge representing languages, models of reasoning, and levels of automation.
2. The need to account for the safety critical nature of the medical domain by ensuring that agents are able to explore all possible lines of reasoning with respect to the issue under deliberation.

These requirements are partially fulfilled by the combined use of schemes and critical questions [16], and a mediator agent implementing protocols in a recently proposed framework for a class of persuasion and conflict resolution dialogues [10]. ASPIC is currently engineering a dialogue component that mediates protocols defined in the framework, and that is based on a prototype implementation described in [3]. A large scale demonstrator [14] is also being built to demonstrate a mediator agent's use of the dialogue component to regulate dialogues between human physicians and automated agents deployed with the ASPIC inference engine. Here, we focus on LCC representations of interaction protocols that the mediator agent can communicate in order to enable agent participation in a dialogue.

We first describe the basic features of the framework described in [10]. This framework imposes an 'explicit reply' structure on dialogues, whereby moves either attack or surrender to a previous move of another participant. The dialogue graph built during a dialogue thus relates each move by a binary relation of 'attack' or 'surrender' to the move it replies to. Given a graph of dialogical moves, [10] defines a procedure for assigning a move's *dialogical status*. In particular, it is the dialogical status of the initial move that is at issue. For example, in fig.3 MA assigns the status *in* to P's initial move $claim(c)$. Q's move $why(c)$ is an attacking reply to $claim(c)$. P's move is now assigned *out* and Q's move assigned *in*. Intuitively, P's claim is under challenge and so the burden of proof now resides with P. For P to win the dialogue it must submit an argument for c in a reply that attacks $why(c)$. Thus, at stage 6 in the dialogue $argue(A)$ is assigned *in*, $why(c)$ *out* and $claim(c)$ *in*. Notice that if Q had moved $concede(c)$ at stage 3 (or after stage 6), then this would be a surrendering reply to $claim(c)$ (respectively $argue(A)$) and $claim(c)$'s dialogical status would remain *in*.

A primary motivation for development of the framework in [10] was to make as few assumptions as possible about participating agents. In abstracting to the level of an explicit reply structure, the framework allows for different sets of speech acts, and different underlying argumentation based logics, thus allowing for participation by heterogenous agents. Furthermore, the framework allows for flexible dialogues (*multi-move* and *multi-reply*). Allowing agents to backtrack to their opponents' previous moves ensures that all possible lines of reasoning / argument can be explored. However, liberal protocols with unconstrained backtracking can lead to 'irrelevant' moves. If backtracking is to be permitted, then some control mechanism is required to restrict backtracking to replies that will affect the outcome in favour of the replying agent. This is where the 'any time' definition of the dialogue outcome discussed in section 3 applies. Various notion of 'relevance' are defined, where, for example, an attacking move is relevant only if it changes the dialogical status of the initial move. Thus, the mediator agent can not only direct a participating agent as to its valid replies, but also which of its opponent's moves can be relevantly replied to. In fig.3, the MA can indicate that a move can

/ cannot be relevantly backtracked to by assigning <*open*>, respectively <*closed*>, to the PIA node's 'reply status' attribute.

We conclude with examples of LCC representations of interaction protocols currently being developed for the ASPIC multi-agent demonstrator. The architecture includes a mediator agent (*MA*) and thus does not use the full strength of the LCC language that was originally intended for peer-to-peer coordination. So, much of the coordination is delegated to this *MA* rather than the protocols themselves. Later in this section, we give an example of LCC flexing its coordination muscles and allowing agents to communicate directly without the mediator.

We restrict ourselves to representation of legal *attacking* replies and their preconditions and postconditions as defined by protocol rules in [9] that conform to the framework in [10]. The dialogue begins with a claim sent by an agent instantiating Id to an agent instantiating Pid with the consequence that Id updates its commitment store (CS) with the claim. In LCC, this step of the dialogue can be specified as:

$$\begin{aligned}
&(1)\\
&a(\_, Id)\textbf{::=}\\
&\quad claim(\phi) \;\Rightarrow\; a(\_, Pid) \;\leftarrow\; update(Id, CS, \phi).
\end{aligned}$$

The *MA* can now include the following in a PIA node, indicating that the replying agent can challenge (attack) a claim with a *why* locution, provided that its commitment store cannot justify (there is no acceptable argument for) that claim.

$$\begin{aligned}
&(2)\\
&a(\_, Id)\textbf{::=}\\
&\quad why(\phi) \;\Rightarrow\; a(\_, Pid) \;\leftarrow\; not(justified(Id, CS, \phi)).
\end{aligned}$$

The legal attacking reply to $why(\phi)$ is $argue(\Phi, \phi)$. This is conditional on previous *why* moves of the form $why(\gamma)$ where $\gamma \in \Phi$ (γ is a premise in Φ). The *MA* could send this LCC clause:

$$\begin{aligned}
&(3)\\
&a(\_, Id)\textbf{::=}\\
&\quad argue(\Phi, \phi) \;\Rightarrow\; a(\_, Pid) \;\leftarrow\; calculate\_protected\_Arg(\Phi, \phi).
\end{aligned}$$

In practice, the agent instantiating Id could satisfy constraint $calculate\_protected\_Arg(\Phi, \phi)$ by checking the argument network for (Φ, ϕ) and ensuring that if there is a premise $\gamma \in \Phi$ which is challenged (attacked) by a *why* locution in the dialogue graph, then that challenge has been been appropriately dealt with by Id (the *why* locution has been assigned the status *out* by *MA*).

The rules have thus far only specified a single attacking reply to a particular locution. However there are two possible attacking replies to $argue$. An agent can either respond to $argue(\Phi, \phi)$ with a $why(\gamma)$ where γ is a premise in Φ, or an $argue(\Omega, \mu)$ that defeats $argue(\Phi, \phi)$.

$$\begin{aligned}
&(4)\\
&a(\_, Id)\textbf{::=}\\
&\quad why(\gamma) \;\Rightarrow\; a(\_, Pid) \;\leftarrow\; calculate\_Arg\_premise(\Phi, \gamma), not(justified(Id, CS, \gamma))\\
&\textbf{or}\\
&\quad argue(\Omega, \mu) \;\Rightarrow\; a(\_, Pid) \;\leftarrow\; calculate\_defeat(\Phi, \phi, \Omega, \mu).
\end{aligned}$$

calculate_defeat could be evaluated by checking that the argument network representations of (Ω, μ) and (Φ, ϕ) can be linked as specified by conflict and preference application nodes. [1]

The mediator agent parcels out appropriate protocols for the agents to execute and is responsible for ensuring that appropriate variables for the protocols are used and the agents receive the messages intended for them. However, LCC enables encoding of the coordinating mechanisms in the protocol itself so that agents can communicate directly without relying on an intermediary. For example, consider clauses 1 and 2 above. These can now be represented by the pairs:

(1a)
1:   $a(claim_s([CSid], CSpid, \phi), Id)$ **::=**
2:      $claim(\phi) \Rightarrow a(claim_h(CSid, CSpid, \phi), Pid)$
3:         **then** $a(why_h([\phi|CSid], CSpid), Id)$.

(1b)
4:   $a(claim_h([CSid], CSpid, \phi), Pid)$ **::=**
5:      $claim(\phi) \Leftarrow a(claim_s(CSid, CSpid, \phi), Id)$
6:         **then** $a(why_s([\phi|CSid], CSpid), Pid)$.

(2a)
7:   $a(why_s(CSid, CSpid), Id)$ **::=**
8:      $why(\phi) \Rightarrow a(why_h(CSid, CSpid), Pid) \leftarrow not(justified(\phi, CSid))$.

(2b)
9:   $a(why_h(CSid, CSpid), Pid)$ **::=**
10:      $why(\phi) \Leftarrow a(why_s(CSid, CSpid), Id)$.

In 1a the agent, whose identification will unify with *Id*, in the role of $claim_s$ (line 1, s denotes 'speaker') sends claim(ϕ) (line 2) to some agent (*Pid*) in the role of $claim_h$ (*h* denotes 'hearer'), after which the agent adopts the role why_h (line 3) and ϕ is added to *Id*'s commitment store $CSid$. Previously, the mediator agent coordinated the legal replies, and their pre and post-conditions. This coordinating role is now subsumed in the protocol language. In 1b the agent playing the role of hearer (line 4) after receiving the claim (line 5) can then adopt the role of the speaker of *why* (line 6). In 2a and 2b we again see how the sending and receiving of messages coordinates the dialogues between the two agents (lines 7 - 10).

---

[1] LCC assumes that the predicate of the constraint is defined by a mutually understood ontology. One can verify that a constraint has been satisfied, but the actual mechanism for verification is not prescribed and is assumed to be implemented internally by the agent. There is a delicate balance to be achieved here between reliability and autonomy. Constraints are needed to create reliable interaction models but should not infringe upon how the agent achieves this. The inclusion of constraints in the protocol helps elucidate the meaning of an agent sending that message. However whether the agent satisfies the constraint by executing a prolog rule, or sends a message to a human who clicks yes or no is a private matter.

6   Conclusions and Future Work

In this paper we have proposed that the AIF's existing core ontology can be used to characterise argumentation based dialogues. Specifically, locutions can be represented as content in I-nodes and interaction protocols can be declaratively specified in a new scheme node type: protocol interaction application nodes. In this way, the AIF representation of argumentation knowledge communicated during the course of a dialogue, i.e. arguments and their premises, and inferential, conflict and preference relations, can be linked to the AIF representation of the dialogue graph. The AIF is intended to provide a formal semantics enabling exchange and automated processing of argumentation knowledge in multi-agent systems. Hence, a PIA node will provide an operational semantics for relating replying locutions in a dialogue. We have therefore proposed an abstract declarative protocol language - the Lightweight Coordination Calculus - for representing interaction protocols. We illustrated the envisaged use of the AIF and LCC representation in the context of an ASPIC multi-agent dialogue scenario currently under development. The scenario illustrated use of the LCC in mediated dialogues. We also showed how the LCC can encode interaction protocols for direct agent to agent communication. In proposing the use of LCC, and PIA nodes as one amongst a number of scheme node types, we believe that our proposal is consistent with recent works in which protocol rules may themselves be part of the domain of discourse, and subject to run time composition. In conclusion, our aim has been to provide a starting point for further discussion and work on development of the AIF in order to characterise communication in multi-agent dialogues. For example, representation of the communication context remains to be addressed. We also suggest that requirements arising from other use case scenarios will usefully inform further development, and possibly revisions, of the proposal described in this paper.

Acknowledgements. This work was funded by the EU FP6 ASPIC and ARGUGRID projects. The authors would also like to acknowledge the authors of [4], including Steven Willmott who was the prime mover in setting up the first AgentLink 3 sponsored AIF meeting, and John Fox who was the first to propose the AIF initiative.

References

1. Amgoud, L., Prade, H., Belabbes, S.: Towards a formal framework for the search of a consensus between autonomous agents. In: Dignum, F., Wooldridge, M., Koenig, S., Kraus, S. (eds.) Proc. 4th International joint Conference on Autonomous Agents and Multi-Agent Systems, AAMAS 2005, pp. 537–543. ACM Press, New York (2005)
2. ASPIC. Deliverable d1.1 - review on argumentation technology: State of the art, technical and user requirements (June 2004),
   http://www.argumentation.org/Public_Deliverables.htm
3. Bodenstaff, L., Prakken, H., Vreeswijk, G.: On formalising dialogue systems for argumentation in the event calculus. In: Proc. Eleventh International Workshop on Nonmonotonic Reasoning, Windermere (UK), pp. 374–382 (2006)
4. Chesnevar, C., McGinnis, J., Modgil, S., Rahwan, I., Reed, C., Simari, G., South, M., Vreeswijk, G., Willmott, S.: Towards an argument interchange format. The Knowledge Engineering Review 21(4), 293–316 (2007)

5. Dung, P.M.: On the acceptability of arguments and its fundamental role in nonmonotonic reasoning, logic programming and n-person games. Artificial Intelligence 77, 321–357 (1995)
6. Estava, M., Rodriguez, J.A., Sierra, C., Garcia, P., Arcos, J.L.: On the formal specifications of electronic institutions. LNAI, 126–147 (2001)
7. McGinis, J., Robertson, D., Walton, C.: Protocol synthesis with dialogue structure theory. In: Parsons, S., Maudet, N., Moraitis, P., Rahwan, I. (eds.) ArgMAS 2005. LNCS (LNAI), vol. 4049, Springer, Heidelberg (2006)
8. Miller, T., McBurney, P.: Towards a lightweight formal language for first-class agent interaction protocols. In: O'Hare, G., Ricci, A., O'Grady, M., Dikenelli, O. (eds.) Workshop Notes of Engineering Societies in the Agents World, pp. 153–168 (2006)
9. Prakken, H.: On dialogue systems with speech acts, arguments, and counterarguments. In: Brewka, G., Moniz Pereira, L., Ojeda-Aciego, M., de Guzmán, I.P. (eds.) JELIA 2000. LNCS (LNAI), vol. 1919, pp. 224–238. Springer, Heidelberg (2000)
10. Prakken, H.: Coherence and flexibility in dialogue games for argumentation. Journal of logic and computation 15, 1009–1040 (2005)
11. Rahwan, I., Sakeer, P.V.: Towards representing and querying arguments on the semantic web. In: Proc. 1st International Conference on Computational Models of Argument, Liverpool, UK, pp. 3–14. IOS Press, Amsterdam (2006)
12. Robertson, D.: Multi-agent coordination as distributed logic programming. In: Proceedings for International Conference on Logic Programming (2004)
13. Rowe, G.W.A., Reed, C., Katzav, J.: Araucaria: Marking up argument. European Conference on Computing and Philosophy (2003)
14. Tolchinsky, P., Cortés, U., Modgil, S., Caballero, F., Lopez-Navidad, A.: Increasing the availability of human organs for transplantation through argumentation based deliberation among agents. IEEE Special Issue on Intelligent Agents in Healthcare 21(6), 30–37 (2006)
15. Vreeswijk, G.A.W.: An algorithm to compute minimally grounded and admissible defence sets in argument systems. In: Proc. 1st International Conference on Computational Models of Argument, Liverpool, UK, pp. 109–120. IOS Press, Amsterdam (2006)
16. Walton, D.N.: Argument Schemes for Presumptive Reasoning. Lawrence Erlbaum Associates, Mahwah (1996)

Preferences and Assumption-Based Argumentation for Conflict-Free Normative Agents

Dorian Gaertner and Francesca Toni

Department of Computing
Imperial College London, UK
{dg00,ft}@doc.ic.ac.uk

Abstract. Argumentation can serve as an effective computational tool and as a useful abstraction for various agent activities and in particular for agent reasoning. In this paper we further support this claim by mapping a form of normative BDI agents onto assumption-based argumentation. By way of this mapping we equip our agents with the capability of resolving conflicts amongst norms, beliefs, desires and intentions. This conflict resolution is achieved by using a variety of agents' preferences, ranging from total to partial orderings over norms, beliefs, desires and intentions, to entirely dynamic preferences defined in terms of rules. We define one mapping for each preference representation. We illustrate the mappings with examples and use an existing computational tool for assumption-based argumentation, the CaSAPI system, to animate conflict resolution within our agents. Finally, we study how the different mappings relate to one another.

Keywords: norms, BDI agents, conflicts, argumentation.

1 Introduction

Normative agents, namely agents that are governed by social norms (see for example [5,7,28]), may be subject to conflicts amongst their individual desires, or beliefs, or intentions. Such conflicts can be resolved by rendering information (such as norms, beliefs, desires and intentions) defeasible and by enforcing preferences [30]. In turn, argumentation has proved to be a useful technique for reasoning with defeasible information and preferences (e.g. see [21,23,25]) when conflicts may arise.

In this paper we adopt a model for normative agents, whereby agents hold beliefs, desires and intentions, as in a conventional BDI model, but these mental attitudes are seen as contexts and the relationships amongst them are given by means of bridge rules (as in [24]). We adopt a norm representation that builds upon and extends the one given for the BDI+C agent model of [15] and refer to our agents as BDI+N agents. In this work, norms are *internalised* as bridge rules. This representation is a natural one, in that norms typically concern different mental attitudes. Bridge rules afford a specific kind of rule-based norm

I. Rahwan, S. Parsons, and C. Reed (Eds.): ArgMAS 2007, LNAI 4946, pp. 94–113, 2008.

representation that lends itself to a mapping onto argumentation frameworks, as we show in this paper.

Furthermore, we assume that preferences over bridge rules and mental attitudes are explicitly given, to be used to resolve (potentially arising) conflicts. We consider three kinds of representations for preferences:

- by means of total orders over conflicting information;
- by means of partial orders over conflicting information;
- by dynamic rules that provide partial, domain-dependent definitions of preferences, e.g. as in [21,23,25].

For the detection and resolution of conflicts arising from choosing to adopt social norms, and for each form of preference representation, we use a specific form of argumentation, known as assumption-based argumentation [4,10,12,17,23]. This has been proven to be a powerful mechanism to understand commonalities and differences amongst many existing frameworks for non-monotonic reasoning [4], for legal reasoning [23], for practical and epistemic reasoning [17], for service selection and composition [32] and for defeasible reasoning [31]. Whereas abstract argumentation [9] focuses on arguments seen as primitive and atomic and attacks as generic relations between arguments, assumption-based argumentation sees arguments as deductions from "assumptions" in an underlying "deductive system" and defines attacks against arguments as deductions for the "contrary" of assumptions supporting those arguments.

Assumption-based argumentation frameworks can be coupled with a number of different semantics, all defined in dialectical terms and borrowed from abstract argumentation, some credulous and some sceptical, of various degrees. Different computational mechanisms can be defined to match the semantics, defined in terms of dialectical proof procedures, in particular, GB-dispute derivations [11] (computing the sceptical "grounded" semantics), AB-dispute derivations [10,11] (computing the credulous "admissible" semantics) and IB-dispute derivations [11,12] (computing the sceptical "ideal" semantics). All these procedures have been implemented within the CaSAPI system [17].

In this paper we provide a mapping from BDI+N agents onto assumption-based argumentation, and make use of the CaSAPI system to animate the agents and provide conflict-free beliefs, desires and intentions, upon which the commitments of the agents are based. The different procedures that CaSAPI implements provide a useful means to characterise different approaches that BDI+N agents may want to adopt in order to build these commitment stores.

The paper is organised as follows. Section 2 gives some background for and a preliminary definition of our BDI+N agents, focusing on the representation of norms. Section 3 gives some background on the form of argumentation we adopt and show how it can be used to detect and avoid conflicts. Section 4 presents our approach to modelling the agents' preferences (in terms of total orderings, partial orderings and dynamic preference definitions) and using these preferences to resolve conflicts in the assumption-based argumentation counterparts of BDI+N agents. Section 5 presents some formal correspondence results between the three translations. Finally, Section 6 discusses related and future work and concludes.

This paper is a revised and extended version of our previous work in [16]. In particular, Section 2 has been restructured and Section 5 has been added.

2   BDI+N Agents: Preliminaries

In this section we briefly present the notion of BDI+N agent, discuss how norms can be represented for such agents and how they are internalised. We also present an example of a normative conflict for such agents.

2.1   Background

Our BDI+N agents are an adaptation and extension of the agent model in [15], which in turn builds upon the work in [24]. The agent model of [15] adapts an architecture based on multi-context systems that have first been proposed by Giunchiglia and Serafini in [19]. Individual theoretical components of an agent are modelled as separate *contexts*, each of which contains a set of statements in a language L_i together with the axioms A_i and inference rules Δ_i of a (modal) logic. A context i is hence a triple of the form: $\langle L_i, A_i, \Delta_i \rangle$. Not only can sentences be deduced in each context using the deduction machinery of the associated logic, but these contexts are also inter-related via *bridge rules* that allow the deduction of a sentence in one context based on the presence of certain sentences in other, linked contexts.

An agent is then defined as a set of context indices $\mathcal{I}$, a function that maps these indices to contexts, another function that maps these indices to theories T_i (providing the initial set of formulae in each context), together with a set of bridge rules BR, namely rules of inference which relate formulae in different contexts. Thus, an agent can be given as follows:

$$Agent = \langle \mathcal{I},\ \mathcal{I} \rightarrow \langle L_i, A_i, \Delta_i \rangle,\ \mathcal{I} \rightarrow T_i,\ BR \rangle$$

The normative agents we are investigating are all extensions of the well-known BDI architecture of Rao and Georgeff [27] and hence the set of context indices $\mathcal{I}$ is {B, D, I}. Bridge rules are inference rules that may be ground, non-ground, or partially instantiated axioms or norm schemata.

2.2   BDI+N Agents

For BDI+N agents, bridge rules have the following syntax:

$$
\begin{aligned}
BridgeRule &::= \frac{\varphi}{\psi} \\
\varphi &::= SeqLiterals \\
SeqLiterals &::= MLiteral \mid MLiteral, SeqLiterals \\
\psi &::= MLiteral \\
MLiteral &::= MentalAtom \mid \neg MentalAtom \\
MentalAtom &::= \text{B}(stateterm) \\
&\quad \mid \text{B}(Eitherterm \rightarrow Eitherterm) \\
&\quad \mid \text{D}(Eitherterm) \mid \text{I}(actionterm) \\
Eitherterm &::= actionterm \mid stateterm
\end{aligned}
$$

and norms are internalised simply as bridge rules, independently of how they are represented in their corresponding norm representation language:

$$Norm ::= BridgeRule$$

Note that we distinguish between two kinds of terms: actions that an agent can execute are called *action terms*; properties that cannot be executed are called *state terms*. State terms can be brought about by executing actions represented by action terms.

This representation of norms is an adaptation of the one proposed for the BDI+C agent model of [15]. However, in [15] norms are meant to feed into a commitment store, where commitments are associated with an agent/institution component which identifies the protagonist and the subject of a commitment. Moreover, in [15], mental atoms are simply defined as follows:

$$MentalAtom ::= \text{B}(term) \mid \text{D}(term) \mid \text{I}(term)$$

Our distinction between action and state terms leads to a refinement of the original BNF definition for a mental atom, so that executable actions are distinguished from properties. Moreover, we allow beliefs within mental atoms to be in implicative form. We restrict intentions to only concern action terms, since, intuitively, an intention is always about some future behaviour. For example, the Bible's Commandment *"You shall not covet your neighbour's wife"* is represented in BDI+N agents as [1]:

$$\frac{\text{B}(correct(bible))}{\neg \text{D}(have(neighbours\_wife))}$$

Indeed, a man cannot intend to have his neighbour's wife: he can desire it, and this may eventually result in an intention (e.g. to leave his wife which in turn is an action). Here, both *correct(bible)* and *have(neighbours_wife)* are state terms.

Simple beliefs are restricted to concern state terms, since one cannot believe an action. Implicative beliefs may have either state or action terms both as antecedent and consequent. Examples of implicative beliefs are: B(*sunny* → *stays_dry(grass)*) or B(*goto(mecca)* → *goto(heaven)*).

Finally, note that we do not allow negative terms of either kind. So, for example, we cannot represent directly B(*rainy* → ¬*stays_dry(grass)*). However, this belief can be expressed equivalently as B(*raining* → *not_stays_dry(grass)*). [2]

---

[1] In this paper we adopt a Prolog-like convention: ground terms and predicates begin with a lower-case letter and variables begin with an upper-case letter.

[2] The relationship between *not_stays_dry(X)* and *stays_dry(X)* can be easily expressed in assumption-based argumentation by setting appropriate definitions of the notion of contrary, as will see later.

The bridge rule given earlier is ground. An examples of a non-ground bridge rule (also referred to as a *schema*) is:

$$\frac{B(X \rightarrow Y),\ D(Y)}{I(X)}$$

expressing that, for any X and Y, if an agent believes that $X \rightarrow Y$ and it desires Y, then the agent should intend X. An example of a partially instantiated bridge rule (schema) is:

$$\frac{B(immediately(armageddon))}{\neg D(X)}$$

namely, if one believes that Armageddon will strike immediately, then one should not desire anything. Note that the first bridge rule given earlier, as well as the bridge rule:

$$\frac{B(correct(quran))}{\neg I(goto(mecca))}$$

are intuitively norms, whereas the other example bridge rules given earlier are not. A detailed analysis of what makes a rule a norm is a complex problem beyond the scope of this paper. Here, we simply assume that agents are equipped with bridge rules including norms, and focus on dealing with conflicts that may arise amongst bridge rules/norms and theories, inference rules and axioms associated to the B, D and I mental attitudes. These conflicts may not arise when agents are created. However, agents communicate with one another (and potentially sense their environment) and by doing so update their beliefs. New beliefs can trigger a norm (possibly by instantiating a norm schema) and subsequently, a new belief, desire or intention could be adopted by the agent. This may be in conflict with existing beliefs, desires or intentions, and thus commitments may be inconsistent. Equipping BDI+N agents with preferences and argumentative abilities, provides a solution to the problem of resolving these conflicts.

2.3   Example

For illustrative purposes, throughout the remainder of this paper we use an example employing agents from the ballroom scenario described in [14]. We consider a single dancer agent at a traditional ballroom. This dancer can be represented as an agent

$$\langle \mathcal{I} = \{B, D, I\},\ \mathcal{I} \rightarrow \langle L_i, A_i, \Delta_i \rangle,\ \mathcal{I} \rightarrow T_i,\ BR \rangle$$

with BR consisting (amongst others) of the following bridge rules:

$$\frac{B(X \rightarrow Y), D(Y)}{I(X)} \quad (\textit{if } X \textit{ is an actionterm}) \tag{1}$$

$$\frac{B(X \rightarrow Y), D(Y)}{D(X)} \quad (if\ X\ is\ a\ stateterm) \tag{2}$$

$$\frac{D(X)}{I(X)} \quad (if\ X\ is\ an\ actionterm) \tag{3}$$

and inference rules in Δ_B:

$$\frac{B(X \rightarrow Y) \wedge B(X)}{B(Y)} \quad (modus\ ponens\ for\ B) \tag{4}$$

Note, that axiom (4) corresponds to modal logic schema K for beliefs, but is not present for desires and intentions since implications can be believed but neither desired nor intended. Furthermore, we do not have positive or negative introspection (modal logic schemata 4 and 5) since we exclude nested beliefs, desires and intentions for simplicity's sake. Moreover, the bridge rules BR include also ground norms using the domain language of the ballroom. We describe a selection of these norms here:

$$\frac{B(attractive(X))}{D(danceWith(X))} \tag{5}$$

$$\frac{B(sameSex(X, self))}{\neg I(danceWith(X))} \tag{6}$$

$$\frac{B(thirsty(self))}{I(goto(bar))} \tag{7}$$

Finally, one needs to define the theories T_i of the agent, detailing his initial beliefs, desires and intentions. Our dancer in question is male, not thirsty and considers his friend and fellow dancer Bob to be attractive. Hence T_B contains $B(attractive(bob))$, $B(sameSex(bob, self))$, $B(not\_thirsty(self))$. From the first belief, norm (5) and an instance of bridge rule schema (3), one can derive that our dancer should intend to dance with Bob. However, from the second belief and norm (6) one can derive the exact opposite, namely that our dancer should not intend to dance with Bob. We believe that this inconsistency is undesirable and intend to address this problem.

3   Conflict Avoidance

In this section we provide some background on assumption-based argumentation (ABA) and show how it can be used to *avoid* conflicts, in the absence of any additional (preference) information that might help to *resolve* them.

3.1   Background

An ABA framework is a tuple $\langle \mathcal{L}, \mathcal{R}, \mathcal{A}, \bar{\ } \rangle$ where

- $(\mathcal{L}, \mathcal{R})$ is a deductive system, with a language $\mathcal{L}$ and a set $\mathcal{R}$ of inference rules,
- $\mathcal{A} \subseteq \mathcal{L}$, is referred to as the *assumption set*,
- a (total) mapping $^{-}$ from $\mathcal{A}$ into $\mathcal{L}$, where $\overline{\alpha}$ is referred to as the *contrary* of α.

We will assume that the inference rules in $\mathcal{R}$ have the syntax $c_0 \leftarrow c_1, \ldots c_n$. (for $n \geq 0$), where $c_i \in \mathcal{L}$. We will represent $c \leftarrow$. simply as c_0.. As in [10], we will restrict attention to *flat* ABA frameworks, such that if $c \in \mathcal{A}$, then there exists no inference rule of the form $c \leftarrow c_1, \ldots, c_n \in \mathcal{R}$ for any $n \geq 0$.

Example 1. $\mathcal{L} = \{p, a, \neg a, b, \neg b\}$, $\mathcal{R} = \{p \leftarrow a. \quad \neg a \leftarrow b. \quad \neg b \leftarrow a.\}$, $\mathcal{A} = \{a, b\}$ and $\overline{a} = \neg a$, $\overline{b} = \neg b$.

An *argument* in favour of a sentence x in $\mathcal{L}$ supported by a set of assumptions X is a backward deduction from x to X, obtained by applying backwards the rules in $\mathcal{R}$. For the simple ABA framework above, an argument in favour of p supported by $\{a\}$ may be obtained by applying $p \leftarrow a$. backwards.

In order to determine whether a conclusion (set of sentences) is to be sanctioned, a set of assumptions needs to be identified that would provide an "acceptable" support for the conclusion, namely a "consistent" set of assumptions including a "core" support as well as assumptions that defend it. This informal definition can be formalised in many ways, using a notion of "attack" amongst sets of assumptions whereby X *attacks* Y iff there is an argument in favour of some $\overline{x}$ supported by (a subset of) X where x is in Y. In Example 1 above, $\{b\}$ attacks $\{a\}$.

Possible formalisations of "acceptable" support are: a set of assumptions is

- *admissible*, iff it does not attack itself and it counter-attacks every set of assumptions attacking it;
- *complete*, iff it is admissible and it contains all assumptions it can defend, by counter-attacking all attacks against them;
- *grounded*, iff it is minimally (wrt set inclusion) complete;
- *ideal*, iff it is admissible and contained in all maximally (wrt set inclusion) admissible sets.

These formalisations are matched by computational mechanisms [10,11,12], defined as disputes between two fictional players: a proponent and an opponent, trying to establish the acceptability of a given conclusion with respect to the chosen semantics. The three mechanisms are GB-dispute derivations, for the grounded semantics, AB-dispute derivations, for the admissible semantics, and IB-derivations, for the ideal semantics. Like the formalisations they implement, these mechanisms differ in the level of scepticism of the proponent player:

- in GB-dispute derivations the proponent is prepared to take no chance and is completely sceptical in the presence of alternatives;
- in AB-dispute derivations the proponent would adopt any alternative that is capable of counter-attacking all attacks without attacking itself;

- in IB-dispute derivations, the proponent is wary of alternatives, but is prepared to accept common ground between them.

The three procedures are implemented within the CaSAPI system for argumentation [17].

In order to employ ABA to avoid (and resolve) conflicts, one has to provide a mapping from the agent representation introduced in Section 2 onto an appropriate ABA framework and choose a suitable semantics. Given such a mapping, one can then run CaSAPI, the argumentation tool, and hence *reason on demand* about a given conclusion.

3.2 Naive Translation into Assumption-Based Argumentation

In our proposed translation, one can see all bridge rules BR, theories T_i, axioms A_i and inference rules Δ_i as inference rules in an appropriate ABA framework (given below). The language $\mathcal{L}$ holds all mental atoms that make up the norms and initial theories. The $\mathcal{R}$ component holds the bridge rules, the inference rules in all theories T_i and the axioms in all A_i. Concretely, we map each norm from the set of bridge rules BR and each element of each of the theories T_i to a fact (and hence to a rule) to an inference rule in $\mathcal{R}$.

The assumption set $\mathcal{A}$ is set to $\emptyset$ in the naive translation. Thus, a definition for $^{-}$ is not required.

Therefore, a naive translation of the ballroom example in Section 2.3 into an ABA framework gives $\langle \mathcal{L}, \mathcal{R}, \mathcal{A}, {}^{-} \rangle$ [3]:

$$\mathcal{L} = L_B \cup L_D \cup L_I$$

$$\mathcal{A} = \emptyset$$

$$\mathcal{R} = \left\{ \begin{array}{l} I(X) \leftarrow B(X \to Y), D(Y), actionterm(X). \\ D(X) \leftarrow B(X \to Y), D(Y), stateterm(X). \\ B(Y) \leftarrow B(X \to Y), B(X). \\ I(X) \leftarrow D(X). \\ D(danceWith(X)) \leftarrow B(attractive(X)). \\ \neg I(danceWith(X)) \leftarrow B(sameSex(X, self)). \\ B(attactive(bob)). \\ B(sameSex(bob, self). \\ actionterm(danceWith(X)). \\ stateterm(attractive(X)). \\ stateterm(sameSex(X, Y)). \end{array} \right\}$$

Having constructed an instance of an ABA framework in this way, one can now use the CaSAPI system [17] to determine (for any semantics supported by CaSAPI) whether a given conclusion holds, and, if so, by which arguments it is

---

[3] All inference rules in $\mathcal{R}$ stand semantically for the set of all their ground instances. However, note that CaSAPI can often handle variables in rules.

supported. In particular, CaSAPI would allow to support the conflicting conclusions

$$I(danceWith(bob)) \text{ and } \neg I(danceWith(bob))$$

simultaneously, under any semantics. These conslusions are supported by a trivial argument with an empty set of assumptions as support. This unwanted behaviour is due to the naivity of the translation

3.3 Avoiding Conflicts Using Assumption-Based Argumentation

The conflict between $I(danceWith(bob))$ and $\neg I(danceWith(bob))$ above can be avoided by rendering the application of the two rules supporting them mutually exclusive. This can be achieved by attaching assumptions to these rules and setting the contrary of the assumption associated to any rule to be the conclusion of the other rule. This would correspond to rendering the corresponding norms/bridge rules defeasible [31,32].

In the ballroom example, the fourth and sixth rules of the naive translation above are replaced by

$$I(X) \leftarrow D(X), \alpha(X).$$

$$\neg I(danceWith(X)) \leftarrow B(sameSex(X, self)), \beta(danceWith(X)).$$

with $\mathcal{A} = \{\alpha(t), \beta(t) | t \text{ is ground}\}$ and $\overline{\alpha(t)} = \neg I(t)$ and $\overline{\beta(t)} = I(t)$.

Within the revised argumentation framework, the conflicting conclusions $I(danceWith(bob))$ and $\neg I(danceWith(bob))$ cannot be justified simultaneously. However, adopting the admissibility semantics (implemented as AB-derivations in CaSAPI), $I(danceWith(bob))$ and $\neg I(danceWith(bob))$ can be justified separately, in a credulous manner. On the other hand, adopting the grounded or ideal semantics (and GB- or IB-derivations), neither $I(danceWith(bob))$ nor $\neg I(danceWith(bob))$ can be justified, sceptically. Thus, the conflict is avoided, but not resolved. Below, we show how to resolve conflicts in the presence of additional information, in the form of preferences over norms, elements of the theories T_i, and inference rules and axioms for the different mental attitudes.

4   Conflict Resolution Using Preferences

In this section we show how to use ABA in order to reason normatively and resolve conflicts (by means of preferences) that come about by accepting or committing to certain norms, beliefs, desires or intentions. Using these preferences, we can, for example, prioritise certain beliefs over a norm or certain norms over desires. Thus, one can think of preferences as the *normative personality* of an agent. We also need to make norms and mental atoms defeasible, by using assumptions as we have done in the earlier section. For the example in Section 2.3, an agent who values norm (3) and (5) more than norm (6) will indeed intend to dance with Bob, whereas another agent who values social conformance, such as norm (6), higher, will not have such an intention. No agent should be allowed to both intend and not intend the same thing. Similarly, simultaneously believing and not believing or desiring and not desiring the same thing is not allowed. We will adopt the following revised agent model:

$$Agent = \langle \mathcal{I},\ \mathcal{I} \to \langle L_i, A_i, \Delta_i \rangle,\ \mathcal{I} \to T_i,\ BR,\ \mathcal{P} \rangle$$

where the new component $\mathcal{P}$ expresses the agent's preferences over norms and mental attitudes. We will consider various representations for $\mathcal{P}$ below, and provide a way to use them to resolve conflicts by means of ABA. Concretely, we start with a total ordering and a cluster-based translation for conflict-resolution. Then we add more flexibility by allowing the order to be partial. Finally, we suggest a way of defining preferences using meta-rules, e.g. as done by [21,25], and following the approach proposed in [23].

In the remainder of the paper, we will refer to an agent

$$\langle \mathcal{I},\ \mathcal{I} \to \langle L_i, A_i, \Delta_i \rangle,\ \mathcal{I} \to T_i,\ BR,\ \mathcal{P} \rangle$$

as $Agent(\mathcal{P})$, and to the ABA framework resulting from applying the naive translation to $\langle \mathcal{I},\ \mathcal{I} \to \langle L_i, A_i, \Delta_i \rangle,\ \mathcal{I} \to T_i,\ BR \rangle$ as $ABA_N = \langle \mathcal{L}_N, \mathcal{R}_N, \emptyset, \overline{}_N \rangle$.

4.1   Preferences as a Total Ordering

The preference information $\mathcal{P}$ can be expressed as a total function that provides a mapping from bridge rules and elements of theories/axioms/inference rules to rational numbers. For now, let us assume that $\mathcal{P}$ provides a total ordering and that the type of $\mathcal{P}$ is

$$BR \cup A_B \cup A_D \cup A_I \cup \Delta_B \cup \Delta_D \cup \Delta_I \cup T_B \cup T_D \cup T_I \to \mathbb{Q}.$$

We stipulate that lower numbers indicate a higher preference for the piece of information in question. In order to translate $Agent(\mathcal{P})$ into a form that ABA can suitably handle, we propose the following mechanism. First, we generate ABA_N. Then, all rules in $\mathcal{R}_N$ are clustered according to their conclusion. Rules in the same cluster all have the same mental atom in their conclusion literal (so that fellow cluster members have either exactly the same or exactly the opposite conclusion). Next, each cluster of rules is considered in turn. All elements of each cluster are sorted in descending order $\pi_1, \dots, \pi_n$ by decreasing preference of their corresponding norm, belief etc. Here and in the remainder of the paper, we assume a naming convention for rules whereby π_i is the name of rule $l_i \leftarrow r_i.$, where l_1 is the literal on the left-hand side of the most important rule and r_n represents the right-hand side of the least important rule.

$$l_1 \leftarrow r_1. \qquad l_2 \leftarrow r_2. \qquad l_3 \leftarrow r_3. \qquad l_4 \leftarrow r_4. \qquad \dots \qquad l_n \leftarrow r_n.$$

Then, we employ a trick suggested in [23,10] and add a new assumption p_i to the right-hand side of each rule:

$$l_1 \leftarrow r_1, p_1. \qquad l_2 \leftarrow r_2, p_2. \qquad l_3 \leftarrow r_3, p_3. \qquad l_4 \leftarrow r_4, p_4. \qquad \dots \qquad l_n \leftarrow r_n, p_n.$$

By introducing additional assumptions into rules we make these rules defeasible and, by appropriately defining contraries, we can render conflicts impossible. We further add rules for new terms q_i of the form:

$$q_2 \leftarrow r_1 \quad q_3 \leftarrow r_2, p_2 \quad q_4 \leftarrow r_3, p_3 \quad \cdots \quad q_n \leftarrow r_{n-1}, p_{n-1}$$
$$q_3 \leftarrow q_2 \quad q_4 \leftarrow q_3 \quad \cdots \quad q_n \leftarrow q_{n-1}$$
$$q_4 \leftarrow q_2 \quad \cdots \quad q_n \leftarrow q_{n-2}$$
$$\cdots \quad \cdots$$
$$q_n \leftarrow q_2$$

Intuitively, q_{i+1} holds if π_i is "selected" (by assuming p_i) and applicable (by r_i holding). Alternatively, q_{i+1} also holds if any of the other more important rules is selected and applicable. Note that there is no definition for q_1, since, as we will see below, the first rule is not intended to be defeasible.

We can now define the contraries of each of the assumptions p_i in such a way as to allow norms with a smaller subscript (higher preference) to override norms with higher subscripts (lower preference). Concretely, by setting $\overline{p_i} = q_i$ for all $i \geq 1$, a rule π_i is only applicable if assumption p_i can be made and this is only the case if q_i cannot be shown. The only way for q_i to hold is when both r_{i-1} and p_{i-1} hold (this would also make rule π_{i-1} applicable) or any of the other more important rules is applicable. Hence π_i is only applicable if π_j is not applicable for any $j < i$. Moreover, if r_1 holds, then π_1 is always applicable, as there is no way for q_1 to hold and thus p_1 can always be assumed.

After applying this procedure to all clusters, none of the clusters of rules can give rise to conflicts and since rules in different clusters have different conclusions, there cannot be any inter-cluster conflicts either. Hence, in the case of a single cluster, the resulting ABA framework $\langle \mathcal{L}, \mathcal{R}, \mathcal{A}, \overline{} \rangle$ with:

$$\mathcal{L} = \mathcal{L}_N \cup \bigcup_{i=1\ldots n}\{p_i, q_i\}$$
$$\mathcal{R} = \{l_i \leftarrow r_i, p_i. \mid (l_i \leftarrow r_i.) \in \mathcal{R}_N\} \cup \{q_{i+1} \leftarrow r_i, p_i. \mid (l_i \leftarrow r_i.) \in \mathcal{R}_N\}$$
$$\cup \; \{q_i \leftarrow q_j \mid 1 < j < i\}$$
$$\mathcal{A} = \bigcup_{i=1\ldots n}\{p_i\}$$
$$\forall p_i \in \mathcal{A} : \overline{p_i} = q_i$$

is conflict-free. Let us consider the ballroom example from Section 2.3 again. Assume that the most important norm is (5) - $\dfrac{B(attractive(X))}{D(danceWith(X))}$ followed by norm (6) - $\dfrac{B(sameSex(X, self))}{\neg I(danceWith(X))}$ and norm schema (4) - $\dfrac{D(X)}{I(X)}$. Assume further that the premises of both norms (5) and (6) are fulfilled, unifying X with bob. [4] Using norm (5) we derive $D(danceWith(bob))$. Now, only norm (6) and norm schema (4) have conflicting conclusions and are grouped together for the purpose of conflict resolution. In this example, we assumed that norm (6) is more important than norm schema (4) and hence we get a cluster:

---

[4] Norm schemata are instantiated at this stage.

$\neg I(danceWith(bob)) \leftarrow B(sameSex(bob, self)), p_1.$
$I(danceWith(bob)) \leftarrow D(danceWith(bob)),\ p_2.$
$q_2 \leftarrow B(sameSex(bob, self)).$

and contraries: $\overline{p_i} = q_i$.

Now the mental literal $\neg I(danceWith(X))$ will be justified, but its complementary literal will not. Note that norm (7) stating that thirsty dancers should go to the bar, does not play a part in resolving the present conflict. One may therefore argue that the requirement of having a total preference order of rules is an unnatural one. For example, one may want to be able to avoid expressing a preference between certain rules that are unrelated (i.e. concerned with different, non-conflicting conclusions).

Note further, that we are adopting the *last-link* principle [25] in using preferences for resolving conflicts, which uses the strength of the last rule used to derive the argument's claim for comparison. According to this principle, the fact that norm schema (4) is *based* on a desire derived using the most important norm is irrelevant.

Once the mapping has been formulated, reasoning with the original framework is mapped onto reasoning with an ABA framework. Alternative semantics are available (in CaSAPI) to compute whether a given claim is supported.

4.2   Preferences as a Partial Ordering

We propose a different representation for preferences if the ordering of norms, beliefs, desires and intentions is not total. We replace the function $\mathcal{P}$ with a set $\mathcal{P}$ which holds facts of the form $pref(\mu_i, \mu_j)$ that intuitively express the agent's preference for norm/belief/etc. named μ_i over the one named μ_j. Note that we assume here a naming for elements of

$$BR \cup A_B \cup A_D \cup A_I \cup \Delta_B \cup \Delta_D \cup \Delta_I \cup T_B \cup T_D \cup T_I.$$

We further stipulate that $\mathcal{P}$ contains only facts about pairs of norms, beliefs, etc whose conclusions are conflicting. We deem it unnecessary to express preferences between rules that do not conflict since they will never be part of the same cluster. We will assume that this relation *pref* is irreflexive and asymmetric. It may also be appropriate to assume that *pref* is not cyclic. The asymmetry and irreflexivity requirements can be expressed as follows [5]:

$\bot \leftarrow pref(\mu_i, \mu_j) \wedge pref(\mu_j, \mu_i) \wedge \mu_i \neq \mu_j$
$\bot \leftarrow pref(\mu_i, \mu_i)$

We define a new mapping into ABA as follows. As before, we first generate ABA_N and cluster rules in $\mathcal{R}_N$ according to their conclusion. But now elements of clusters are no longer sorted by their quantitative preference, given by the total order, but instead are considered one at a time. Moreover, each rule in $\mathcal{R}_N$

---

[5] We refrain in this paper from axiomatising the *pref* relation and will assume instead that $\mathcal{P}$ is given so that these requirements hold.

is implicitly assumed to have the same name as the corresponding norm, belief, desire or intention.

Within the new mapping, if for a given rule we find a conflicting rule, but there is no appropriate fact in the *pref* relation, we apply the mechanism of Section 3.3 that guarantees mutual exclusion. For example, let us consider two rules π_i and π_j in the same cluster, of the form $l_i \leftarrow r_i$. and $l_j \leftarrow r_j$., named μ_i and μ_j respectively, where l_i and l_j are in conflict (i.e. opposite mental literals) but neither $pref(\mu_i, \mu_j)$ nor $pref(\mu_j, \mu_i)$ belongs to $\mathcal{P}$. We follow the same mechanism as in Section 3.3, adding two assumptions to the rules, yielding:

$$l_i \leftarrow r_i, p_i. \qquad l_j \leftarrow r_j, p_j.$$

and directly setting: $\overline{p_i} = l_j$ and $\overline{p_j} = l_i$. In this way, each rule is only applicable if the other one is not.

If, however, j_n facts exist in $\mathcal{P}$ ($j_n \geq 1$) expressing the agent's preference of rules named $\mu_{j_1}, \ldots, \mu_{j_n}$ over some rule named μ_i:

$$pref(\mu_{j_1}, \mu_i), \ldots, pref(\mu_{j_n}, \mu_i)$$

where $\mu_i : l_i \leftarrow r_i$. and $\mu_{j_1} : l' \leftarrow r_{j_1}. \ldots \mu_{j_n} : l' \leftarrow r_{j_n}$. are such that l' is the complement of l_i, then the mechanism illustrated below is employed, ensuring that the lower priority rule is only applied in case none of the "more important" ones are applicable. The rules named μ_i, $\mu_{j_1}, \ldots \mu_{j_n}$ are rewritten as

$$l_i \leftarrow r_i, p_i.$$
$$l' \leftarrow r_{j_1}, p_{j_1}. \quad \ldots \quad l' \leftarrow r_{j_n}, p_{j_n}.$$
$$q_i \leftarrow r_{j_1}, pref(\mu_{j_1}, \mu_i).$$
$$\ldots$$
$$q_i \leftarrow r_{j_n}, pref(\mu_{j_n}, \mu_i).$$
$$q_{j_1} \leftarrow r_i, pref(\mu_i, \mu_{j_1}).$$
$$\ldots$$
$$q_{j_n} \leftarrow r_i, pref(\mu_i, \mu_{j_n}).$$

where $p_i, p_{j_1}, \ldots, p_{j_n}$ are new assumptions. Finally, we set $\overline{p_i} = q_i$ and $\overline{p_{j_1}} = q_{j_1}$, $\ldots, \overline{p_{j_n}} = q_{j_n}$, and add all facts in $\mathcal{P}$ to the set of inference rules. For a more formal definition of this mapping see [32]. The resulting ABA is conflict-free.

In order to illustrate this mapping, consider again the ballroom example, where rules are named $\mu_1, \ldots \mu_{11}$ following the order in which they are presented in Section 3.2. If $pref(\mu_6, \mu_4) \in \mathcal{P}$ then in the resulting ABA framework, a subset of the set of inference rules is:

$$I(X) \leftarrow D(X), p_4(X).$$
$$q_4(X) \leftarrow B(sameSex(X, self)), pref(\mu_6, \mu_4).$$

$$\neg I(danceWith(X)) \leftarrow B(sameSex(X, self)), p_6(X).$$
$$q_6(X) \leftarrow D(X), pref(\mu_4, \mu_6).$$

$$pref(\mu_6, \mu_4).$$

The first rule applies, only if $D(X)$ and $p_4(X)$ both hold. However, it is defeated by the fact that the contrary of $p_4(X)$ holds. This contrary ($q_4(X)$) is dependent on $pref(\mu_6, \mu_4)$, which is true in this example. Similarly, the rule with the conclusion $\neg I(danceWith(X))$ applies, only if both $B(sameSex(X, self))$ and $p_6(X)$ hold. In our example, this rule is not defeated, since the contrary of $p_6(X)$ cannot be shown. This contrary depends on $pref(\mu_4, \mu_6)$, which does not hold. It can hence be seen how the content of $\mathcal{P}$ influences the applicability of rules.

4.3   Defining Dynamic Preferences Via Meta-rules

The relation $\mathcal{P}$ described in the previous subsection held simple facts. One can easily extend these facts into rules [6] by adding extra conditions. As an example, one could replace the fact $pref(\mu_1, \mu_2)$ with two meta-rules one stating $pref(\mu_1, \mu_2) \leftarrow sunny$ and another one stating $pref(\mu_2, \mu_1) \leftarrow rainy$. This allows the agent to change the preference between two norms, beliefs etc depending on the weather.

The addition of conditions makes the applicability of a certain norm dependent on the fulfilment of the condition and hence allows more fine-grained control over arguments. The transformation defined in the previous subsection still applies here.

Note that one can view these meta-rules themselves as norms in the sense of "one should prefer norm 1 over norm 2 whenever the sun shines". We are currently considering another kind of conflict, that contrasts $goto(bar)$ with $danceWith(X)$ since nobody can go to the bar and be on the dance-floor at the same time. Imagine the possibility of such a conflict. Then norm (7), referring to thirsty dancers, conflicts with an instance of norm schemata (4), that refers to dance intentions. A dancer that considers himself a gentleman then prefers μ_4 over μ_7, resisting the temptation to go for a drink. A selfish dancer on the other hand prefers μ_7 over μ_4. Considering yourself as a gentleman is itself a dynamic notion, that can change once the dancer has been to the bar a few times. Considering the meta-rules for preferences themselves as norms opens up many potential future investigations that we are looking forward to conduct.

5   Theoretical Considerations

In this section we show that each of the translation mechanisms proposed in the previous section is a conservative extension of the earlier mechanism, if any. For simplicity we will always assume a single cluster of preferences.

The following result, stating that given a partial order, the tranformations given in Sections 4.2 and 4.3 are equivalent, is trivial, since the two mappings return the same outcome given a partial order:

---

[6] Note, that these meta-rules here only concern the *pref* predicate and should not be confused with the object-level rules that act as arguments to these preference predicates.

Theorem 1. *Consider an Agent($\mathcal{P}$) such that $\mathcal{P}$ is a partial order as in section 4.2. Let $ABA_{PO} = \langle \mathcal{L}_{PO}, \mathcal{R}_{PO}, \mathcal{A}_{PO}, \overline{}_{PO} \rangle$ be the ABA framework resulting from applying the transformation in Section 4.2 to Agent($\mathcal{P}$) and let $ABA_D = \langle \mathcal{L}_D, \mathcal{R}_D, \mathcal{A}_D, \overline{}_D \rangle$ be the ABA framework resulting from applying the transformation in Section 4.3 to Agent($\mathcal{P}$). Then, for any sentence $s \in L_B \cup L_D \cup L_I$:*

- *there is an acceptable support for s wrt ABA_{PO} iff there is an acceptable support for s wrt ABA_D*

for any notion of acceptable support given in section 3.1.

The analogous result linking the mapping for total orders and partial order, given a total order as input, is easy to prove. Below, since trivially every total order is a partial order, we will use the same symbol ($\mathcal{P}$) to stand for a total order as represented in Section 4.1 and as represented in Section 4.2. Indeed, given a total order as in Section 4.1, this can be automatically mapped onto the representation in Section 4.2, by creating an element $pref(\pi_i, \pi_j)$ for every pair of elements of the cluster such that $i < j$. For a cluster with n elements, we thus obtain $\frac{n^2-n}{2}$ facts in the *pref* predicate.

Theorem 2. *Consider an Agent($\mathcal{P}$) such that $\mathcal{P}$ is a total order as in section 4.1. Let $ABA_{TO} = \langle \mathcal{L}_{TO}, \mathcal{R}_{TO}, \mathcal{A}_{TO}, \overline{}_{TO} \rangle$ be the ABA framework resulting from applying the transformation in Section 4.1 to Agent($\mathcal{P}$) and let $ABA_{PO} = \langle \mathcal{L}_{PO}, \mathcal{R}_{PO}, \mathcal{A}_{PO}, \overline{}_{PO} \rangle$ be the ABA framework resulting from applying the transformation in Section 4.2 to Agent($\mathcal{P}$). Then, for any sentence $s \in L_B \cup L_D \cup L_I$:*

- *there is an acceptable support for s wrt ABA_{TO} iff there is an acceptable support for s wrt ABA_{PO}*

for any notion of acceptable support given in Section 3.1.

This theorem can be proven as follows. First, note that, trivially, the underlying languages of the deductive systems in the two ABAs differ only in the abducibles, their contraries, and the *pref* facts, namely:

$$\mathcal{L}_{TO} - (\mathcal{A}_{TO} \cup \{x | x = \overline{a} \text{ for some } a \in \mathcal{A}_{TO}\}) =$$
$$\mathcal{L}_{PO} - (\mathcal{A}_{PO} \cup \{x | x = \overline{a} \text{ for some } a \in \mathcal{A}_{PO}\} \cup \mathcal{P}) =$$
$$L_B \cup L_D \cup L_I.$$

Moreover, there is a one-to-one correspondence between assumptions in the two ABAs and contraries in the two ABAs, as follows.

Suppose we have a cluster of three conflicting rules named μ_1, μ_2 and μ_3 such that each μ_i is of the form $l_i \leftarrow r_i$., $l_1 = l_3$ and l_2 is the complement of l_1 and l_3. Let us further assume that μ_1 is preferred to μ_2 which in turn is preferred to μ_3. This total order can be expressed in terms of the representation of Section 4.2 by the facts $pref(\mu_1, \mu_2), pref(\mu_2, \mu_3)$ and $pref(\mu_1, \mu_3)$. In ABA_{TO}, the relevant part of the $\mathcal{R}_{TO}$ component for this cluster is:

$$l_1 \leftarrow r_1, p_1. \qquad l_2 \leftarrow r_2, p_2. \qquad l_3 \leftarrow r_3, p_3.$$
$$q_2 \leftarrow r_1. \qquad q_3 \leftarrow r_2, p_2.$$
$$q_3 \leftarrow q_2.$$

The corresponding part of $\mathcal{R}_{PO}$ in ABA_{PO} is:

$$l_1 \leftarrow r_1, p'_1. \qquad l_2 \leftarrow r_2, p'_2. \qquad l_3 \leftarrow r_3, p'_3.$$
$$q'_1 \leftarrow r_2, pref(\mu_2, \mu_1). \quad q'_2 \leftarrow r_1, pref(\mu_1, \mu_2). \quad q'_3 \leftarrow r_2, pref(\mu_2, \mu_3).$$
$$q'_2 \leftarrow r_3, pref(\mu_3, \mu_2).$$
$$pref(\mu_1, \mu_2). \qquad pref(\mu_2, \mu_3). \qquad pref(\mu_1, \mu_3)$$

By partially evaluating the *pref* conditions, this set of inference rules can be seen to be equivalent to

$$l_1 \leftarrow r_1, p'_1. \qquad l_2 \leftarrow r_2, p'_2. \qquad l_3 \leftarrow r_3, p'_3.$$
$$q'_2 \leftarrow r_1. \qquad q'_3 \leftarrow r_2.$$

Clearly there is a one-to-one correspondence between each p_i in $\mathcal{A}_{TO}$ and p'_i in $\mathcal{A}_{PO}$. Furthermore, there is a one-to-one correspondence between each q_i in $\mathcal{L}_{TO}$ and q'_i in $\mathcal{L}_{PO}$.

Formally, we define two mappings α_{TO-PO} and α_{PO-TO} between the languages of the two frameworks as follows:

- let p_i, p'_i be the assumptions associated with rule named μ_i in $\mathcal{R}_{TO}$ and $\mathcal{R}_{PO}$, respectively; then:
  - $\alpha_{TO-PO}(p_i) = p'_i$
  - $\alpha_{PO-TO}(p'_i) = p_i$
- let q_i, q'_i be the contraries of assumptions p_i, p'_i associated with rule named μ_i in $\mathcal{R}_{TO}$ and $\mathcal{R}_{PO}$, respectively; then:
  - $\alpha_{TO-PO}(q_i) = q'_i$
  - $\alpha_{PO-TO}(q'_i) = q_i$

  let s be any non-assumption, non-contrary, non-preference sentences in $\mathcal{L}_{TO}$ and $\mathcal{L}_{PO}$; then $\alpha_{TO-PO}(s) = \alpha_{PO-TO}(s) = s$

This mappings can be easily extended to sets of sentences.

Lemma 1. *Given any sentence $s \in \mathcal{L}_{TO}$,*

- *there is a deduction for s wrt ABA_{TO} iff there is a deduction for $\alpha_{TO-PO}(s)$ wrt ABA_{PO}.*

Given any sentence $s \in \mathcal{L}_{PO} - \mathcal{P}$,

- *there is a deduction for s wrt ABA_{TO} iff there is a deduction for $\alpha_{PO-TO}(s)$ wrt ABA_{PO}.*

As a consequence, it is easy to see that, by definition of attack:

Lemma 2. *Given any sets of assumptions $S_1, S_2 \subseteq \mathcal{A}_{TO}$,*

- *S_1 attacks S_2 wrt ABA_{TO} iff $\alpha_{TO-PO}(S_1)$ attacks $\alpha_{TO-PO}(S_2)$ wrt ABA_{PO}.*

Given any sets of assumptions $S_1, S_2 \subseteq \mathcal{A}_{PO}$,

- *S_1 attacks S_2 wrt ABA_{PO} iff $\alpha_{PO-TO}(S_1)$ attacks $\alpha_{PO-TO}(S_2)$ wrt ABA_{TO}.*

Theorem 2 is a straightforward consequence of this lemma, since all definitions of "acceptable" support are solely defined in terms of the notion of attack.

6   Conclusions

In this paper we have proposed to use assumption-based argumentation to solve conflicts that a normative agent can encounter, arising from applying conflicting norms but also due to conflicting beliefs, desires and intentions. We employ qualitative preferences over an agent's beliefs, desires and intentions and over the norms it is subjected to in order to resolve conflicts.

We provided a translation from the agent definition to an assumption-based argumentation framework that can be executed using a working prototype implementation of the query-oriented argumentation system CaSAPI. After manually applying the translation described in this paper (from the contexts, theories and preferences of a normative BDI+N agent to an argumentation framework $\langle \mathcal{L}, \mathcal{R}, \mathcal{A}, ^{-} \rangle$), one can execute CaSAPI and obtain a defence set containing all assumptions employed in the argument for a given claim. From these, one can derive which rules (norms or mental atoms) have been relied upon during the argumentation process. It would be useful to embed the implementation of this translation into the CaSAPI system or develop a wrapper that does the translation and employs CaSAPI.

We have considered three different notions of preference with different degrees of flexibility and expressiveness. Some theoretical considerations allowed us to show how these notions are related. Notice how our preference model (that ranks individual rules and mental attitudes) is different from the one chosen by Amgoud and Cayrol in [2], who have a preference relation over arguments such that an attack between arguments is only relevant if the attackee is not preferred to the attacker. A related approach, based on Bench-Capon's value-based argumentation framework [3] is that of Dunne et al. who developed a preference model which takes audiences into account (see [8] and [13]).

Normative conflicts have previously been addressed from a legal reasoning perspective by Sartor [30] and from a practical reasoning point of view by Kollingbaum and Norman [22]. It is traditional in the legal domain to order laws hierarchically, using criteria such as source, chronology and speciality. One such system by Garcia-Camino et al. [18] employs these criteria and a meta-order over them to solve conflicts in compound activities. As far as we know, argumentation and in particular assumption-based argumentation, has received little attention in the agent community with respect to normative conflicts.

Argumentation-based negotiation (see for example [26]) is a field of artificial intelligence that concerns itself with resolving conflicts in a multi-agent society. However, to the best of our knowledge it has hardly been used to resolve normative conflicts of the kind we study in this paper. To the best of our knowledge, the only architecture for individual agents that uses argumentation is the KGP model [20] that follows the approach of [21] to support its control component and its goal decision capability. The KGP model has been extended to support normative reasoning [29] but no conflict resolution amongst the outcomes of norm enforcement and beliefs is performed in this extension.

We have adopted a "last-link" approach to dealing with preferences in deriving conflicting conclusions along the lines of [25]. This principle employs of the strength of the last rule used to derive the argument's claim for comparison; other (potentially stronger) rules uses earlier in the derivation process are irrelevant for determining preferences. An alternative from the standard literature is the principle of the "weakest link" [1] which compares the minimum strength of the sentences used in each argument.

In the near future, we plan to research the effects of splitting the preference function into four separate ones for beliefs, desires, intentions and norms. One may be able to draw conclusions about the kind of normative personality an agent possesses depending on how these individual preference functions relate. Such relationships have been used quantitatively by Casali et al. [6] in their work on graded BDI agents.

Acknowledgements

This research was partially funded by the Sixth Framework IST programme of the EC, under the 035200 ARGUGRID project. The first author is partially supported by a PhD bursary from the Engineering and Physical Sciences Research Council (EPSRC) of the United Kingdom. The second author has also been supported by a UK Royal Academy of Engineering/Leverhulme Trust senior fellowship.

References

1. Amgoud, L., Cayrol, C.: Inferring from inconsistency in preference-based argumentation frameworks. J. Autom. Reason. 29(2), 125–169 (2002)
2. Amgoud, L., Cayrol, C.: A reasoning model based on the production of acceptable arguments. Annals of Mathematics and Artificial Intelligence 34(1-3), 197–215 (2002)
3. Bench-Capon, T.J.M.: Persuasion in practical argument using value-based argumentation frameworks. Journal of Logic and Computation 13(3), 429–448 (2003)
4. Bondarenko, A., Dung, P., Kowalski, R., Toni, F.: An abstract, argumentation-theoretic framework for default reasoning. Artificial Intelligence 93(1-2), 63–101 (1997)
5. Broersen, J., Dastani, M., Hulstijn, J., Huang, Z., van der Torre, L.: The BOID architecture: Conflicts between beliefs, obligations, intentions and desires. In: Proceedings of AGENTS 2001, pp. 9–16. ACM Press, New York (2001)
6. Casali, A., Godo, L., Sierra, C.: Graded BDI models for agent architectures. In: Jantke, K.P., Lunzer, A., Spyratos, N., Tanaka, Y. (eds.) Federation over the Web. LNCS (LNAI), vol. 3847, pp. 126–143. Springer, Heidelberg (2006)
7. Dignum, F., Morley, D., Sonenberg, E., Cavendon, L.: Towards socially sophisticated BDI agents. In: Proceedings of ICMAS 2000, pp. 111–118. IEEE Computer Society, Los Alamitos (2000)
8. Doutre, S., Bench-Capon, T.J.M., Dunne, P.E.: Explaining preferences with argument positions. In: Kaelbling, L.P., Saffiotti, A. (eds.) IJCAI, pp. 1560–1561. Professional Book Center (2005)

9. Dung, P.: The acceptability of arguments and its fundamental role in non-monotonic reasoning and logic programming and n-person game. Artificial Intelligence 77 (1995)

10. Dung, P., Kowalski, R., Toni, F.: Dialectic proof procedures for assumption-based, admissible argumentation. Artificial Intelligence 170, 114–159 (2006)

11. Dung, P., Mancarella, P., Toni, F.: Computing ideal sceptical argumentation. Technical report, Imperial College London (2006)

12. Dung, P., Mancarella, P., Toni, F.: A dialectic procedure for sceptical, assumption-based argumentation. In: Proceedings of COMMA (2006)

13. Dunne, P.E., Bench-Capon, T.J.M.: Identifying audience preferences in legal and social domains. In: Proceedings of the 15th International Conference on Database and Expert Systems Applications, Zaragoza, Spain, pp. 518–527 (September 2004)

14. Gaertner, D., Clark, K., Sergot, M.: Ballroom etiquette: A case study for norm-governed multi-agent systems. In: Proceedings of the 1st International Workshop on Coordination, Organisation, Institutions and Norms (2006)

15. Gaertner, D., Noriega, P., Sierra, C.: Extending the BDI architecture with commitments. In: Proceedings of the 9th International Conference of the Catalan Association of Artificial Intelligence (2006)

16. Gaertner, D., Toni, F.: Conflict-free normative agents using assumption-based argumentation. In: Proceedings of the Fourth International Workshop on Argumentation in Multi-Agent Systems (2007)

17. Gaertner, D., Toni, F.: A credulous and sceptical argumentation system. In: Proceedings of ArgNMR (2007), www.doc.ic.ac.uk/~dg00/casapi.html

18. García, A., Noriega, P., Rodríguez-Aguilar, J.-A.: An Algorithm for Conflict Resolution in Regulated Compound Activities. In: ESAW workshop (2006)

19. Giunchiglia, F., Serafini, L.: Multi-language hierarchical logics or: How we can do without modal logics. Artificial Intelligence 65(1), 29–70 (1994)

20. Kakas, A., Mancarella, P., Sadri, F., Stathis, K., Toni, F.: The KGP model of agency. In: Proceedings of the European Conference on Artificial Intelligence, pp. 33–37 (August 2004)

21. Kakas, A., Moraitis, P.: Argumentation based decision making for autonomous agents. In: Proceedings of AAMAS 2003, pp. 883–890 (2003)

22. Kollingbaum, M., Norman, T.: Strategies for resolving norm conflict in practical reasoning. In: ECAI Workshop Coordination in Emergent Agent Societies (2004)

23. Kowalski, R.A., Toni, F.: Abstract argumentation. Journal of AI and Law, Special Issue on Logical Models of Argumentation 4(3-4), 275–296 (1996)

24. Parsons, S., Sierra, C., Jennings, N.: Agents that reason and negotiate by arguing. Journal of Logic and Computation 8(3), 261–292 (1998)

25. Prakken, H., Sartor, G.: Argument-based extended logic programming with defeasible priorities. Journal of Applied Non-Classical Logics 7(1), 25–75 (1997)

26. Rahwan, I., Ramchurn, S., Jennings, N., McBurney, P., Parsons, S., Sonenberg, L.: Argumentation-based negotiation. Knowledge Engineering Review (2004)

27. Rao, A.S., Georgeff, M.P.: BDI-agents: from theory to practice. In: Proceedings of the First International Conference on Multiagent Systems, San Francisco (1995)

28. Sadri, F., Stathis, K., Toni, F.: Normative KGP agents. Computational and Mathematical Organization Theory 12(2/3), 101–126 (2006)

29. Sadri, F., Stathis, K., Toni, F.: Normative kgp agents. Computational & Mathematical Organization Theory 12(2-3) (October 2006)

30. Sartor, G.: Normative conflicts in legal reasoning. Artificial Intelligence and Law 1(2-3), 209–235 (1992)
31. Toni, F.: Assumption-based argumentation for closed and consistent defeasible reasoning. In: Satoh, K., Inokuchi, A., Nagao, K., Kawamura, T. (eds.) JSAI 2007. LNCS (LNAI), vol. 4914, Springer, Heidelberg (2007)
32. Toni, F.: Assumption-based argumentation for selection and composition of services. In: Proceedings of the 8th International Workshop on Computational Logic in Multi-Agent Systems (CLIMA VIII) (2007)

The Hedgehog and the Fox*
An Argumentation-Based Decision Support System

Maxime Morge

Dipartimento di Informatica, Università di Pisa
via F. Buonarroti, 2 I-56127 Pisa, Italy
morge@di.unipi.it
http://maxime.morge.org

Abstract. In this paper, we present a decision support system which is built upon an argumentation framework for practical reasoning. A logic language is used as a concrete data structure for holding statements representing knowledge, goals, and decisions. Different priorities are attached to these items, corresponding to the probability of the knowledge, the preferences between goals, and the expected utilities of decisions. These concrete data structures consist of information providing the backbone of arguments. Due to the abductive nature of practical reasoning, arguments are built by reasoning backwards, and possibly by making suppositions over missing information. Moreover, arguments are defined as tree-like structures. In this way, our computer system, implemented in Prolog, suggests some solutions and provides an interactive and intelligible explanation of this choice.

1 Introduction

Decision making is the cognitive process leading to the selection of a course of action among alternatives based on estimates of the values of those alternatives. Indeed, when a human identifies her needs and specifies them with high-level and abstract terms, there should be a possibility to select some existing solutions. Decision Support Systems (DSS) are computer-based systems that support decision making activities including expert systems and multi-criteria decision analysis. However, these approaches are not suitable when the decision maker has partial and conflicting information. Further, standard decision theory provides little support in giving intelligible explanation of the choice made.

Since a decision can be resolved by confronting and evaluating the justifications of different positions, argumentation can support such a process. This is the reason why many works in the area of Artificial Intelligence focus on computational models of argumentation. In particular, nonmonotonic logic techniques have been used as a model with hierarchies of possibly conflicting rules (see [1]

---

* The author would like to thank Paolo Mancarella for his contribution on a previous version of this paper. This work is supported by the Sixth Framework IST programme of the EC, under the 035200 ARGUGRID project.

I. Rahwan, S. Parsons, and C. Reed (Eds.): ArgMAS 2007, LNAI 4946, pp. 114–131, 2008.

for a survey). However, even if modern techniques are used, this logical approach is still limited to the epistemic reasoning and do not encompass practical reasoning. The point is that a decision is not limited to draw conclusions but must suggest a solution, i.e. take a decision.

In this paper, we present a Decision Support System (DSS) with the help of an example for selecting a business location. This system is built upon an Argumentation Framework (AF) for practical reasoning. A logic language is used as a concrete data structure for holding statements representing knowledge, goals, and decisions. Different priorities are attached to these items corresponding to the uncertainty of the knowledge about the circumstances, the preferences between goals, and the expected utilities of decisions. These concrete data structures consist of information providing the backbone of arguments. Due to the abductive nature of practical reasoning, arguments are built by reasoning backwards, and possibly by making suppositions over missing information. Moreover, arguments are defined as tree-like structures. In this way, our DSS, implemented in Prolog, suggests some solutions and provides an interactive and intelligible explanation of this choice.

Section 2 presents the principle of our DSS. Section 3 introduces the walkthrough example. In order to present our Argumentation Framework (AF) for practical reasoning, we will browse the following fundamental notions. First, we define the *object language* (cf Section 4) and the priorities (cf Section 5). Second, we will focus on the internal structure of *arguments* (cf Section 6). We present in Section 7 the *interactions* amongst them. These relations allow us to give a declarative model-theoretic *semantics* to this framework (cf section 8) and we adopt a dialectical proof *procedure* to implement it (cf Section 9). Section 10 discusses some related works. Section 11 concludes with some directions for future work.

2   Principle

Basically, decision makers are categorized as either "hedgehogs", which know one big thing, or "foxes", which know many little things [2]. While most of the DSS are addressed to "hedgehogs", we want to provide one for both.

An "hedgehog" is an expert of a particular domain, who has intuitions and strong convictions. A "fox" is not an expert but she knows many different things in different domains. She decides by interacting with others and she is able to change her mind. Most of the DSS are addressed to "hedgehogs". These computer systems provide a way to express qualitative and/or quantitative judgements and show how to synthesize them in order to suggest some solutions. A decision taken with the help of a hedgehog could be great, but a full decision of hedgehogs could be a disaster. Since executives do not want to hear that a problem is complex and uncertain, decision makers need many hedgehog qualities. However the analytic skills needed for good judgments are those of foxes. We want to provide a DSS for the effective management of teams including both hedgehogs and foxes.

Figure 1 represents the principle of our DSS based upon an assistant agent. The mind of the agent relies upon MARGO (Multiattribute ARGumentation framework for Opinion explanation), i.e. our argumentative engine. The hedgehog informs the assistant agent in order to structure and evaluate the decision making problem, by considering the different needs, by identify the alternative actions (alternatives, for short), and by gathering the required knowledge. As we will see in the next section, the agent uses concrete data structures for holding the hedgehog's knowledge, goals, and decisions. These concrete data structures consist of information providing the backbone of arguments used to interact with the fox. The latter can ask for a possible solutions (*challenge*). MARGO suggests some solutions (*argue*). The reasons supporting these admissible solutions can be interactively explored (*challenge/argue*).

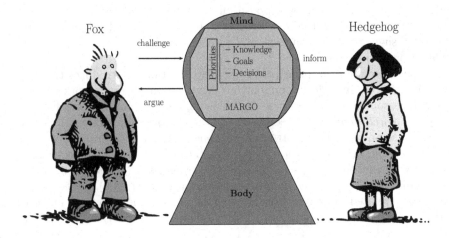

Fig. 1. Principle of the decision support system

3   Walk-Through Example

Inspired by [3], we consider here the decision making problem for selecting a suitable business location. An investment requires a proper understanding of all relevant aspects. Detailed needs for the business location such as the government regulation, taxes, and so on as well as the knowledge about the quality of infrastructures and services, such as the availability of sea transports, is also of vital importance. The assistant agent is responsible for suggesting some suitable locations, based on the explicit users'needs and on their knowledge. The main goal, that consists in selecting the location (`Location`), is addressed by a decision, i.e. a choice amongst some alternatives, i.e. Hochiminh or Hanoi (`hochiminh`, `hanoi`). The main goal (`suitable`) is split into independent sub-goals and independent sub-goals of these sub-goals. The location must offer a "good" regulation (`regulation`) and a "great" accessibility (`accessibility`). These high-level goals, which are *abstract*, reveal the user's needs. The location offers a "good" regulation, if the taxes are low (**taxes**), the permit can be easily obtained (**permit**) and an assistance is available (**assistance**). In the same way, the location offers a "good" accessibility, if the sewage is good (**sewage**) and transport are available (**transport**). These low-level goals are *concrete*, i.e. some criteria for evaluating different alternatives. The knowledge about the location is expressed with predicates such as: $Sea(x)$ (the location x is accessible by sea transports), or $Road(x)$ (the location x is accessible by road transports).

Figure 2 provides a simple graphical representation of the decision problem called influence diagram [4]. The elements of the decision problem, i.e. *values* (represented by rectangles with rounded corners), *decisions* (represented by rectangles) and *knowledge* (represented by ovals), are connected by arcs where predecessors affect successors. We consider here a multiattribute decision problem captured by a hierarchy of values where the abstract value (represented by rectangles with rounded corner and double line) aggregates the independent values in the lower level. When the structure of the decision is built, the alternatives must be identified, the preferences must be expressed and the knowledge gathered.

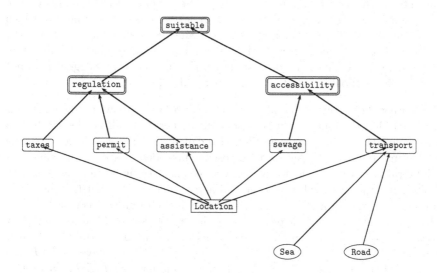

Fig. 2. Influence diagramm to structure the decision

While the influence diagram displays the structure of the decision, the object language and the priorities reveal the hidden details of the decision making informed by the hedgehog.

4   The Object Language

Since we want to provide a computational model of argumentation for decision making and we want to instantiate it for our example, we need to specify a particular logic allowing the hedgehog to express statements representing knowledge, goals, and decisions.

The object language expresses rules and facts in logic-programming style. In order to address a decision making problem, we distinguish:

- a set of *abstract goals*, i.e. some propositional symbols which represent the abstract features that the decisions must exhibit (in the example `suitable`, `regulation`, and `accessibility`);
- a set of *concrete goals*, i.e. some propositional symbols which represent the concrete features that the decisions must exhibit (in the example `taxes`, `permit`, `assistance`, `sewage` and `transport`);
- a set of *decisions*, i.e. some predicate symbols which represent the actions which must be performed or not (in the example `Location` is the only one);
- a set of *alternatives*, i.e. some constants symbols which represent the mutually exclusive solutions for each decision (in the example `hochiminh`, or `hanoi`);
- a set of *beliefs*, i.e. some predicate symbols which represent epistemic statements of the hedgehog (in the example `Sea`, `Road`). In the language, we explicitly distinguish *assumable* beliefs (resp. *non-assumable*) beliefs, which can (resp. cannot) be taken for granted. Since the hedgehog can make the supposition that Hanoi is accessible by road, `Road(hanoi)` is assumable. Obviously, some beliefs are non-assumable. For instance, the hedgehog cannot make the supposition that Vienna is accessible by Sea.

Since we want to consider conflicts in this object language, we need some forms of negation. For this purpose, we consider strong negation, also called explicit or classical negation, and weak negation, also called negation as failure. A strong literal is an atomic first-order formula, possible preceded by strong negation $\neg$. A weak literal is a literal of the form $\sim L$, where L is a strong literal. $\neg L$ says "L is definitely not the case", while $\sim L$ says "There is no evidence that L is the case". In order to express in a compact way the mutual exclusion between statements, such as the different alternatives for a decision, we define the incompatibility relation (denoted by $\mathcal{I}$) as a binary relation over atomic formulas which is asymmetric. Whatever the atom L is a belief or a goal, we have $L \mathcal{I} \neg L$ and $\neg L \mathcal{I} L$, while we have $L \mathcal{I} \sim L$ but we do not have $\sim L \mathcal{I} L$. Obviously, $D_1(a_1) \mathcal{I} D_1(a_2)$ and $D_1(a_2) \mathcal{I} D_1(a_1)$, D_1 being a decision predicate, a_1 and a_2 being different[1] alternatives for D. We say that two sets of sentences Φ_1 and Φ_2 are incompatible ($\Phi_1 \mathcal{I} \Phi_2$) iff there is a sentence ϕ_1 in Φ_1 and a sentence ϕ_2 in Φ_2 such as $\phi_1 \mathcal{I} \phi_2$. A theory gathers the statements of the hedgehog about the decision making problem.

Definition 1 (Theory). *A theory $\mathcal{T}$ is an extended logic program, i.e a finite set of rules such as $R : L_0 \leftarrow L_1, \ldots, L_j, \sim L_{j+1}, \ldots, \sim L_n$ with $n \geq 0$, each L_i being a strong literal. The literal L_0, called the* head *of the rule, is denoted* head(R). *The finite set $\{L_1, \ldots, \sim L_n\}$, called the* body *of the rule, is denoted*

---

[1] Notice that in general a decision can be addressed by more than two alternatives.

body(R). The body of a rule can be empty. In this case, the rule, called a fact, *is an unconditional statement. R, called the* name *of the rule, is an atomic formula. All variables occurring in a rule are implicitly universally quantified over the whole rule. A rule with variables is a scheme standing for all its ground instances.*

Considering a decision making problem, we distinguish:

- *goal rules* of the form $R : G_0 \leftarrow G_1, \ldots, G_n$ with $n > 0$. Each G_i is a goal literal. The head of the rule is an abstract goal (or its strong negation). According to this rule, the abstract goal is promoted (or demoted) by the combination of goal literals in the body;
- *epistemic rules* of the form $R : B_0 \leftarrow B_1, \ldots, B_n$ with $n \geq 0$. Each B_i is a belief literal. According to this rule, the belief B_0 is true if the conditions $B_1, \ldots, B_n$ are satisfied;
- *decision rules* of the form $R : G \leftarrow D(a), B_1, \ldots, B_n$ with $n \geq 0$. The head of the rule is a concrete goal (or its strong negation). The body includes a decision literal $(D(a))$ and a possible empty set of belief literals. According to this rule, the concrete goal is promoted (or demoted) by the decision $D(a)$, provided that conditions $B_1, \ldots, B_n$ are satisfied.

Considering statements in the theory is not sufficient to take a decision.

5   Priority

In order to evaluate the previous hedgehog's statements, all relevant pieces of information should be taken into account, such as the likelihood of beliefs, the preferences between goals, or the expected utilities of the decisions.

In Mathematics, order relations are binary relations on a set. Since these relations classify the elements from the 'best' to the 'worst', with or without *ex æquo*, they are qualitative. For this purpose, we can consider either a preorder, i.e. a reflexive and transitive relation considering possible *ex æquo*, or an order, i.e. an antisymmetric preorder relation. The preorder (resp. the order) is total iff all elements are comparable. In this way, we consider that the *priority* $\mathcal{P}$ is a (partial or total) preorder on the rules in $\mathcal{T}$. $R_1 \mathcal{P} R_2$ can be read "R_1 has priority over R_2". $R_1 \bar{\mathcal{P}} R_2$ can be read "R_1 has no priority over R_2", either because R_1 and R_2 are *ex æquo* (denoted $R_1 \sim R_2$), i.e. $R_1 \mathcal{P} R_2$ and $R_2 \mathcal{P} R_1$, or because R_1 and R_2 are not comparable, i.e. $\neg(R_1 \mathcal{P} R_2)$ and $\neg(R_2 \mathcal{P} R_1)$.

In this work, we consider that all rules are potentially defeasible and that the priorities are extra-logical and domain-specific features. The priority over concurrent rules depends of the nature of rules. Rules are *concurrent* if their heads are identical or incompatible. We define three priority relations:

- the priority over *goal rules* comes from the *preferences* overs goals. The priority of such rules corresponds to the relative importance of the combination of (sub)goals in the body as far as reaching the goal in the head is concerned;

- the priority over *epistemic rules* comes from the *uncertainty* of knowledge. The prior the rule is, the more likely the rule holds;
- the priority over *decision rules* comes from the *expected utility* of decisions. The priority of such rules corresponds to the expectation of the conditional decision in promoting/demoting the goal literal.

In order to illustrate the notions introduced previously, let us go back to the example. The goal theory, the epistemic theory, and the decision theory are represented in Table 1. A rule above another one has priority over it. To simplify the graphical representation of the theories, they are stratified in non-overlapping subsets, i.e. different levels. The *ex æquo* rules are grouped in the same level. Non-comparable rules are arbitrarily assigned to a level.

Table 1. The goal theory (upper),the epistemic theory (lower left), and the decision theory (lower right)

r_{012} : suitable ← regulation, accessibility
r_{1345} : regulation ← taxes, permit, assistance
r_{267} : accessibility ← sewage, transport

r_{145} : regulation ← permit, assistance

r_{01} : suitable ← regulation
r_{13} : regulation ← taxes
r_{26} : accessibility ← sewage

r_{02} : suitable ← accessibility
r_{14} : regulation ← permit
r_{27} : accessibility ← transport
r_{15} : regulation ← assistance

r_{31} : taxes ← $D(\text{hanoi})$
r_{42} : permit ← $D(\text{hochiminh})$
r_{52} : assistance ← $D(\text{hochiminh})$
$r_{71}(x)$: transport ← $D(x), \text{Sea}(x)$

f_1 : Road(hochiminh) ←
f_2 : Sea(hochiminh) ←
f_3 : ¬Road(hochiminh) ←

r_{32} : taxes ← $D(\text{hochiminh})$
r_{41} : permit ← $D(\text{hanoi})$
r_{51} : assistance ← $D(\text{hanoi})$
r_{61} : sewage ← $D(\text{hanoi})$
r_{62} : sewage ← $D(\text{hochiminh})$
$r_{72}(x)$: transport ← $D(x), \text{Road}(x)$

According to the decision theory, both alternatives are relevant for the concrete goals taxes (r_{31} and r_{32}), permit (r_{41} and r_{42}), assistance (r_{51} and r_{52}), sewage (r_{61} and r_{62}), and transport ($r_{71}(x)$ and $r_{72}(x)$). Actually, taxes are lower in Hanoi ($r_{31}\ \mathcal{P}\ r_{32}$). The permit and the assistance are easier to obtain in Hochiminh ($r_{42}\ \mathcal{P}\ r_{41}$ and $r_{52}\ \mathcal{P}\ r_{51}$). We do not know if the sewage is better in Hochiminh or in Hanoi ($r_{61} \sim r_{62}$). Moreover, the utilities of these alternatives with respect to transport depends on the surrounding circumstances. Sea accessible locations have a better utility than road accessible locations ($r_{71}(x)\ \mathcal{P}\ r_{72}(x)$). Our formalism allows to capture the mutual influence of decisions over the independent goals.

Accordingtothegoaltheory,achievingthegoalsregulation,andaccessibility is required to reach suitable (cf. r_{012}). However, these constraints can be relaxed. The achievement of accessibility (resp. regulation) can be relaxed, $r_{012} \mathcal{P} r_{01}$ (resp. $r_{012} \mathcal{P} r_{02}$). Moreover, the achievement of regulationis more important than accessibility($r_{01} \mathcal{P} r_{02}$).Ourformalismallowstocapturecomplexandincomplete information about the preferences amongst goals.

According to the epistemic theory, Hochiminh is accessible by sea transports (cf. f_2). Due to conflicting sources of information, the agent has conflicting beliefs about the road accessibility of Hochiminh (f_1 and f_3). The sources of information can be more or less reliable. For instance, we have $f_1 \mathcal{P} f_3$. We can notice that no information about the accessibility of Hanoi is available. Our formalism allows to capture complex (and incomplete) information about the likelihood of the surrounding circumstances. We will build now arguments upon these (incomplete) statements in order to compare the alternatives.

6   Arguments

Due to the abductive nature of the practical reasoning, we define and construct arguments by reasoning backwards, and possibly by making suppositions over missing information. Since we adopt a tree-like structure of arguments, our framework not only suggests some solutions but also provides an intelligible explanation of them for the fox.

The simplest way to define an argument is by a pair ⟨ premises, conclusion ⟩ as in [5]. This definition leaves implicit that the underlying logic validates a proof of the conclusion from the premises. When the argumentation framework is built upon an extended logic program, an argument is often defined as a sequence of rules [6]. These definitions ignore the recursive nature of arguments: arguments are composed of subarguments, subarguments for these subarguments, and so on. For this purpose, we adopt the tree-like structure for arguments proposed in [7] and we extend it with suppositions on the missing information.

Definition 2 (Argument). *An argument is composed by a conclusion, a top rule, some premises, some suppositions, and some sentences. These elements are abbreviated by the corresponding prefixes. An argument A is:*

1. *a* hypothetical argument *built upon an unconditional ground statement.*
   If L is a assumable belief literal, then the argument built upon this ground and assumable literal is defined as follows:

   $$conc(A) = L, top(A) = \emptyset, premise(A) = \emptyset, supp(A) = \{L\}, sent(A) = \{L\}.$$

   or
2. *a* built argument *built upon a rule such that all the literals in the body are the conclusion of subarguments.*
   If R is a rule in $\mathcal{T}$*, we define the argument A built upon this rule as follows. Let* $body(R) = \{L_1, \ldots, L_n\}$ *and* $sbarg(A) = \{A_1, \ldots, A_n\}$ *be a collection*

of arguments such that, for each $L_i \in body(R)$, $conc(A_i) = L_i$ (each A_i is called a subargument of A). Then: $conc(A) = head(R)$, $top(A) = R$, $premise(A) = body(R)$, $supp(A) = \cup_{A' \in sbarg(A)} supp(A')$, $sent(A) = \cup_{A' \in sbarg(A)} sent(A') \cup body(R) \cup head(R)$.

As in [7], we consider *composite* arguments and *atomic* arguments where the top rule is a fact. Contrary to the other definitions of arguments (pair of premises - conclusion, sequence of rules), our definition considers that the different premises can be challenged and can be supported by subarguments. In this way, arguments are intelligible explanations. Moreover, we distinguish *hypothetical* arguments (1) and *built* arguments (2). While the latters are built upon a top rule which is a rule (or a fact) of the theory, the formers are built upon missing information. In this way, our framework allows to reason further by making suppositions related to the unknow beliefs and over possible decisions under which arguments can be built. Due to the abductive nature of practical reasoning, we define and construct arguments by reasoning backwards. Therefore, arguments do not include irrelevant information such as sentences not used to derive the conclusion.

Let us consider the previous example. Some of the arguments concluding transport are depicted in Figure 3. According to the argument B_7^1 (resp. B_7^2), Hochiminh promotes the transport since this location is accessible by sea (resp. road). According to the argument A_7^1 (resp. A_7^2), Hanoi promotes the transport if we suppose that this location is accessible by sea (resp. by road). An argument can be represented as tree where the root is the conclusion (represented by a triangle) directly connected to the premises (represented by losanges) if they exist, and where leefs are either some suppositions (represented by circles) or θ^2. Each plain arrow corresponds to a rule (or a fact) where the head node corresponds to the head of the rule and the tall nodes are in the body of the rule. While the tree argument B_7^1 (resp. B_7^2) is built upon two subarguments: one hypothetical argument supporting Location(hochiminh) and one trivial argument supporting Sea(hochiminh) (resp. Road(hochiminh)), the tree argument A_7^1 (resp. A_7^2) is built upon two subarguments which are hypothetical: one supporting Location(hanoi) and one supporting Sea(hanoi) (resp. Road(hanoi)). Neither trivial arguments nor hypothetical arguments contain subarguments. Due to their structures and their natures, arguments interact with one another.

7   Interactions between Arguments

The interactions between arguments may come from the incompatibility of their sentences, from their nature (hypothetical or built) and from the priority over rules. We examine in turn these different sources of interaction.

Since their sentences are conflicting, arguments interact with one another. For this purpose, we define the attack relation.

Definition 3 (Attack relation). *Let A and B be two arguments. A attacks B (denoted by attacks (A,B)) iff $sent(A) \mathcal{I} sent(B)$.*

---

[2] θ denotes that no literal is required.

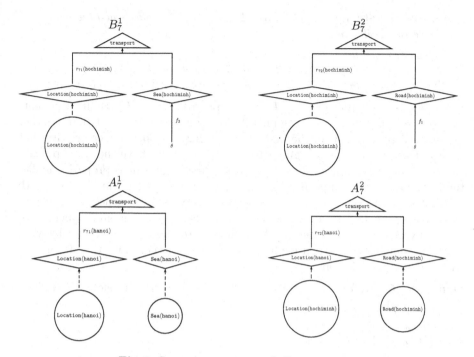

Fig. 3. Some arguments concluding `transport`

This relation encompasses both the direct (often called *rebuttal*) attack due to the incompatibility of the conclusions, and the indirect (often called *undermining*) attack, i.e. directed to a "subconclusion". According to this definition, if an argument attacks a subargument, the whole argument is attacked. The attack relation is useful to build arguments which are homogeneous explanations for the fox.

Due to the nature of argument, arguments are more or less hypothetical. This is the reason why we define the size of their suppositions.

Definition 4 (Supposition size). *Let A be an arguments. The size of suppositions for A, denoted **suppsize**(A), is defined such that:*

1. *if A is a hypothetical argument, then **suppsize**$(A) = 1$;*
2. *if A is a built argument and **sbarg**$(A) = \{A_1, \ldots, A_n\}$ is the collection of subarguments of A, then **suppsize**$(A) = \Sigma_{A' \in sbarg(A)}$**suppsize**$(A')$.*

The size of suppositions for an argument does not only count the number of hypothetical subarguments which compose the argument but also counts the number of hypothetical subarguments of these subarguments, and so on.

Since arguments have different natures (hypothetical or built) and the top rules of built arguments are more or less strong, they interact with one another. For this purpose, we define the strength relation.

Definition 5 (Strength relation). *Let A_1 be a hypothetical argument, and A_2, A_3 be two built arguments.*

1. *A_2 is stronger than A_1 (denoted $A_2 \ \mathcal{P}^{\mathcal{A}} A_1$);*
2. *If $(top(A_2) \ \mathcal{P} \ top(A_3)) \wedge \neg(top(A_3) \ \mathcal{P} \ top(A_2))$, then $A_2 \ \mathcal{P}^{\mathcal{A}} A_3$;*
3. *If $(top(A_2) \sim top(A_3)) \wedge (suppsize(A_2) < suppsize(A_3))$, then $A_2 \ \mathcal{P}^{\mathcal{A}} A_3$;*

Since $\mathcal{P}$ is a preorder on $\mathcal{T}$, $\mathcal{P}^{\mathcal{A}}$ is a preorder on $\mathcal{A}(\mathcal{T})$. Built arguments are preferred to hypothetical arguments. An argument is stronger than another argument if the top rule of the first argument has a proper higher priority that the top rule of the second argument or if the top rules have the same priority but the number of suppositions made in the first argument is properly smaller than the number of suppositions made in the second argument. The strength relation is useful to choose (when it is possible) between homogeneous concurrent explanations for the fox, i.e. non conflicting arguments with the same conclusions.

The two previous relations can be combined to choose (if possible) between non-homogeneous concurrent explanations for the fox, i.e. conflicting arguments with the same conclusions.

Definition 6 (Defeats). *Let A and B be two arguments. A defeats B (written defeats (A, B)) iff:*

1. *attacks (A, B);*
2. *$\neg(B \ \mathcal{P}^{\mathcal{A}} A)$.*

Similarly, we say that a set S of arguments defeats an argument A if A is defeated by one argument in S.

Let us consider our previous example. The arguments in favor of Hochiminh (B_7^1 and B_7^2) and the arguments in favor of Hanoi (A_7^1 and A_7^2) attack each other.

Since the top rule of B_7^1 and A_7^1 (i.e. $r_{71}(x)$) is stronger than the top rule of B_7^2 and A_7^2 (i.e. $r_{72}(x)$), B_7^1 (resp. A_7^1) defeats A_7^2 (resp. B_7^2). Moreover, B_7^1 which includes one hypothetical argument is stronger than A_7^1, which includes two hypothetical arguments. Determining whether a suggestion and an explanation are ultimately suggested to the fox requires a complete analysis of all arguments and subarguments. In this section, we have defined the interactions between arguments in order to give them a status.

8   Semantics

We can consider our AF abstracting away from the logical structures of arguments. This abstract AF consists of a set of arguments associated with a binary defeat relation.

Given an AF, [8] and [9] define the following notions of "acceptable" sets of arguments:

Definition 7 (Semantics). *An AF is a pair $\langle \mathcal{A}, \text{ defeats} \rangle$ where $\mathcal{A}$ is a set of arguments and defeats $\subseteq \mathcal{A} \times \mathcal{A}$ is the defeat relationship[3] for AF. For $A \in \mathcal{A}$ an argument and $S \subseteq \mathcal{A}$ a set of arguments, we say that:*

---

[3] Actually,the defeat relation is called attack in [8] and in [9].

- A *is* acceptable *with respect to S (denoted $A \in \mathcal{S}_{\mathcal{A}}^{S}$) iff $\forall B \in \mathcal{A}$,   defeats (B, A) $\exists C \in S$ such that   defeats (C, B);*
- S *is* conflict-free *iff $\forall A, B \in S \neg$ defeats (A, B);*
- S *is* admissible *iff S is conflict-free and $\forall A \in S,\ A \in \mathcal{S}_{\mathcal{A}}^{S}$;*
- S *is* preferred *iff S is maximally admissible;*
- S *is* complete *iff S is admissible and S contains all arguments A such that S defeats all defeaters against A;*
- S *is* grounded *iff S is minimally complete;*
- S *is* ideal *iff S is admissible and it is contained in every preferred sets.*

The semantics of an admissible (or preferred) set of arguments is credulous, in that it sanctions a set of arguments as acceptable if it can successfully dispute every arguments against it, without disputing itself. However, there might be several conflicting admissible sets. Various sceptical semantics have been proposed for AF, notably the grounded semantics, the ideal semantics, and the sceptically preferred semantics, whereby an argument is accepted if it is a member of all maximally admissible sets of arguments.

Since some ultimate choices amongst various admissible sets of alternatives are not always possible, we consider in this paper only the credulous semantics. Let us focus on the goal `sewage` in the previous example. Since the arguments supporting Hanoi and Hochiminh are admissible, both alternatives can be suggested to reach this goal. If we consider now the whole problem, the argument depicted in Figure 4 is the only one reaching `suitable` which is admissible.

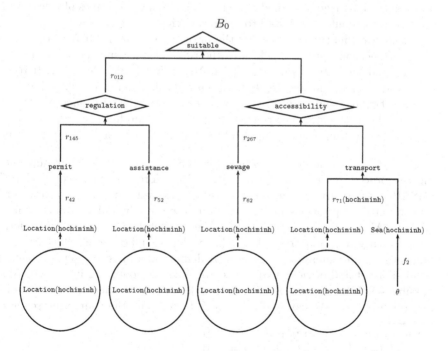

Fig. 4. An argument concluding `suitable`

In our example, there is only one admissible argument deriving the main goal. However, in the general case, a decision $D_1(a_1)$ is *suggested* iff $D_1(a_1)$ is a supposition of one argument in an admissible set deriving the main goal. Therefore, our AF involves some ultimate choices of the fox between various admissible sets of alternatives. In this section, we have given a status to the arguments.

9   Procedure

A dialectical proof procedure is required to compute the model-theoretic semantics of our argumentation framework. The procedures proposed in [9,10] compute the credulous semantics. Since our practical application requires to specify the internal structure of arguments, we adopt the procedure proposed in [9].

In order to compute admissible arguments in our AF, we have translated our AF in an Assumption-based AF (ABF for short). This general framework considers a deductive system $(\mathcal{L}, \mathcal{R})$ (with a language $\mathcal{L}$ and a set $\mathcal{R}$ of inference rules) augmented by a non-empty set of assumptions $\mathcal{A} \subseteq \mathcal{L}$ and a (total) mapping $\mathcal{C}on : \mathcal{A} \to \mathcal{L}$ from assumptions to their contrary. In this framework, an argument for a conclusion is a deduction of its conclusion supported by a set of assumptions. An argument attacks another argument iff the first argument supports a conclusion that is the contrary of one assumption of the second argument. The ABF corresponding to our AF is defined in the following way:

- $\mathcal{L}$ is the language described in section 4 including the names of rules and the predicate symbols `deleted` to represent when a rule does not hold;
- $\mathcal{R}$ comes from the theories and the priorities over them. If R is a goal/decision/epistemic rule then the rule r defined such as head$(r) =$ head (R) and body$(r) =$ body$(R) \cup \{\sim \texttt{deleted}(R)\}$ is included in $\mathcal{R}$. If R_1 and R_2 are concurrent and $R_1 \mathcal{P} R_2$, then the rule r defined such as head$(r) =$ $\texttt{deleted}(R_2)$ and body$(r) = \{\sim \texttt{deleted}(R_1)\}$ is also included in $\mathcal{R}^4$;
- $\mathcal{A}$ includes the inference rules and the the decision literals;
- $\mathcal{C}on$ comes from the incompatibility relation $\mathcal{I}$ over atomic formulas in $\mathcal{L}$.

CaSAPI[5] [12] computes the admissible semantics in the ABF by implementing the procedure originally proposed in [13]. Moreover, we have developed a CaSAPI meta-interpreter to relax the goals achievements in the priority order and to make suppositions in order to compute the admissible semantics in our concrete AF[6]. Suppose we wish to investigate whether an argument is preferred, i.e. it belongs to a preferred set. We know that it suffices to check that this argument is in an admissible set, since, by definition, a preferred set is a maximal admissible set and obviously all admissible sets are contained in a maximal admissible set. If the procedure succeeds, we know that the argument is contained in a preferred set. We can easily extend it to compute the competing semantics

---

[4] Our treatment of priority is inspired by [11].
[5] http://www.doc.ic.ac.uk/~dg00/casapi.html
[6] For brevity, we do not describe this mechanism in the paper.

which have been proposed in [9]. The implementation of our framework, called MARGO (Multiattribute ARGumentation framework for Opinion explanation), is written in Prolog and available in GPL (GNU General Public License) at `http://margo.sourceforge.net/`.

In order to be computed by MARGO, the problem description must contain:

- a set of decisions, i.e. some lists which contain the alternatives courses of actions (in the example,
  `decisions([location(hochiminh), location(hanoi)]))`;
- a set of incompatibilities, i.e. some couples which contain incompatible literals (in the example,
  `incompatibility(noroad(hochiminh),road(hochiminh)))`;
- a set of goal rules, i.e. some triples of name - head - body which are simple Prolog representations of the goal rules in our AF (in the example,
  `goalrule(r012, suitable, [regulation, accesibility]),...)`;
- a set of decisions rules, i.e. some triples of name - head - body which are simple Prolog representations of the decision rules in our AF (in the example,
  `decisionrule(r31, taxes, [location(hanoi)]),...)`;
- a set of epistemic rules, i.e. some triples of name - head - body which are simple Prolog representations of the epistemic rules in our AF (in the example,
  `epistemicrule(f1,road(hochiminh),[]),...)`;
- a set of goal priorities, i.e. some ordered lists of sublists of goal rules where the rules in a previous sublists have priorities and the rules in the same sublists are *ex æquo* (in the example, `goalpriority([[r267], [r27], [r26] ])`, since $r_{267} \mathcal{P} r_{27} \mathcal{P} r_{26}, \ldots$);
- a set of decision priorities, i.e. some couples of decision rules such that the former have priority over the latter (in the example,
  `decisionpriority(r31,r32),...)`;
- a set of epistemic priorities, i.e. some couples of decision rules such that the former have priority over the latter (in the example,
  `epistemicpriority(f1,f2))`;
- a set of possible suppositions, i.e. some couples such that the former is the name of the supposition and the latter is an assumable belief literal (in the example, `supposition(a12,road(hanoi)),...)`.

The main predicate for argument manipulation `admissibleArgument(+C, ?P, ?S)` succeeds when P are the premises and S are the suppositions of an admissible argument deriving the conclusion C. For instance, `admissibleArgument(suitable,P,S)` returns:

```
SUPPOSITIONS = [location(hochiminh),sea(hochiminh)],
PREMISES = [regulation,accesibility].
```

These sub-goals can be challenged. For instance, `admissibleArgument(regulation,P,S)` returns:

```
SUPPOSITIONS = [location(hochiminh)],
PREMISES = [permit,assistance].
```

The top rule of this argument is r_{145}, which is no the strongest goal rule. However, P is the strongest combination of (sub)goals which can be reach by a course of actions. In this section, we have shown how to compute admissible arguments in our AF in order to provide an interactive and intelligible explanation of the suggestion to the fox.

10   Related Works

Argumentation has been put forward as a promising approach to support decision making [14]. While influence diagrams and belief networks [15] require that all the factors relevant for a decision are identified *a priori*, arguments are defeasible or reinstantiated in the light of new information not previously available.

Contrary to the theoretical reasoning, practical reasoning is not only about whether some beliefs are true, but also about whether some actions should or should not be performed. The practical reasoning [16] follows three main steps: i) *deliberation*, i.e. the generation of goals; ii) *means-end reasoning*, i.e. the generation of plans; iii) *decision-making*, i.e. the selection of plans that will be performed to reach the selected goals. For instance, [17] proposes an AF focusing on the deliberation (closed to the principle of [18] where argumentation is implicit) and [19,20] have provided formal models for deliberation and means-end reasoning. While some frameworks are based upon defeasible logic programming (e.g. [21,22]), most of them instantiate the abstract argumentation framework of Dung [8]. Since the latter abstracts away from the internal structure of arguments in order to focus on the manner in which arguments interact, [23] instantiates an argument scheme in the context of practical reasoning in order to capture the interaction in terms of internal structure.

In this work, we have proposed an AF for decision-making. In this perspective, [24] proposes a critical survey of some computational models of argumentation over actions. For this purpose, [25,26] have considered several principles according to the different types of arguments which are considered (PROS/CONS, strong/weak, related to a positive/negative goal) are aggregated. However, contrary to our approach, the potential interaction amongst arguments, as studied in the seminal work of Dung [8] is not considered. Moreover, we allow the epistemic theory and the goal theory to be inconsistent. In this paper we have considered the example borrowed from [3] and we have adopted like [27] an abductive approach to the practical reasoning which is directly modelled within in our framework.

Finally, to the best of our knowledge, few implementation of argumentation over actions exist. CaSAPI and DeLP [7] are restricted to the theoretical reasoning. PARMENIDES[8] is a software to structure the debate over actions by adopting a particular argumentation scheme. GORGIAS [9] implements an argumentation

---

[7] http://lidia.cs.uns.edu.ar/DeLP

[8] http://cgi.csc.liv.ac.uk/~katie/Parmenides.html

[9] http://www.cs.ucy.ac.cy/~nkd/gorgias/

based framework to support the decision making of an agent within a modular architecture. Like the latter, MARGO incorporate abduction on missing information. Moreover, we can easily extend it to compute the competing semantics which have been proposed in [9] since we have instantiated the abstract argumentation framework of Dung.

11   Conclusions

In this paper we have presented a DSS based upon a concrete and implemented AF for practical reasoning which suggests different alternative courses of actions and provides an interactive and intelligible explanation of the choices. A logic language is used as a concrete data structure for holding statements representing knowledge, goals, and decisions. Different priorities are attached to these items corresponding to the uncertainty of the knowledge about the circumstances, the preferences between goals, and the expected utilities of decisions. These concrete data structures consist of information providing the backbone of arguments. Due to the abductive nature of practical reasoning, arguments are built by reasoning backwards, and possibly by making suppositions over missing information. To be intelligible, arguments are defined as tree-like structures. The interactions between arguments may come from the incompatibility of their sentences, from their nature (hypothetical or built) and from the priority over rules. Since an ultimate choice amongst various admissible sets of alternatives is not always possible, we have adopted a credulous semantics. In order to compute it, we have implemented our AF in Prolog.

In future works, we wants to incorporate decision-theoretic techniques within the model. Standard decision theory weighs the cost and benefits of possible outcomes with their probabilities to produce a preference on the expected utilities of the alternatives. However in many practical applications, it is not natural to give a quantitative representation of many objectives, or it could not deal with the cases of decision makers that only have partial information. Further standard decision theory provides little support in giving intelligible explanation of the choices. For this purpose, it would be best to have a hybrid approach combining both quantitative and qualitative decision theory. Argumentation provides a natural framework for these hybrid systems by providing a link between qualitative objectives and its quantitative representation.

References

1. Prakken, H., Vreeswijk, G.: Logical systems for defeasible argumentation. In: Handbook of Philosophical Logic, vol. 4, pp. 219–318. Kluwer Academic Publishers, Dordrecht (2002)
2. Berlin, S.I.: The Hedgehog and the Fox. Simon & Schuster (1953)
3. Stournaras, T. (ed.): Concrete scenarios identification & simple use cases. Deliverable document D1.1 ARGUGRID (2007)
4. Clemen, R.T.: Making Hard Decisions. Duxbury. Press (1996)

5. Amgoud, L., Cayrol, C.: A reasoning model based on the production of acceptable arguments. Annals of Maths and AI 34(1-3), 197–215 (2002)
6. Ralf Schweimeier, M.S.: Notions of attack and justified arguments for extended logic programs. In: van Harmelen, F. (ed.) Proc. of the 15th European Conference on Artificial Intelligence (ECAI 2002), Amsterdam, pp. 536–540. IOS Press, Amsterdam (2002)
7. Vreeswijk, G.: Abstract argumentation systems. Artificial Intelligence 90, 225–279 (1997)
8. Dung, P.M.: On the acceptability of arguments and its fundamental role in non-monotonic reasoning, logic programming and n-person games. Artif. Intell. 77(2), 321–357 (1995)
9. Dung, P.M., Mancarella, P., Toni, F.: Computing ideal sceptical argumentation. Artificial Intelligence, Special Issue on Argumentation in Artificial Intelligence 171(10-15), 642–674 (2007)
10. Vreeswijk, G., Prakken, H.: Credulous and sceptical argument games for preferred semantics. In: Brewka, G., Moniz Pereira, L., Ojeda-Aciego, M., de Guzmán, I.P. (eds.) JELIA 2000. LNCS (LNAI), vol. 1919, pp. 239–253. Springer, Heidelberg (2000)
11. Kowalski, R., Toni, F.: Abstract argumentation. Artificial Intelligence and Law Journal Special Issue on Logical Models of Argumentation 4(3-4), 275–296 (1996)
12. Gartner, D., Toni, F.: CaSAPI: a system for credulous and sceptical argumentation. In: Simari, G., Torroni, P. (eds.) Proc. Workshop on Argumentation for Non-monotonic Reasoning, pp. 80–95 (2007)
13. Dung, P.M., Kowalski, R.A., Toni, F.: Dialectic proof procedures for assumption-based, admissible argumentation. Artificial Intelligence 170(2), 114–159 (2006)
14. Fox, J., Parsons, S.: On using arguments for reasoning about actions and values. In: Doyle, J., Thomason, R.H. (eds.) Proceedings of the Working Papers of the AAAI Spring Symposium on Qualitative Preferences in Deliberation and Practical Reasoning, Standford, pp. 55–63 (1997)
15. Oliver, R.M., Smith, J.Q. (eds.): Influence Diagrams, Belief Nets and Decision Analysis. John Wiley and Sons, Chichester (1988)
16. Raz, J. (ed.): Practical Reasoning. Oxford University Press, Oxford (1978)
17. Amgoud, L., Kaci, S.: On the generation of bipolar goals in argumentation-based negotiation. In: Rahwan, I., Moraïtis, P., Reed, C. (eds.) ArgMAS 2004. LNCS (LNAI), vol. 3366, pp. 192–207. Springer, Heidelberg (2005)
18. Thomason, R.H.: Desires and defaults: A framework for planning with inferred goals. In: Proc. of the seventh International Confenrence on Principle of Knowledge Representation and Reasoning (KR), pp. 702–713 (2000)
19. Hulstijn, J., van der Torre, L.W.N.: Combining goal generation and planning in an argumentation framework. In: Proc. of the 9h International Workshop on Non-Monotonic Reasoning (NMR 2004), pp. 212–218 (2004)
20. Rahwan, I., Amgoud, L.: An argumentation-based approach for practical reasoning. In: Proc. of the 5th International Joint Conference on Autonomous Agents and Multiagent Systems (AAMAS), pp. 347–354. ACM Press, New York (2006)
21. Simari, G.R., García, A.J., C., M.: Actions, planning and defeasible reasoning. In: Proc. of the 10th International Workshop on Non-Monotonic Reasoning, Whistler BC, Canada, pp. 377–384 (2004)
22. Kakas, A., Moraitis, P.: Argumentative-based decision-making for autonomous agents. In: Proceedings of the 2nd International Joint Conference on Autonomous Agents and Multi-Agent Systems (AAMAS), pp. 883–890. ACM Press, New York (2003)

23. Atkinson, K., Bench-Capon, T., McBurney, P.: Computational representation of practical argument. Synthese, special issue on Knowledge, Rationality and Action 152(2), 157–206 (2006)
24. Ouerdane, W., Maudet, N., Tsoukias, A.: Arguing over actions that involve multiple criteria: A critical review. In: Mellouli, K. (ed.) ECSQARU 2007. LNCS (LNAI), vol. 4724, Springer, Heidelberg (2007)
25. Amgoud, L., Prade, H.: Comparing decisions in an argumentation-based setting. In: Proc. of the 11th International Workshop on Non-Monotonic Reasoning (NMR 2006), Session on Argumentation, Dialogue, and Decision Making, Lake District, UK, pp. 426–432 (2006)
26. Amgoud, L., Prade, H.: Explaining qualitative decision under uncertainty by argumentation. In: Proc. of the 21st National Conference on Artificial Intelligence (AAAI 2006), Boston, Boston, pp. 16–20 (2006)
27. Bench-Capon, T., Prakken, H.: Justifying actions by accruing arguments. In: Proc. of the 1st International Conference on Computational Models of Argument, pp. 247–258. IOS Press, Amsterdam (2006)

An Extended Value-Based Argumentation Framework for Ontology Mapping with Confidence Degrees

Cássia Trojahn[1], Paulo Quaresma[1], and Renata Vieira[2]

[1] Departamento de Informática, Universidade de Évora, Portugal
[2] Pós-Graduacão em Computacão Aplicada,
Universidade do Vale do Rio dos Sinos, Brazil
cassia@di.uevora.pt, pq@di.uevora.pt, renatav@unisinos.br

Abstract. Heuristics to combine different approaches for ontology mapping have been proposed in the literature. This paper proposes to use abstract argumentation frameworks to combine such approaches. We extend the Value-based Argumentation Framework (VAF)[2], in order to represent arguments with confidence degrees. Our agents apply individual mapping algorithms and cooperate in order to exchange their local results (arguments). Next, based on their preferences and confidence of the arguments, the agents compute their preferred mapping sets. The arguments in such preferred sets are viewed as the set of globally acceptable arguments.

1   Introduction

Ontology mapping is the process of linking corresponding terms from different ontologies. The mapping result can be used for ontology merging, agent communication, query answering, or for navigation on the Semantic Web.

Well-known approaches to the problem can be grouped into lexical, semantic, and structural ones, as terms may be mapped by a measure of lexical similarity, or they can be evaluated semantically, usually on the basis of semantic oriented linguistic resources, or considering the term positions in the ontology hierarchy. It is assumed that the approaches are complementary to each other and combining different ones reflect better solutions when compared to the solutions of the individual approaches. Heuristics to combine such approaches have been proposed [18][14][9][15].

This paper proposes to use abstract argumentation frameworks [6] to combine approaches for ontology mapping. We extend a state of art argumentation framework, namely Value-based Argumentation Framework (VAF)[2], in order to represent arguments with confidence degrees. The VAF allows to determine which arguments are acceptable, with respect to the different *audiences* represented by different agents. We then associate to each argument a confidence degree, representing how confident an agent is in the similarity of two ontology terms.

I. Rahwan, S. Parsons, and C. Reed (Eds.): ArgMAS 2007, LNAI 4946, pp. 132–144, 2008.

Our agents apply different mapping approaches and cooperate in order to exchange their local results (arguments). Next, based on their preferences and confidence of the arguments, the agents compute their preferred mapping sets. The arguments in such preferred sets are viewed as the set of globally acceptable arguments. Our approach is able to give a formal motivation for the composite mapping approaches.

This paper is structured as follows. Section 2 comments on argumentation framework. Section 3 introduces the ontology mapping approaches. Section 4 presents our agent argumentation model. Section 5 presents a walk through example. Section 6 comments on related work. Finally, section 7 presents the final remarks and the future work.

2   Argumentation Framework

Our argumentation model is based on the Value-based Argumentation Frameworks (VAF)[2], a development of the classical argument system of Dung [6]. First, we present the Dung's framework, upon which the VAF rely. Next, we present the VAF and our extended framework.

2.1   Classical Argumentation Framework

Dung [6] defines an argumentation framework as follows.

Definition 2.1.1. An Argumentation Framework is a pair $AF = (AR, attacks)$, where AR is a set of arguments and *attacks* is a binary relation on AR, i.e., $attacks \subseteq AR \times AR$. An $attack$(A,B) means that the argument A attacks the argument B. A set of arguments S attacks an argument B if B is attacked by an argument in S.

The key question about the framework is whether a given argument A, $A \in AR$, should be accepted. One reasonable view is that an argument should be accepted only if every attack on it is rebutted by an accepted argument [6]. This notion produces the following definitions:

Definition 2.1.2. An argument $A \in AR$ is *acceptable* with respect to set arguments $S(acceptable(A,S))$, if $(\forall x)(x \in AR)$ & $(attacks(x,A)) \longrightarrow (\exists y)(y \in S)$ & $attacks(y,x)$

Definition 2.1.3. A set S of arguments is *conflict-free* if $\neg(\exists x)(\exists y)((x \in S)$&$(y \in S)$ & $attacks(x,y))$

Definition 2.1.4. A conflict-free set of arguments S is *admissible* if $(\forall x)(x \in S) \longrightarrow acceptable(x,S)$

Definition 2.1.5. A set of arguments S is a *preferred extension* if it is a maximal (with respect to inclusion set) admissible set of AR.

A *preferred extension* represent a consistent position within AF, which can defend itself against all attacks and which cannot be further extended without introducing a conflict.

The purpose of [2] in extending the AF is to allow associate arguments with the social values they advance. Then, the attack of one argument on another is evaluated to say whether or not it succeeds by comparing the strengths of the values advanced by the arguments concerned.

2.2   Value-Based Argumentation Framework

In Dung's frameworks, attacks always succeed. However, in many domains, including the one under consideration, arguments lack this coercive force: they provide reasons which may be more or less persuasive [11]. Moreover, their persuasiveness may vary according to their audience.

The VAF is able to distinguish attacks from successful attacks, those which defeat the attacked argument, with respect to an ordering on the values that are associated with the arguments. It allows accommodate different audiences with different interests and preferences.

Definition 2.2.1. A Value-based Argumentation Framework (VAF) is a 5-tuple $VAF = (AR,attacks,V,val,P)$ where $(AR,attacks)$ is an argumentation framework, V is a nonempty set of values, val is a function which maps from elements of AR to elements of V and P is a set of possible audiences. For each $A \in AR$, $val(A) \in V$.

Definition 2.2.2. An Audience-specific Value Based Argumentation Framework (AVAF) is a 5-tuple $VAF_a = (AR,attacks,V,val,valpref_a)$ where AR, $attacks, V$ and val are as for a VAF, a is an audience and $valpref_a$ is a preference relation (transitive, irreflexive and asymmetric) $valpref_a \subseteq V \times V$, reflecting the value preferences of audience a. $valpref(v_1,v_2)$ means v_1 is preferred to v_2.

Definition 2.2.3. An argument $A \in AR$ defeats$_a$ (or *successful attacks*) an argument $B \in AR$ for audience a if and only if both $attacks(A,B)$ and not $valpref(val(B), val(A))$.

An attack succeeds if both arguments relate to the same value, or if no preference value between the values has been defined.

Definition 2.2.4. An argument $A{\in}AR$ is *acceptable* to audience a (*acceptable$_a$*) with respect to set of arguments S, acceptable$_a$$(A,S)$) if $(\forall x)$ $((x \in AR$ & defeats$_a$ $(x,A)) \longrightarrow (\exists y)((y \in S)$ & defeats$_a$ $(y,x)))$.

Definition 2.2.5. A set S of arguments is *conflict-free* for audience a if $(\forall x)(\forall y)((x \in S$ & $y \in S) \longrightarrow (\neg attacks(x,y) \lor valpref(val(y),val(x)) \in valpref_a))$.

Definition 2.2.6. A *conflict-free* set of argument S for audience a is *admissible* for an audience a if $(\forall x)(x \in S \longrightarrow$ acceptable$_a$ $(x,S))$.

Definition 2.2.7. A set of argument S in the VAF is a *preferred extension* for audience a *(preferred$_a$)* if it is a maximal (with respect to set inclusion) *admissible* for audience a of AR.

In order to determine the preferred extension with respect to a value ordering promoted by distinct audiences, [2] introduces the notion of *objective* and *subjective* acceptance.

Definition 2.2.8. An argument $x \in AR$ is *subjectively* acceptable if and only if x appears in the preferred extension for some specific audiences but not all. An argument $x \in AR$ is *objectively* acceptable if and only if, x appears in the preferred extension for every specific audience. An argument which is neither objectively nor subjectively acceptable is said to be *indefensible*.

2.3   An Extended Value-Based Argumentation Framework

We extend the VAF in order to represent arguments with confidence degrees. Two elements have been added to the VAF: a set with confidence degrees and a function which maps from arguments to confidence degrees. The confidence value represents the confidence that an individual agent has in some argument. We assumed that the confidence degrees is a criteria which is necessary to represent the ontology mapping domain.

Definition 2.3.1. An Extended Value-based Argumentation Framework (E-VAF) is a 7-tuple *E-VAF = (AR, attacks,V,val,P,C,valC)* where *(AR, attacks,V,val,P)* is a value-based argumentation framework, C is a nonempty set of values representing the confidence degrees, *valC* is a function which maps from elements of AR to elements of C. *valC* $\subseteq C \times C$ and *valprefC(c_1, c_2)* means c_1 is preferred to c_2.

Definition 2.3.2. An argument $x \in AR$ defeats$_a$ (or *successful attacks*) an argument $y \in AR$ for audience a if and only if *attacks(x,y)* $\wedge$ *(valprefC(valC(x), valC(y))* $\vee$ *($\neg$ valpref(val(y),val(x))* $\wedge \neg$ *valprefC(valC(y), valC(x))))*.

An attack succeeds if (a) the confidence degree of the attacking argument is greater than the confidence degree of the argument being attacked; or if (b) the argument being attacked does not have greater preference value than attacking argument (or if both arguments relate to the same preference values) and the confidence degree of the argument being attacked is not greater than the attacking argument.

Definition 2.3.3. A set S of arguments is *conflict-free* for audience a if *($\forall x$)($\forall y$)* *((x $\in$ S & y $\in$ S)* $\longrightarrow$ *($\neg$attacks(x, y)* $\vee$ *($\neg$valprefC(valC(x),valC(y))* $\wedge$ *(valpref(val(y), val(x))* $\vee$ *valprefC(valC(y),valC(x)))))*.

3   Ontology Mapping

The approaches for ontology mapping vary from lexical (see [18][14]) to semantic and structural levels (see [9]). In the lexical level, metrics to compare string similarity are adopted. One well-known measure is the Levenshtein distance or edit distance [12], which is given by the minimum number of operations (insertion, deletion, or substitution of a single character) needed to transform one string into another. Other common metrics can be found in [14], [17], and [7].

The semantic level considers the semantic relations between concepts to measure the similarity between them, usually on the basis of semantic oriented linguistic resources. The well-known WordNet[1] database, a large repository of English semantically related items, has been used to provide these relations. This kind of mapping is complementary to the pure string similarity metrics. It is common that string metrics yield high similarity between strings that represent completely different concepts (i.e, the words "score" and "store"). Moreover, semantic-structural approaches have been explored [3][9]. In this case, the positions of the terms in the ontology hierarchy are considered, i.e, terms more generals and terms more specifics are also considered as input to the mapping process.

Heuristics to combine different approaches for ontology mapping have been proposed in the literature. It is assumed that the approaches are complementary to each other and combining different ones reflect better solutions when compared to the solutions of the individual approaches.

We propose to use the E-VAF to combine such approaches. Our agents apply different mapping algorithms and cooperate in order to exchange their local results (arguments). Next, based on their preferences and confidence of the arguments, the agents compute their preferred mapping sets. The arguments in such preferred sets are viewed as the set of arguments globally acceptable (objectively or subjectively).

4   E-VAF for Ontology Mapping

In our model, dedicated agents encapsulate different mapping approaches. Each approach represents a different audience in an E-VAF, i.e, the agents' preferences are based on specific approach used by the agent. In this paper we consider three audiences: lexical (L), semantic (S), and structural (E) (i.e. $P = \{L, S, E\}$, where $P \in$ E-VAF). We point out that our model is extensible to other audiences.

4.1   Argumentation Generation

First, the agents work in an independent manner, applying the mapping approaches and generating mapping sets. The mapping result will consist of a set of all possible correspondences between terms of two ontologies. A mapping m can be described as a 3-tuple $m = (t_1, t_2, R)$, where t_1 corresponds to a term

---

[1] http://www.wordnet.princeton.edu

in the ontology 1, t_2 corresponds to a term in the ontology 2, and R is the mapping relation resulting from the mapping between these two terms. The lexical and semantic agents are able to return *equivalence* value to R, while the structural agents return *sub-class* or *super-class* values to R. Each mapping m is represented as a argument. Now, we can define arguments as follows:

Definition 4.1. An *argument* $\in AR$ is a 4-tuple $x = (m,a,c,h)$, where m is a mapping; $a \in P$ is the agent's audience generating that argument (agent's preference, i.e, lexical, semantic or structural); $c \in C$ is the confidence degree associated to that mapping (*certainty* or *uncertainty*, as it will be commented below); h is one of $\{-,+\}$ depending on whether the argument is that m does or does not hold.

The confidence degree is defined by the agent when applying the specific mapping approach. Here, we assumed $C = \{\text{certainty, uncertainty}\}$, where $C \in$ E-VAF. Table 1 shows the possible values to h and c, according to the agent's audiences. The agents generate their arguments based on rules from Table 1.

Table 1. h and c to audiences

h	c	Audiences	
		Lexical	Semantic
+	certainty	1	synonym
+	uncertainty	$1 > r > t$	related
-	certainty	$0 < r <= t$	
-	uncertainty	0	unknown

Lexical Agent. The output of lexical agents (r) is a value from the interval $[0,1]$, where 1 indicates high similarity between two terms. This way, if the output is 1, the lexical agent generates an argument $x = (m,L,certainty,+)$, where $m = (t_1,t_2,equivalence)$. If the output is 0, the agent generates an argument $x = (m,L,certainty,-)$, where $m = (t_1,t_2, equivalence)$. A threshold (t) is used to classify the output in uncertain categories. The threshold value can be specified by the user.

Semantic Agent. The semantic agents consider semantic relations between terms, such as synonym, antonym, holonym, meronym, hyponym, and hypernym (i.e., such as in WordNet database). When the terms being mapped are synonymous, the agent generates an argument $x = (m,S,certainty,+)$, where $m = (t_1,t_2, equivalence)$. The terms related by holonym, meronym, hyponym, or hypernym are considered related and an argument $x = (m,S, uncertainty,+)$ is generated, where $m = (t_1,t_2, equivalence)$; when the terms can not be related by the WordNet (the terms are unknown for the WordNet database), an argument $x = (m,L,uncertainty, -)$, where $m = (t_1,t_2,equivalence)$, is then generated.

Structural Agent. The structural agents consider the super-classes (or sub-classes) intuition to verify if the terms can be mapped. First, it is verified if the super-classes of the compared terms are lexically similar. If not, the semantic similarity between they is used. If the super-classes of the terms are lexically or semantically similar, the terms are considered equivalent to each other. The argument is generated according to the lexical or semantic comparison. For instance, if the super-classes of the terms are not lexically similar, but they are synonymous (semantic similarity), an argument $x = (m, E, certainty, +)$, where $m = (t_1, t_2, super\text{-}class)$, is generated.

4.2   Preferred Extension Generation

After generating their set of arguments, the agents exchange with each other their arguments. Following a specific protocol, an agent asks (*ask* sign) the others about their arguments. The other agents then, send their arguments to the first agent. An *ack* sign is then sent to requesting agents, in order to indicate that the arguments have been correctly received. Otherwise, an *error* sign is sent.

When all agents have received the set of argument of the each other, they generate their *attacks* set. An *attack* (or counter-argument) will arise when we have arguments for the mapping between the same terms, but with conflicting values of h. For instance, an argument $x = (m_1, L, certainty, +)$ have as an *attack* an argument $y = (m_2, E, certainty, -)$, where m_1 and m_2 refer to the same terms in the ontologies. The argument y also represents an *attack* to the argument x.

As an example, consider the mapping between the terms "Reference/ Dissertation" and "Citation/Thesis" and the lexical and structural agents. The lexical agent generates an argument $x = (m, L, uncertainty, -)$, where $m =$ (dissertation, thesis, *equivalence*); and the structural agent generates an argument $y = (m, E, certainty, +)$, where $m =$ (dissertation, thesis, *super-class*). For both lexical and structural audiences, the set of arguments is $AR= \{x, y\}$ and the *attacks* $= \{(x,y), (y,x)\}$. However, the relations of *successful attacks* will be defined according to specific audience (see *Definition 2.3.2*), as it is commented below.

When the set of arguments and attacks have been produced, the agents need to define which of them must be accepted. To do this, the agents compute their preferred extension, according to the audiences and confidence degrees. A set of arguments is *globally subjectively acceptable* if each element appears in the preferred extension for some agent. A set of arguments is *globally objectively acceptable* if each element appears in the preferred extension for every agent. The arguments which are neither objectively nor subjectively acceptable are considered *indefensible*.

In the example above, considering the lexical(L) and structural(E) audiences, where $L \succ E$ and $E \succ L$, respectively. For the lexical audience, the argument y successful attacks the argument x, while the argument x does not successful attack the argument y for the structural audience. Then, the preferred extension of both lexical and structural agents is composed by the argument y, which can be seen as globally *objectively* acceptable. The mapping between the terms "Reference/ Dissertation" and "Citation/Thesis", indicated by y is correct.

5 A Walk through Example

Let us consider that three agents need to obtain a consensus about mappings that link corresponding class names in two different ontologies.

First, we used part of the ontology of Google and Yahoo web directories[2], and the argumentation model output has been compared with manual matches[3].

We considered lexical (L), semantic (S), and structural (E) audiences (mapping approaches) in order to verify the behavior of our argumentation model. The lexical agent was implemented using the edit distance measure (Levenshtein measure). We used the algorithm available in the API for ontology alignment (INRIA)[4] (EditDistNameAlignment). The semantic agent has used the JWord-Net API[5], which is an interface to the WordNet database. For each WordNet synset, we retrieved the synonymous terms and considered the hypernym, hyponym, member-holonym, member-meronym, part-holonym, and part-meronym as related terms. The structural agent was based on super-classes similarity. The threshold used to classify the matcher agents output was 0.6. This value was defined based on previous analysis of the edit distance values between the terms of the ontologies used in the experiments. The terms with edit distance values greater than 0.6 have presented lexical similarity.

We have selected three possible mappings between terms of the ontologies: "Music/History" and "Architecture/History", "Art/ArtHistory" and "ArtHumanity/ArtHistory", and "Art" and "ArtHumanity". Table 2 shows arguments and attacks (counter-arguments) generated for each audience. The mappings between these terms have been selected because they were identified as conflicting cases when using our previous cooperative negotiation model [20][21], which is based on voting mechanism.

Table 2. Arguments and attacks

ID	Argument	Attacks
1	(history,history,*equivalence*,L,*certainty*,+)	3
2	(history,history,*equivalence*,S,*certainty*,+)	3
3	(history,history,*super-class*,E,*certainty*,-)	1,2
4	(art-history,art-history,*equivalence*,L,*certainty*,+)	-
5	(art-history,art-history,*equivalence*,S,*certainty*,+)	-
6	(art-history,art-history,*super-class*,E,*certainty*,+)	-
7	(art,art-humanity,L,*equivalence*,*uncertainty*,-)	8,9
8	(art,art-humanity,S,*equivalence*,*certainty*,+)	7
9	(art,art-humanity,E,*super-class*,*uncertainty*,+)	7

---

[2] http://dit.unitn.it/~accord/Experimentaldesign.html (Test 3)
[3] http://dit.unitn.it/ accord/Experimentaldesign.html
[4] http://alignapi.gforce.inria.fr
[5] http://jwn.sourceforge.net (using WordNet 2.1)

For the mapping between the terms "Music/History" and "Architecture/History", each agent has as arguments $AR = \{1,2,3\}$ and as relations of attack $attacks = \{(3,1),\ (3,2),\ (1,3),\ (2,3)\}$. These sets are generated by each agent, after receiving the arguments of other agents. Next, the arguments that defeat each other are computed, according to the agent's audience. For the lexical audience, where $L \succ S$ and $L \succ E$, there is no argument that successfully attacks another, because all agents have certainty in the mappings. The same occurs for the semantic ($S \succ L$ and $S \succ E$) and structural ($E \succ L$ and $E \succ S$) audiences.

The preferred extensions of the agents are composed by the arguments generated by the corresponding audience (i.e, the preferred extension of the lexical agent is $\{1\}$; the preferred extension of the semantic agent is $\{2\}$; and the preferred extension of the structural agent is $\{3\}$). This way, there is no argument globally *objectively* acceptable. Then, we can consider that the mapping between the terms is not possible, what is correct according to the manual mapping.

Using our cooperative negotiation model, the final mapping between the "Music/History" and "Architecture/ History" terms was incorrect. The semantic and lexical agents returned mappings with certainty, while the structural agent returned a non mapping with certainty. By voting, a mapping with certainty was obtained. This conflict is then resolved by our argumentation model.

For the mapping between the terms "Art/ArtHistory" and "ArtHumanity/ArtHistory", each agent has as arguments $AR = \{4,5,6\}$, but there are not relations of attack. Then, all agents accept the mapping with certainty between these terms. This mapping is considered a correct mapping by the manual mapping.

Finally, for the mapping between the terms "Art" and "ArtHumanity", each agent has as arguments $AR = \{7,8,9\}$ and as relations of attack $attacks = \{(8,7), (9,7), (7,8), (7,9)\}$. For the lexical audience, the argument 8 successfully attacks the argument 7. Then, the preferred extension has the argument 8. For the semantic audience, the argument 8 also successful attacks the argument 7, and for structural audience, the arguments 8 and 9 successful attack theirs counter-arguments. Then, the preferred extension of the structural agent is $\{8,9\}$. The argument 8 is present in all preferred extension, then it is globally *objectively* acceptable, confirming the mapping indicated by manual mapping.

We have used different agents' output which use distinct mapping algorithms in order to verify the behavior of our model. Our argumentation model has identified correctly the three mappings defined by expert mappings, being two mapping positives (h is +) and one negative (h is -).

Second, we compared the argumentation output with the results obtained by the cooperative negotiation model. Table 3 shows the comparative results. Although the negotiation model having obtained better precision than argumentation model, the F-measure of the argumentation model is better than negotiation model. The negotiation model identified 7 true positive mappings and it did not classify correctly 4 true positive mappings. The argumentation model identified 8 true positive, returning 1 false positive mapping not identifying 3 true positives mappings.

Table 3. Argumentation vs. negotiation

Ontology	Argumentation			Negotiation		
	P	R	F	P	R	F
Company profiles (160)	0.88	0.72	0.79	1	0.63	0.77

Third, we compared our argumentation model with three state of the art schema-based matching systems: Cupid [10], COMA [5], and S-Match [8]. We consider the class and the attribute names of the ontologies in the comparison. Table 4 shows the results. Our argumentation model had better F-measures than all others systems.

Table 4. Comparative mapping results – argumentation model

Ontology	Arg			Cupid			COMA			S-Match		
	P	R	F	P	R	F	P	R	F	P	R	F
Company profiles (160)	0.88	0.72	0.79	0.50	0.60	0.54	0.80	0.70	0.74	1.0	0.65	0.78

6   Related Work

In the field of ontology negotiation we find distinct proposals. [19] presents an ontology to serve as the basis for agent negotiation, the ontology itself is not the object being negotiated. A similar approach is proposed by [4], where ontologies are integrated to support the communication among heterogeneous agents.

[1] presents an ontology negotiation model which aims to arrive at a common ontology which the agents can use in their particular interaction. We, on the other hand, are concerned with delivering mapping pairs found by a group of agents using abstract argumentation frameworks. The links between related concepts are the result of the preferred mappings of each agent, instead of an integrated ontology upon which the agents will be able to communicate for a specific purpose. We do not consider negotiation steps such as the ones presented in [1], namely clarification and explanation. But we consider different mapping methods represented by different audiences selecting by argumentation the best solution for the mapping problem.

[16] describes an approach for ontology mapping negotiation, where the mapping is composed by a set of semantic bridges and their inter-relations, as proposed in [13]. The agents are able to achieve a consensus about the mapping through the evaluation of a confidence value that is obtained by utility functions. According to the confidence value the mapping rule is accepted, rejected or negotiated. Differently from [16], we do not use utility functions. Our model is based on cooperation and argumentation, where the agents exchange their arguments and by argumentation they select the preferred mapping. The arguments in each preferred set are considered globally acceptable.

[11] proposes to use an argument framework to deal with arguments that support or oppose candidate correspondences between ontologies. The mapping candidates are provided by a single service. The accepted mappings resulting from argumentation are used for agent communication. Differently from [11], the mappings are obtained by different agents specialized on different mapping algorithms and not only in a single service. In [11], the mappings are assumed to be correct, and we are interested in how to obtain mapping sets by combining different approaches for ontology mapping. Moreover, in [11] it is assumed that arguments being negotiated have the same confidence. We are proposing to associate to each argument a confidence degree. This way, in order to compute the preferred mapping, the audiences and confidence degrees must be considered.

7   Final Remarks and Future Work

This paper proposed to use abstract argumentation frameworks to combine approaches for ontology mapping. We extended a state of art argumentation framework, namely Value-based Argumentation Framework (VAF), in order to represent arguments with confidence degrees. The VAF allows to determine which arguments are acceptable, with respect to the different preferences represented by different agents. Our extension associates to each argument a confidence degree, representing the confidence that a specific agent has in that argument. We assumed that the confidence degrees is a criteria which is necessary to represent the ontology mapping domain.

We have used different agents' output which use distinct mapping algorithms in order to verify the behavior of our model. The terms presented here were identified as conflicting cases in our previous negotiation model. Our argumentation model has identified correctly the three mapping defined by expert mappings, being two mapping positives (h is +) and one negative (h is -). This model has obtained better results for the conflicting cases when compared with our previous model. When comparing our model with the three state of the art matching systems, our model obtained better F-measure than all other systems. The results, although preliminary, are promising especially for what concerns F-measure values.

In the future, we intend to develop further tests considering also agents using constraint-based mapping approaches; and use the ontology's application context in our matching approach. Next, we will use the mapping result as input to an ontology merge process in the question answering domain.

Acknowledgments

The first author is supported by the Programme Alban, the European Union Programme of High Level Scholarships for Latin America, scholarship no.E05D05-9374BR.

References

1. Bailin, S., Truszkowski, W.: Ontology negotiation between intelligent information agents. The Knowledge Engineering Review 17(1), 7–19 (2002)
2. Bench-Capon, T.: Persuasion in practical argument using value-based argumentation frameworks. Journal of Logic and Computation 13, 429–448 (2003)
3. Chaves, M.: Mapeamento e comparacao de similaridade entre estruturas ontologicas. Master's thesis, Pontificia Universidade Catolica do Rio Grande do Sul (2002)
4. Diggelen, J.v., Beun, R., Dignum, F., Eijk, v.R., Meyer, J.C.: Anemone: An effective minimal ontology negotiation environment. In: Proceedings of the V International Conference on Autonomous Agents and Multi-Agent Systems, pp. 899–906 (2006)
5. Do, H.H., Rahm, E.: Coma - a system for flexible combination of schema matching approaches. In: Proceedings of the 28th Conference on Very Large Databases (VLDB) (2002)
6. Dung, P.: On the acceptability of arguments and its fundamental role in nonmonotonic reasoning, logic programming and n–person games. Artificial Intelligence 77, 321–358 (1995)
7. Euzenat, J., Le Bach, T., Barrasa, J., Bouquet, P., De Bo, J., Dieng-Kuntz, R., Ehrig, M., Hauswirth, M., Jarrar, M., Lara, R., Maynard, D., Napoli, A., Stamou, G., Stuckenschmidt, H., Shvaiko, P., Tessaris, S., Van Acker, S., Zaihrayeu, I.: State of the art on ontology alignment. Technical report (2004)
8. Giunchiglia, F., Shvaiko, P., Yatskevich, M.: S-match: An algorithm and an implementation of semantic matching. In: First European Semantic Web Symposium (2004)
9. Hakimpour, F., Geppert, A.: Resolving semantic heterogeneity in schema integration: An ontology approach. In: Proceedings of the International Conference on Formal Ontology in Informational Systems (2001)
10. Madhavan, P.B.J., Rahm, E.: Generic schema matching with cupid. In: Proceedings of the Very Large Data Bases Conference (VLDB), p. 49 (2001)
11. Laera, L., Tamma, V., Euzenat, J., Bench-Capon, T., Payne, T.R.: Reaching agreement over ontology alignments. In: Cruz, I., Decker, S., Allemang, D., Preist, C., Schwabe, D., Mika, P., Uschold, M., Aroyo, L.M. (eds.) ISWC 2006. LNCS, vol. 4273, Springer, Heidelberg (2006)
12. Levenshtein, I.: Binary codes capable of correcting deletions, insertions an reversals. In: Cybernetics and Control Theory (1966)
13. Maedche, A., Motik, B., Silva, N., Volz, R.: Mafra - a mapping framework for distributed ontologies. In: 13th International Conference on Knowledge Engineering and Knowledge Management, pp. 235–250 (2002)
14. Maedche, A., Staab, S.: Measuring similarity between ontologies. In: Proceedings of the European Conference on Knowledge Acquisition and Management, pp. 251–263 (2002)
15. Rodriguez, A., Egenhofer, M.: Determining semantic similarity among entity classes from different ontologies. IEEE Transactions on Knowledge and Data Engineering 15(2), 442
16. Silva, N., Maio, P., Rocha, J.: An approach to ontology mapping negotiation. In: Proceedings of the K-CAP Workshop on Integrating Ontologies
17. Smith, T., Waterman, M.: Identification of common molecular subsequences. Journal of Molecular Biology 147, 195–197 (1981)

18. Stoilos, G., Stamou, G., Kollias, S.: A string metric for ontology alignment. In: Gil, Y., Motta, E., Benjamins, V.R., Musen, M.A. (eds.) ISWC 2005. LNCS, vol. 3729, pp. 624–637 Springer, Heidelberg (2005)
19. Tamma, V., Wooldridge, M., Blacoe, I., Dickinson, I.: An ontology based approach to automated negotiation. In: Proceedings of the IV Workshop on Agent Mediated Electronic Commerce, pp. 219–237 (2002)
20. Trojahn, C., Moraes, M., Quaresma, P., Vieira, R.: A negotiation model for ontology mapping. In: Proceedings of the IEEE/WIC/ACM International Conference on Intelligent Agent Technology (2006)
21. Trojahn, C., Moraes, M., Quaresma, P., Vieira, R.: Using cooperative agent negotiation for ontology mapping. In: Proceedings of Fourth European Workshop on Multi-Agent Systems (EUMAS) (2006)

Defeasible Argumentation Support for an Extended BDI Architecture*

Nicolás D. Rotstein, Alejandro J. García, and Guillermo R. Simari

Consejo Nacional de Investigaciones Científicas y Técnicas (CONICET)
Artificial Intelligence Research and Development Laboratory
Department of Computer Science and Engineering
Universidad Nacional del Sur, Bahía Blanca, Argentina
{ndr,ajg,grs}@cs.uns.edu.ar

Abstract. In this work, an agent architecture that combines defeasible argumentation and the BDI model is described. Argumentation will be used as a mechanism for reasoning about beliefs, for filtering desires considering the agent's current environment, and for selecting proper intentions. The approach allows to define different types of agents and this will affect the way in which desires are filtered and hence, which intention is selected. For performing defeasible reasoning, the approach uses a concrete framework based on a working defeasible argumentation system: Defeasible Logic Programming (DeLP). A set of filtering rules, represented as a defeasible logic program, will be used to represent reasons for and against adopting desires. Thus, based on its perceived or derived beliefs, the agent will argue about which of its desires are achievable in the current situation. To clarify the ideas two applications will be introduced to show two significantly different types of agent that can be implemented using this approach.

1 Introduction and Motivation

In this work, an agent architecture that combines defeasible argumentation and the BDI model is described. Argumentation will be used for reasoning about beliefs, for filtering desires considering the agent's current environment, and for selecting proper intentions. The approach allows to define different types of agents and this will affect the way in which desires are filtered and hence, which intention is selected. For performing defeasible reasoning, the approach uses a concrete framework based on a working defeasible argumentation system: Defeasible Logic Programming (DeLP).

This work is an extension of the article "Reasoning from Desires to Intentions: A Dialectical Framework" published in AAAI 2007 by the same authors [1]. Here, besides presenting the approach, we focus on two types of applications: a security system and robotic soccer. They were chosen because they represent two significantly different kinds of agents that can be implemented using our approach. As explained below, the security-system agent will have the goal of handling unexpected problematic situations, whereas the soccer agent will control the behavior of a robot in order to play somehow successfully.

---

* Partially supported by CONICET, ANPCyT, and UNSur.

I. Rahwan, S. Parsons, and C. Reed (Eds.): ArgMAS 2007, LNAI 4946, pp. 145–163, 2008.

In the first application domain, we consider a security system agent supervising a building with several rooms (*e.g.*, a museum). The agent's goal will be to act in case of unexpected problems (*e.g.*, fire or intruders) and to decide which is the best action to take in each case. The agent will have sources of information from which to gather beliefs: video cameras and smoke, motion and temperature sensors. These sensors can be thought as coupled and thus work as two mutual backup subsystems: the smoke/temperature sensors pair would detect fire and the camera/motion sensor pair, intruders. As it will be explained in detail in Section 7, agent's intentions could be: *"send a guard to a room"*, *"call the police"* or *"call the firemen"*.

The security system agent perceives information from the environment through the mentioned sensors and this information represents its *perceived belief.* (*e.g.*, *"there is motion in room 2"* or *" there is no smoke in room 3"*). Besides perceived beliefs the agent may have more knowledge represented as a defeasible logic program (Section 2) that will be used for warranting *derived beliefs*.

Our approach provides a defeasible reasoning mechanism for filtering agent's desires in order to obtain a set of current desires, *i.e.*, those that are achievable in the current situation. A set of *filtering rules*, represented as a defeasible logic program, will be used to represent reasons for and against adopting desires. For example, the defeasible rule $call(firemen) \prec smoke(R)$ means "if there is smoke in a room R then there are reasons for calling the firemen". Thus, the security system agent will be provided with a set of filtering rules that will represent reasons for and against adopting one of its desires, *i.e.*, *call the firemen*, *call the police* or *send a guard*. Thus, based on its perceived or derived beliefs, the agent will debate which of its desires are achievable in the current situation. For example, if the agent perceive that there is smoke in one room then *"call firemen"* could be one of its *current desires*. Since the approach allows to define different agent types, in the case of the security system application we will develop a cautious agent, that is, an agent that only selects warranted desires. Once the set of current desires is obtained, then the agent will be able to select one intention. The security system agent will be explained in detail in Section 7.

The other application domain that we will consider in this work is robotic soccer. Our robotic soccer agent senses its environment through a video camera that takes the whole playing field, and from that perception it can build its set of perceived beliefs (*e.g.*, *it is marked, a mate has the ball*). Our proposed agent will have rules in order to derived other beliefs, for instance, the defeasible rule *"if a mate has the ball then the agent may receive the ball"* will allow the agent to build an argument for the belief that it may receive the ball, based on the perception that a mate has the ball. However, as we will show in detail in the next section, other rule like *"if the agent is marked and a mate has the ball then it will not receive the ball"* can be used for building a counter-argument for the previous one. The set of desires of the soccer agent could be *shoot, carry, pass* and *move*, *i.e.*, shoot to goal, carry the ball, pass the ball to a teammate and move to a different position in the field.

A significant difference between the two application domains is how they select intentions. The security-system agent is allowed to select and fulfill possibly many intentions at the same time, because it would have to deal with multiple hazardous situations simultaneously. In opposition to this, a robotic-soccer agent can pursue just one intention at a time, since, for instance, it cannot shoot on goal and pass the ball to a teammate at once.

2   The Proposed Architecture

An outline of this architecture appears in Fig. 1 [1]. Briefly, the main input is the *perception* from the environment, which is part of the set of *belief rules* (Π_B, Δ_B) that, through an *argumentation process*, leads to the set B of warranted beliefs. For example, suppose that a soccer agent perceives that *it is marked* and *a teammate has the ball*, then it can warrant the belief *"I will not receive the ball"*.

As shown in the figure, the set of filtering rules, along with a set D of desires and the specification of a *filtering function* are the input to a *dialectical filtering process*, whose output is the set D^c of the agent's *current desires*. Following our example, consider that our soccer agent has the filtering rule *"if I will not receive the ball then there is a reason to move to a different place"*. Since there is a warrant for *"I will not receive the ball"*, then *move* will be a current desire. The final stage of the *agent behavior loop* shown in the figure involves the usage of a set of *intention rules*, embedded in an *intention policy* that will determine the preferred rule. The current desire in the head of this rule will be the *selected intention*.

As shown in Fig. 1, there are three main processes. They use defeasible argumentation based on Defeasible Logic Programming (DeLP). Next, we give a brief summary of DeLP (for more details see [2]). In DeLP, knowledge is represented using facts, strict rules, and defeasible rules:

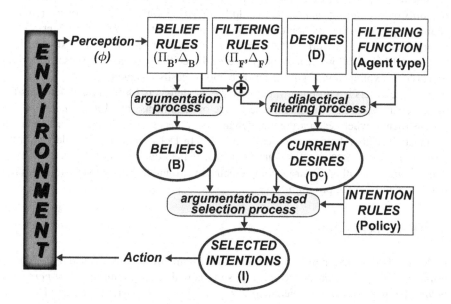

Fig. 1. DeLP-based BDI architecture

- *Facts* are ground literals representing atomic information or the negation of atomic information using strong negation "$\sim$" (*e.g.*, $hasBall(opponent)$).
- *Strict Rules* are denoted $L_0 \leftarrow L_1, \ldots, L_n$, where L_0 is a ground literal and $\{L_i\}_{i>0}$ is a set of ground literals (*e.g.*, $\sim hasBall(myTeam) \leftarrow hasBall(opponent)$).
- *Defeasible Rules* are denoted $L_0 \prec L_1, \ldots, L_n$, where L_0 is a ground literal and $\{L_i\}_{i>0}$ is a set of ground literals. (*e.g.*, $\sim pass(mate1) \prec marked(mate1)$).

Rules are distinguished by the type of arrows, and a defeasible rule "$Head \prec Body$" expresses that "*reasons to believe in the antecedent Body give reasons to believe in the consequent Head*" representing tentative information that may be used if nothing could be posed against it.

A Defeasible Logic Program (*de.l.p.*) $\mathcal{P}$ is a set of facts, strict rules and defeasible rules. When required, $\mathcal{P}$ is denoted (Π, Δ) distinguishing the subset Π of facts and strict rules, and the subset Δ of defeasible rules. Strict and defeasible rules are ground, however, following the usual convention [3], some examples will use "schematic rules" with variables.

Strong negation could appear in the head of program rules, and can be used to represent contradictory knowledge. From a program (Π, Δ) contradictory literals could be derived, however, the set Π (used to represent non-defeasible information) must be non-contradictory, *i.e.*, no pair of contradictory literals can be derived from Π. Given a literal L, $\overline{L}$ represents the complement with respect to strong negation. If contradictory literals are derived from (Π, Δ), a dialectical process is used for deciding which literal prevails. In short, an *argument* for a literal L, denoted $\langle \mathcal{A}, L \rangle$, is a minimal set of defeasible rules $\mathcal{A} \subseteq \Delta$, such that $\mathcal{A} \cup \Pi$ is non-contradictory, and there is a derivation for L from $\mathcal{A} \cup \Pi$. A literal L is *warranted* from (Π, Δ) if there exists a non-defeated argument $\mathcal{A}$ supporting L. To establish if $\langle \mathcal{A}, L \rangle$ is a non-defeated argument, *argument rebuttals* or *counter-arguments* that could be *defeaters* for $\langle \mathcal{A}, L \rangle$ are considered, *i.e.*, counter-arguments that by some criterion are preferred to $\langle \mathcal{A}, L \rangle$. A defeater $\mathcal{A}_1$ for an argument $\mathcal{A}_2$ can be proper ($\mathcal{A}_1$ *stronger than* $\mathcal{A}_2$) or *blocking* (same strength). In the examples that follow we assume generalized specificity as the comparison criterion, however, as explained in [2] the criterion could be easily changed.

Since defeaters are arguments, there may exist defeaters for them, and defeaters for these defeaters, and so on. Thus, a sequence of arguments called *argumentation line* is constructed, where each argument defeats its predecessor in the line (for a detailed explanation of this dialectical process see [2]). In DeLP, a query Q could have four possible answers: YES, if Q is warranted; NO, if the complement of Q is warranted; UNDECIDED, if neither Q nor its complement is warranted; and UNKNOWN, if Q is not in the signature of the program.

3   Warranting Beliefs

Following [4], agent's beliefs correspond to the semantics[1] of a *defeasible logic program* $\mathcal{P}_B = (\Pi_B, \Delta_B)$. In Π_B two disjoint subsets will be distinguished: Φ of *perceived beliefs* that will be updated dynamically (see Fig. 1), and Σ of strict rules and facts that

---

[1] Since the semantics of DeLP is skeptical, there is only one.

will represent static knowledge, $\Pi_B = \Phi \cup \Sigma$. Besides the perceived beliefs, the agent may use strict and defeasible rules from $\mathcal{P}_B$ to obtain a *warrant* for its *derived beliefs* (see Definition 1).

We require Π_B to be non-contradictory, and also assume that perception is correct in the sense that it will never give a pair of contradictory literals. The next definition introduces the different types of belief that an agent will obtain from a defeasible logic program (Π_B, Δ_B).

Definition 1 (Belief types). *A **Perceived belief** is a fact in Φ that the agent has perceived directly from its environment. A **Strict belief** is a literal that is not a perceived belief, and it is derived from $\Pi_B = \Phi \cup \Sigma$ (i.e., no defeasible rules are used for its derivation). A **Defeasible belief** is a warranted literal L supported by an non-empty argument $\mathcal{A}$ (i.e., it uses at least one defeasible rule). Finally, a **Derived belief** is a strict or a defeasible belief. We will denote with B_s the set of strict beliefs, and with B_d the set of defeasible beliefs. Therefore, in any given situation, the beliefs of an agent will be $B = \Phi \cup B_s \cup B_d$.*

Example 1. *Consider a robotic-soccer agent with the following program (Π_B, Δ_B), where Π_B was divided distinguishing the set $\Phi = \{hasBall(t1),\ marked(t1)\}$ of perceived facts representing "player t1 has the ball", and "teammate t1 is marked", the set Σ of non-perceived information, and the set Δ_B of defeasible knowledge:*

$$\Sigma = \left\{ \begin{array}{l} mate(t1),\ opponent(o1), \\ (\sim mate(X) \leftarrow opponent(X)), \\ (\sim receive(self) \leftarrow hasBall(self)) \end{array} \right\}$$

$$\Delta_B = \left\{ \begin{array}{l} (receive(self) \prec hasBall(X), mate(X)), \\ (\sim receive(self) \prec marked(self)), \\ (\sim receive(self) \prec hasBall(X), \sim mate(X)) \end{array} \right\}$$

From (Π_B, Δ_B) the agent can infer the strict belief: $\sim mate(o1)$. The argument built from (Π_B, Δ_B) for $receive(self)$: $\{receive(self) \prec hasBall(t1), mate(t1)\}$, has no defeaters, and therefore, there is a warrant for one defeasible belief: $receive(self)$ (the agent may receive a pass).

The sets Φ, B_s and B_d are disjoint sets. It can be shown that the set B of beliefs of an agent is a non-contradictory set of warranted literals. Although perceived beliefs are facts in Π_B, there could be other facts in Π_B which are not perceived, for instance, facts that represent agent's features, roles, *etc.* These facts that do not represent perceived information are persistent in the sense that they cannot change with perception, like $myRole(defender)$, or $mate(t1)$.

We assume a perception function that provides the agent with information about its environment. This function will be invoked by the agent to update its perceived beliefs set Φ. When this happens the new information overrides the old one following some criterion. Updating a set of literals is a well-known problem and many proposals exist in the literature [5,6]. Since we require Π_B to be non-contradictory, when Φ is updated, a revision function will ensure that Π_B remains a non-contradictory set. The specification of a proper revision operator is out of the scope of this paper.

Example 2. *In the context of Ex. 1, with the perception that the agent is now marked, the set Φ becomes $\{hasBall(t1), marked(t1), marked(self)\}$. Now the argument for $receive(self)$ has a "blocking defeater", which means that the DeLP answer for both $receive(self)$ and $\sim receive(self)$ will be* UNDECIDED.

Consider a different situation, where the perception is $\Phi = \{hasBall(o1)\}$. Here, the answer for $receive(self)$ is NO, *since there is a warrant for $\sim receive(self)$ supported by the non-defeated argument $\{\sim receive(self) \prec hasBall(o1), \sim mate(o1)\}$.*

4   Filtering Desires

Agents desires will be represented by a given set D of literals that will contain a literal representing each desire the agent might want to achieve. Clearly, D may be contradictory, that is, both a literal L and its complement $\overline{L}$ might belong to D. We will assume that beliefs and desires are represented with separate names, *i.e.*, D $\cap$ B $= \emptyset$. Hence, a desire cannot be perceived or derived as a belief.

Set D represents all the desires that the agent may want to achieve. However, depending on the situation in which it is involved, there could be some desires impossible to be carried out. For example, if the agent does not have the ball and the ball is in a place p, then, the desire *shoot* could not be effected, whereas $goto(p)$ is a plausible option. Therefore, agents should reason about their desires to select the ones that could be actually realized. Following the spirit of the BDI model, once appropriate desires are detected, the agent may select (and commit to) a specific intention (goal), and then select appropriate actions to fulfill that intention (see Figure 1).

In [4] a reasoning formalism was introduced for selecting from D those desires that are suitable to be brought about. To perform this selection, the agent uses its beliefs (representing the current situation) and a defeasible logic program (Π_F, Δ_F) composed by *filtering rules*. The filtering rules represent reasons for and against adopting desires. In other words, filtering rules eliminate those desires that cannot be effected in the situation at hand. Once the set of achievable desires is obtained, the agent can adopt one of them as an intention.

Definition 2 (Filtering rule). *Let D be the set of desires of an agent, a* filtering rule *is a strict or defeasible rule that has a literal $L \in$ D in its head and a non-empty body.*

Observe that a filtering rule can be either strict or defeasible and, as will be explained below, that will influence the filtering process. Note also that a filtering rule cannot be a single literal (*i.e.*, a fact). Below we will explain how to use filtering rules in order to select desires, but first we will introduce an example to provide some motivation.

Example 3. *A robotic-soccer agent A^r could have the following sets of desires and filtering rules:*

$$D = \left\{ \begin{array}{l} shoot \\ carry \\ pass \\ move \end{array} \right\} \quad \Pi_F = \left\{ \begin{array}{l} \sim carry \leftarrow \sim ball \\ \sim shoot \leftarrow \sim ball \\ \sim pass \leftarrow \sim ball \end{array} \right\}$$

$$\Delta_F = \left\{ \begin{array}{l} shoot \prec theirGoalieAway \\ carry \prec noOneAhead \\ pass \prec freeTeammate \\ \sim shoot \prec farFromGoal \\ \sim carry \prec shoot \\ move \prec \sim ball \end{array} \right\}$$

Consider a particular situation in which an agent does not have the ball (*i.e.*, $\sim ball \in \Phi$). If the agent has $\Delta_B = \emptyset$, $\Pi_B = \Phi$ and the filtering rules (Π_F, Δ_F) from Ex. 3, then, there are warrants for $\sim carry$, $\sim pass$ and $\sim shoot$ from this information. Hence, in this particular situation, the agent should not consider selecting the desires *carry*, *pass*, and *shoot*, because there are justified reasons against them. Observe that these reasons are not defeasible.

Consider now a different situation with a new set of perceived beliefs: $B = \Phi = \{ball, theirGoalieAway, farFromGoal\}$, that is, a situation in which the agent has the ball and the opponent goalie is away from its position, but the agent is far from the goal. Then, from the agent's beliefs and the filtering rules (Π_F, Δ_F) of Ex. 3, there are arguments for both *shoot* and $\sim shoot$. Since these two arguments defeat each other, a blocking situation occurs and the answer for both literals is UNDECIDED. In our approach (as will be explained later) an undecided desire could be eligible.

In this formalism, beliefs and filtering rules should be used in combination. Hence, we need to explain how two defeasible logic programs can be properly combined. Agents will have a *de.l.p.* (Π_B, Δ_B) containing rules and facts for deriving beliefs, and a *de.l.p.* (Π_F, Δ_F) with filtering rules for selecting desires. We need to combine these two *de.l.p.*, but the union of them might not be a *de.l.p.*, because the union of the sets of strict rules could be contradictory. To overcome this issue, we use a merge revision operator "$\circ$" [6]. Hence, in our case, the join of (Π_B, Δ_B) and (Π_F, Δ_F) will be a program (Π, Δ), where $\Pi = \Pi_B \circ \Pi_F$ and $\Delta = \Delta_B \cup \Delta_F \cup \Delta_X$. A set X is introduced, containing those strict rules r_i that derive complementary literals. This set is eliminated when merging Π_B and Π_F, then every r_i is transformed into a defeasible rule, and the set Δ_X is generated, carrying the resulting defeasible rules (see [4] for more details).

Definition 3 (Agent's Knowledge Base)
Let (Π_B, Δ_B) be the set containing rules and facts for deriving beliefs; (Π_F, Δ_F), the set of filtering rules; and $\Delta_X = \{(\alpha \prec \gamma) \mid (\alpha \leftarrow \gamma) \in (\Pi_B \cup \Pi_F) \text{ and } (\Pi_B \cup \Pi_F) \vdash \{\alpha, \overline{\alpha}\}\}$. Then $K_{Ag} = (\Pi_B \circ \Pi_F, \Delta_B \cup \Delta_F \cup \Delta_X)$ will be the agent's knowledge base.

The next definition introduces a mechanism for filtering D obtaining only those desires that are achievable in the *current* situation. We allow the representation of different *agent types*, each of which will specify a different filtering process.

Definition 4 (Current desires). *Let T be a boolean function representing a selection criterion. The set D^c of Current Desires is defined as:*

$$D^c = filter(T, D) = \{\delta \in D \mid T(\delta, K_{Ag}) = true\}.$$

Observe that the filtering function can be defined in a modular way. Methodologically, it would be important to make this function related to the K_{Ag}, in order to obtain a rational filtering. Implementing a sensible filtering function is not a trivial task, as it is domain-dependent, and a general criterion cannot be stated. Different agent types or personalities can be obtained depending on the chosen selection criterion T. The following are interesting alternatives:

- CAUTIOUS AGENT: $T(\delta, K_{Ag})$ is true when there is a warrant for δ from K_{Ag}.
- BOLD AGENT: $T(\delta, K_{Ag})$ is true when there is no warrant for $\overline{\delta}$ from K_{Ag}.

Notice that when neither δ nor $\overline{\delta}$ has a warrant built from K_{Ag}, then both literals will be included into the set D^c of a bold agent. Therefore, the agent will consider these two options (among others), albeit in contradiction.

The way a bold agent selects its current desires (see Ex. 4) becomes clearer considering the relation of warrant states with DeLP answers. In DeLP, given a literal Q, there are four possible answers for the query Q: YES, NO, UNDECIDED, and UNKNOWN. Thus, agent types using DeLP can be defined as follows:

- CAUTIOUS AGENT: $T(\delta, K_{Ag})$ is true when the answer for δ from K_{Ag} is YES.
- BOLD AGENT: $T(\delta, K_{Ag})$ is true when the answer for δ from K_{Ag} is YES, UNDECIDED or UNKNOWN.

Example 4. *Extending Ex. 3, if we consider a bold agent as defined above and the set of beliefs:*
$$\mathsf{B} = \Phi = \{\, farFromGoal,\ noOneAhead,\ ball \,\}$$
the agent will generate the following set of current desires:
$$\mathsf{D}^c = \{carry, pass\}$$
In this case, we have $K_{Ag} = (\Phi \circ \Pi_F, \emptyset \cup \Delta_F \cup \emptyset)$. Regarding D^c, DeLP's answer for shoot is NO, for carry is YES, and for pass is UNDECIDED. Finally, note that a cautious agent would choose carry as the only current desire.

As stated above, it is required that B and D be two separate sets to avoid the confusion when joining the $(\Pi_\mathsf{B}, \Delta_\mathsf{B})$ and (Π_F, Δ_F) programs. This is not a strong restriction, because a literal being both a belief and a desire brings about well-known representational issues, *e.g.*, symbol overload.

5   Selecting Intentions

In our approach, an intention will be a current desire $d \in \mathsf{D}^c$ that the agent can commit. To specify under what conditions the intention could be achieved, the agent will be provided with a set of *intention rules*. Next, these concepts and the formal notion of *applicable intention rule* are introduced.

Definition 5 (Intention Rule)
An intention rule is a device used to specify under what conditions an intention could be effected. It will be denoted as $(d \Leftarrow \{p_1, \ldots, p_n\}, \{not\ c_1, \ldots, not\ c_m\})$, where d is a literal representing a desire that could be selected as an intention, $p_1, \ldots, p_n$ $(n \geq 0)$ are literals representing preconditions, and $c_1, \ldots, c_m$ $(m \geq 0)$ are literals representing constraints.

Example 5. *The robotic-soccer agent* A^r *might have the following set of intention rules:*

$$IR_1 : (carry \Leftarrow \{ball\}, \{\})$$
$$IR_2 : (pass \Leftarrow \{ball\}, \{not\ shoot\})$$
$$IR_3 : (shoot \Leftarrow \{ball\}, \{not\ marked\})$$
$$IR_4 : (carry \Leftarrow \{winning\}, \{\})$$
$$IR_5 : (move \Leftarrow \{\}, \{\})$$

Now we describe how an intention becomes applicable.

Definition 6 (Applicable Intention Rule)
Let $K_{Ag} = (\Pi_B \circ \Pi_F, \Delta_B \cup \Delta_F \cup \Delta_X)$ *be the knowledge base of an agent, and* D^c, *its set of current desires. Let* B *be the set of beliefs obtained from* (Π_B, Δ_B). *An intention rule* $(d \Leftarrow \{p_1, \ldots, p_n\}, \{not\ c_1, \ldots, not\ c_m\})$ *is applicable iff*

1. $d \in D^c$,
2. *for each precondition* p_i $(0 \leq i \leq n)$ *it holds* $p_i \in (B \cup D^c)$
3. *for each constraint* c_i $(0 \leq i \leq m)$ *it holds* $c_j \notin (B \cup D^c)$.

Thus, in every applicable intention rule it holds:

1. the head d is a current desire of the agent selected by the filtering function,
2. every precondition p_i that is a belief is warranted from K_{Ag},
3. every precondition p_i that is a desire belongs to set D^c,
4. every belief constraint c_i has no warrant from K_{Ag}, and
5. every c_i that is a desire does not belong to D^c.

Example 6. *Consider a bold agent, and* K, B *and* D^c *as given in Example 4. Now it is possible to determine which of the intention rules of Example 5 are applicable. Rule* IR_1 *is applicable because* $carry \in D^c$. *Rule* IR_2 *is applicable because* $pass \in D^c$, $ball \in B$, *and* $shoot \notin D^c$. *Rule* IR_3 *is not applicable because* $shoot \notin D^c$. *Rule* IR_4 *is not applicable because the precondition is not a literal from* K. *Finally,* IR_5 *is not applicable because* $move \notin D^c$. *Thus,* $\{IR_1, IR_2\}$ *is the set of applicable rules.*

Intention rules' goal is to select the final set of intentions. In general, this selection among current desires cannot be done by using filtering rules. For instance, if we have to select just one intention, and there are two warranted current desires, how can we choose one? There is a need for an external mechanism to make that decision.

Intention rules and filtering rules (Definition 2) have different semantics and usage:

– Filtering rules are used to build arguments for and against desires (thus, they are the basis of the dialectical process for warranting a desire), whereas intention rules are used on top of the dialectical process.
– Intention rules do not interact, whereas filtering rules do interact because they can be in conflict or can be used for deriving a literal in the body of another filtering rule.

– Applicable intention rules depend on the result of the filtering process over desires and warranted beliefs, whereas a filtering rule is "applicable" when its body literals arc supported by perceived beliefs, or hy other defeasible or strict rules.

The set of all applicable intention rules contains rules whose heads represent *applicable intentions* achievable in the current situation. Depending on the application domain, there are many possible policies to select from the set of applicable intentions. For example, the agent could try to pursue some of them simultaneously, or it might be forced to commit to one. Furthermore, each of these two options has, in turn, several solutions. The idea behind having intention rules and policies is to give a more flexible mechanism than plain priorities. Next, we define how to obtain a set of selected intentions.

Definition 7 (Set of Selected Intentions)
Let IR be the set of intention rules, and $App \subseteq IR$ be the set of all the applicable intention rules. Let $p : IR \rightarrow D$ be a given selection policy. Then, the set of selected intentions I will be $p(App)$.

The policy $p(App)$ could be defined in many ways. For instance, $p(App)$ could be "return all the heads of rules in App". However, depending on the application domain, more restrictive definitions for $p(App)$ could be necessary. For example, in our robotic soccer domain, agents must select a single applicable intention at a time (*i.e.*, an agent cannot shoot and pass the ball at the same time). One possibility for defining a policy that returns a single intention is to provide a sequence with all the intention rules $[IR_1,...,IR_n]$ that represents a preference order among them. Then, the policy $p(App)$ selects the first rule IR_k ($1 \leq k \leq n$) in the sequence that belongs to App, returning the head of IR_k.

Example 7. *Continuing with Ex. 6. The set of applicable intention rules is $App = \{IR_1, IR_2, IR_5\}$, and suppose that the policy p is the one introduced above. Then, if the preference order is $[IR_1, IR_2, IR_3, IR_4, IR_5]$, the selected intention will be the head of IR_1, i.e., $p(App) = \{carry\}$.*

Now we can formally define the structure of an agent.

Definition 8 (DeLP-Based BDI Agent)
An agent A is a tuple $\langle D, (\Pi_B, \Delta_B), (\Pi_F, \Delta_F), T, IR, p \rangle$, where: D is the set of desires of the agent, (Π_B, Δ_B) is the agent knowledge (that will include perceived beliefs), (Π_F, Δ_F) are filtering rules, T is an agent type, IR is a set of intention rules, and $p(\cdot)$ is a policy for selecting intentions.

6 Application Example: Robotic Soccer

In this section a robotic-soccer agent A^r will be introduced and then we will show, using different examples, how A^r selects appropriate intentions when faced with different scenarios. In each example, the difference of defining a bold or a cautious agent will be made clear.

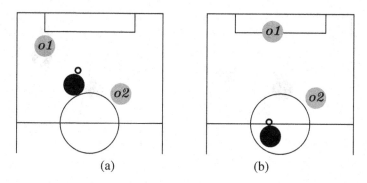

Fig. 2. Two scenarios for a robotic soccer agent

The robotic-soccer agent will be $A^r = \langle D, (\Pi_B, \Delta_B), (\Pi_F, \Delta_F), T, IR, p \rangle$ where the set D and (Π_F, Δ_F) are the ones from Ex. 3, the set IR is the one defined in Ex. 5, the policy p was defined in Ex. 7, and the set $\Delta_B = \emptyset$.

Example 8. *Consider the agent A^r and the situation depicted in Fig. 2(a) where "o1" and "o2" represent the positions of two opponents and "self" is the position of the agent A^r who has the ball (small circle).*
Here, the perception of A^r is $\Phi_1 = \{ball, noOneAhead, theirGoalieAway\}$. In this situation, A^r can build the following arguments:

$\mathcal{A}_1 : \{shoot \prec theirGoalieAway\}$,
$\mathcal{A}_2 : \{carry \prec noOneAhead\}$,
$\mathcal{A}_3 : \{(\sim carry \prec shoot), (shoot \prec theirGoalieAway)\}$.

Hence, shoot is warranted, whereas carry, $\sim$carry, pass and $\sim$pass are not. As stated above the filter function will determine the type of agent (e.g., bold or cautious), which could affect the set of selected intentions. For example:

- *for a cautious agent, $D_{C1}^c = \{shoot\}$, intention rule IR_3 is applicable, and $I_{C1} = \{shoot\}$;*
- *for a bold agent, $D_{B1}^c = \{shoot, carry, pass\}$, intention rules IR_1 and IR_3 are applicable, and $I_{B1} = \{carry\}$.*

Note that the cautious agent obtains only one current desire that is its selected intention. On the other hand, since the bold agent includes "undecided" literals in its current desires, D_{B1}^c has more elements than D_{C1}^c, there are two applicable intention rules, and the policy "p" has to be used.

Example 9. *Consider the agent A^r but in a different scenario (depicted in Fig. 2(b)). The perception of the agent is here $\Phi_2 = \{ball, noOneAhead, farFromGoal\}$. In this situation, A^r can build the following arguments:*

$\mathcal{A}_4 : \{\sim shoot \prec farFromGoal\}$,
$\mathcal{A}_5 : \{carry \prec noOneAhead\}$.

Hence, $\sim$shoot and carry are warranted, whereas pass and $\sim$pass are not, and:

- *for a cautious agent, $D_{C2}^c = \{carry\}$, intention rule IR_1 is applicable, and $I_{C2} = \{carry\}$;*

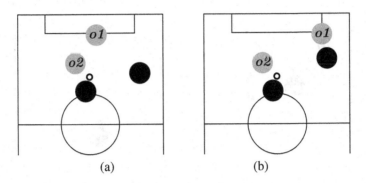

Fig. 3. Two scenarios for a robotic soccer agent

– *for a bold agent,* $D_{B2}^c = \{carry, pass\}$, *intention rules* IR_1 *and* IR_2 *are applicable, and* $I_{B2} = \{carry\}$.

Example 10. *Consider now that* A^r *is in the situation depicted in Fig. 3(a), where "t1" represents the position of a teammate of* A^r. *The perception of* A^r *is* $\Phi_3 = \{ball, freeTeammate, farFromGoal\}$. *In this situation,* A^r *can build the following arguments:*

$\quad \mathcal{A}_6 : \{\sim shoot \multimap farFromGoal\}$,
$\quad \mathcal{A}_7 : \{pass \multimap freeTeammate\}$,

Hence, we have that pass and $\sim shoot$ *are warranted, whereas carry and* $\sim carry$ *are not, and:*

– *for a cautious agent,* $D_{C3}^c = \{pass\}$, *intention rule* IR_2 *is applicable, and* $I_{C3} = \{pass\}$;
– *for a bold agent,* $D_{B3}^c = \{carry, pass\}$, *intention rules* IR_1 *and* IR_2 *are applicable, and* $I_{B3} = \{carry\}$;

Example 11. *Consider finally that* A^r *is in the situation of (Fig. 3(b)). The perception of* A^r *will be* $\Phi_4 = \{ball, freeTeammate, theirGoalieAway\}$, *and we can build the following arguments:*

$\quad \mathcal{A}_8 : \{shoot \multimap theirGoalieAway\}$,
$\quad \mathcal{A}_9 : \{pass \multimap freeTeammate\}$,
$\quad \mathcal{A}_{10} : \{(\sim carry \multimap shoot), (shoot \multimap theirGoalieAway)\}$.

Hence, pass, shoot and $\sim carry$ *are warranted, and:*

– *for a cautious agent,* $D_{C4}^c = \{shoot\}$, *intention rule* IR_3 *is applicable, and* $I_{C4} = \{shoot\}$;
– *for a bold agent,* $D_{B4}^c = \{shoot\}$, *intention rules* IR_3 *is applicable, and* $I_{B4} = \{shoot\}$.

7   Application Example: Security System

In this section, we present an example consisting of a security-system agent. The system will be simplified in order to keep it easy to understand.

The security-system agent senses rooms of a building from four different sources: temperature, smoke, motion sensors, and video cameras. Whenever a temperature or smoke sensor is on, the agent will have a reason to call the firemen; analogously, if a motion sensor or a camera tells that an intruder might have entered to a room, the police should be called. These are not strict rules, but defeasible, as will be clear next (see Figure 4). The idea behind this setting is to have pairs of sensors acting as mutual backup, that is, we have smoke sensors as the backup for temperature sensors (and *vice versa*), and motion sensors as the backup for cameras (and *vice versa*).

Although sensor pairs provide robustness, they also bring about a few shortcomings, *e.g.*, a motion sensor in a room might detect that something is moving, while the corresponding camera is not showing any change in the image. Images coming from a camera may remain static for several reasons: perhaps someone attached a photograph to it, or the device could be simply malfunctioning. An analogous situation occurs when a room is signaled as having smoke but the temperature sensor placed there shows no activity. This generally means that one of the two sensors is not working properly. The filtering rules modelling abnormal situations like these are shown in Figure 4.

Abnormal situations within a room are handled by the agent, who will send a guard to that room (rules in Π_F, Figure 4). If the guard confirms that an intruder has entered to the room or that the room is on fire, it will manually trigger the corresponding alarm, providing a reason to the agent for calling the firemen or the police (last rule in Figure 4). Thus, once an alarm is fired, it will stop when a call (either to the police or firemen) is made, or when a guard arrives to a room and finds that everything is normal.

In this section, we will define an agent $A^s = \langle \mathsf{D}^s, (\Pi^s_{\mathsf{B}}, \Delta^s_{\mathsf{B}}), (\Pi^s_F, \Delta^s_F), \mathsf{T}^s, IR^s, p^s \rangle$. We start the description of the agent with its set of desires:

$$\mathsf{D}^s = \{send\_guard(R), call(firemen, R), call(police, R)\}$$

Desire $send\_guard(R)$ means that a guard could be sent to room R, and desires $call(firemen, R)$ and $call(police, R)$ give the possibility of calling the firemen and police because room R is on fire or an intruder entered to R, respectively.

In this case, there is no need to include negated literals in the set of desires, since, for instance, the security agent will never intend to fulfill the desire $\sim call(firemen, R)$. The system just will not make a call or send a guard to a room if there are no justified reasons to do it. This can be seen as just a design decision, but it turned to be a sensible representation.

A fundamental difference with the soccer domain examples is that the security-system agent does not require the selection of just one intention. This agent will select an arbitrary amount of intentions; it may even select no current desire as an intention (*i.e.*, $I^s = \emptyset$). For instance, the agent could send several guards to certain rooms while making calls to both police and firemen regarding other rooms.

The security system will be managed by a cautious agent, *i.e.*, agent A^s will put in its set of current desires only the desires that are warranted from the DeLP-program $(\Pi^s_{\mathsf{B}} \circ \Pi^s_F, \Delta^s_{\mathsf{B}} \cup \Delta^s_F \cup \Delta^s_X)$. This choice will be justified at the end of this section.

The beliefs program $\mathcal{P}^s_{\mathsf{B}}$ has no rules, it will just consist of the set of perceived facts. The program (Π^s_F, Δ^s_F) of strict and defeasible filtering rules is shown in Figure 4.

$$\Pi_F^s = \left\{ \begin{array}{l} send\_guard(R) \leftarrow hi\_temp(R), \sim smoke(R) \\ send\_guard(R) \leftarrow \sim hi\_temp(R), smoke(R) \\ send\_guard(R) \leftarrow motion(R), \sim camera(R) \\ send\_guard(R) \leftarrow \sim motion(R), camera(R) \end{array} \right\}$$

$$\Delta_F^s = \left\{ \begin{array}{l} call(firemen, R) \mathrel{-\!\!\!\prec} hi\_temp(R) \\ call(firemen, R) \mathrel{-\!\!\!\prec} smoke(R) \\ \sim call(firemen, R) \mathrel{-\!\!\!\prec} hi\_temp(R), \sim smoke(R) \\ \sim call(firemen, R) \mathrel{-\!\!\!\prec} \sim hi\_temp(R), smoke(R) \\ call(police, R) \mathrel{-\!\!\!\prec} motion(R) \\ call(police, R) \mathrel{-\!\!\!\prec} camera(R) \\ \sim call(police, R) \mathrel{-\!\!\!\prec} motion(R), \sim camera(R) \\ \sim call(police, R) \mathrel{-\!\!\!\prec} \sim motion(R), camera(R) \\ call(Who, R) \mathrel{-\!\!\!\prec} manual\_alarm(Who, R) \end{array} \right\}$$

Fig. 4. Filtering rules for the security agent A^s

The set Π_F^s of strict rules models situations in which a couple of sensor differs and a guard has to be sent to a room, *e.g.*, when a camera detects no change, but the motion sensor placed in the same room says that something has moved.

Defeasible rules in Δ_F^s model reasons for and against making a call to police or firemen; for instance, if the temperature sensor signals heat in a certain room, the agent has a reason to call the firemen. However, if the corresponding smoke sensor has not fired, the agent will prefer not to make that call, but send a guard instead (modelled via strict rules). Regarding the last rule, if the manual alarm is fired by that guard, the call should be made immediately.

Note also that the filtering rules supporting calls to firemen or police refer to the room in which the danger was detected through variable R. This is important for the dialectical analysis to be performed over the same "situation". That is, if an argument for calling the police is posed and is under attack, it must be attacked by a counterargument that speaks of the same room. This parameter also tells where firemen or police must go to.

The set IR^s of intention rules for the security agent are:

$$IR_1 : (send\_guard(R) \Leftarrow \{\}, \{not\ manual\_alarm(W, R)\})$$
$$IR_2 : (call(firemen, R) \Leftarrow \{\}, \{\})$$
$$IR_3 : (call(police, R) \Leftarrow \{\}, \{\})$$

Observe that intention rule IR_1 has a constraint: a guard will not be sent to a room R in which a manual alarm has been triggered (variable W refers to whom should be called: police or firemen). This is because a guard is already there: the one who sounded the alarm. As will be clear below, this is best written as a constraint, rather than included into the filtering rules. Intention rules IR_2 and IR_3 specify that firemen and police should be called to go to room R whenever the head of the rule is a current desire.

It is important to note that, if the manual-alarm constraint of IR_1 is coded in the strict filtering rules, we should add this constraint in the body of each of the four rules. Keeping this constraint at intention-rules level allows us to write simpler filtering rules. For the agent A^s the policy p^s for selecting intentions will be simple, taking the set App of applicable intention rules and returning the set containing their heads:

$$p^s(App) = \{h \mid (h \Leftarrow P, C) \in App\}$$

Next, we introduce a series of sets of beliefs (B_0 through B_3) describing different scenarios. For each of them, the set of selected intentions will be calculated. In order to keep the example small and simple, we place our security agent in a building with two rooms: $r1$ and $r2$. The initial set of beliefs is:

$$B_0 = \left\{ \begin{array}{l} hi\_temp(r1), \quad smoke(r1), \\ \sim camera(r1), \ \sim motion(r1), \\ \sim hi\_temp(r2), \sim smoke(r2), \\ \sim camera(r2), \ \sim motion(r2) \end{array} \right\}$$

Where positive literals represent a sensor that has fired, whereas negative literals mean the opposite. These beliefs, along with the filtering rules, give us two undefeated arguments for $call(firemen, r1)$:

$$\langle \{call(firemen, r1) \prec hi\_temp(r1)\}, call(firemen, r1) \rangle,$$
$$\langle \{call(firemen, r1) \prec smoke(r1)\}, call(firemen, r1) \rangle.$$

Then, the set of current desires is $D_0^c = \{call(firemen, r1)\}$, which means that the only applicable intention rule is IR_2, and the set of selected intentions consists of the head of IR_2, that is $I_0^s = D_0^c = \{call(firemen, r1)\}$.

Observation: To avoid the system to keep sending guards to a room, we will assume that queries about desires are performed only when the set of beliefs has changed.

Suppose now a different situation, in which not only the temperature and smoke sensors in room $r1$ had fired, but also did the motion sensor in room $r2$. The new set of beliefs is:

$$B_1 = \left\{ \begin{array}{l} hi\_temp(r1), \quad smoke(r1), \\ \sim camera(r1), \ \sim motion(r1), \\ \sim hi\_temp(r2), \sim smoke(r2), \\ \sim camera(r2), \ motion(r2) \end{array} \right\}$$

As before, $call(firemen, r1)$ has two undefeated arguments. In addition, now there is one argument for calling the police:

$$\langle \{call(police, r2) \prec motion(r2)\}, call(police, r2) \rangle,$$

which is attacked by:

$$\langle \{\sim call(police, r2) \prec motion(r2), \sim camera(r2)\}, \sim call(police, r2) \rangle.$$

Since the argument for not calling the police is more specific than the other, the argument supporting $call(police, r2)$ is defeated and does not belong to D_1^c (note that $\sim call(police, r2)$ is warranted). In addition to this, there is an empty argument for $send\_guard(r2)$ from the strict rule $(send\_guard(R) \leftarrow motion(R), \sim camera(R))$. Thus, we have $D_1^c = \{call(firemen, r1), send\_guard(r2)\}$. Intention rule IR_1 is applicable, because its precondition holds: $send\_guard(r2) \in D_1^c$, and its constraint is satisfied: $manual\_alarm(W, r2) \notin B_1$. Intention rule IR_2 is also applicable, because $call(firemen, r1) \in D_1^c$. Hence, again we have that the current set of selected intentions equals the set of current desires, $i.e.,$ $I_1^s = D_1^c$. This will happen whenever the manual alarm is not triggered, since the set of intention rules IR^s is quite simple (rules have no preconditions nor constraints, excepting IR_1), and so is the policy (to take the head of every applicable intention rule as a selected intention).

Now suppose that the situation in room $r1$ is now normal, but the motion sensor in room $r2$ fired, and a guard has been sent to that room to check if an intruder has effectively entered there. Let us assume that the guard finds a thief in room $r2$. Then, the guard triggers the manual alarm, which changes the set of beliefs of the security-system agent:

$$B_2 = \begin{cases} \sim hi\_temp(r1), & \sim smoke(r1), \\ \sim camera(r1), & \sim motion(r1), \\ \sim hi\_temp(r2), & \sim smoke(r2), \\ \sim camera(r2), & motion(r2), \\ manual\_alarm(police, r2) \end{cases}$$

The following arguments for and against $call(police, r2)$ are built:

$$\mathcal{A}_1^s = \langle\{call(police, r2) \prec motion(r2)\}, call(police, r2)\rangle,$$
$$\mathcal{A}_2^s = \langle\{\sim call(police, r2) \prec motion(r2), \sim camera(r2)\}, \sim call(police, r2)\rangle,$$
$$\mathcal{A}_3^s = \langle\{call(police, r2) \prec manual\_alarm(police, r2)\}, call(police, r2)\rangle.$$

Argument $\mathcal{A}_1^s$ has $\mathcal{A}_2^s$ as proper defeater, since the latter is more specific than the former. In turn, $\mathcal{A}_2^s$ is blocked by defeater $\mathcal{A}_3^s$, reinstating $\mathcal{A}_1^s$. Thus, the desire $call(police, r2)$ is now warranted, and belongs to D_2^c. Desire $send\_guard(r2)$ is also in D_2^c from the strict rule $(send\_guard(R) \leftarrow motion(R), \sim camera(R))$. Therefore, $D_2^c = \{call(police, r2), send\_guard(r2)\}$. Note that now intention rule IR_1 is not applicable, because its constraint $(not\ manual\_alarm(police, r2))$ does not hold. Here, the only applicable intention rule is IR_3. Thus, the set of selected intentions is $I_2^s = \{call(police, r2)\}$, which differs from D_2^c. It is a sensible decision not to send a guard to a room when the police is already being sent there by a guard in that room.

Finally, consider that sensors do not detect anything abnormal, then:

$$B_3 = \begin{cases} \sim hi\_temp(r1), \sim smoke(r1), \\ \sim camera(r1), \sim motion(r1), \\ \sim hi\_temp(r2), \sim smoke(r2), \\ \sim camera(r2), \sim motion(r2), \end{cases}$$

This set of beliefs builds no arguments for any desire from the filtering rules. Then, the set of current desires is empty, and so is the set of selected intentions, $i.e.,$ $D_3^c = I_3^s = \emptyset$. The system will remain in this state until a sensor is fired.

The choice of a cautious agent instead of a bold one is clear when analyzing the latter case. A bold agent would select every desire as a current desire, since there are no arguments for nor against any of them:

$$D_3'^c = \left\{ \begin{array}{l} send\_guard(r1), send\_guard(r2), \\ call(firemen, r1), call(firemen, r2), \\ call(police, r1), call(police, r2) \end{array} \right\}$$

Regarding intention rules, all of them will be applicable, and therefore $I_3'^s = D_3'^c$. This means that guards will be sent to rooms $r1$ and $r2$, and both the police and firemen will be called to check on both rooms. Clearly, this is not the intended behavior for the security-system agent.

8 Related Work

The use of defeasible argumentation in BDI architectures is not new and it was originally suggested in [7], and more recently in [8]. Also in [9] and [10] a formalism for reasoning about beliefs and desires is given, but they do not use argumentation.

Recently, Rahwan and Amgoud [11] have proposed an argumentation-based approach for practical reasoning that extends [12] and [13], introducing three different instantiations of Dung's framework to reason about beliefs, desires and plans, respectively. This work is, in our view, the one most related to ours. Both approaches use defeasible argumentation for reasoning about beliefs and desires (in their work, they also reason about plans, but this is out of the scope of our presentation). Like us, they separate in the language those rules for reasoning about belief from those rules for reasoning about desires; and, in both approaches, it is possible to represent contradictory information about beliefs and desires. Both approaches construct arguments supporting competing desires, and they are compared and evaluated to decide which one prevails. Their notion of *desire rule* is similar to our *filtering rules*.

In their approach, two different argumentation frameworks are needed to reason about desires: one framework for beliefs rules and another framework for desires rules. The last one depends directly on the first one, and since there are two kinds of arguments, a policy for comparing mixed arguments is given. In our case, only one argumentation formalism is used for reasoning with both types of rules. In their object language, beliefs and desires include a certainty factor for every formula, and no explicit mention of perceived information is given. In our case, uncertainty is represented by defeasible rules [2] and perceived beliefs are explicitly treated by the model. Besides, the argumentation formalism used in their approach differs from ours: their comparison of arguments relies on the certainty factor given to each formula, and they do not distinguish between proper and blocking defeaters. Another fundamental difference is that we permit the definition of different types of agents. This feature adds great flexibility in the construction of an agent.

9 Conclusions

We have shown how a deliberative agent can represent its perception and beliefs using a defeasible logic program. The information perceived directly from the environment is represented with a subset of perceived beliefs that is dynamically updated, and a set formed with strict rules and facts represent other static knowledge of the agent. In addition to this, defeasible argumentation is used to warrant agents (derived) beliefs. Strict and defeasible filtering rules have been introduced to represent knowledge regarding desires. Defeasible argumentation is used for selecting a proper desire that fits in the particular situation the agent is involved. With this formalism, agents can reason about its desires and select the appropriate ones.

We allow the representation of different agent types, each of which will specify a different way to perform the filtering process. In our approach, an intention is a current desire that the agent can commit to pursue. The agent is provided with a set of intention rules that specify under what conditions an intention could be achieved. If there is more than one applicable intention rule, then a policy is used to define a preference criterion among them. Thus, intention policies give the agent a mechanism for deciding which intentions should be selected in the current situation.

In this work, we have shown how to implement two rather different kinds of agents using our model. We discussed their similarities and differences, stressing the point of the selection of the set of intentions, which is bound to be a singleton in one application, whereas is unrestricted in the other. Another difference regards to the way each of these agents perceive and gather beliefs. Regarding the sets of desires of both applications, they do not have any important structural difference; in fact, they coincide in not having complementary literals. However, it is difficult to conceive an application domain with a set of desires containing complementary literals. Usually, an argument concluding the complement of a desire has the purpose of "stopping" the justification (in the sense of warrant) of that desire, rather than supporting the opposite desire.

As future work, further research will be directed towards the improvement of the implementation of the proposed architecture. We plan to use a DeLP-Server [14], which provides a Defeasible Logic Programming reasoning service and allows client-agents to perform contextual queries.

References

1. Rotstein, N., García, A., Simari, G.: Reasoning from desires to intentions: A dialectical framework. In: Proceedings of the 22nd. AAAI Conference on Artificial Intelligence, pp. 136–141 (2007)
2. García, A., Simari, G.: Defeasible logic programming: An argumentative approach. Theory Practice of Logic Programming 4(1), 95–138 (2004)
3. Lifschitz, V.: Foundations of logic programming. In: Brewka, G. (ed.) Principles of Knowledge Representation. CSLI, pp. 69–127 (1996)
4. Rotstein, N., García, A.: Defeasible reasoning about beliefs and desires. In: Proc. of the 11th NMR, pp. 429–436 (2006)
5. Falappa, M., Kern-Isberner, G., Simari, G.: Belief revision, explanations and defeasible reasoning. Artificial Intelligence Journal 141, 1–28 (2002)
6. Fuhrmann, A.: An Essay on Contraction. In: Studies in Logic, Language and Information, CSLI Publications, Stanford, CA (1997)
7. Bratman, M.E., Israel, D., Pollack, M.: Plans and resource-bounded practical reasoning. In: Cummins, R., Pollock, J.L. (eds.) Philosophy and AI: Essays at the Interface, pp. 1–22. MIT Press, Cambridge (1991)

8. Parsons, S., Sierra, C., Jennings, N.: Agents that reason and negotiate by arguing. Journal of Logic and Computation 8(3), 261–292 (1998)
9. Thomason, R.: Desires and defaults: A framework for planning with inferred goals. In: Proc. of the seventh KR, pp. 702–713 (2000)
10. Broersen, J., Dastani, M., Hulstijn, J., Huang, Z., van der Torre, L.: The boid architecture: conficts between beliefs, obligations, intentions and desires. In: Proc. of 5th Int. Conf. on Autonomous Agents, pp. 9–16. ACM Press, New York (2001)
11. Rahwan, I., Amgoud, L.: An argumentation-based approach for practical reasoning. In: Proc. of the 5th AAMAS (2006)
12. Amgoud, L.: A formal framework for handling conflicting desires. In: Nielsen, T.D., Zhang, N.L. (eds.) ECSQARU 2003. LNCS (LNAI), vol. 2711, pp. 552–563. Springer, Heidelberg (2003)
13. Amgoud, L., Cayrol, C.: A reasoning model based on the production of acceptable arguments. Annals of Mathematics and Artificial Intelligence 34(1-3), 197–215 (2002)
14. García, A., Rotstein, N., Tucat, M., Simari, G.: An Argumentative Reasoning Service for Deliberative Agents. In: Zhang, Z., Siekmann, J.H. (eds.) KSEM 2007. LNCS (LNAI), vol. 4798, Springer, Heidelberg (2007)

Arguing and Explaining Classifications

Leila Amgoud and Mathieu Serrurier

Institut de Recherche en Informatique de Toulouse (IRIT)
118, route de Narbonne,
31062 Toulouse Cedex 4 France
{amgoud,serrurier}@irit.fr

Abstract. Argumentation is a promising approach used by autonomous agents for reasoning about inconsistent knowledge, based on the construction and the comparison of arguments. In this paper, we apply this approach to the classification problem, whose purpose is to construct from a set of training examples a model (or hypothesis) that assigns a class to any new example.

We propose a general formal argumentation-based model that constructs arguments for/against each possible classification of an example, evaluates them, and determines among the conflicting arguments the acceptable ones. Finally, a "valid" classification of the example is suggested. Thus, not only the class of the example is given, but also the reasons behind that classification are provided to the user as well in a form that is easy to grasp.

We show that such an argumentation-based approach for classification offers other advantages, like for instance classifying examples even when the set of training examples is inconsistent, and considering more general preference relations between hypotheses. Moreover, we show that in the particular case of concept learning, the results of version space theory are retrieved in an elegant way in our argumentation framework.

Keywords: Argumentation, Classification.

1 Introduction

Argumentation has become an Artificial Intelligence keyword for the last fifteen years, especially in sub-fields such as non monotonic reasoning, inconsistency-tolerant reasoning, multiple-source information systems [1,7,9,3]. Argumentation follows basically three steps: i) to construct arguments and counter-arguments for a statement, ii) to select the "acceptable" ones and, finally, iii) to determine whether the statement can be accepted or not.

This paper claims that argumentation can also be used as an alternative approach for the problem of classification. Classification aims at building *models* that describe a *concept* from a set of *training examples*. The models are intended to be sufficiently general in order to be reused on new examples. When the concept to learn is binary, i.e. examples of that concept can be either true or false, the problem is called *concept learning*.

I. Rahwan, S. Parsons, and C. Reed (Eds.): ArgMAS 2007, LNAI 4946, pp. 164–177, 2008.

In our argumentation-based approach, the classification problem is reformulated as follows: given a set of examples (the training ones, and/or additional examples) and a set of hypotheses, what should be the class of a given example? To answer this question, arguments are constructed in favor of all the possible classifications of that example. A classification can come either from an hypothesis, or from a training example. The obtained arguments may be conflicting since it may be the case that the same example is affected to different classes. Finally, a "valid" classification of the example is suggested. Thus, not only the class of the example is given, but also the reasons behind that classification are provided to the user as well in a form that is easy to grasp.

We show that such an argumentation-based approach for classification offers other advantages, like for instance classifying examples even when the set of training examples is inconsistent, and considering more general preference relations between hypotheses. Moreover, we show that in the particular case of concept learning, the results of the version space theory developed by Mitchell in [4] are retrieved in an elegant way in our argumentation framework. We show that the acceptability semantics defined in [2] allow us to identify and characterize the version space as well as its lower and upper bounds. In sum, this paper proposes a formal theoretical framework for handling, analysing and explaining the problem of classification. The framework presents the following features that make it original and flexible:

1. it handles i) the case of a consistent set of training examples; ii) the case of an inconsistent set of training examples; and iii) the case of an empty set of training examples;
2. it allows one to reason directly on the set of hypotheses;
3. examples are classified on the basis of the whole set of hypotheses rather than only one hypothesis as it is the case in standard classification models. Indeed, in the standard approach, a unique hypothesis is chosen, and all the examples are classified on the basis of that hypothesis.
4. it presents several original and intuitive decision criteria for choosing the class of an example.

The paper is organized as follows. We first present the classification problem, then we introduce the basic argumentation framework of Dung [2]. The third section introduces our argumentation-based framework for classification as well as its properties.

2   Classification Problem

The aim of this section is to introduce the classification problem. Let $\mathcal{X}$ denote a *feature space* used for describing examples. Elements of $\mathcal{X}$ may then be pairs (attribute, value), first order facts, etc. This set $\mathcal{X}$ is supposed to be equipped with an equivalence relation $\equiv$. Let $\mathcal{C} = \{c_1, \ldots, c_n\}$ be a *concept space*, or a set of possible distinct classes.

A classification problem takes as input a *hypothesis space* $\mathcal{H}$, and a set $\mathcal{S}$ of *m training examples*.

$$\mathcal{S} = \{(x_i, c_i)_{i=1,\ldots,m} \text{ s.t } x_i \subset \mathcal{X} \text{ and } c_i \in C\}$$

An important notion in classification is that of consistency. In fact, a set of examples is said to be consistent if it does not contain two logically equivalent examples with two different classes. Formally:

Definition 1 (Consistency). *Let* $\mathcal{T} = \{(x_i, c_i)_{i=1,\ldots,n}$ *s.t* $x_i \in \mathcal{X}$ *and* $c_i \in C\}$ *be a set of examples.* $\mathcal{T}$ *is* consistent *iff* $\nexists$ (x_1, c_1), $(x_2, c_2) \in \mathcal{T}$ *such that* $x_1 \equiv x_2$ *and* $c_1 \neq c_2$. *Otherwise,* $\mathcal{T}$ *is said to be* inconsistent.

Regarding the *hypothesis space* $\mathcal{H}$, it may be, for instance, decision trees, propositional sets of rules, neural nets, etc. An *hypothesis h* is a mapping from $\mathcal{X}$ to $\mathcal{C}$ (i.e. $h: \mathcal{X} \mapsto \mathcal{C}$). Before defining the output of the framework, let us first introduce a key notion, that of *soundness*.

Definition 2 (Soundness). *Let* $h \in \mathcal{H}$. *An hypothesis h is* sound *with respect to a training example* $(x, c) \in \mathcal{S}$ *iff* $h(x) = c$. *If* $\forall (x_i, c_i) \in \mathcal{S}$, *h is sound w.r.t* (x_i, c_i), *then h is said to be* sound *with* $\mathcal{S}$.

The general task of classification is to identify an $h \in \mathcal{H}$ that is sound with respect to the training examples. This hypothesis will be next used for classifying new examples. The most common approach for identifying this hypothesis is to use a greedy exploration of the hypothesis space, guided by a preference relation on hypothesis. This preference relation may be encoded by a utility function or by a syntactic or a semantic relation. Utility functions are generally based on the accuracy of the hypothesis (proportion of well classified examples) weighted by some complexity criteria (number of rules, etc.). Utility functions encode usually a total order. Syntactic relations may be for instance entailment or subsumption in the logical case. In this case it encodes a partial preorder on $\mathcal{H}$.

Example 1 (Learning the concept sunny day). In this example, the feature space is a pair (attribute, value). Three attributes are considered: pressure, temperature, and humidity. The concept to learn is supposed to be binary, thus $C = \{0, 1\}$. Four training examples are given, and are summarized in the Table below. For instance (pressure, low), (temperature, medium), and (humidity, high) is a negative example for the concept a sunny day, whereas the (pressure, medium), (temperature, medium), and (humidity, low) is a positive one.

pressure	temperature	humidity	sunny
low	medium	high	0
medium	medium	low	1
low	medium	medium	0
medium	high	medium	1

Let us suppose that the hypothesis space $\mathcal{H}$ is the space of *constraints* on the values of each attribute. Indeed, the constraints are conjunctions of accepted values of attributes. The special constraint $\emptyset$ (resp. ?) means that no (resp. all) values of attributes are accepted. If a vector of values of attributes match all the constraints, then it is considered as a *positive* example, otherwise it is a *negative* one. The hypotheses $\langle \emptyset, \emptyset, \emptyset \rangle$ and $\langle ?, ?, ? \rangle$ are respectively the lower and the upper bound of the hypothesis space $\mathcal{H}$.

3 Abstract Argumentation Framework

Argumentation is a reasoning model that follows the following steps:

1. Constructing *arguments* and counter-arguments.
2. Defining the *strengths* of those arguments.
3. Evaluating the *acceptability* of the different arguments.
4. Concluding or defining the *justified conclusions*.

In [2], an argumentation system is defined as follows:

Definition 3 (Argumentation system). *An* argumentation system *(AS) is a pair* $\langle \mathcal{A}, \mathcal{R} \rangle$. $\mathcal{A}$ *is a set of arguments and* $\mathcal{R} \subseteq \mathcal{A} \times \mathcal{A}$ *is a defeat relation. We say that an argument A defeats an argument B iff* $(A, B) \in \mathcal{R}$ *(or* $A \mathcal{R} B$*).*

Note that to each argumentation system is associated an oriented graph whose nodes are the different arguments, and the edges represent the defeasibility relationship between them. Among all the conflicting arguments, it is important to know which arguments to keep for inferring conclusions or for making decisions. In [2], different semantics for the notion of acceptability have been proposed. Let us recall them here.

Definition 4 (Conflict-free, Defence). *Let* $\mathcal{B} \subseteq \mathcal{A}$.

– $\mathcal{B}$ *is* conflict-free *iff there exist no* A_i, $A_j \in \mathcal{B}$ *such that* $A_i \mathcal{R} A_j$.
– $\mathcal{B}$ defends *an argument* A_i *iff for each argument* $A_j \in \mathcal{A}$, *if* $A_j \mathcal{R} A_i$, *then there exists* $A_k \in \mathcal{B}$ *such that* $A_k \mathcal{R} A_j$.

Definition 5 (Acceptability semantics). *Let* $\mathcal{B}$ *be a conflict-free set of arguments, and let* $\mathcal{F}: 2^{\mathcal{A}} \mapsto 2^{\mathcal{A}}$ *be a function such that* $\mathcal{F}(\mathcal{B}) = \{ A \mid \mathcal{B} \text{ defends } A \}$.

– $\mathcal{B}$ *is a* complete extension *iff* $\mathcal{B} = \mathcal{F}(\mathcal{B})$.
– $\mathcal{B}$ *is a* grounded extension *iff it is the minimal (w.r.t. set-inclusion) complete extension.*
– $\mathcal{B}$ *is a* preferred extension *iff it is a maximal (w.r.t. set-inclusion) complete extension.*
– $\mathcal{B}$ *is a* stable extension *iff it is a preferred extension that defeats all arguments in* $\mathcal{A} \backslash \mathcal{B}$.

Let $\{\mathcal{E}_1, ..., \mathcal{E}_n\}$ *be the set of all possible extensions under a given semantics.*

Note that there is only one grounded extension which may be empty. It contains all the arguments that are not defeated, and also the arguments which are defended directly or indirectly by non-defeated arguments.

The last step of an argumentation process consists of determining, among all the conclusions of the different arguments, the "good" ones, called *justified conclusions*.

4   An Argumentation Framework for Classification

The aim of this section is to propose an instantiation of the general and abstract framework of Dung that allows the classification of examples. Throughout this section, we will consider a features space $\mathcal{X}$, a concept space $\mathcal{C} = \{c_1, \ldots, c_n\}$, a (maybe *inconsistent*) set $\mathcal{S}$ of $m > 0$ training examples, a hypotheses space $\mathcal{H}$ that is equipped with an arbitrary preference relation $\succeq$. Thus, $\succeq \subseteq \mathcal{H} \times \mathcal{H}$, and $\mathcal{H}$ is supposed to be a *partial preorder*.

In order to instantiate the abstract framework of Dung, one needs to define the set $\mathcal{A}$ of arguments as well as the defeat relation between those arguments.

In our particular application, one needs to argue about particular classifications, thus arguments are constructed in favor of assigning particular classes from $\mathcal{C}$ to an example in $\mathcal{X}$. Indeed, an argument in favor of the pair (x, c) represents the reason for assigning the class c to the example x. Two reasons can be distinguished:

1. (x, c) is a training example in $\mathcal{S}$,
2. there exists a hypothesis $h \in \mathcal{H}$ that classifies x in c.

Definition 6 (Argument). *An argument is a triplet $A = \langle h, x, c \rangle$ such that:*

1. *$h \in \mathcal{H}$, $x \in \mathcal{X}$, $c \in \mathcal{C}$*
2. *If $h \neq \emptyset$, then $c = h(x)$*
3. *If $h = \emptyset$, then $(x, c) \in \mathcal{S}$*

h is called the support *of the argument, and (x, c) its* conclusion. *Let* Example$(A) = x$, *and* Class$(A) = c$.
Let $\mathcal{A}$ be the set of arguments built from $(\mathcal{H}, \mathcal{X}, \mathcal{C})$.

Note that from the above definition, for any training example $(x_i, c_i) \in \mathcal{S}$, $\exists \langle \emptyset, x_i, c_i \rangle \in \mathcal{A}$. Let $\mathcal{A}_\mathcal{S} = \{\langle \emptyset, x, c \rangle \in \mathcal{A}\}$ (i.e. the set of arguments coming from the training examples). Since the set $\mathcal{S}$ of training examples is not empty, then $\mathcal{A}_\mathcal{S}$ is not empty as well.

Property 1. Let $\mathcal{S}$ be a set of training examples.

- $|\mathcal{S}| = |\mathcal{A}_\mathcal{S}|$[1].
- $\mathcal{A}_\mathcal{S} \neq \emptyset$.

Proof. The first point follows from the above definition, and from the fact that an hypothesis h cannot be empty. The second point follows directly from the first property, i.e. $|\mathcal{S}| = |\mathcal{A}_\mathcal{S}|$, and the assumption that $\mathcal{S} \neq \emptyset$.

Let us illustrate the notion of argument through example 1.

Example 2. In example 1, there are exactly four arguments with an empty support, and they correspond to the training examples: $\mathcal{A}_\emptyset = \{a_1 = \langle \emptyset, (\text{pressure, low}) \wedge (\text{temperature, medium}) \wedge (\text{humidity,high}), 0 \rangle$,

---

[1] || denotes the cardinal of a given set.

$a_2 = \langle \emptyset, \text{(pressure, medium)} \wedge \text{(temperature, medium)} \wedge \text{(humidity, low)}, 1 \rangle$,
$a_3 = \langle \emptyset, \text{(pressure, low)} \wedge \text{(temperature, medium)} \wedge \text{(humidity, medium)}, 0 \rangle$,
$a_4 = \langle \emptyset, \text{(pressure, medium)} \wedge \text{(temperature, high)} \wedge \text{(humidity, medium)}, 1 \rangle \}$.
There are also arguments with a non-empty support such as:
$\langle a_5 = \langle \ ? \ , \text{medium} \vee \text{high}, \ ? \rangle, \text{(pressure, low)} \wedge \text{(temperature, high)} \wedge \text{(humidity, high)}, 1 \rangle \}$,
$a_6 = \langle \langle \text{medium} \vee \text{high}, \ ?, \ ? \rangle, \text{(pressure, low)} \wedge \text{(temperature, high)} \wedge \text{(humidity, high)}, 0 \rangle$,
$a_7 = \langle \langle \text{medium}, \text{medium} \vee \text{high}, \ ? \rangle, \text{(pressure, low)} \wedge \text{(temperature, high)} \wedge \text{(humidity, high)}, 0 \rangle$.

In [1,7,9], it has been argued that arguments may have different strengths depending on the quality of information used to construct them. In [9], for instance, arguments built from specific information are stronger than arguments built from more general ones. In our particular application, it is clear that arguments with an empty support are stronger than arguments with a non-empty one. This reflects the fact that classifications given by training examples take precedence over ones given by hypotheses in $\mathcal{H}$. It is also natural to consider that arguments using most preferred hypothesis are stronger than arguments with less preferred ones.

Definition 7 (Comparing arguments). *Let* $\langle h, x, c \rangle$, $\langle h', x', c' \rangle$ *be two arguments of* $\mathcal{A}$. $\langle h, x, c \rangle$ *is preferred to* $\langle h', x', c' \rangle$, *denoted by* $\langle h, x, c \rangle$ *Pref* $\langle h', x', c' \rangle$, *iff:*

- $h = \emptyset$ *and* $h' \neq \emptyset$, *or*
- $h \succeq h'$.

Property 2. The relation Pref is a partial preorder.

Proof. This is due to the fact that the relation $\succeq$ is a partial preorder.

Now that the set of arguments is defined, it is possible to define the defeasibility relation $\mathcal{R}$ between arguments in $\mathcal{A}$. Here again, there are two ways in which an argument A can attack another argument B:

1. by *rebutting* its *conclusion*. This situation occurs when the two arguments have contradictory conclusions, i.e. the same example is classified in different ways.
2. by *undercutting* its *support*. This occurs when the support of B classifies in a different way the example of the conclusion of A. However, this relation is only restricted to training examples. Indeed, only arguments built from training examples are allowed to undercut other arguments. The idea behind this is that training examples are the only, in some sense, certain information one has, and thus cannot be defeated by hypothesis. However, hypothesis have controversial status.

Definition 8 (Rebutting). *Let* $\langle h, x, c \rangle$, $\langle h', x', c' \rangle$ *be two arguments of* $\mathcal{A}$. $\langle h, x, c \rangle$ *rebuts* $\langle h', x', c' \rangle$ *iff* $x \equiv x'$, $c \neq c'$.

Example 3. In example 2, we have for instance :
a_5 rebuts a_6, a_5 rebuts a_7, a_6 rebuts a_5, and a_7 *rebuts* a_5.

Definition 9 (Undercutting). *Let* $\langle h, x, c \rangle$, $\langle h', x', c' \rangle$ *be two arguments of* $\mathcal{A}$. $\langle h, x, c \rangle$ *undercuts* $\langle h', x', c' \rangle$ *iff* $h = \emptyset$ *and* $h'(x) \neq c$.

Example 4. In example 2, we have for instance :
a_1 undercuts a_5, a_2 undercuts a_5, a_3 undercuts a_5, and a_4 *undercuts* a_5.

Note that the rebutting and undercutting relations are used in most argumentation systems that handle inconsistency in knowledge bases.

Property 3. If $\mathcal{S}$ is consistent, then $\nexists$ A, $B \in \mathcal{A}_\mathcal{S}$ such that A rebuts B, or A undercuts B.

Proof. Let $A = \langle \emptyset, x, u \rangle$, $B = \langle \emptyset, x', u' \rangle \in \mathcal{S}$ such that A rebuts B. According to Definition 8, $x \equiv x'$ and $u \neq u'$. This contradicts the fact that $\mathcal{S}$ is consistent.

The two above conflict relations are brought together in a unique relation, called "Defeat".

Definition 10 (Defeat). *Let* $A = \langle h, x, c \rangle$, $B = \langle h', x', c' \rangle$ *be two arguments of* $\mathcal{A}$. *A defeats B iff:*

1. *A rebuts (resp. undercuts) B, and*
2. *(A Pref B), or (not(A Pref B) and not(B Pref A))*

Example 5. With the argument defined in ex. 2 we have for instance : a_1 *defeats* a_5, a_2 *defeats* a_5, a_3 *defeats* a_5, a_4 *defeats* a_5, a_5 *defeats* a_6, a_5 *defeats* a_7 and a_6 *defeats* a_5.

From the above definition, it is easy to check that an argument with an empty-support cannot be defeated by an argument with a non-empty support.

Property 4. $\forall$ $A \in \mathcal{A}_\mathcal{S}$, $\nexists$ $B \in \mathcal{A} \backslash \mathcal{A}_\mathcal{S}$ s.t B defeats A.

Proof. Let $A \in \mathcal{A}_\mathcal{S}$ and $B \in \mathcal{A} \backslash \mathcal{A}_\mathcal{S}$ such that B defeats A. This means that B rebuts A (because according to Definition 9, an argument with a non-empty support cannot undercut an argument with an empty one. Moreover, according to Definition 10, we have either B Pref A, or (not(B Pref A) and not(A Pref B)). This is impossible because according to Definition 7, arguments in $\mathcal{A}_\mathcal{S}$ are always preferred to arguments with a non-empty support.

The argumentation system for classification is then the following:

Definition 11 (Argumentation system). *An* argumentation system *for classification (ASC) is a pair* $\langle \mathcal{A}, defeat \rangle$, *where* $\mathcal{A}$ *is the set of arguments (see Definition 6) and defeat is the relation defined in Definition 10.*

Let us now identify the acceptable arguments of the above ASC. It is clear that the arguments that are not defeated at all will be acceptable. Let $\mathcal{U}$ denote that set of undefeated arguments.

Proposition 1. *If $\mathcal{S}$ is consistent, then $\mathcal{A}_{\mathcal{S}} \subseteq \mathcal{U}$.*

Proof. Let $A \in \mathcal{A}_{\mathcal{S}}$. Let us assume that $\exists B \in \mathcal{A}$ such that B defeats A. According to Property 4, $B \notin \mathcal{A} \backslash \mathcal{A}_{\mathcal{S}}$. Thus, $B \in \mathcal{A}_{\mathcal{S}}$. Moreover, B defeats A means that B rebuts A. This means then that A classifies a training example in u, and B classifies an equivalent example in $u' \neq u$. This contradicts the fact that the set $\mathcal{S}$ is consistent.

As said in Section 3, one of the acceptability semantics is the so-called 'grounded extension'. Such an extension is unique and maybe empty. However, we show that when the set $\mathcal{S}$ of training examples is consistent, this grounded extension is not empty.

Proposition 2 (Grounded extension). *If $\mathcal{S}$ is consistent, then the argumentation system $\langle \mathcal{A}, defeat \rangle$ has a non empty grounded extension $\mathcal{E}$.*

Proof. This is due to the fact that $\mathcal{A}_{\mathcal{S}} \neq \emptyset$ and $\mathcal{A}_{\mathcal{S}} \subseteq \mathcal{U}$.

Note that the system $\langle \mathcal{A}, defeat \rangle$ is not always finite. By finite we mean that each argument is defeated by a finite number of arguments. This is due to the fact that $\mathcal{H}$ and $\mathcal{X}$ are not always finite.

Proposition 3. *If $\mathcal{H}$ and $\mathcal{X}$ are finite, then the system $\langle \mathcal{A}, defeat \rangle$ is finite.*

When an argumentation system is finite, its characteristic function $\mathcal{F}$ is continuous. Consequently, the least fixed point of this function can be defined by an iterative application of $\mathcal{F}$ to the empty set.

Proposition 4. *If the argumentation system $\langle \mathcal{A}, defeat \rangle$ is finite, then the grounded extension $\mathcal{E}$ is:*

$$\mathcal{E} = \bigcup \mathcal{F}^{i \geq 0}(\emptyset) = \mathcal{U} \cup [\bigcup_{i \geq 1} \mathcal{F}^i(\mathcal{U})].$$

Let us now analyze the other acceptability semantics, namely preferred and stable ones. In general, the ASC has at least one preferred extension that may be empty. However, as for the case of grounded extension, we can show that in the particular case of a consistent set of training examples, the ASC has at least one non-empty preferred extension.

Proposition 5. *If $\mathcal{S}$ is consistent, then the ASC $\langle \mathcal{A}, defeat \rangle$ has $n \geq 1$ nonempty preferred extensions.*

Proof. In [2], it has been shown that the grounded extension is included in very preferred extension. Since the grounded extension is not empty (according to Proposition 2, then there exists at least one non-empty preferred extension).

In general, the preferred extensions of an argumentation system are not stable. However, we can show that when the set $\mathcal{C}$ contains only two possible classes, this means that the concept to learn is binary, these extensions coincide. This result is due to the fact that the oriented graph associated to the above ASC has no odd length circuits in this case. However, it may contain circuits of even length.

Proposition 6. *If $C = \{c_1, c_2\}$ with $c_1 \neq c_2$, then:*

- *The graph associated with the system $\langle \mathcal{A}, defeat \rangle$ has no odd length circuits.*
- *The preferred extensions and stable extensions of the system $\langle \mathcal{A}, defeat \rangle$ coincide.*

Proof (Sketch). **Part 1:** Let A, B, C be three arguments such that A defeats B, B defeats C, and C defeats A.

Case 1: Let us suppose that $A \in \mathcal{A}_S$.
According to Property 3, $B \in \mathcal{A} \backslash \mathcal{A}_S$. According to Property 4, C should be in $\mathcal{A} \backslash \mathcal{A}_S$. Contradiction because according to Property 4, C cannot defeat A, which is in $\mathcal{A}_S$.

Case 2: Let us suppose that $A, B, C \in \mathcal{A} \backslash \mathcal{A}_S$. This means that A rebuts B, B rebuts C, and C rebuts A (according to Definition 9). Consequently, $\mathtt{Example}(A) \equiv \mathtt{Example}(B) \equiv \mathtt{Example}(C)$, and $\mathtt{Value}(A) \neq \mathtt{Value}(B)$, $\mathtt{Value}(B) \neq \mathtt{Value}(C)$. Due to the fact that $\mathcal{U} = \{0, 1\}$, we have $\mathtt{Value}(A) = \mathtt{Value}(C)$. This contradicts the assumption that C rebuts A.

Part 2: This is a consequence of the fact that there is no odd circuits in the system.

Moreover, in this case the intersection of all the preferred (stable) extensions coincides with the grounded extension.

Proposition 7. *Let $\langle \mathcal{A}, defeat \rangle$ be an ASC. Let $\mathcal{E}$ be its grounded extension, and $\mathcal{E}_1, \ldots, \mathcal{E}_n$ its preferred (stable) extensions. If $C = \{c_1, c_2\}$ with $c_1 \neq c_2$, then $\mathcal{E} = \bigcap_{i=1,\ldots,n} \mathcal{E}_i$.*

The last step of an argumentation process consists of defining the *status* of the conclusions, in our case, the classification of examples. In what follows we present two decision criteria: The first one, called universal vote, consists of accepting those classifications that are in any extension. However, it is clear that this kind of voting may not classify all the examples. Thus, we propose a second criterion, called majority vote, that allows to associate a class with each example. The conclusions here are the ones that are supported by a majority of arguments that appear in the different extensions. Formally:

Definition 12. *Let $\langle \mathcal{A}, defeat \rangle$ be a ASC, and $\mathcal{E}_1, \ldots, \mathcal{E}_n$ its extensions under a given semantics. Let $x \in \mathcal{X}$ and $c \in \mathcal{C}$.*

Universal vote: x is universally classified in c iff $\forall \mathcal{E}_i$, $\exists <h, x, c> \in \mathcal{E}_i$. *UV denotes the set of all (x, c), such that x is universally classified in c.*

Majority vote: x is majoritarily classified in c iff $|\{<h, x, c> | \exists \mathcal{E}_i, <h, x, c> \in \mathcal{E}_i\}| \geq |\{<h, x, c'> | c' \neq c, \exists \mathcal{E}_i, <h, x, c'> \in \mathcal{E}_i\}|$. *MV denotes the set of all (x, c), such that x is majoritarily classified in c.*

The universally classified examples are those that are supported by arguments in all the extensions. From a classification point of view, these correspond to examples classified by the most preferred hypotheses. It is easy to check that the set of universally classified examples is included in the set of majoritarily classified ones.

Property 5. Let $\langle \mathcal{A}, defeat \rangle$ be a ASC, and $\mathcal{E}_1, \ldots, \mathcal{E}_n$ its extensions under a given semantics :

$$UV \subseteq MV$$

We can show that the above argumentation framework delivers "safe" results, since its sets of conclusions UV, MV are consistent. Formally:

Proposition 8. *Let* $\langle \mathcal{A}, defeat \rangle$ *be a ASC, and* UV, MV *its sets of conclusions. The sets* UV *and* MV *are consistent.*

5 Retrieving Version Space Theory

As said before, *concept learning* is a particular case of classification, where the concept to learn is binary. In [4], Mitchell has proposed the famous general and abstract framework, called *version space learning*, for concept learning. That framework takes as input a *consistent* set of *training examples* on the concept to learn. $\mathcal{C}$ contains only two classes, denoted respectively by 0 and 1. Thus, $\mathcal{C} = \{0, 1\}$. The set $\mathcal{H}$ is supposed to be equipped with a "particular" *partial preorder* $\succeq$ that reflects the idea that some hypothesis are more general than others in the sense that they classify positively more examples. This preorder defines a lattice on the hypothesis space. Formally:

Definition 13 (Generality order on hypothesis). *Let* h_1, $h_2 \in \mathcal{H}$. h_1 *is more general than* h_2, *denoted by* $h_1 \succeq h_2$, *iff* $\{x \in \mathcal{X} | h_1(x) = 1\} \supseteq \{x \in \mathcal{X} | h_2(x) = 1\}$.

The framework identifies the *version space*, which is the set $\mathcal{V}$ of all the hypothesis of $\mathcal{H}$ that are sound with $\mathcal{S}$. The idea is that a "good" hypothesis should at least classify the training examples correctly.

Definition 14 (Version space)

$$\mathcal{V} = \{h \in \mathcal{H} | \ h \text{ is sound with } \mathcal{S}\}$$

Version space learning aims at identifying the *upper* and the *lower* bounds of this version space $\mathcal{V}$. The upper bound will contain the most general hypothesis, i.e the ones that classify more examples, whereas the lower bound will contain the most specific ones, i.e the hypothesis that classify less examples.

Definition 15 (General hypotheses). *The set of* general hypothesis *is* $\mathcal{V}_G = \{h \in \mathcal{H} \mid h \text{ is sound with } \mathcal{S} \text{ and } \not\exists \ h' \in \mathcal{H} \text{ with } h' \text{ sound with } \mathcal{S}, \text{ and } h' \succeq h\}$.

Definition 16 (Specific hypotheses). *The set of* specific hypothesis *is* $\mathcal{V}_S = \{h \in \mathcal{H} \mid h \text{ is sound with } \mathcal{S} \text{ and } \not\exists \ h' \in \mathcal{H} \text{ with } h' \text{ sound with } \mathcal{S}, \text{ and } h \succeq h'\}$.

From the above definition, we have the following simple property characterizing the elements of $\mathcal{V}$.

Property 6. [4]

$$\mathcal{V} = \{h \in \mathcal{H} | \exists h_1 \in \mathcal{V}_S, \exists h_2 \in \mathcal{V}_G, h_2 \succeq h \succeq h_1\}$$

In [4], an algorithm that computes the version space $\mathcal{V}$ by identifying its upper and lower bounds $\mathcal{V}_S$ and $\mathcal{V}_G$ has been proposed.

The above framework has some limits. First, finding the version space is not sufficient for classifying examples out of the training set. This is due to possible conflicts between hypothesis. Second, it has been shown that the complexity of the algorithm that identifies $\mathcal{V}_S$ and $\mathcal{V}_G$ is very high. In order to palliate that limit, learning algorithms try in general to reach only one hypothesis in the version space by using heuristical exploration of $\mathcal{H}$ (from general to specific exploration, for instance FOIL [8], or from specific to general exploration, for instance PROGOL [6]). That hypothesis is then used for classifying new objects. Moreover, it is obvious that this framework does not support inconsistent set of examples:

Property 7. [4] If the set $\mathcal{S}$ is inconsistent, then the version space $\mathcal{V} = \emptyset$.

A consequence of the above result is that no concept can be learned. This problem may appear in the case of noisy training data set.

Let us now show how the above ASC can retrieve the results of the version space learning, namely the version space and its lower and upper bounds. Before doing that, we start first by introducing some useful notations.

Let Hyp be a function that returns for a given set of arguments, their non empty supports. In other words, this function returns all the hypothesis used to build arguments:

Definition 17. *Let $T \subseteq \mathcal{A}$.*

$$\mathrm{Hyp}(T) = \{h \mid \exists \langle h, x, u \rangle \in T \text{ and } h \neq \emptyset\}$$

Now we will show that the argumentation-based model for concept learning computes in an elegant way the version space $\mathcal{V}$.

Proposition 9. *Let $\langle \mathcal{A}, defeat \rangle$ be a ASC. Let $\mathcal{E}$ be its grounded extension, and $\mathcal{E}_1, \ldots, \mathcal{E}_n$ its preferred (stable) extensions. If the set $\mathcal{S}$ is consistent then:*

$$\mathrm{Hyp}(\mathcal{E}) = \mathrm{Hyp}(\mathcal{E}_1) = \ldots = \mathrm{Hyp}(\mathcal{E}_n) = \mathcal{V}$$

where $\mathcal{V}$ is the version space.

Proof. Let $\mathcal{E}_i$ be an extension under a given semantics.

$\mathrm{Hyp}(\mathcal{E}_i) \subseteq \mathcal{V}$: Let $h \in \mathrm{Hyp}(\mathcal{E}_i)$, then $\exists \langle h, x, u \rangle \in \mathcal{E}_i$.
Let us assume that $\exists (x_i, u_i) \in \mathcal{S}$ such that $h(x_i) \neq u_i$. This means $\langle \emptyset, x_i, u_i \rangle$ undercuts $\langle h, x, u \rangle$ (according to Definition 9). Consequently, $\langle \emptyset, x_i, u_i \rangle$ defeats $\langle h, x, u \rangle$. However, according to Property 1, $\langle \emptyset, x_i, u_i \rangle \in \mathcal{A}_\mathcal{S}$, thus $\langle \emptyset, x_i, u_i \rangle \in \mathcal{E}_i$. Contradiction because $\mathcal{E}_i$ is an extension, thus by definition it is conflict-free.

$\mathcal{V} \subseteq \mathrm{Hyp}(\mathcal{E}_i)$: Let $h \in \mathcal{V}$, and let us assume that $h \notin \mathrm{Hyp}(\mathcal{E}_i)$. Since $h \in \mathcal{V}$, then
$\forall (x_i, u_i) \in \mathcal{S}, h(x_i) = u_i$ (1)
Let $(x, u) \in \mathcal{S}$, thus $h(x) = u$ and consequently $\langle h, x, u \rangle \in \mathcal{A}$. Moreover, since $h \notin \mathrm{Hyp}(\mathcal{E})$, then $\langle h, x, u \rangle \notin E$. Thus, $\exists \langle h', x', u' \rangle$ that defeats $\langle h, x, u \rangle$.

- Case 1: $h' = \emptyset$. This means that $\langle \emptyset, x', u' \rangle$ undercuts $\langle h, x, u \rangle$ and $h(x') \neq u'$ Contradiction with (1).
- Case 2: $h' \neq \emptyset$. This means that $\langle h', x', u' \rangle$ rebuts $\langle h, x, u \rangle$. Consequently, $x \equiv x'$ and $u \neq u'$. However, since $h \in \mathcal{V}$, then h is sound with $\mathcal{S}$. Thus, $\langle \emptyset, x, u \rangle$ defeats $\langle h', x', u' \rangle$, then $\langle \emptyset, x, u \rangle$ defeats $\langle h, x, u \rangle$. Since $\langle \emptyset, x, u \rangle \in \mathcal{S}$, then $\langle h, x, u \rangle \in \mathcal{F}(\mathcal{C})$ and consequently, $\langle h, x, u \rangle \in \mathcal{E}_i$. Contradiction.

The above result is of great importance. It shows that to get the version space, one only needs to compute the grounded extension.

We can also show that if a given argument is in an extension $\mathcal{E}_i$, then any argument based on an hypothesis from the version space that supports the same conclusion is in that extension. Formally:

Proposition 10. *Let* $\langle \mathcal{A}, defeat \rangle$ *be a ASC, and* $\mathcal{E}_1, \ldots, \mathcal{E}_n$ *its extensions under a given semantics. If* $< h, x, u > \in \mathcal{E}_i$, *then* $\forall h' \in \mathcal{V}$ *s.t.* $h' \neq h$ *if* $h'(x) = u$ *then* $< h', x, u > \in \mathcal{E}_i$.

Using the grounded extension, one can characterize the upper and the lower bounds of the version space. The upper bound corresponds to the most preferred arguments (w.r.t Pref) of the grounded extension, whereas the lower bound corresponds to the less preferred ones.

Proposition 11. *Let* $\langle \mathcal{A}, defeat \rangle$ *be a ASC, and* $\mathcal{E}$ *its grounded extension.*

- $\mathcal{V}_G = \{h \mid \exists <h, x, u> \in \mathcal{E} \text{ s.t } \forall <h', x', u'> \in \mathcal{E}, \text{ not } (<h', x', u'> Pref <h, x, u>)\}$.
- $\mathcal{V}_S = \{h \mid \exists <h, x, u> \in \mathcal{E} \text{ s.t } \forall <h', x', u'> \in \mathcal{E}, \text{ not } (<h, x, u> Pref <h', x', u'>)\}$.

Proof.
$\mathcal{V}_G = \{h \mid \exists <h, x, u> \in \mathcal{E} \text{ s.t } \forall <h', x', u'> \in \mathcal{E}, \text{ not } (<h', x', u'> Pref <h, x, u>)\}$.
- Let $h \in \mathcal{V}_G$, thus $h \in \mathcal{V}$, and $\forall h' \in \mathcal{V}$, $h \succeq h'$. Since $h \in \mathcal{V}$, thus, $h \in \text{Hyp}(\mathcal{E})$, with $\mathcal{E}$ an extension. Then, $\exists \langle h, x, u \rangle \in \mathcal{E}$. Since $h \succeq h'$ for any $h' \in \mathcal{V}$, then $h \succeq h'$ for any $h' \in \text{Hyp}(\mathcal{E})$. Thus, $\langle h, x, u \rangle$ Pref $\langle h', x', u' \rangle$, $\forall \langle h', x', u' \rangle \in \mathcal{E}$.
- Let $\langle h, x, u \rangle \in \mathcal{E}$ such that $\forall \langle h', x', u' \rangle \in \mathcal{E}$, and $\text{not}(\langle h', x', u' \rangle Pref \langle h, x, u \rangle)$. Thus, $h \in \text{Hyp}(\mathcal{E})$, and $\forall h' \in \text{Hyp}(\mathcal{E})$, $\text{not}(h' \succeq h)$, thus $h \in \mathcal{V}_G$.

$\mathcal{V}_S = \{h \mid \exists <h, x, u> \in \mathcal{E} \text{ s.t } \forall <h', x', u'> \in \mathcal{E}, \text{ not } (<h, x, u> Pref <h', x', u'>)\}$.
- Let $h \in \mathcal{V}_S$, thus $\nexists h' \in \mathcal{V}$ such that $h \succeq h'$. Since $h \in \mathcal{V}_S$, then $h \in \mathcal{V}$ and consequently, $h \in \text{Hyp}(\mathcal{E})$. This means that $\exists \langle h, x, u \rangle \in \mathcal{E}$. Let us assume that $\exists \langle h', x', u' \rangle \in \mathcal{E}$ such that $\langle h, x, u \rangle$ *Pref* $\langle h', x', u' \rangle$, thus $h \succeq h'$. Contradiction with the fact that $h \in \mathcal{V}_S$.
- Let $\langle h, x, u \rangle \in \mathcal{E}$ such that $\forall \langle h', x', u' \rangle \in \mathcal{E}$, and $\text{not}(\langle h, x, u \rangle Pref \langle h', x', u' \rangle)$, thus $\text{not}(h \succeq h')$. Since $h \in \mathcal{V}$, and $\forall h' \in \mathcal{V}$, $\text{not}(h \succeq h')$, then $h \in \mathcal{V}_S$.

6   Conclusion

Recently, some researchers have tried to use argumentation techniques in machine learning [10,5]. The basic idea behind their work is to improve existing algorithms in learning by providing arguments. However, they don't exploit the whole power of argumentation theory. This paper has proposed, to the best of our knowledge, the first framework for classification that is completely argumentation-based, and that uses Dung's semantics.

This framework considers the classification problem as a process that follows four main steps: it first constructs arguments in favor of classifications of examples from a set of training examples, and a set of hypothesis. Conflicts between arguments may appear when two arguments classify the same example in different classes. Once the arguments identified, it is possible to compare them on the basis of their strengths. The idea is that arguments coming from the set of training examples are stronger than arguments built from the set of hypothesis. Similarly, arguments based on most preferred hypothesis are stronger than arguments built from less preferred hypothesis. We have shown that acceptability semantics of the ASC retrieves and even characterizes the version space and its upper and lower bounds. Thus, the argumentation-based approach gives another interpretation of the version space as well as its two bounds in terms of arguments. We have also shown that when the set of training examples is inconsistent, it is still possible to classify examples. Indeed, in this particular case, the version space is empty as it is the case in the version space learning framework. A last and not least feature of our framework consists of defining the class of each example on the basis of all the hypothesis and not only one, and also to suggest four intuitive decision criteria for that purpose.

A first extension of this framework would be to explore the proof theories in argumentation that test directly whether a given argument is in the grounded extension without computing this last. This means that one may know the class of an example without exploring the whole hypothesis space.

References

1. Amgoud, L., Cayrol, C.: Inferring from inconsistency in preference-based argumentation frameworks. Int. Journal of Automated Reasoning 29(2), 125–169 (2002)
2. Dung, P.M.: On the acceptability of arguments and its fundamental role in non-monotonic reasoning, logic programming and n-person games. Artificial Intelligence 77, 321–357 (1995)
3. Gómez, S.A., Chesñevar, C.I.: Integrating defeasible argumentation with fuzzy art neural networks for pattern classification. In: Lavrač, N., Gamberger, D., Todorovski, L., Blockeel, H. (eds.) ECML 2003. LNCS (LNAI), vol. 2837, Springer, Heidelberg (2003)
4. Mitchell, T.: Generalization as search. Artificial intelligence 18, 203–226 (1982)
5. Mozina, M., Zabkar, J., Bratko, I.: Argument based rule learning. In: Proc. of the In 17th European Conference on Artificial Intelligence, ECAI 2006
6. Muggleton, S.: Inverse entailment and Progol. New Generation Computing 13, 245–286 (1995)

7. Prakken, H., Sartor, G.: Argument-based extended logic programming with defeasible priorities. Journal of Applied Non-Classical Logics 7, 25–75 (1997)
8. Quinlan, J.R.: Learning logical definitions from relations. Machine Learning 5, 239–266 (1990)
9. Simari, G.R., Loui, R.P.: A mathematical treatment of defeasible reasoning and its implementation. Artificial Intelligence and Law 53, 125–157 (1992)
10. Zabkar, J., Mozina, M., Videcnik, J., Bratko, I.: Argument based machine learning in a medical domain. In: Press, I. (ed.) Proc. of the 1st International Conference on Computational Models of Argument, pp. 59–70 (2006)

An Argumentation-Based Framework for Deliberation in Multi-agent Systems

Santi Ontañón[1] and Enric Plaza[2]

[1] CCL, Cognitive Computing Lab,
Georgia Institute of Technology
Atlanta, GA 30332/0280
santi@cc.gatech.edu
[2] IIIA, Artificial Intelligence Research Institute,
CSIC, Spanish Council for Scientific Research
Campus UAB, 08193 Bellaterra, Catalonia (Spain)
enric@iiia.csic.es

Abstract. This paper focuses of the group judgments obtained from a committee of agents that use deliberation. The deliberative process is realized by an argumentation framework called **AMAL**. The AMAL framework is completely based on learning from examples: the argument preference relation, the argument generation policy, and the counterargument generation policy are case-based techniques. For join deliberation, learning agents share their experience by forming a committee to decide upon some joint decision. We experimentally show that the deliberation in committees of agents improves the accuracy of group judgments. We also show that a voting scheme based on assessing the confidence of arguments improves the accuracy of group judgments than majority voting.

1 Introduction

Argumentation frameworks for multi-agent systems can be used for different purposes like joint deliberation, persuasion, negotiation, and conflict resolution. In this paper we focus on committees of agents that use deliberation to achieve more informed and accurate group judgments. Since most work on multi-agents systems is oriented towards bargain-based decision-making (like negotiation or persuasion) it is important to remark the following difference: while bargain-based decision-making assumes that individual preferences are "given" (i.e. preferences preexisting and/or fixed), deliberation-based decision-making preferences are formed [15].

Argumentation-based joint deliberation involves discussion over the outcome of a particular situation or the appropriate course of action for a particular situation. Learning agents are capable of learning from experience, in the sense that past examples (situations and their outcomes) are used to predict the outcome for the situation at hand. However, since individual agents experience may be limited, individual knowledge and prediction accuracy is also limited. Thus, learning agents that are capable of arguing their individual predictions with other agents may reach better prediction accuracy after such an argumentation process.

I. Rahwan, S. Parsons, and C. Reed (Eds.): ArgMAS 2007, LNAI 4946, pp. 178–196, 2008.

Most existing argumentation frameworks for multi-agent systems are based on deductive logic or some other deductive logic formalism specifically designed to support argumentation, such as default logic [3]. Usually, an argument is seen as a logical statement, while a counterargument is an argument offered in opposition to another argument [4,14]; agents use a preference relation to resolve conflicting arguments. However, logic-based argumentation frameworks assume agents with preexisting knowledge and preference relations. This is similar to the difference in assumptions between bargain-based decision-making and deliberation-based decision-making: our interest is in an adaptive and dynamic approach for deliberation processes where agents are responsive to external arguments or factual statements and, by integrating them, being able changing their minds.

In this paper, we focus on an *Argumentation-based Multi-Agent Learning* (AMAL) framework where both knowledge and preference relation are learned from experience. Thus, we consider a scenario with agents that (1) work in the same domain using a shared ontology, (2) are capable of learning from examples, and (3) communicate using an argumentative framework. Having learning capabilities allows agents effectively use a specific form of counterargument, namely the use of *counterexamples*. Counterexamples offer the possibility of agents learning *during* the argumentation process. Moreover, learning agents allow techniques that use learnt experience to generate adequate arguments and counterarguments. Specifically, we will need to address two issues: (1) how to define a technique to generate arguments and counterarguments by generalizing from examples, and (2) how to define a preference relation over two conflicting arguments that have been generalized from examples.

This paper presents a case-based approach to address both issues. The agents use case-based reasoning (CBR) [1] to learn from past cases (where a case is a situation and its outcome) in order to predict the outcome of a new situation. We propose an argumentation protocol inside the AMAL framework at supports agents in reaching a joint prediction over a specific situation or problem — moreover, the reasoning needed to support the argumentation process will also be based on cases. In particular, we present two *case-based measures*, one for generating the arguments and counterarguments adequate to a particular situation and another for determining preference relation among arguments. Finally, we experimentally show that the deliberation in committees of agents improves the accuracy of group judgments compared to voting without deliberation. We also show that a voting scheme based on assessing the confidence of arguments improves the accuracy of group judgments compared to majority voting.

The paper is structured as follows. Section 2 discusses the relation among committees, deliberation and social choice. Then Section 3 introduces our multi-agent CBR framework and the notion of justified prediction. After that, Section 4 formally defines our argumentation framework. Sections 5 and 6 present our case-based preference relation and argument generation policies respectively. Later, Section 7 presents the argumentation protocol in our AMAL framework. After that, Section 8 presents an exemplification of the argumentation framework. Finally, Section 9 presents an empirical evaluation of our apparoach. The paper closes with related work and conclusions sections.

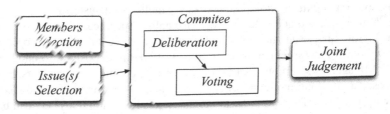

Fig. 1. The main aspects of a deliberative committees of agents

2   Deliberation, Committees and Social Choice

While there is ample research work on multi-agent systems concerning teams (agents associated in some joint action) and coalitions (agents not temporarily combine their action for a specific purpose), this paper focuses on committees. A common definition of committee is "A group of people officially delegated (voted or appointed) to perform a function, such as investigating, considering, reporting, or acting on a matter." Considered as an institution, the committee is a widespread form of coordination, deliberation, and joint decision-making. Philip Pettit in *Republicanism* say that "the committee is the enzyme of the body politic" (page 239, [9]) because committees are ubiquitous and because of the importance of their proper functioning to sustain a reliable working of the whole body politic.

In our approach, a committee of agents is a form of electronic institution designed to perform *group judgments*. The issue of *group judgments*, following Cass Sunstein [16], is answering the following question: How can groups obtain or use the information that their members have? The author then studies three approaches: deliberation, statistical means, and information markets. In our previous work on committees of agents [11] we focused on statistical means, in the sense of using voting schemes as the aggregation function to achieve group judgments. These approaches are based on what is called the *ensemble effect* [11] in Machine Learning and the *Condorcet Jury Theorem* [16] in social choice theory — stating succinctly that the accuracy of the group judgement is higher than that of the best individual member when some properties are satisfied by the members and an adequate aggregation function (e.g. majority voting) is used.

Since human committees also employ deliberation, we focus on this paper on developing a framework for deliberative committees of agents. Figure 1 shows the main aspects of a committee of agents: a way to select the members of the committee, the selection of the issues to be addressed by that committee, a deliberation stage and (if a consensual agreement is not achieved) a voting stage. Notice that if the committee addresses not a single issue but several related issues the stages of deliberation and voting can be iterated. In this paper we focus on single-issue committees of agents and on the deliberation and voting stages. We offer no contribution to the problems of selecting relevant issues and member selection, focusing on the internal workings of a committee proposing an argumentation-based approach to deliberation and new confidence-based voting mechanism.

The argumentation-based framework assumes agents capable of learning — in particular in agents capable of reasoning with (and learning from) cases. This approach gives an empirical grounding to several important issues of argumentation frameworks, like generation and selection of arguments and counterarguments. In our approach, the agents using case-based reasoning (CBR) will argue based on what they have learnt, and they will accept or reject counterarguments posited by other agents based on what they have learnt. Finally, since deliberation is only useful if agents are capable of changing their mind as a result of their argumentation with others, learning offers a basis from which individual changes in judgment are integrated with (and based on) the acquisition of new information from communicating with other agents. The next section introduces CBR agents and the requirements for sustaining an argumentation framework.

3   Multi-agent CBR Systems

A *Multi-Agent Case Based Reasoning System* (MAC) $\mathcal{M} = \{(A_1, C_1), ..., (A_n, C_n)\}$ is a multi-agent system composed of $\mathcal{A} = \{A_i, ..., A_n\}$, a set of CBR agents, where each agent $A_i \in \mathcal{A}$ possesses an individual case base C_i. Each individual agent A_i in a MAC is completely autonomous and each agent A_i has access only to its individual and private case base C_i. A case base $C_i = \{c_1, ..., c_m\}$ is a collection of cases. Agents in a MAC system are able to individually solve problems, but they can also collaborate with other agents to solve problems.

In this framework, we will restrict ourselves to analytical tasks, i.e. tasks like classification, where the solution of a problem is achieved by selecting a solution class from an enumerated set of solution classes. In the following we will note the set of all the solution classes by $S = \{S_1, ..., S_K\}$. Therefore, a *case* $c = \langle P, S \rangle$ is a tuple containing a case description P and a solution class $S \in S$. In the following, we will use the terms *problem* and *case description* indistinctly. Moreover, we will use the dot notation to refer to elements inside a tuple; e.g., to refer to the solution class of a case c, we will write $c.S$.

Therefore, we say a group of agents perform *joint deliberation*, when they collaborate to find a joint solution by means of an argumentation process. However, in order to do so, an agent has to be able to *justify* its prediction to the other agents (i.e. generate an argument for its predicted solution that can be examined and critiqued by the other agents). The next section addresses this issue.

3.1   Justified Predictions

Both expert systems and CBR systems may have an explanation component [17] in charge of justifying why the system has provided a specific answer to the user. The line of reasoning of the system can then be examined by a human expert, thus increasing the reliability of the system.

Most of the existing work on explanation generation focuses on generating explanations to be provided to the user. However, in our approach we use explanations (or justifications) as a tool for improving communication and coordination among agents.

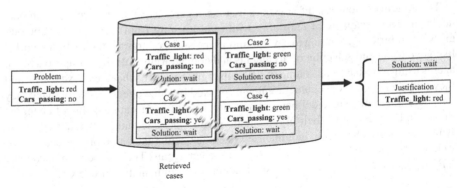

Fig. 2. An example of justification generation in a CBR system. Notice that, since the only relevant feature to decide is *Traffic_light* (the only one used to retrieve cases), it is the only one appearing in the justification.

We are interested in justifications since they can be used as arguments. For that purpose, we will benefit from the ability of some machine learning methods to provide justifications.

A *justification* built by a CBR method after determining that the solution of a particular problem P was S_k is a description that contains the relevant information from the problem P that the CBR method has considered to predict S_k as the solution of P. In particular, CBR methods work by retrieving similar cases to the problem at hand, and then reusing their solutions for the current problem, expecting that since the problem and the cases are similar, the solutions will also be similar. Thus, if a CBR method has retrieved a set of cases $C_1, ..., C_n$ to solve a particular problem P the justification built will contain the relevant information from the problem P that made the CBR system retrieve that particular set of cases, i.e. it will contain the relevant information that P and $C_1, ..., C_n$ have in common.

For example, Figure 2 shows a justification build by a CBR system for a toy problem (in the following sections we will show justifications for real problems). In the figure, a problem has two attributes (*Traffic_light*, and *Cars_passing*), the retrieval mechanism of the CBR system notices that by considering only the attribute *Traffic_light*, it can retrieve two cases that predict the same solution: *wait*. Thus, since only this attribute has been used, it is the only one appearing in the justification. The values of the rest of attributes are irrelevant, since whatever their value the solution class would have been the same.

In general, the meaning of a justification is that all (or most of) the cases in the case base of an agent that satisfy the justification (i.e. all the cases that are *subsumed* by the justification) belong to the predicted solution class. In the rest of the paper, we will use $\sqsubseteq$ to denote the subsumption relation. In our work, we use LID [2], a CBR method capable of building symbolic justifications such as the one exemplified in Figure 2. When an agent provides a justification for a prediction, the agent generates a *justified prediction*:

Definition 1. *A* Justified Prediction *is a tuple* $J = \langle A, P, S, D \rangle$ *where agent A considers S the correct solution for problem P, and that prediction is justified a symbolic description D such that* $J.D \sqsubseteq J.P$.

Justifications can have many uses for CBR systems [8,10]. In this paper, we are going to use justifications as arguments, in order to allow learning agents to engage in argumentation processes.

4 Arguments and Counterarguments

For our purposes an *argument* α generated by an agent A is composed of a statement S and some evidence D supporting S as correct. In the remainder of this section we will see how this general definition of argument can be instantiated in specific kind of arguments that the agents can generate. In the context of $\mathcal{MAC}$ systems, agents argue about predictions for new problems and can provide two kinds of information: a) specific cases $\langle P, S \rangle$, and b) justified predictions: $\langle A, P, S, D \rangle$. Using this information, we can define three types of arguments: justified predictions, counterarguments, and counterexamples.

A *justified prediction* α is generated by an agent A_i to argue that A_i believes that the correct solution for a given problem P is $\alpha.S$, and the evidence provided is the justification $\alpha.D$. In the example depicted in Figure 2, an agent A_i may generate the argument $\alpha = \langle A_i, P, \mathit{Wait}, (\mathit{Traffic\_light} = \mathit{red}) \rangle$, meaning that the agent A_i believes that the correct solution for P is *Wait* because the attribute *Traffic_light* equals *red*.

A *counterargument* β is an argument offered in opposition to another argument α. In our framework, a counterargument consists of a justified prediction $\langle A_j, P, S', D' \rangle$ generated by an agent A_j with the intention to rebut an argument α generated by another agent A_i, that endorses a solution class S' different from that of $\alpha.S$ for the problem at hand and justifies this with a justification D'. In the example in Figure 2, if an agent generates the argument $\alpha = \langle A_i, P, \mathit{Walk}, (\mathit{Cars\_passing} = \mathit{no}) \rangle$, an agent that thinks that the correct solution is *Wait* might answer with the counterargument $\beta = \langle A_j, P, \mathit{Wait}, (\mathit{Cars\_passing} = \mathit{no} \land \mathit{Traffic\_light} = \mathit{red}) \rangle$, meaning that, although there are no cars passing, the traffic light is red, and the street cannot be crossed.

A *counterexample* c is a case that contradicts an argument α. Thus a counterexample is also a counterargument, one that states that a specific argument α is not always true, and the evidence provided is the case c. Specifically, for a case c to be a counterexample of an argument α, the following conditions have to be met: $\alpha.D \sqsubseteq c$ and $\alpha.S \neq c.S$, i.e. the case must satisfy the justification $\alpha.D$ and the solution of c must be different than the predicted by α.

By exchanging arguments and counterarguments (including counterexamples), agents can argue about the correct solution of a given problem, i.e. they can engage a joint deliberation process. However, in order to do so, they need a specific interaction protocol, a preference relation between contradicting arguments, and a decision policy to generate counterarguments (including counterexamples). In the following sections we will present these elements.

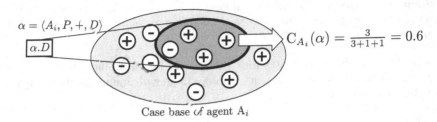

$$\alpha = \langle A_i, P, +, D \rangle$$

$$C_{A_i}(\alpha) = \frac{3}{3+1+1} = 0.6$$

Case base of agent A_i

Fig. 3. Confidence of arguments is evaluated by contrasting them against the case bases of the agents

5   Preference Relation

A specific argument provided by an agent might not be consistent with the information known to other agents (or even to some of the information known by the agent that has generated the justification due to noise in training data). For that reason, we are going to define a preference relation over contradicting justified predictions based on cases. Basically, we will define a *confidence* measure for each justified prediction (that takes into account the cases owned by each agent), and the justified prediction with the highest confidence will be the preferred one.

The idea behind case-based confidence is to count how many of the cases in an individual case base *endorse* a justified prediction, and how many of them are counterexamples of it. The more the endorsing cases, the higher the confidence; and the more the counterexamples, the lower the confidence. Specifically, to assess the confidence of a justified prediction α, an agent obtains the set of cases in its individual case base that are subsumed by $\alpha.D$. With them, an agent A_i obtains the Y (*aye*) and N (*nay*) values:

- $Y_\alpha^{A_i} = |\{c \in C_i | \alpha.D \sqsubseteq c.P \wedge \alpha.S = c.S\}|$ is the number of cases in the agent's case base *subsumed* by the justification $\alpha.D$ that belong to the solution class $\alpha.S$,
- $N_\alpha^{A_i} = |\{c \in C_i | \alpha.D \sqsubseteq c.P \wedge \alpha.S \neq c.S\}|$ is the number of cases in the agent's case base *subsumed* by justification $\alpha.D$ that do *not* belong to that solution class.

An agent estimates the confidence of an argument as:

$$C_{A_i}(\alpha) = \frac{Y_\alpha^{A_i}}{1 + Y_\alpha^{A_i} + N_\alpha^{A_i}}$$

i.e. the confidence on a justified prediction is the number of endorsing cases divided by the number of endorsing cases plus counterexamples. Notice that we add 1 to the denominator, this is to avoid giving excessively high confidences to justified predictions whose confidence has been computed using a small number of cases. Notice that this correction follows the same idea than the Laplace correction to estimate probabilities. Figure 3 illustrates the individual evaluation of the confidence of an argument, in particular, three endorsing cases and one counterexample are found in the case base of agents A_i, giving an estimated confidence of 0.6

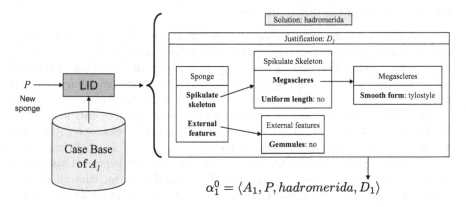

Fig. 4. Example of a real justification generated by LID in the marine Sponges data set

Moreover, we can also define the *joint confidence* of an argument α as the confidence computed using the cases present in the case bases of all the agents in the group:

$$C(\alpha) = \frac{\sum_i Y_\alpha^{A_i}}{1 + \sum_i \left(Y_\alpha^{A_i} + N_\alpha^{A_i} \right)}$$

Notice that, to collaboratively compute the joint confidence, the agents only have to make public the aye and nay values locally computed for a given argument.

In our framework, agents use this joint confidence as the preference relation: a justified prediction α is preferred over another one β if $C(\alpha) \geq C(\beta)$.

6   Generation of Arguments

In our framework, arguments are generated by the agents from cases, using learning methods. Any learning method able to provide a justified prediction can be used to generate arguments. For instance, decision trees and LID [2] are suitable learning methods. Specifically, in the experiments reported in this paper agents use LID. Thus, when an agent wants to generate an argument endorsing that a specific solution class is the correct solution for a problem P, it generates a justified prediction as explained in Section 3.1.

For instance, Figure 4 shows a real justification generated by LID after solving a problem P in the domain of marine Sponges identification. In particular, Figure 4 shows how when an agent receives a new problem to solve (in this case, a new sponge to determine its order), the agent uses LID to generate an argument (consisting on a justified prediction) using the cases in the case base of the agent. The justification shown in Figure 4 can be interpreted saying that "the predicted solution is hadromerida because the smooth form of the megascleres of the spiculate skeleton of the sponge is of type tylostyle, the spiculate skeleton of the sponge has no uniform length, and there is no gemmules in the external features of the sponge". Thus, the argument generated will be $\alpha = \langle A_1, P, hadromerida, D_1 \rangle$.

6.1 Generation of Counterarguments

As previously stated, agents may try to rebut arguments by generating counterargument or by finding counterexamples. Let us explain how they can be generated.

An agent A_i wants to generate a counterargument β to rebut an argument α when α is in contradiction with the local case base of A_i. Moreover, while generating such counterargument β, A_i expects that β is preferred over α. For that purpose, we will present a specific policy to generate counterarguments based on the *specificity* criterion [12].

The specificity criterion is widely used in deductive frameworks for argumentation, and states that between two conflicting arguments, the most specific should be preferred since it is, in principle, more informed. Thus, counterarguments generated based on the specificity criterion are expected to be preferable (since they are more informed) to the arguments they try to rebut. However, there is no guarantee that such counterarguments will always win, since, as we have stated in Section 5, agents in our framework use a preference relation based on joint confidence. Moreover, one may think that it would be better that the agents generate counterarguments based on the joint confidence preference relation; however it is not obvious how to generate counterarguments based on joint confidence in an efficient way, since collaboration is required in order to evaluate joint confidence. Thus, the agent generating the counterargument should constantly communicate with the other agents at each step of the induction algorithm used to generate counterarguments (presently one of our future research lines).

Thus, in our framework, when an agent wants to generate a counterargument β to an argument α, β has to be more specific than α (i.e. $\alpha.D \sqsubseteq \beta.D$).

The generation of counterarguments using the specificity criterion imposes some restrictions over the learning method, although LID or ID3 can be easily adapted for this task. For instance, LID is an algorithm that generates a description starting from scratch and heuristically adding features to that term. Thus, at every step, the description is made more specific than in the previous step, and the number of cases that are subsumed by that description is reduced. When the description covers only (or almost only) cases of a single solution class LID terminates and predicts that solution class. To generate a counterargument to an argument α LID just has to use as starting point the description $\alpha.D$ instead of starting from scratch. In this way, the justification provided by LID will always be subsumed by $\alpha.D$, and thus the resulting counterargument will be more specific than α. However, notice that LID may sometimes not be able to generate counterarguments, since LID may not be able to specialize the description $\alpha.D$ any further, or because the agent A_i has no case in C_i that is subsumed by $\alpha.D$. Figure 5 shows how an agent A_2 that disagreed with the argument shown in Figure 4, generates a counterargument using LID. Moreover, Figure 5 shows the generation of a counterargument β_2^1 for the argument α_1^0 (in Figure 4) that is a specialization of α_1^0.

Specifically, in our experiments, when an agent A_i wants to rebut an argument α, uses the following policy:

1. Agent A_i uses LID to try to find a counterargument β more specific than α; if found, β is sent to the other agent as a counterargument of α.
2. If not found, then A_i searches for a counterexample $c \in C_i$ of α. If a case c is found, then c is sent to the other agent as a counterexample of α.
3. If no counterexamples are found, then A_i cannot rebut the argument α.

$$\alpha_1^0 = \langle A_1, P, hadromerida, D_1 \rangle$$

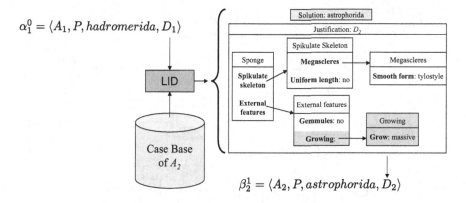

Fig. 5. Generation of a counterargument using LID in the Sponges data set

$$\beta_2^1 = \langle A_2, P, astrophorida, D_2 \rangle$$

7   Argumentation-Based Multi-agent Learning

The interaction protocol of AMAL allows a group of agents $A_1, ..., A_n$ to deliberate about the correct solution of a problem P by means of an argumentation process. If the argumentation process arrives to a consensual solution, the joint deliberation ends; otherwise a weighted vote is used to determine the joint solution. Moreover, AMAL also allows the agents to learn from the counterexamples received from other agents.

The AMAL protocol consists on a series of rounds. In the initial round, each agent states which is its individual prediction for P. Then, at each round an agent can try to rebut the prediction made by any of the other agents. The protocol uses a token passing mechanism so that agents (one at a time) can send counterarguments or counterexamples if they disagree with the prediction made by any other agent. Specifically, each agent is allowed to send one counterargument or counterexample each time he gets the token (notice that this restriction is just to simplify the protocol, and that it does not restrict the number of counterargument an agent can sent, since they can be delayed for subsequent rounds). When an agent receives a counterargument or counterexample, it informs the other agents if it accepts the counterargument (and changes its prediction) or not. Moreover, agents have also the opportunity to answer to counterarguments when they receive the token, by trying to generate a counterargument to the counterargument.

When all the agents have had the token once, the token returns to the first agent, and so on. If at any time in the protocol, all the agents agree or during the last n rounds no agent has generated any counterargument, the protocol ends. Moreover, if at the end of the argumentation the agents have not reached an agreement, then a voting mechanism that uses the confidence of each prediction as weights is used to decide the final solution (Thus, AMAL follows the same mechanism as human committees, first each individual member of a committee exposes his arguments and discuses those of the other members (joint deliberation), and if no consensus is reached, then a voting mechanism is required).

At each iteration, agents can use the following performatives:

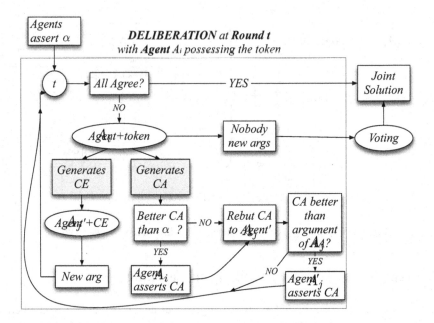

Fig. 6. Graphical representation of the argumentation protocol at round t with the token in possession of agent A_i

- $assert(\alpha)$: the justified prediction held during the next round will be α. An agent can only hold a single prediction at each round, thus is multiple asserts are send, only the last one is considered as the currently held prediction.
- $rebut(\beta, \alpha)$: the agent has found a counterargument β to the prediction α.

We will define $H_t = \langle \alpha_1^t, ..., \alpha_n^t \rangle$ as the predictions that each of the n agents hold at a round t. Moreover, we will also define $contradict(\alpha_i^t) = \{\alpha \in H_t | \alpha.S \neq \alpha_i^t.S\}$ as the set of contradicting arguments for an agent A_i in a round t, i.e. the set of arguments at round t that support a different solution class than α_i^t.

The protocol is initiated because one of the agents receives a problem P to be solved. After that, the agent informs all the other agents about the problem P to solve, and the protocol starts:

1. At round $t = 0$, each one of the agents individually solves P, and builds a justified prediction using its own CBR method. Then, each agent A_i sends the performative $assert(\alpha_i^0)$ to the other agents. Thus, the agents know $H_0 = \langle \alpha_i^0, ..., \alpha_n^0 \rangle$. Once all the predictions have been sent the token is given to the first agent A_1.
2. At each round t (other than 0), the agents check whether their arguments in H_t agree. If they do, the protocol moves to step 5. Moreover, if during the last n rounds no agent has sent any counterexample or counterargument, the protocol also moves to step 5. Otherwise, the agent A_i owner of the token tries to generate a counterargument for each of the opposing arguments in $contradict(\alpha_i^t) \subseteq H_t$ (see Section 6.1). Then, the counterargument β_i^t against the prediction α_j^t with the lowest confidence $C(\alpha_j^t)$ is selected (since α_j^t is the prediction more likely to be successfully rebutted).

- If β_i^t is a counterargument, then, A_i locally compares α_i^t with β_i^t by assessing their confidence against its individual case base C_i (see Section 5) (notice that A_i is comparing its previous argument with the counterargument that A_i itself has just generated and that is about to send to A_j). If $C_{A_i}(\beta_i^t) > C_{A_i}(\alpha_i^t)$, then A_i considers that β_i^t is stronger than its previous argument, changes its argument to β_i^t by sending $assert(\beta_i^t)$ to the rest of the agents (the intuition behind this is that since a counterargument is also an argument, A_i checks if the newly coun-terargument is a better argument than the one he was previously holding) and $rebut(\beta_i^t, \alpha_j^t)$ to A_j. Otherwise (i.e. $C_{A_i}(\beta_i^t) \le C_{A_i}(\alpha_i^t)$), A_i will send only $rebut(\beta_i^t, \alpha_j^t)$ to A_j. In any of the two situations the protocol moves to step 3.
  - If β_i^t is a counterexample c, then A_i sends $rebut(c, \alpha_j^t)$ to A_j. The protocol moves to step 4.
  - If A_i cannot generate any counterargument or counterexample, the token is sent to the next agent, a new round $t + 1$ starts, and the protocol moves to state 2.

3. The agent A_j that has received the counterargument β_i^t, locally compares it against its own argument, α_j^t, by locally assessing their confidence. If $C_{A_j}(\beta_i^t) > C_{A_j}(\alpha_j^t)$, then A_j will accept the counterargument as stronger than its own argument, and it will send $assert(\beta_i^t)$ to the other agents. Otherwise (i.e. $C_{A_j}(\beta_i^t) \le C_{A_j}(\alpha_j^t)$), A_j will not accept the counterargument, and will inform the other agents accordingly. Any of the two situations start a new round $t + 1$, A_i sends the token to the next agent, and the protocol moves back to state 2.

4. The agent A_j that has received the counterexample c retains it into its case base and generates a new argument α_j^{t+1} that takes into account c, and informs the rest of the agents by sending $assert(\alpha_j^{t+1})$ to all of them. Then, A_i sends the token to the next agent, a new round $t + 1$ starts, and the protocol moves back to step 2.

5. The protocol ends yielding a joint prediction, as follows: if the arguments in H_t agree then their prediction is the joint prediction, otherwise a voting mechanism is used to decide the joint prediction. The voting mechanism uses the joint confidence measure as the voting weights, as follows:

$$S = \arg\max_{S_k \in \mathcal{S}} \sum_{\alpha_i \in H_t | \alpha_i.S = S_k} C(\alpha_i)$$

Moreover, in order to avoid infinite iterations, if an agent sends twice the same argu-ment or counterargument to the same agent, the message is not considered.

Figure 6 graphically illustrates this process. Where the greyed area is the loop formed by steps 2, 3, and 4.

8   Exemplification

Let us consider a system composed of three agents A_1, A_2 and A_3. One of the agents, A_1 receives a problem P to solve, and decides to use **AMAL** to solve it. For that reason, invites A_2 and A_3 to take part in the argumentation process. They accept the invitation, and the argumentation protocol starts.

Initially, each agent generates its individual prediction for P, and broadcasts it to the other agents. Thus, all of them can compute $H_0 = \langle \alpha_1^0, \alpha_2^0, \alpha_3^0 \rangle$. In particular, in this example.

- $\alpha_1^0 = \langle A_1, P, hadromerida, D_1 \rangle$
- $\alpha_2^0 = \langle A_2, P, astrophorida, D_2 \rangle$
- $\alpha_3^0 = \langle A_3, P, axinellida, D_3 \rangle$

A_1 starts (Round 0) owning the token and tries to generate counterarguments for α_2^0 and α_3^0, but does not succeed, however it has one counterexample c_{13} for α_3^0. Thus, A_1 sends the the message $rebut(c_{13}, \alpha_3^0)$ to A_3. A_3 incorporates c_{13} into its case base and tries to solve the problem P again, now taking c_{13} into consideration. A_3 comes up with the justified prediction $\alpha_3^1 = \langle A_3, P, hadromerida, D_4 \rangle$, and broadcasts it to the rest of the agents with the message $assert(\alpha_3^1)$. Thus, all of them know the new $H_1 = \langle \alpha_1^0, \alpha_2^0, \alpha_3^1 \rangle$.

Round 1 starts and A_2 gets the token. A_2 tries to generate counterarguments for α_1^0 and α_3^1 and only succeeds to generate a counterargument $\beta_2^1 = \langle A_2, P, astrophorida, D_5 \rangle$ against α_3^1. The counterargument is sent to A_3 with the message $rebut(\beta_2^1, \alpha_3^1)$. Agent A_3 receives the counterargument and assesses its local confidence. The result is that the individual confidence of the counterargument β_2^1 is lower than the local confidence of α_3^1. Therefore, A_3 does not accept the counterargument, and thus $H_2 = \langle \alpha_1^0, \alpha_2^0, \alpha_3^1 \rangle$.

Round 2 starts and A_3 gets the token. A_3 generates a counterargument $\beta_3^2 = \langle A_3, P, hadromerida, D_6 \rangle$ for α_2^0 and sends it to A_2 with the message $rebut(\beta_3^2, \alpha_2^0)$. Agent A_2 receives the counterargument and assesses its local confidence. The result is that the local confidence of the counterargument β_3^2 is higher than the local confidence of α_2^0. Therefore, A_2 accepts the counterargument and informs the rest of the agents with the message $assert(\beta_3^2)$. After that, $H_3 = \langle \alpha_1^0, \beta_3^2, \alpha_3^1 \rangle$.

At Round 3, since all the agents agree (all the justified predictions in H_3 predict $hadromerida$ as the solution class) The protocol ends, and A_1 (the agent that received the problem) considers $hadromerida$ as the joint solution for the problem P.

9   Experimental Evaluation

In this section we empirically evaluate the AMAL argumentation framework for deliberative committees. We have made experiments in two different data sets: *Soybean* (from the UCI machine learning repository) and *Sponges* (a relational data set). The Soybean data set has 307 examples and 19 solution classes, while the Sponges data set has 280 examples and 3 solution classes. In an experimental run, the data set is divided in 2 sets: the training set and the test set. The training set examples are distributed among 5 different agents without replication, i.e. there is no example shared by two agents. In the testing stage, problems in the test set arrive randomly to one of the agents, and their goal is to predict the correct solution.

The experiments are designed to test the hypothesis that argumentation-based deliberation is useful for group judgment and improves over other typical methods such as majority voting. Moreover, we also expect that the improvement achieved from argumentation will increase as the number of agents participating in the argumentation increases (since more information will be taken into account). For this purpose, we ran four experiments,

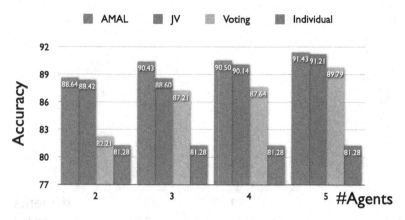

Fig. 7. Accuracy in Sponges data set for committees of 2 to 5 agents where predictions are achieved individually, by majority voting, by justification-based voting, and by the full **AMAL** argumentation framework

using committees of 2, 3, 4, and 5 agents respectively (in all experiments each agent has a 20% of the training data, since the training is always distributed among 5 agents).

Figures 7 and 8 show the result of those experiments in the Sponges and Soybean data sets. Classification accuracy is plotted in the vertical axis, and in the horizontal axis the number of agents that took part in the argumentation processes is shown. For each number of agents, four bars are shown: *Individual*, *Voting*, *JV*, and **AMAL**. The individual bar shows the average accuracy of individual agents predictions; the Voting bar shows the average accuracy of the agents using a majority voting system to aggregate their predictions (i.e. without deliberation); the last **AMAL** bar shows the average accuracy of the joint prediction using argumentation and (if need be) the confidence-based voting explained in the step 5 of the protocol. Therefore, since the **AMAL** framework has in fact to phases, namely deliberation and voting, then it is fair to ask how much contributes each phase to the final result. For this purpose, we have included the JV bar in Figures 7 and 8 that correspond to an experiment performed where the deliberation phase is skipped. More specifically, the agents simply present their justified predictions once (i.e. H_0 is generated) and then a confidence-based voting is performed immediately (i.e. without sending any counterargument or counterexample). The results shown are the average of 5 10-fold cross validation runs.

Figures 7 and 8 show that collaboration (Voting, JV, and **AMAL**) outperforms individual problem solving. Moreover, as we expected, the accuracy improves as more agents collaborate, since more information is taken into account. Since **AMAL** always outperforms *Majority Voting*, it is clear that having deliberation is better than not having it. Moreover, **AMAL** always outperforms JV, indicating that having a confidence-based voting stage *after* the deliberation stage is better than skipping deliberation and use a confidence-based voting stage *before*. Thus, we conclude that joint predictions are based on better information that has been provided by the deliberation stage.

Moreover, Figures 7 and 8 show that the magnitude of the improvement obtained due to the argumentation process depends on the data set. For instance, the joint accuracy for 2 agents in the Sponges data set is of 88.64% for **AMAL**, 88.42% for JV, and 82.21% for

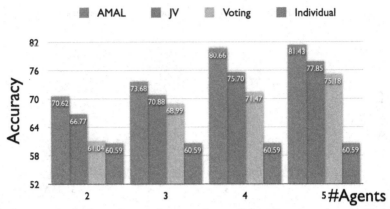

Fig. 8. Accuracy in Soybean data set for committees of 2 to 5 agents where predictions are achieved individually, by majority voting, by justification-based voting, and by the full AMAL argumentation framework

majority voting (while individual accuracy is just 81.28%). Moreover, the improvement achieved by AMAL over voting is larger in the Soybean data set. The reason is that the Soybean data set is more "difficult" (in the sense that agents need a higher percentage of the data set to achieve a reasonably good accuracy level). These experimental results show that AMAL effectively exploits the opportunity for improvement: the accuracy is higher only because more agents have changed their prediction during argumentation (otherwise they would achieve the same result as Voting). For instance, the joint accuracy for 2 agents in the Soybean data set is of 70.62% for AMAL, 66.77% for JV, and 61.04% for majority voting (while individual accuracy is just 60.59%)

Figure 9 shows the frequency in which the agent committee was able to reach consensus or needed a final voting stage for committees with 2, 3, 4, and 5 agents in the Sponges and Soybean data set. The first bar (*Unanimity*) shows the percentage in which the agents predictions on Round 0 of the protocol are equal (and no deliberation in needed), the second bar (*Consensus*) shows the percentage in which all the agents agree on a joint prediction after deliberation, and the third bar (*Voting*) shows the remaining percentage in which the agents vote to determine the joint prediction. A first difference is between data sets: Soybean, being more "difficult" (average error is higher than in Sponges) has as expected higher disagreement and the percentage of times a vote is needed is higher than in the Sponges data set. We can also observe that larger committees have less unanimity (as expected), but since smaller committees also have larger errors, the additional deliberation and voting needed is also to be expected. Concerning deliberation, we see the committees can use the information exchanged using AMAL to reach a consensual solution in a fairly large number of occasions (more often in Sponges, since in Soybean the higher error rate makes consensus more difficult).

Table 1 shows the average number rounds of argumentation performed (and also the maximum number rounds in one deliberation) for committees of 2, 3, 4, and 5 agents. The difficulty of the Soybean data set is reflected in the higher number of argumentation

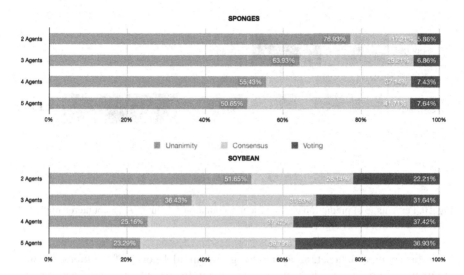

Fig. 9. Percentage of times that agents agree before the deliberation, after deliberation, and times when final voting is needed

rounds performed compared to the Sponges data set, as well as in the higher maximum number of rounds some deliberation stages achieve.

Let us analyze in more detail the difference in accuracy obtained by the **AMAL** argumentation process versus *Voting* and *JV* in the scenario with 5 agents. This improvement is only possible if agents change their mind about the correct prediction during the deliberation phase due to the argumentation process. Figure 10 shows as percentage the average number of times that an agent changes its prediction during the deliberation phase, according too three possible mechanisms:

Counterargument (CA). when a counterargument received by the agent is accepted (since it has higher individual confidence than the previously held argument)

Counterexample (CE). when a counterexample is received and since added to the individual case base the agent finds that now another argument has higher individual confidence (this may be due to this single counterexample or to a number of previously received counterexamples in addition to this one)

Self-Argument (SA). when an agent changes its mind because, while trying to generate a counterargument for another agent, it explores a different region of the hypothesis space and finds an argument with higher individual confidence than the one currently holding.

Table 1. Average and maximum rounds of argumentation

	Sponges				Soybean			
	2 Agents	3 Agents	4 Agents	5 Agents	2 Agents	3 Agents	4 Agents	5 Agents
Average rounds	1.32	1.68	2.07	2.51	1.76	2.80	4.19	5.27
Maximum rounds	5	15	25	20	16	16	179	141

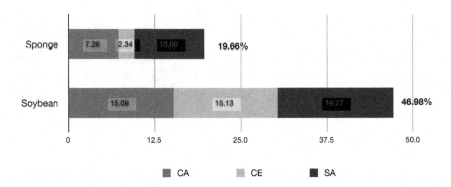

Fig. 10. Percentage of prediction change due to a counterargument (CA), a counterexample (CE), or to the finding a better argument (SA)

In the Sponges data set, an agent changes its mind 19.66% of the times due to the argumentation process: 7.26% of the times due to the reception of a counterargument, 2.34% of the times due to the reception of a counterexample, and the remaining 10.06% is due to a self-argument. If we look at the same numbers in the Soybean data set, agents change their minds a 46.98% of the times due to argumentation: 15.09% of the times due to counterarguments, 15.13% of the times due to counterexamples, and the remaining 16.77% is due to a self-argument. Clearly, we can establish a relation between the number of times an agent changes its mind with the increase in classification accuracy. In the Sponges data set, agents change their minds less times, and thus the increase in accuracy (from Voting to AMAL) is lower, while in the Soybean data set they change their minds more often, and thus the increase (from Voting to AMAL) of accuracy is higher.

Moreover, we can further analyze these numbers. In the Sponges data set, agents receive a counterexample to their arguments a 35.23% of the times, but they only change their minds due to them a 2.34% of the times due to them (i.e. only 1 out of 15 counterexamples makes an agent change its mind). That means that the extra information that an agent receives with one counterexample is small, and may need several counterexamples before effectively making the agent change its prediction. However, in the Soybean data set, agents receive a counterexample to their arguments a 31.49% of the times, and they change their minds due to them a 15.13% of the times (i.e. 1 out of 2 counterexamples makes an agent change its mind). Therefore, we can see that the amount of information that an agent receives with one counterexample is larger in the Soybean data set (in the sense that 1 or 2 examples may suffice to change an agent's prediction).

Finally, notice that an agent can change its mind due to only two different reasons: due to learning new information (i.e. learning new cases), or due to seeing the information it already had from a different point of view. When an agent changes its mind due to a counterexample, it is changing its mind due to learning new information. When an agent changes its mind due to a counterargument or due to a self-argument (searching through a new area in the generalizations space while trying to find a counterargument), the reason is that the agent sees its cases from a new point of view. The agents in our experiments use LID as their method to generate predictions that uses a heuristic method to explore the *generalizations space*. The heuristic approach avoids exploring the whole space of generalizations but does not assure that the part of the space effectively explored is always the one with the best generalization. Thus, from a generalizations space point of view, the argumentation process is useful for the agents in two respects: it provides new information (by means of counterexamples) an it provides new points of view to analyze data (i.e. it forces the agents to explore parts of the generalizations space that they have not explored following their heuristics).

10   Related Work

Our work on multi-agent case-based learning started in 1999 [6]; later Mc Ginty and Smyth [7] presented a multi-agent collaborative CBR approach (CCBR) for planning. Finally, another interesting approach is *multi-case-base reasoning* (MCBR) [5], that deals with distributed systems where there are several case bases available for the same task and addresses the problems of cross-case base adaptation. The main difference is that our $\mathcal{MAC}$ approach is a way to distribute the *Reuse* process of CBR (using a voting system) while *Retrieve* is performed individually by each agent; the other multi-agent CBR approaches, however, focus on distributing the *Retrieve* process.

Research on MAS argumentation focus on several issues like a) logics, protocols and languages that support argumentation, b) argument selection and c) argument interpretation. Approaches for logic and languages that support argumentation include defeasible logic [4] and BDI models [14]. Although argument selection is a key aspect of automated argumentation (see [13] and [14]), most research has been focused on preference relations among arguments. In our framework we have addressed both argument selection and preference relations using a case-based approach.

11   Conclusions and Future Work

In this paper we have presented an argumentation-based framework for multiagent deliberation. Specifically, we have presented AMAL, a framework that allows a committee of agents to argue about the solution of a given problem and we have shown how the learning capabilities can be used to generate arguments and counterarguments. The experimental evaluation shows that the increased amount of information provided to the agents during the deliberation stage increases the predictive accuracy of group judgments, and specially when an adequate number of agents take part in the argumentation.

The main contributions of this work are: a) an argumentation framework for learning agents; b) a case-based preference relation over arguments, based on computing an overall confidence estimation of arguments; c) a case-based policy to generate counterarguments and select counterexamples, and d) a voting scheme based on assessing the confidence of arguments (instead of assessing the trust on agents). Although we introduced justification-based voting (JV) in a previous paper [8], the full capability of this approach has not been established until now. JV is as good as the arguments provided, and we show here that the arguments sustained by the agents are refined and improved during deliberation; thus JV is better used not as a technique per se (as proposed in [8]) but as the later stage of a deliberation process where the arguments have been challenged and improved.

Future work will focus on extending this approach from single-issue to multiple-issue deliberation and group judgment. Social choice theory calls this the task of aggregating sets of judgments, and there is an impossibility theorem similar to Arrow's The problems arise from the fact that the interdependencies between different judgments may cause logical paradoxes (e.g. logical contradiction between the votes on the premises and the votes on the conclusion). However, relaxing some properties of aggregation strategies may be feasible for specific application purposes.

Acknowledgments. This research is partially supported by the MID-CBR (TIN2006-15140-C03-01) project and the Agreement Technologies (CONSOLIDER CSD2007-0022, INGENIO 2010) project.

References

1. Aamodt, A., Plaza, E.: Case-based reasoning: Foundational issues, methodological variations, and system approaches. Artificial Intelligence Communications 7(1), 39–59 (1994)
2. Armengol, E., Plaza, E.: Lazy induction of descriptions for relational case-based learning. In: Flach, P.A., De Raedt, L. (eds.) ECML 2001. LNCS (LNAI), vol. 2167, pp. 13–24. Springer, Heidelberg (2001)
3. Brewka, G.: Dynamic argument systems: A formal model of argumentation processes based on situation calculus. Journal of Logic and Computation 11(2), 257–282 (2001)
4. Chesñevar, C.I., Simari, G.R.: Formalizing Defeasible Argumentation using Labelled Deductive Systems. Journal of Computer Science & Technology 1(4), 18–33 (2000)
5. Leake, D., Sooriamurthi, R.: Automatically selecting strategies for multi-case-base reasoning. In: Craw, S., Preece, A.D. (eds.) ECCBR 2002. LNCS (LNAI), vol. 2416, pp. 204–219. Springer, Heidelberg (2002)
6. Martín, F.J., Plaza, E., Arcos, J.-L.: Knowledge and experience reuse through communications among competent (peer) agents. International Journal of Software Engineering and Knowledge Engineering 9(3), 319–341 (1999)
7. McGinty, L., Smyth, B.: Collaborative case-based reasoning: Applications in personalized route planning. In: Aha, D.W., Watson, I. (eds.) ICCBR 2001. LNCS (LNAI), vol. 2080, pp. 362–376. Springer, Heidelberg (2001)
8. Ontañón, S., Plaza, E.: Justification-based multiagent learning. In: ICML 2003, pp. 576–583. Morgan Kaufmann, San Francisco (2003)
9. Pettit, P.: Republicanism. Oxford University Press, Oxford (1997)
10. Plaza, E., Armengol, E., Ontañón, S.: The explanatory power of symbolic similarity in case-based reasoning. Artificial Intelligence Review 24(2), 145–161 (2005)
11. Plaza, E., Ontañón, S.: Learning collaboration strategies for committees of learning agents. Journal of Autonomous Agents and Multi-Agent Systems 13, 429–461 (2006)
12. Poole, D.: On the comparison of theories: Preferring the most specific explanation. In: IJCAI 1985, pp. 144–147 (1985)
13. Sycara, K., Kraus, S., Evenchik, A.: Reaching agreements through argumentation: a logical model and implementation. Artificial Intelligence Journal 104, 1–69 (1998)
14. Jennings, N.R., Parsons, S., Sierra, C.: Agents that reason and negotiate by arguing. Journal of Logic and Computation 8, 261–292 (1998)
15. Sunstein, C.R. (ed.): The partial Constitution. Harvard University Press (1993)
16. Sunstein, C.R.: Group judgments: Deliberation, statistical means, and information markets. New York University Law Review 80, 962–1049 (2005)
17. Bruce, A.: Wooley. Explanation component of software systems. ACM CrossRoads, 5.1 (1998)

A Hybrid Argumentation of Symbolic and Neural Net Argumentation (Part I)

Wataru Makiguchi[1] and Hajime Sawamura[2]

[1] Graduate School of Science and Technology, Niigata University
8050, 2-cho, Ikarashi, Niigata, 950-2181 Japan
makiguti@cs.ie.niigata-u.ac.jp
[2] Institute of Natural Science and Technology
Academic Assembly, Niigata University
8050 2-cho Ikarashi, Niigata, 950-2181 Japan
sawamura@ie.niigata-u.ac.jp

Abstract. A novel approach to argumentation has been started by A. Garcez et al. Inspired by their work, we further go on investigating it, but turn to a more syncretic direction such as the interplay between neural net argumentation and symbolic argumentation. More specifically, we address ourselves to the following basic questions that can not be overlooked.
1. Can the neural argumentation algorithm deal with self-defeating or other pathological arguments?
2. Can the argument status of the neural net argumentation correspond to the well-known argument status?

Consequently, we give the positive answers to them. They are beneficial for understanding or characterizing the computation power and outcome of the neural net argumentation from the perspective of the symbolic argumentation. We also exemplify these results.

1 Introduction

Much attention and effort have been devoted to the symbolic argumentation so far [1] [2], and its application to agent-oriented computing in which societal view on computation is emphasized.

On the other hand, it is a long time since connectionism appeared as an alternative movement in cognitive science or computing science which hopes to explain human intelligence or soft information processing. It has been a matter of hot debate how and to what extent the connectionism paradigm constitutes a challenge to classicism or symbolic AI [3].

Recently, quite a novel approach to argumentation has been started by A. Garcez et al., aiming to provide a model in which the learning of arguments can be combined with reasoning capabilities within the same framework. On account, they presented a neural argumentation algorithm that is responsible for translating argumentation networks into standard neural networks, and showed that the translated neural network executes a sound computation of the prevailing arguments in the original argumentation network [4].

I. Rahwan, S. Parsons, and C. Reed (Eds.): ArgMAS 2007, LNAI 4946, pp. 197–215, 2008.

Inspired by their work, we further go on investigating it, but turn to a more syncretic direction such as the interplay between neural net argumentation and symbolic argumentation. More specifically, in this paper we address ourselves to the former two questions of the following basic ones that can not be overlooked. For the latter two, we will deal with them in the consecutive paper (Part II) [5] since space is not enough to cover all of them in a single paper.

1. *Can the neural argumentation algorithm deal with self-defeating or other pathological arguments?*
   A. Garcez et al. dissolve such an anomaly as circular arguments (odd circle) through the use of neural network argumentation. We are further concerned with self-defeating arguments and other pathological arguments that are stated in the paper "Logics for defeasible argumentation" by Prakken and Vreeswijk [6], and show that their neural argumentation network yields a sound computation for them as well although self-defeating arguments tend to be ruled out in presenting the argumentation frameworks. Of course, self-defeating arguments and pathological arguments are not entitled to rebutting others in our daily life. However, we think we do not need to exclude them from the definition of the underlying argumentation framework (in fact, A. Garcez et al. employ Bench-Capon's value-based argumentation framework [7]).

2. *Can the argument status of the neural net argumentation correspond to the well-known status?*
   A. Garcez et al. classified the argument status into three: prevailing, fail to prevail and defeated. But it is not clear how they correspond to those of other symbolic argumentation frameworks. Having in mind the well-known argumentation framework by Prakken and Vreeswijk[6], we give an appropriately devised neural net with specially tailored computation so that the neural network yields the same argumentation status as the original argumentation. That is, we show that the notions of prevailing, fail to prevail and defeated correspond to the notions of justified, overruled and defensible respectively.

3. *Can the neural net argumentation compute the fixpoint semantics for argumentation?*
   The fixpoint semantics for formal argumentation frameworks is now standard since the influential work on argumentation by Dung [8]. We are concerned with what kind of neural net argumentation and how it can compute the fixpoint semantics. For this we give a correspondence theorem and its inductive proof under an appropriately devised neural net with specially tailored computation.

4. *Can argumentative dialogues be extracted from the neural net argumentation?*
   Here we are interested in returning to symbolic dialogues from the neural net computing. We illustrate a method of transforming neural net computations into symbolic dialogue processes. The symbolic presentation of arguments would be much better for us since it makes the neural net argumentation process verbally understandable.

We think the solutions to them would be helpful for us to understand and further promote the syncretic approach of symbolism and connectionism in the field of computational argumentation. In this paper, we are mainly concerned only with analyzing and characterizing the relationship between symbolic and neural net argumentation. In the next section, we present some preliminaries for the neural net argumentation by A. Garcez et al. Then the remaining part of the paper will be spent on describing in detail the former two questions described above and their solutions, giving one section to each of them. This paper does not have a section for related work since there is no directly related work on our topics and purposes except the work of Garcez et al. as far as we know. The final section summarizes contributions of this paper, and discusses some future works on another intriguing interplay of symbolism and connectionism in the field of computational argumentation.

2   Preliminaries to Neural Net Argumentation

In this section, we describe some preliminaries to the neural net argumentation that originated from the work by A. S. D. Garcez at al [4].

2.1   Argumentation Network

We start by introducing a definition of argumentation network, following Dung's argumentation framework[8].

Definition 1. (Argumentation network)
An argumentation network has the form $\mathcal{AN} =< \alpha, attack >$, where α is a set of arguments, and $attack \subseteq \alpha^2$ is a relation indicating which arguments attack which other arguments.

2.2   Neural Argumentation Algorithm

We assume readers are familiar with basic notions of neural network. The neural argumentation algorithm [4] is one that translates an argumentation network into a neural network. We describe its version adjusted to our purposes of this paper below.

Neural Argumentation Algorithm: For an argumentation network $\mathcal{AN}$ with arguments $\alpha_1, \alpha_2, \cdots, \alpha_n$,

1. Number each argument of $\mathcal{AN}$ from 1 to n, and create the input and output layers of a neural network $\mathcal{N}$ such that ith neuron represents the ith argument of $\mathcal{AN}$.
2. For each argument α_l of $\mathcal{AN}$ $(1 \leq l \leq n)$:
   (a) add neuron N_l to the hidden layer of $\mathcal{N}$;
   (b) connect neuron α_l in the input layer of $\mathcal{N}$ to hidden neuron N_l and set the connection weight to $W = 1$;

    (c) connect hidden neuron N_l to neuron α_l in the output layer of $\mathcal{N}$ and set the connection weight to $W = 1$.

3. For each $(\alpha_i, \alpha_j) \subset$ *attack*:
    (a) connect hidden neuron N_l to output neuron α_j;
    (b) set the connection weight to $W' = -1$
4. Set the threshold of each neuron in $\mathcal{N}$ to 0.
5. Set $g(x) = x$ as the activation function of the neurons in the input layer of $\mathcal{N}$.
6. Set $h(x) = 1$ if $x \geq 1$, $h(x) = -1$ if $x \leq -1$, and $h(x) = x$ for $-1 < x < 1$ as the activation function of the neurons in hidden and output layers of $\mathcal{N}$.

2.3   Neural Net Computation

The neural network obtained by the neural net algorithm in the previous subsection is a very simple recurrent neural network in which recurrence occurs only in the connections from output neurons to input neurons. In this subsection, we specify how and what the neural net argumentation under such a neural network computes.

One of the three argument's statuses (prevailing, failure to prevail, defeated) is given to an argument by the following neural net computation in $\mathcal{N}$.

Step 1. Give 1 to every input neuron of $\mathcal{N}$, go to Step 2.
Step 2. Obtaining an output vector:
    (a) if the output vector is the same as the input vector, go to Step 3.
    (b) if the output vector is different from the input vector, provide the output vector as a new input to $\mathcal{N}$ and repeat Step 2 again.
Step 3. For each neuron:
    (a) if neuron α_l outputs 1 in Step 2 (a), let argument α_l be prevailing.
    (b) if neuron α_l outputs 0 in Step 2 (a), let argument α_l be failure to prevail.
    (c) if neuron α_l outputs -1 in Step 2 (a), let argument α_l be defeated.

It is noted that it does not contain any learning mechanism in it, but is powerful enough to deal with notorious or puzzling pathological arguments that are to be considered in Sect. 3. In other words, it is a primitive one that has no mechanism for adaptation of weights based on, for example, back propagation, and neither supervised learning mechanism nor unsupervised one. Garcez et al. introduces the so-called back propagation to his neural net argumentation in dealing with such problems as circular arguments like one introduced in Sect. 4.3 or a situation in which we have to decide prevailing arguments in the Nixon diamond problem. In the next section, we show that we do not need any learning mechanism for dealing with only pathological arguments.

We illustrate a neural net computation that follows the above steps 1-3.

Example 1. Consider six arguments A, B, C, D, E and F in an argumentation network $\mathcal{AN}$ such that B attacks A, D attacks A, C attacks B and D, E attacks

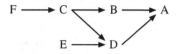

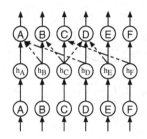

Fig. 1. Example of an argumentation network[4]

Fig. 2. Neural network translated from Fig. 1

Table 1. Outputs of the neural net computation in Fig. 2

	A	B	C	D	E	F
1st input	1	1	1	1	1	1
1st output	−1	0	0	−1	1	1
2nd output	0	0	−1	−1	1	1
3rd output	1	1	−1	−1	1	1
4th output	1	1	−1	−1	1	1

D and F attacks C (See Fig. 1.[1]) Then, we have a neural network $\mathcal{N}$ translated from $\mathcal{AN}$ by the neural argumentation algorithm in Fig. 2.[2]

For the neural net computation, we start with the input vector $[1, 1, 1, 1, 1, 1]$ (Step 1), and obtain an output vector $[-1, 0, 1, -1, 1, 1]$. We then use $[-1, 0, 1, -1, 1, 1]$ as input to obtain output $[-1, 0, -1, -1, 1, 1]$ (Step 2). Let us use $\mapsto$ to denote the above mapping from input to output vectors, so that we have: $[1, 1, 1, 1, 1, 1] \mapsto [-1, 0, 1, -1, 1, 1] \mapsto [0, 0, -1, -1, 1, 1] \mapsto [1, 1, -1, -1, 1, 1] \mapsto [1, 1, -1, -1, 1, 1]$. This computation reaches to a stable state $[1, 1, -1, -1, 1, 1]$. From the stable state $[1, 1, -1, -1, 1, 1]$, we can decide each argument's status as follows: A is prevailing, B is prevailing, C is defeated, D is defeated, E is prevailing, F is prevailing (Step 3). We give an output table of this neural net computation in Table 1. A more visual computation flow of Fig. 2 is given in Appendix A.

In Sect. 4, we introduce a new neural net argumentation with specially tailored computation, which has a special mechanism for changing the weights and the thresholds for neurons without relying upon the back propagation.

3   Can the Neural Argumentation Algorithm Deal with Self-defeating or other Pathological Arguments?

In this section, we show that the neural argumentation algorithm yields a sound computation for the self-defeating or other pathological arguments as well. In

---

[1] Each arrow in Fig. 1 represents which argument attacks which other arguments.

[2] Solid arrows represent positive weights (1) and dotted arrows represent negative weights (−1).

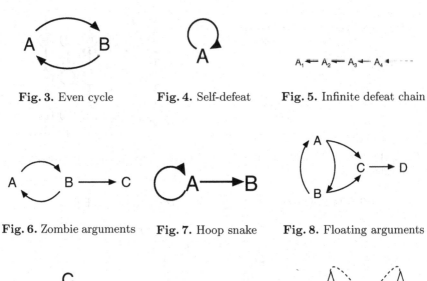

Fig. 3. Even cycle   Fig. 4. Self-defeat   Fig. 5. Infinite defeat chain

  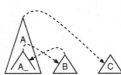 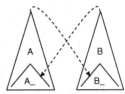

Fig. 6. Zombie arguments   Fig. 7. Hoop snake   Fig. 8. Floating arguments

Fig. 9. Odd loop   Fig. 10. Zombie arguments 2 Fig. 11. Crossover defeat

doing so, we compare our computational results with Prakken and Vreeswijk's remarks on them [6]. The pathological arguments which we deal with in this section are as follows: Even cycle, Self-defeat, Infinite defeat chain, Zombie arguments, Hoop snake,[3] Floating arguments, Odd loop, Zombie arguments 2 and Crossover defeat. Their argumentation networks are given in Fig. 3 ⋯ Fig. 11. We verify correspondences between the results of the neural net argumentation and Prakken and Vreeswijk's remarks about these pathological arguments. We take Even cycle, Self-defeat, Zombie arguments 2 as examples in the succeeding subsections, results of other pathological arguments are given in Table 5 and Table 6.

3.1 Even Cycle

Consider the arguments A and B such that A attacks B and B attacks A.[4] The argumentation network for these network is given in Fig. 3 and the neural

---

[3] "Hoop snake" is a name we gave for convenience since this pathological argument has no name in [6].

[4] Note that Prakken and Vreeswijk use the term 'defeat' instead of 'attack' in [6].

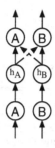

Table 2. Outputs of Fig. 12

	A	B
1st input	1	1
1st output	0	0
2nd output	0	0

Fig. 12. Neural network translated from Even cycle

network translated from it is given in Fig. 12. The values of the output neuron vectors from the neural network of Fig. 12 is tabulated every time round in Table 2.

Now, we can know that both of the two arguments A and B fail to prevail in the neural net argumentation [4] since the network converges to a stable state $[0, 0]$ as can be seen in Table 2. Prakken and Vreeswijk analyze this even cycle argument as "Both of the conflicting arguments receive the status 'not justified'." [6] Both of them can be said to be defensible if the argument status notions of 'overruled' and 'defensible' to be used at this point. Consequently, we here can see a rough coincidence of the neural argumentation results with Prakken and Vreeswijk's interpretation on Even cycle.

3.2   Self-defeat

Consider an argument A such that it attacks itself. The argumentation network for it is given in Fig. 4. The neural argumentation algorithm by A. Garcez does not permit such a reflexive attack relation in the argumentation networks.

In order to make it possible to translate the self-defeating argumentation network with the reflexive attack relation into an appropriate neural network, we slightly modify the original neural argumentation algorithm by A. Garcez. We then associate not only a positive weight arrow from a hidden neuron h_A with an output neuron A, but also another negative weight arrow from the h_A with it. The resulting neural net is shown in Fig. 13. The outputs from the neural network is tabulated in Table 3.

Now, we can know that argument A fails to prevail in the neural net argumentation since the network converges to $[0]$. Prakken and Vreeswijk analyze this as "It is hard to find generally applicable solutions to this problem." [6], and he rules out the self-defeating arguments in presenting the argumentation framework from the beginning. So we will not compare our computational result by the neural net with Prakken and Vreeswijk's remark for Self-defeating argumentation. Instead we verify that this neural argumentation brings us a good result for an pathological argument including a self-defeating argument in Table 6 (Hoop snake).

Table 3. Outputs of Fig. 4

	A
1st input	1
1st output	0
2nd output	0

Fig. 13. Argumentation network of Self-defeat

3.3 Zombie Arguments 2

Consider the arguments A_-, A, B and C such that A_- and B attack each other and A attacks C. A_- is a proper subargument of A. The argumentation network for it is given in Fig. 10. The neural net is not available from the argumentation network since the neural argumentation algorithm by A. Garcez can not deal with argumentation networks including subarguments.

In order to allow the algorithm to translate subarguments, we modify the neural argumentation algorithm as follows. If an argument A has a subargument A_- that is attacked by other arguments, we translate not only A but also A_- into the neural network as an extra neuron. And if an argument B attacks A_-, the hidden neuron h_B is connected by two negative arrows to not only output neuron A_- but also output neuron A respectively. This is due to the fact that B's attack against A_- should cause B to attack A at the same time, and prevent A from being prevailed. Thus we can translate the argumentation network including subarguments into a relevant neural network. The translated neural network in this way is given in Fig. 14. The table of outputs is Table 4.

Now, we can know that all arguments fail to prevail in the neural net argumentation since the network converges to $[0, 0, 0, 0]$. Prakken and Vreeswijk analyze it as "All arguments are defensible." [6] Consequently, we can see a coincidence of the neural argumentation results with Prakken and Vreeswijk's interpretation on Zombie arguments 2.

The results of the neural net argumentation for other pathological arguments (Infinite defeat chain, Zombie arguments, Hoop snake, Floating arguments, Odd loop are Crossover defeat) and Prakken and Vreeswijk's remarks for them are also tabulated in Table 5. The coincidences between the results and the remarks are in Table 6.

For the other kinds of pathological arguments and their solutions, readers should refer to [9]. We so far have had much concern with how and to what extent the neural argumentation algorithm can deal with self-defeating arguments and many pathological arguments that are well-known but tend to be hated or excluded very often in almost all the symbolic argumentation frameworks [6]. For those arguments, we have seen that the argument status almost coincides with

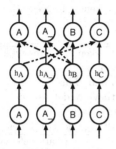

Fig. 14. Neural network translated from Zombie arguments 2

Table 4. Outputs of Fig. 10

	A	A_	B	C
1st input	1	1	1	1
1st output	0	0	0	0
2nd output	0	0	0	0

each other in both symbolic and neural argumentation. It, however, has been examined and verified based on the hypotheses that three notions for argument status by 'prevailing', 'fail to prevail' and 'defeated' by A. Garcez et al. would correspond to 'justified', 'defensible' and 'overruled' by Prakken and Vreeswijk respectively. In fact, A. Garcez et al. do not discuss such a correspondence.

In the next section, we will examine those coincidences between symbolic argumentation and neural net argumentation in a mathematical rigor. For example, we are interested in these questions: Is the notion of 'prevailing' equivalent to the notion of 'justified'? Is there an appropriate neural net that computes the original symbolic argumentation? We will address ourselves to these questions and give positive answers to them.

4 Can the Argument Status of the Neural Net Argumentation correspond to the Well-Known Status?

We begin with observing an example in which the two statuses do not coincide with each other and analyzing the reason why they don't. Then, we propose an appropriately devised neural net with specially tailored computation so that the neural network yields the same argumentation status as the original argumentation. First of all, we fix a naive definition of the well-known argument status by Prakken and Vreeswijk, which in fact is a mixture of Definition 1 and 14 in [6].

Definition 2. (**Arguments' status**[6])

1. An argument is justified iff all arguments attacking it (if any) are overruled.
2. An argument is overruled iff it is not justified, and attacked by a justified argument.
3. An argument is defensible iff it is not justified and not overruled.

A. Garcez et al., on the other hand, classified the argument status into three: prevailing, fail to prevail and defeated [4]. In the following example, we will show that Prakken and Vreeswijk's status and Garcez's one do not coincide with each other.

Table 5. Results of the neural net argumentation and Prakken and Vreeswijk's remarks for pathological arguments

Argument types	Result of the neural net argumentation	Prakken and Vreeswijk's remark
Even cycle	A and B fail to prevail.	A and B are not justified (they are defensible).
Self-defeat	A fails to prevail.	This argument is ruled out.
Infinite defeat chain	All arguments fail to prevail.	All arguments are defensible.
Zombie arguments	A, B and C fail to prevail.	A, B and C are defensible.
Hoop snake	A and B fail to prevail.	A and B are defensible.
Floating arguments	A and B fail to prevail, C is defeated and D is prevailing.	One remark is that all arguments are defensible. Another remark is that A and B are defensible, C is overruled and D is justified.
Odd loop	A, B and C fail to prevail.	A, B and C are defensible.
Zombie arguments 2	A, A_-, B and C fail to prevail.	A, A_-, B and C are defensible.
Crossover defeat	A, A_-, B and B_- fail to prevail.	One remark is that all arguments are defensible. Another remark is that one in which only A_- and A are justified, or one in which only B_- and B are justified.

Example 2. Consider the six arguments A, B, C_1, C_2, D_1 and D_2 such that B, C_1 and C_2 attack A, D_1 attacks C_1, D_2 attacks C_2 (See Fig. 15). In this argumentation network, A is directly attacked by B, and indirectly supported by D_1 and D_2, via C_1 and C_2 respectively.[5] The neural network translated from the argumentation network is Fig. 16. The input-output table of the neural network of Fig. 16 in each time round is Table 7.

The table shows that the arguments A, B, D_1 and D_2 are prevailing, C_1 and C_2 are defeated in the neural net argumentation since the network converges to $[1, 1, -1, -1, 1, 1]$.

Let us consider these arguments' status according to Definition 2. The arguments B, D_1 and D_2 are justified since they are unattacked arguments. The arguments A, C_1 and C_2 are overruled since they are attacked by the justified argument B, D_1 and D_1 respectively. Thus, the status 'prevailing' and 'justified' do not agree with each other with respect to the argument A in this example. This is because an argument can be prevailing even if it is attacked by prevailing arguments in the neural net argumentation, whereas an argument can not be justified if it is attacked by justified arguments (Definition 2). Additionally, in the neural net argumentation, an argument can be prevailing in the situation

---

[5] If argument A is attacked by argument B and B is attacked by argument C, we say that C indirectly supports A.

Table 6. Correspondences between the results of the neural net argumentation and Prakken and Vreeswijk's remarks

Argument types	Coincident?
Even cycle	Yes
Self-defeat	N/A
Infinite defeat chain	Yes
Zombie arguments	Yes
Hoop snake	Yes
Floating arguments	Prakken and Vreeswijk have two interpretations. Neural net argumentation coincides with one of them.
Odd loop	Yes
Zombie arguments 2	Yes
Crossover defeat	Prakken and Vreeswijk have two interpretations. Neural net argumentation coincides with one of them.

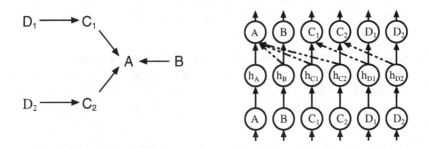

Fig. 15. An argumentation network   **Fig. 16.** The neural network for Fig. 15

in which it is indirectly supported by arguments whose number is more than or equal to the number of arguments directly attacking it, even if it is attacked by prevailing arguments. In Fig. 15, A has one argument which directly attacks it and two arguments which indirectly support A. Thus, A is entitled to be given the status 'prevailing' in the neural argumentation.

4.1   A Neural Net Computation that Yields the Same Argumentation Status

We tailor the neural net computation towards removing the difference of argumentation status, so that it yields the same argumentation status as Definition 2. The translation algorithm is the same as that of [4]. For the new neural net computation, we first prepare notational conventions. In what follows, $\mathcal{AN}$ denotes an argumentation network, and $\mathcal{N}$ a neural network translated from $\mathcal{AN}$ by the neural argumentation algorithm.

Definition 3. (Time round) *In the neural argumentation with a neural network $\mathcal{N}$, the passage of time till the output vector are read off at the output*

Table 7. The input-output table of the neural network of Fig. 16

	A	B	C_1	C_2	D_1	D_2
1st input	1	1	1	1	1	1
1st output	−1	1	0	0	1	1
2nd output	−1	1	−1	−1	1	1
3rd output	0	1	−1	−1	1	1
4nd output	1	1	−1	−1	1	1
5nd output	1	1	−1	−1	1	1

neurons since the input neurons are given an input vector is called time round, symbolically denoted by τ. It has 0 as an initial value, and is incremented by 1 every time an input vector is repeatedly given to $\mathcal{N}$.

So for example, we give the first input vector to $\mathcal{N}$ and read off the first output vector at $\tau = 0$, give the second input vector and get the second output vector at $\tau = 1$, and so on.

Definition 4 (Justified, overruled and undecided neuron)
Let A_i, A_h and A_o be an input neuron, a hidden neuron and an output neuron in $\mathcal{AN}$ which are translated from an argument A in $\mathcal{AN}$ respectively. The neurons in $\mathcal{N}$ are classified into three categories: justified, overruled and undecided as follows:

1. *Given an input vector at $\tau = 0$, let every neuron be 'undecided neuron' (the initial classification of every neuron is an undecided neuron).*
2. *If A_o outputs 1 at even τ, let the three neurons A_i, A_h and A_o be 'justified neurons'.*
3. *If A_o outputs −1 at odd τ, let the three neurons A_i, A_h and A_o be 'overruled neurons'.*

In the Garcez's computation, the output vector is repeatedly given as the next input vector. But, the way of giving input vectors is defined in a different way as follows:

Definition 5 (Input vector in the neural net computation)
The inputs to $\mathcal{N}$ are given for all input neurons every time round as follows:

1. *At $\tau = 0$, 1 is input to every input neuron in $\mathcal{N}$.*
2. *For $\tau \geq 1$,*
   (a) *1 is given to every justified neuron in the input layer of $\mathcal{N}$*
   (b) *−1 is given to every overruled neuron in the input layer of $\mathcal{N}$*
   (c) *0 is given to every undecided neuron in the input layer of $\mathcal{N}$.*

Taking Definition 2 into account, to let an argument which is attacked by only overruled arguments in $\mathcal{AN}$ be a justified neuron in $\mathcal{N}$, we introduce the following Definitions 6 and 7 with the special conditions for changing weights and thresholds during the neural net computation. They play an important role in tailoring the neural net computation that was originally specified in the subsection 2.3 so as to reflect Definition 2. It should be noted that in the Garcez's neural computation in $\mathcal{N}$, the weight and the threshold of each neuron is not changed during the computation, but it is changed only when the learning rule is applied to $\mathcal{N}$ [4].

Definition 6 (Condition for changing thresholds)
Let A_i, A_h and A_o be as in Definition 4. Let the number of the negative weight connections from any hidden neurons to A_o be n, and the threshold of A_o be θ. If A_i, A_h and A_o is undecided neuron, the threshold of A_o is changed to $\theta = n - 1$ only when $\tau \geq 2$ and τ is even.

This definition allows an argument attacked by the overruled neurons in the output layer to be active at even τ. At $\tau = 0$, and when τ is odd, the threshold of every neuron is set to zero.

To let an argument attacked by the justified arguments in $\mathcal{AN}$ be an overruled neuron in $\mathcal{N}$, we introduce the condition for changing weights as follows.

Definition 7 (Condition for changing weights)
If the hidden neuron A_h for a neuron A in $\mathcal{N}$ is a justified neuron, then the negative weights on the connections from A_h to the output neurons in $\mathcal{N}$ are set to $-\infty$.

This definition allows every output neuron which has the negative weight connections to it from justified neurons to be an overruled neuron.

In the Garcez's computation, if an output vector is identical with the corresponding input vector, then the computation is said to be in a stable state. But, here we redefine a stable state from the viewpoint of the neurons' classification in Definition 4 as follows.

Definition 8 (Stable state)
If all neurons in $\mathcal{N}$ do not change their categories of Definition 4 during any two contiguous τ, then the computation of $\mathcal{N}$ is said to be in a stable state.

In the Garcez's computation, arguments' status are to be decided from the output vector only in a stable state. But, for the argument status judgement in our neural net computation, we introduce a slightly complicated definition to provide relevant arguments' status as follows.

Definition 9 (Justified, overruled, defensible at a stable state)
When an iterative computation in $\mathcal{N}$ reaches to a stable state, the arguments' status are given to each argument as follows:

1. *If A_i, A_h and A_o are justified neurons in $\mathcal{N}$, argument A is justified in $\mathcal{N}$.*
2. *If A_i, A_h and A_o are overruled neurons in $\mathcal{N}$, argument A is overruled in $\mathcal{N}$.*
3. *If A_i, A_h and A_o are undecided neurons in $\mathcal{N}$, argument A is defensible in $\mathcal{N}$.*

4.2   An Augmented Neural Net Computation

In this subsection, we give a neural net computation that yields the same argument status as those by the argumentation network derived by Prakken and Vreeswijk's argumentation framework [6], based on the definitions prepared in the previous subsection.

Step 1: Let $\tau = 0$, the threshold of every neuron be 0, and every neuron be an undecided neuron. The initial value 1 is given to every input neuron of the neural network $\mathcal{N}$. Go to Step 2.

Step 2: Check whether τ is even or odd.
  - If a neuron A_o outputs 1 at even τ, then let A_i, A_h and A_o be justified neurons, and let every weight of the negative weight connections from these justified neurons be $-\infty$.
  - If a neuron A_o outputs -1 at odd τ, then let A_i, A_h and A_o be overruled neurons.

  Go to Step 3.

Step 3: If $\tau \neq 0$, check whether the classifications at τ and $\tau - 1$ changed or not.
  - If they changed, increment τ and go to Step 4.
  - If they do not change, go to Step 6.

  If $\tau = 0$, increment τ go to Step 6.

Step 4: Check whether τ is even or odd.
  - If τ is even, set the threshold for every undecided neuron in output layer to $\theta = n - 1$.
  - If τ is odd, set the threshold of every neuron to $\theta = 0$.

  Go to Step 5.

Step 5: Give the input vector to $\mathcal{N}$ as follows:
  - Give 1 to each justified neuron in the input layer as input
  - Give -1 to each overruled neuron in the input layer as input
  - Give 0 to each undecided neuron in the input layer as input

  Go to Step 2.

Step 6: Now that the computation of $\mathcal{N}$ is in a stable state, the arguments' status in $\mathcal{N}$ are given following Definition 9 as follows:
  - An argument A is justified in $\mathcal{N}$ if A_i, A_h and A_o is all justified neurons in $\mathcal{N}$.
  - An argument A is overruled in $\mathcal{N}$ if A_i, A_h and A_o is all overruled neurons in $\mathcal{N}$.
  - An argument A is defensible in $\mathcal{N}$ if A_i, A_h and A_o is all undecided neurons in $\mathcal{N}$.

The following theorem states that this augmented neural net computation provides a sound computation in the sense that it yields the same argument status as those by the argumentation network $\mathcal{AN}$ derived by Prakken and Vreeswijk's argumentation framework [6].

Theorem 1. (Soundness of the augmented neural net computation)
Given an argumentation network $\mathcal{AN}$ and its translated neural net $\mathcal{N}$. Then, we have,

1. *A justified argument in $\mathcal{N}$ is a justified argument in $\mathcal{AN}$.*
2. *An overruled argument in $\mathcal{N}$ is an overruled argument in $\mathcal{AN}$.*
3. *A defensible argument in $\mathcal{N}$ is a defensible argument in $\mathcal{AN}$.*

Proof. Refer to [9] for the proof.

4.3   Traced Examples

Let us consider Example 2 again, but this time following the computation steps in the previous subsection. The computation proceeds every time round as follows.

$\tau = 0$

Input: According to Step 1, set the threshold of every neuron to $\theta = 0$ and give the input vector $[1, 1, 1, 1, 1, 1]$.

Output: We get an output vector $[-1, 1, 0, 0, 1, 1]$. The neurons that output 1 are B_o, D_{1o} and D_{2o}. According to Step 2, B, D_1 and D_2 are justified neurons since τ is 0 (even). Change the weights of the connections from B_h to A_o, from D_{1h} to C_{1o} and D_{2h} to C_{2o} into $-\infty$ respectively. Other neurons that output 0 or -1 are undecided neurons, that is, their status categories don't change. According to Step 3, τ is incremented to 1 from 0.

$\tau = 1$

Input: According to Step 4, set the threshold of every undecided neuron in the output layer to $\theta = 0$ since τ is 1 (odd). According to Step 5, the input vector is $[0, 1, 0, 0, 1, 1]$.

Output: We get an output vector $[-1, 1, -1, -1, 1, 1]$. Neurons that output -1 are A, C_1 and C_2. According to Step 2, A, C_1 and C_2 are overruled neurons since τ is 1 (odd). Now, B, D_1 and D_2 are justified neurons, A, C_1 and C_2 are overruled neurons. According to Step 3, both at $\tau = 1$ and $\tau = 0$, the categories of neurons status changed. Thus τ is incremented to 2 from 1.

$\tau = 2$

Input: According to Step 4, set the threshold for every undecided neuron in the output layer to $\theta = n - 1$ since τ is 2 (even). But, the threshold of every neuron is 0 since there is no undecided neurons. And according to Step 5, the input vector is $[-1, 1, -1, -1, 1, 1]$.

Output: We get an output vector $[-1, 1, -1, -1, 1, 1]$. Neurons that output 1 are B, D_1 and D_2. According to Step 2, B, D_1 and D_2 are justified neurons. But these neurons are already justified neurons. Now, B, D_1 and D_2 are justified neurons, A, C_1 and C_2 are overruled neurons. According to Step 3, although at $\tau = 2$ the categories of neurons didn't change, but at $\tau = 1$ they changed, thus τ is incremented to 3 from 2.

Table 8. Outputs of the neural network of Fig. 16

		A	B	C_1	C_2	D_1	D_2
$\tau = 0$	input	1	1	1	1	1	1
	output	−1	1	0	0	1	1
$\tau = 1$	input	0	1	0	0	1	1
	output	−1	1	−1	−1	1	1
$\tau = 2$	input	−1	1	−1	−1	1	1
	output	−1	1	−1	−1	1	1
$\tau = 3$	input	−1	1	−1	−1	1	1
	output	−1	1	−1	−1	1	1

$\tau = 3$

Input: According to Step 4, set the threshold for every undecided neuron input layer to $\theta = 0$ since τ is 3 (odd). But, the threshold of every neuron is zero since there is no undecided arguments. And, according to Step 5, the input vector is $[-1, 1, -1, -1, 1, 1]$.

Output: We get an output vector $[-1, 1, -1, -1, 1, 1]$. Neurons that output -1 are A, C_1 and C_2. According to Step 2, A, C_1 and C_2 are overruled neurons since τ is 3 (odd). But these neurons are already overruled neurons. Now, B, D_1 and D_2 are justified neurons, A, C_1 and C_2 are overruled neurons. According to Step 3, both at $\tau = 3$ and $\tau = 2$, the categories of neurons didn't change. So, stop the computation and go to Step 6.

Stable state. In this stable state, B, D_1 and D_2 are justified neurons, A, C_1 and C_2 are overruled neurons. According to Step 6, B, D_1 and D_2 are justified arguments, A, C_1 and C_2 are overruled arguments in Fig. 15.

The table of input and output every time round is shown in Table 8. It shows that the computation results of the augmented neural network argumentation coincides with those of the argumentation network induced from Prakken and Vreeswijk's argumentation framework.

Example 3. (**A baffling argument** [4]) Consider the arguments A, B, C and D such that A attacks B and C, B attacks D, C attacks D and D attacks A. The argumentation network is given in Fig. 17. It is a baffling argumentation network brought up in [4], which leads to infinite loop in the computation as follows: $[1, 1, 1, 1] \mapsto [0, 0, 0, -1] \mapsto [1, 0, 0, -1] \mapsto [1, -1, -1, -1] \mapsto [1, -1, -1, 1] \mapsto [0, -1, -1, 1] \mapsto [-1, -1, -1, 1] \mapsto [-1, 0, 0, 1] \mapsto [-1, 1, 1, 1] \mapsto [-1, 1, 1, -1] \mapsto [0, 1, 1, -1] \mapsto [1, 1, 1, -1] \mapsto [1, 0, 0, -1] \mapsto \cdots \mapsto [1, 0, 0, -1] \cdots$. To untangle such an infinite loop, A. Garcez applies a learning rule of a neural network. But we do not need the learning rule to obtain a stable result if we apply to it our augmented neural net computation devised in this section. Below we list the neural network translated by the neural argumentation algorithm in Fig. 18, and the output table in Table 9. The table shows that our neural net computation can halt at time round 2 and all arguments are defensible. We believe it is comparatively a good outcome of argumentation.

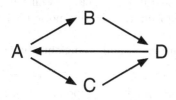

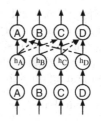

Fig. 17. A baffling argumentation network [4]

Fig. 18. The neural network translated from Fig. 17

Table 9. Outputs of the neural network of Fig. 18

		A	B	C	D
$\tau = 0$	input	1	1	1	1
	output	0	0	0	-1
$\tau = 1$	input	0	0	0	0
	output	0	0	0	0
$\tau = 2$	input	0	0	0	0
	output	0	0	0	-1

5   Concluding Remark and Future Work

The neural net argumentation has a great potential for computing argumentation from the perspective of neural network computation. In particular, it enables us to hybridize symbolic argumentation with neural net one, resolving anomalies such as self-defeating arguments and pathological arguments appearing in argumentation. The contributions of this paper are twofold. We have shown that

1. The neural argumentation algorithm can deal with self-defeating or other pathological arguments.
2. The argument status of the neural net argumentation can be corresponded to the well-known argument status under the appropriately chosen neural net.

Self-defeating arguments or pathological arguments have been ruled out from almost all argumentation frameworks developed so far. The first result guarantees that the neural net argumentation makes it possible for us to accept those kinds of arguments without causing any difficulty and problem. Therefore we could say there is no rationale for ruling them out from the standpoint of the neural net argumentation. It is also a reification of, as it were, Occam's Razor. It is not so obvious what the neural net argumentation first proposed by Garcez et al. actually computes. Our second result has made it clear by characterizing their argumentation status from the perspective of the symbolic argumentation. Overall, these results provide a significant mechanism to better integrate symbolic and neural net argumentation.

In this paper, we have obtained these results, paying much attention to Prakken and Vreeswijk's argumentation framework. This, however, is not a must.

We could apply our results to other argumentation models as well since the symbolic argumentation networks are derived from the abstract notion of attack relations among arguments.

In the succeeding paper [5], we further continue to addressing ourselves to the following remaining questions of interest:

3. Can the neural argumentation algorithm compute the fixpoint semantics for formal argumentation?
4. Can argumentative dialogues be extracted from the neural net argumentation reciprocally?

From the arrival point of the paper, we further deepen the syncretic relations of symbolic and neural net argumentation, in particular by employing our Logic of Multiple-valued Argumentation (LMA) for uncertain argumentation as a fleged value-based argumentation model [10]. We expect that other soft computing techniques such as fuzzy theory, genetic algorithm, rough set theory, etc. could have something to do with argumentation as well via considerations and results obtained in this paper. Finally, it is planned to incorporate the neural net argumentation based on the results of this paper in our symbolic argumentation system [11]. It would help to augment or enrich the dialectical proof theory of LMA.

Furthermore, we are going to explore its applicability to agent-oriented computing since neural nets and argumentation have close relationship with agents' capabilities such as environment-sensitivity and perceptibility. It is expected that the hybridization of symbolic and neural net argumentation could enhance those capabilities further in agent-oriented computing. We will deal with these issues separately in our future paper.

Acknowledgments. We are grateful to Dr. Artur d'Avila Garcez for giving us his comments on our initial results on the topics of this paper.

References

1. Chesñevar, C.I., Maguitman, G., Loui, R.P.: Logical models of argument. ACM Computing Surveys 32, 337–383 (2000)
2. Prakken, H., Sartor, G.: Argument-based extended logic programming with defeasible priorities. J. of Applied Non-Classical Logics 7(1), 25–75 (1997)
3. Fodor, J.A., Pylyshyn, Z.W.: Connectionism and cognitive architecture. A critical analysis, Cognition 28(1-2), 3–71 (1988)
4. d'Avila Garcez, A.S., Gabbay, D.M., Lamb, L.C.: Value-based argumentation frameworks as neural-symbolic learning systems. Journal of Logic and Computation 15(6), 1041–1058 (2005)
5. Makiguchi, W., Sawamura, H.: A Hybrid Argumentation of Symbolic and Neural Net Argumentation (Part II). In: Proc. of Fourth International Workshop on Argumentation in Multi-Agent Systems, pp. 104–121 (2007)
6. Prakken, H., Vreeswijk, G.: Logics for defeasible argumentation. In: Gabbay, D., Guenthner, F. (eds.) Handbook of Philosophical Logic, vol. 4, pp. 219–318. Kluwer Academic, Dordrecht (2002)

7. Bench-Capon, T.J.M.: Persuasion in practical argument using value-based argumentation frameworks. Journal of Logic and Computation 13(3), 429–448 (2003)
8. Dung, P.M.: On the acceptability of arguments and its fundamental role in nonmonotonic reasoning, logic programming and n-person games. Artificial Intelligence 77(2), 321–358 (1995)
9. Makiguchi, W.: A hybrid argumentation of symbolic and neural net argumentation. In: Graduation Thesis for Bachelor's degree (in Japanese, 2007), http://www.cs.ie.niigata-u.ac.jp/~makiguti/HA_gt.pdf
10. Takahashi, T., Sawamura, H.: A logic of multiple-valued argumentation. In: Proceedings of the third international joint conference on Autonomous Agents and Multi Agent Systems (AAMAS 2004), pp. 800–807. ACM, New York (2004)
11. Isogai, T., Fukumoto, T., Sawamura, H.: An integrated argumentation environment for arguing agents. In: 2006 IEEE / WIC / ACM International Conference on Web Intelligence(WI 2006), pp. 1077–1078. IEEE Computer Society Press, Los Alamitos (2006)

A   An Untangled Computation Flow of Fig. 2

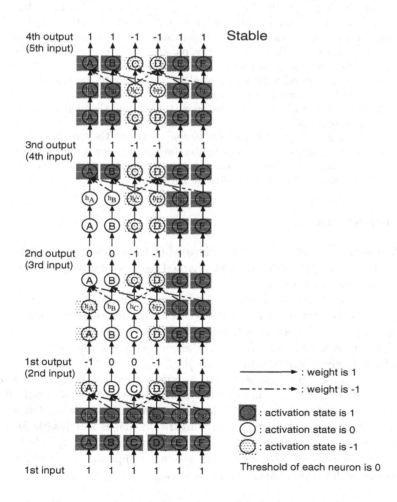

A Hybrid Argumentation of Symbolic and Neural Net Argumentation (Part II)

Wataru Makiguchi[1] and Hajime Sawamura[2]

[1] Graduate School of Science and Technology, Niigata University
8050, 2-cho, Ikarashi, Niigata, 950-2181 Japan
makiguti@cs.ie.niigata-u.ac.jp
[2] Institute of Natural Science and Technology
Academic Assembly, Niigata University
8050 2-cho Ikarashi, Niigata, 950-2181 Japan
sawamura@ie.niigata-u.ac.jp

Abstract. A novel approach to argumentation has been started by A. Garcez et al. Inspired by their work, we further go on investigating it, but turn to a more syncretic direction such as the interplay between neural net argumentation and symbolic argumentation. This paper is a sequel to our former one (Part I) [1]. In this paper we address ourselves to the following basic questions that can not be overlooked.

1. Can the neural argumentation algorithm compute the fixpoint semantics for formal argumentation?
2. Can argumentative dialogues be extracted from the neural net argumentation?

Consequently, we give the positive answers to them. They are beneficial for understanding or characterizing the computation power and outcome of the neural net argumentation from the perspective of the symbolic argumentation. We also exemplify these results.

1 Introduction

Much attention and effort have been devoted to the symbolic argumentation so far [2] [3], and its application to agent-oriented computing in which societal view on computation is emphasized.

On the other hand, it is a long time since connectionism appeared as an alternative movement in cognitive science or computing science which hopes to explain human intelligence or soft information processing. It has been a matter of hot debate how and to what extent the connectionism paradigm constitutes a challenge to classicism or symbolic AI [4].

Recently, quite a novel approach to argumentation has been started by A. Garcez et al., aiming to provide a model in which the learning of arguments can be combined with reasoning capabilities within the same framework. On account, they presented a neural argumentation algorithm that is responsible for translating argumentation networks into standard neural networks, and showed that the translated neural network executes a sound computation of the prevailing arguments in the original argumentation network [5].

I. Rahwan, S. Parsons, and C. Reed (Eds.): ArgMAS 2007, LNAI 4946, pp. 216–233, 2008.

Inspired by their work, we further go on investigating it, but turn to a more syncretic direction such as the interplay between neural net argumentation and symbolic argumentation. More specifically, in this paper we address ourselves to the latter two questions of the following basic ones that can not be overlooked. For the former two, we dealt with them in the paper (Part I) [1].

1. *Can the neural argumentation algorithm deal with self-defeating or other pathological arguments?*
   A. Garcez et al. dissolve such an anomaly as circular arguments (odd circle) through the use of neural network argumentation. We are further concerned with self-defeating arguments and other pathological arguments that are stated in the paper "Logics for defeasible argumentation" by Prakken and Vreeswijk [6], and show that their neural argumentation network yields a sound computation for them as well although self-defeating arguments tend to be ruled out in presenting the argumentation frameworks. Of course, self-defeating arguments and pathological arguments are not entitled to rebutting others in our daily life. However, we think we do not need to exclude them from the definition of the underlying argumentation framework (in fact, A. Garcez et al. employ Bench-Capon's value-based argumentation framework [7]).

2. *Can the argument status of the neural net argumentation correspond to the well-known status?*
   A. Garcez et al. classified the argument status into three: prevailing, fail to prevail and defeated. But it is not clear how they correspond to those of other symbolic argumentation frameworks. Having in mind the well-known argumentation framework by Prakken and Vreeswijk[6], we give an appropriately devised neural net with specially tailored computation so that the neural network yields the same argumentation status as the original argumentation. That is, we show that the notions of prevailing, fail to prevail and defeated correspond to the notions of justified, overruled and defensible respectively.

3. *Can the neural net argumentation compute the fixpoint semantics for argumentation?*
   The fixpoint semantics for formal argumentation frameworks is now standard since the influential work on argumentation by Dung [8]. We are concerned with what kind of neural net argumentation and how it can compute the fixpoint semantics. For this we give a correspondence theorem and its inductive proof under an appropriately devised neural net with specially tailored computation.

4. *Can argumentative dialogues be extracted from the neural net argumentation ?*
   Here we are interested in returning to symbolic dialogues from the neural net computing. We illustrate a method of transforming neural net computations into symbolic dialogue processes. The symbolic presentation of arguments would be much better for us since it makes the neural net argumentation process verbally understandable.

We think the solutions to them would be helpful for us to understand and further promote the syncretic approach of symbolism and connectionism in the field of computational argumentation. In this paper, we are mainly concerned only with analyzing and characterizing the relationship between symbolic and neural net argumentation. In the next section, we present some preliminaries for the neural net argumentation by A. Garcez et al. Then the remaining part of the paper will be spent on describing in detail the latter two questions described above and their solutions, giving one section to each of them. This paper does not have a section for related work since there is no directly related work on our topics and purposes except the work of Garcez et al. as far as we know. The final section summarizes contributions of this paper, and discusses some future works on another intriguing interplay of symbolism and connectionism in the field of computational argumentation.

2   Preliminaries to Neural Net Argumentation

In this section, we describe some preliminaries to the neural net argumentation that originated from the work by A. S. D. Garcez at al [5].

2.1   Argumentation Network

We start by introducing a definition of argumentation network, following Dung's argumentation framework[8].

Definition 1 (Argumentation network)
An argumentation network has the form $\mathcal{AN} =< \alpha, attack >$, where α is a set of arguments, and attack $\subseteq \alpha^2$ is a relation indicating which arguments attack which other arguments.

2.2   Neural Argumentation Algorithm

We assume readers are familiar with basic notions of neural network. The neural argumentation algorithm [5] is one that translates an argumentation network into a neural network. We describe its version adjusted to our purposes of this paper below.

Neural Argumentation Algorithm: For an argumentation network $\mathcal{AN}$ with arguments $\alpha_1, \alpha_2, \cdots, \alpha_n$,

1. Number each argument of $\mathcal{AN}$ from 1 to n, and create the input and output layers of a neural network $\mathcal{N}$ such that ith neuron represents the ith argument of $\mathcal{AN}$.
2. For each argument α_l of $\mathcal{AN}$ $(1 \leq l \leq n)$:
   (a) add neuron N_l to the hidden layer of $\mathcal{N}$;
   (b) connect neuron α_l in the input layer of $\mathcal{N}$ to hidden neuron N_l and set the connection weight to $W = 1$;

(c) connect hidden neuron N_l to neuron α_l in the output layer of $\mathcal{N}$ and set the connection weight to $W = 1$.

3. For each $(\alpha_i, \alpha_j) \in attack$:
   (a) connect hidden neuron N_l to output neuron α_j;
   (b) set the connection weight to $W' = -1$
4. Set the threshold of each neuron in $\mathcal{N}$ to 0.
5. Set $g(x) = x$ as the activation function of the neurons in the input layer of $\mathcal{N}$.
6. Set $h(x) = 1$ if $x \geq 1$, $h(x) = -1$ if $x \leq -1$, and $h(x) = x$ for $-1 < x < 1$ as the activation function of the neurons in hidden and output layers of $\mathcal{N}$.

2.3   Neural Net Computation

The neural network obtained by the neural net algorithm in the previous subsection is a very simple recurrent neural network in which recurrence occurs only in the connections from output neurons to input neurons. In this subsection, we specify how and what the neural net argumentation under such a neural network computes.

One of the three argument's statuses (prevailing, failure to prevail, defeated) is given to an argument by the following neural net computation in $\mathcal{N}$.

Step 1. Give 1 to every input neuron of $\mathcal{N}$, go to Step 2.
Step 2. Obtaining an output vector:
   (a) if the output vector is the same as the input vector, go to Step 3.
   (b) if the output vector is different from the input vector, provide the output vector as a new input to $\mathcal{N}$ and repeat Step 2 again.
Step 3. For each neuron:
   (a) if neuron α_l outputs 1 in Step 2 (a), let argument α_l be prevailing.
   (b) if neuron α_l outputs 0 in Step 2 (a), let argument α_l be failure to prevail.
   (c) if neuron α_l outputs -1 in Step 2 (a), let argument α_l be defeated.

We illustrate a neural net computation that follows the above steps 1-3.

Example 1. Consider six arguments A, B, C, D, E and F in an argumentation network $\mathcal{AN}$ such that B attacks A, D attacks A, C attacks B and D, E attacks D and F attacks C. (See Fig. 1.[1]) Then, we have a neural network $\mathcal{N}$ translated from $\mathcal{AN}$ by the neural argumentation algorithm in Fig. 2.[2]

For the neural net computation, we start with the input vector $[1,1,1,1,1,1]$ (Step 1), and obtain an output vector $[-1,0,1,-1,1,1]$. We then use $[-1,0,1,-1,1,1]$ as input to obtain output $[-1,0,-1,-1,1,1]$(Step 2). Let us use $\mapsto$ to denote the above mapping from input to output vectors, so that we have: $[1,1,1,1,1,1] \mapsto [-1,0,1,-1,1,1] \mapsto [0,0,-1,-1,1,1] \mapsto [1,1,-1,-1,1,1] \mapsto [1,1,-1,-1,1,1]$. This computation reaches to a stable state $[1,1,-1,-1,1,1]$.

---

[1] Each arrow in Fig. 1 represents which argument attacks which other arguments.
[2] Solid arrows represent positive weights (1) and dotted arrows represent negative weights (-1).

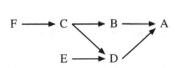

Fig. 1. Example of an argumentation network[5]

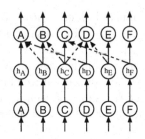

Fig. 2. Neural network translated from Fig. 1

Table 1. Outputs of the neural net computation in Fig. 2

	A	B	C	D	E	F
1st input	1	1	1	1	1	1
1st output	−1	0	0	−1	1	1
2nd output	0	0	−1	−1	1	1
3rd output	1	1	−1	−1	1	1
4th output	1	1	−1	−1	1	1

From the stable state $[1, 1, −1, −1, 1, 1]$, we can decide each argument's status as follows: A is prevailing, B is prevailing, C is defeated, D is defeated, E is prevailing, F is prevailing (Step 3). We give an output table of this neural net computation in Table 1.

The neural net computation does not contain any learning mechanism in it and hence is a primitive one that has no mechanism for adaptation of weights based on, for example, back propagation, and neither supervised learning mechanism nor unsupervised one. Garcez et al. introduce the so-called back propagation to his neural net argumentation in dealing with such problems as semantic circular arguments. In the next section, we provide a neural net with specially tailored computation so that it can compute the fixpoint semantics for argumentation. It has a special mechanism for changing the thresholds for neurons without relying upon the back propagation.

3   Can the Neural Argumentation compute the Fixpoint Semantics for Argumentation?

Arguably, the fixpoint semantics for argumentation (specified in [8][3]) is one of the most influential approaches to argumentation semantics for formal argumentation frameworks. We are concerned with the use of neural net argumentation that coincides with the fixpoint semantics, more specifically a question of how the neural net argumentation can compute the fixpoint semantics.

In this section, we employ the definition of the arguments' status discussed by Prakken and Vreeswijk[6], and give a main theorem that guarantees the coincidence of the neural net argumentation with the fixpoint of symbolic argumentation under Prakken and Vreeswijk's definition. For this aim, we introduce a neural net with specially tailored computation. First of all, we outline the fixpoint semantics for argumentation in the next section.

3.1   The Fixpoint Semantics for Argumentation

The core of the fixed point semantics for argumentation by Dung is undoubtedly the notion of acceptability.

Definition 2 (Acceptability of arguments[8])
An argument A is acceptable with respect to a set S of arguments iff each argument attacking A is attacked by an argument in S.

Definition 3 (Operator F [6])
Let Args be a set of arguments ordered by a binary relation of attack, and let $S \subseteq Args$. Then the operator F is defined as follow:

- *$F(S) = \{A \in Args \mid A$ is acceptable with respect to $S\}$*

It is well known that the operator has a least fixed point since F is monotonic.

Definition 4 (Argument status: justified, overruled, and defensible [6])
Let A be an argument.

- *A is justified with respect to Args iff A is a member of the least fixed point of F.*
- *A is overruled with respect to Args iff A is not justified and attacked by justified arguments.*
- *A is defensible with respect to Args iff A is not justified and not overruled.*

Proposition 1. [6] *Consider the following sequence of arguments.*

- *$F^0 = \emptyset$*
- *$F^{i+1} = \{A \in Args \mid A$ is acceptable with respect to $F^i\}$*

The following observations hold [8].

1. *All arguments in $\cup_{i=0}^{\infty}(F^i)$ are justified.*
2. *If each argument is attacked by at most a finite number of arguments, then an argument is justified iff it is in $\cup_{i=0}^{\infty}(F^i)$.*

3.2   Definitions for Tailoring the Neural Net Computation to the Fixpoint Semantics

We tailor the neural net computation so as to be able to compute the fixpoint semantics. For this, we introduce definitions for the new computation in this subsection. The translation algorithm is the same as that of [5]. In what follows, $\mathcal{AN}$ denotes an argumentation network, and $\mathcal{N}$ a neural network translated from $\mathcal{AN}$ by the neural argumentation algorithm.

Definition 5 (Time round)
In the neural argumentation with a neural network $\mathcal{N}$, the passage of time till the output vector is read off at the output neurons since the input neurons are given an input vector is called time round, symbolically denoted by τ. It has 0 as an initial value, and is incremented by 1 every time an input vector is repeatedly given to $\mathcal{N}$.

So for example, we give the first input vector to $\mathcal{N}$ and read off the first output vector at $\tau = 0$, give the second input vector and get the second output vector at $\tau = 1$, and so on.

Definition 6 (Acceptable, strictly defeated and undecided neuron)
Let A_i, A_h and A_o be an input neuron, a hidden neuron and an output neuron in $\mathcal{AN}$ which are translated from an argument A in $\mathcal{AN}$ respectively. The neurons in $\mathcal{N}$ are classified into three categories: acceptable, strictly defeated and undecided as follows:

1. *Given an input vector at $\tau = 0$, let every neuron be 'undecided neuron' (the initial classification of every neuron is undecided neuron).*
2. *If A_o outputs 1 at even τ, let the three neurons A_i, A_h and A_o be 'acceptable neuron'.*
3. *If A_o outputs -1 at odd τ, let the three neurons A_i, A_h and A_o be 'strictly defeated neuron'.*

When we start the computation, all neurons are undecided neurons. At even τ, we decide which neurons are acceptable neurons. And at odd τ, we decide which neurons are strictly defeated neurons.

In the Garcez's computation, the output vector is repeatedly given as the next input vector. But, the way of giving input vectors is defined in a different way for our purpose as follows:

Definition 7 (Input vector in the neural net computation)
The inputs to $\mathcal{N}$ are given for all input neurons every time round as follows:

1. *At $\tau = 0$, the value 1 is input to every input neuron in $\mathcal{N}$.*
2. *For $\tau \geq 1$,*
   (a) 1 is given to every acceptable neuron in the input layer of $\mathcal{N}$
   (b) -1 is given to every strictly defeated neuron in the input layer of $\mathcal{N}$
   (c) 0 is given to every undecided neuron in the input layer of $\mathcal{N}$.

Taking Definition 2 into account, to let an argument which is an acceptable in $\mathcal{AN}$ be an acceptable neuron in $\mathcal{N}$, we introduce the following Definition 8 with the special condition for changing thresholds during the neural net computation. It plays an important role in tailoring the neural net computation that was originally specified in the Sect. 2.3 so as to reflect Definition 2 and to relate the neural net argumentation to the fixpoint semantics. It should be noted that in the Garcezs neural computation in $\mathcal{N}$, the threshold of each neuron is not changed during the computation, but it is changed only when the learning rule is applied to $\mathcal{N}$ [5].

Definition 8 (Condition for changing thresholds)
Let A_i, A_h and A_o be as in Definition 6. Let the threshold of A_o be θ. If A_i, A_h and A_o are undecided neurons, the threshold of A_o is changed as follows:

1. *Let the number of the negative weight connections from any hidden neurons to A_o be n, and only when $\tau \geq 2$ and τ is even, the threshold of A_o is changed to $\theta = n - 1$.*
2. *Only when τ is odd, first check if either of two following conditions are satisfied on A_o or not.*
   (a) *If output neuron B_o is an undecided neuron and is given a negative weight connection by A_h, and A_o is given a negative connection by hidden neuron B_h, then B_o has no negative weight connection from other hidden neurons except A_h.*
   (b) *If output neuron B_o is an undecided neuron and is given a negative weight connection by A_h, and A_o is given a negative connection by hidden neuron B_h, then every hidden neuron which gives a negative connection to B_o except A_h is given a negative connection by only strictly defeated neurons.*
   Then, letting n be the number of the negative weight connections to A_o from B_h which does not satisfy the two conditions above, the threshold of A_o is changed to $\theta = 1 - n$.

This definition allows every output neuron A_o which is given any negative weight connections from only the strictly defeated neurons in the hidden layer to be active at even τ. And it allows every output neuron A_o which is given any negative weight connections from only the acceptable neurons except from neurons B_h which satisfies the conditions of (a) or (b) in Definition 8 to deactivate at odd τ. At $\tau = 0$, the threshold of every neuron is set to zero.

In the Garcez's computation, if an output vector is identical to the corresponding input vector, then the computation is said to be in a stable state. But, here we redefine a stable state from the viewpoint of the neurons' classification in Definition 6 as follows:

Definition 9 (Stable state)
If all neurons in $\mathcal{N}$ do not change their categories of Definition 6 during any two contiguous τ, then the computation of $\mathcal{N}$ is said to be in a stable state.

In our computation, we want to decide the argument status with acceptable neurons in $\mathcal{N}$. We introduce a special step for deciding each argument status in $\mathcal{N}$ after the stable state in following definition. In this step, we give inputs to $\mathcal{N}$ such as every acceptable neuron in output layer outputs 1, every neuron in output layer which has a negative weight connection with any acceptable neurons outputs -1 and every neuron in output layer which is neither an acceptable neuron nor a neuron which has a negative weight connection with any acceptable neurons outputs 0.

Definition 10 (Justified, overruled, defensible at a stable state)
When an iterative computation in $\mathcal{N}$ reaches to a stable state, we reset the threshold of every neuron to 0, and then, give the inputs to $\mathcal{N}$ again as follows:

- *1 is given to every acceptable neuron in the input layer of $\mathcal{N}$.*
- *0 is given to every strictly defeated neuron and every undecided one in the input layer of $\mathcal{N}$.*

From each output for this input, we define the argument status of each argument as follows:

1. *If A_o outputs 1 in $\mathcal{N}$, argument A is justified in $\mathcal{N}$.*
2. *If A_o outputs -1 in $\mathcal{N}$, argument A is overruled in $\mathcal{N}$.*
3. *If A_o outputs 0 in $\mathcal{N}$, argument A is defensible in $\mathcal{N}$.*

3.3   Yet another Augmented Neural Net Computation

In this subsection, we describe the neural net computation steps that yield the same argument status as those by the argumentation network derived by Prakken and Vreeswijk's argumentation framework[6], based on the definitions prepared in the Sect. 3.1.

Step 1: Let $\tau = 0$, the threshold of every neuron be 0, and every neuron be an undecided neuron. The initial value 1 is given to every input neuron of the neural network $\mathcal{N}$. Go to Step 2.

Step 2: Check whether τ is even or odd.
- If A_o outputs 1 at even τ, then let A_i, A_h and A_o be acceptable neurons.
- If A_o outputs -1 at odd τ, then let A_i, A_h and A_o be strictly defeated neurons.

Go to Step 3.

Step 3: If $\tau \neq 0$, check whether the classifications at τ and $\tau - 1$ changed or not.
- If they change, increment τ by 1 and go to Step 4.
- If they do not change, increment τ by 1 and go to Step 6.

If $\tau = 0$, increment τ by 1 and go to Step 6.

Step 4: Check whether τ is even or odd.
- If τ is even, set the threshold for every undecided neuron in the output layer to $\theta = n - 1$.[3]
- If τ is odd, set the threshold for every undecided neuron in the output layer to $\theta = 1 - n$.

Go to Step 5.

Step 5: Give the input vector as follows:
- Give 1 to each acceptable neuron in the input layer as input.
- Give -1 to each strictly defeated neuron in the input layer as input.
- Give 0 to each undecided neuron in the input layer as input.

Go to Step 2.

Step 6: Now that the computation of $\mathcal{N}$ is in a stable state, the arguments' status in $\mathcal{N}$ are given following Definition 10. Set the threshold for every output neuron to $\theta = 0$. The inputs are given as follows:

---

[3] n is the number defined in Definition 8.

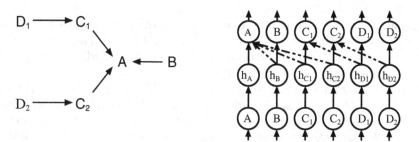

Fig. 3. An argumentation network   **Fig. 4.** The neural network for Fig. 3

- Give 1 to each acceptable neuron in the input layer as input.
- Give 0 to each strictly defeated neuron in the input and undecided neuron in input layer as input.

Then, each output neuron A_o determines its argument status in $\mathcal{N}$ as follows:

- If A_o outputs 1, an argument A is justified in $\mathcal{N}$.
- If A_o outputs -1, an argument A is overruled in $\mathcal{N}$.
- If A_o outputs 0, an argument A is defensible in $\mathcal{N}$.

3.4   A Traced Example

Let us consider an example of the argumentation network in Fig. 3 and the neural network in Fig. 4, following the computation steps in the Sect. 3.3.

$\tau = 0$

Input According to Step 1, set 0 to the threshold of every neuron, give the input vector $[1, 1, 1, 1, 1, 1]$.

Output We get an output vector $[-1, 1, 0, 0, 1, 1]$. The Neurons that output 1 are B, D_1 and D_2. According to Step 2, They are acceptable neurons since τ is zero (even). Other neurons that output 0 or -1 are undecided neurons, that is, their status categories do not change. According to Step 3, τ is incremented to 1 from 0.

$\tau = 1$

Input According to Step 4, set the threshold of every undecided neuron in the output layer to $\theta = 1 - m$ since τ is 1 (odd). That is, the threshold of A_o is -2, C_{1o} and C_{2o} are -1, D_{1o} and D_{2o} are 0. According to Step 5, the input vector is $[0, 1, 0, 0, 1, 1]$.

Output We get output vector $[1, 1, -1, -1, 1, 1]$. Neurons that output -1 are C_{1o} and C_{2o}. According to Step 2, C_1 and C_2 are strictly defeated neurons since τ is 1 (odd). Now, B, D_1 and D_2 are acceptable neurons, C_1 and C_2 are strictly defeated neurons, and A is undecided neuron. According to Step 3, both at $\tau = 1$ and $\tau = 0$, the categories of neurons changed. Thus τ is incremented to 2 from 1.

$\tau = 2$

Input   According to Step 4, set the threshold of every undecided neurons in the output layer to $\theta = n - 1$ since τ is 2 (even). Thus, the threshold of A_o is 2, and other neurons are zero. And according to Step 5, the input vector is $[0, 1, -1, -1, 1, 1]$.

Output We get an output vector $[-1, 1, -1, -1, 1, 1]$. Neurons that output 1 are B_o, D_{1o} and D_{2o}. According to Step 2, B, D_1 and D_2 are acceptable neurons. But these neurons are already acceptable neurons. Now, B, D_1 and D_2 are acceptable neurons, C_1 and C_2 are strictly defeated neurons, and A is undecided neuron. According to Step 3, although at $\tau = 2$ the categories of neurons did not change, but at $\tau = 1$ they changed, thus τ is incremented to 3 from 2.

$\tau = 3$

Input   According to Step 4, set the threshold of every undecided neuron in output layer to $\theta = 1 - m$ since τ is 3 (odd). Thus, the threshold of A_o is -2, and the other neurons are 0. And according to Step 5, the input vector is $[0, 1, -1, -1, 1, 1]$.

Output We get an output vector $[1, 1, -1, -1, 1, 1]$. Neurons that output -1 are C_{1o} and C_{2o}. According to Step 2, C_1 and C_2 are strictly defeated neurons since τ is 3 (odd). But these neurons are already strictly defeated neurons. Now, B, D_1 and D_2 are acceptable neurons, C_1 and C_2 are strictly defeated neurons, and A is undecided neuron. According to Step 3, both at $\tau = 3$ and $\tau = 2$, the categories of neurons did not change. So, τ is incremented to 4 from 3, and go to Step 6.

$\tau = 4$

Input   According to Step 6, set the threshold of every neuron $\theta = 0$. And the input vector is $[0, 1, 0, 0, 1, 1]$.

Output We get an output vector $[-1, 1, -1, -1, 1, 1]$. Neurons that output 1 are B, D_{1o} and D_{2o}. According to Step 6, argument B, argument D_1 and argument D_2 are justified in $\mathcal{N}$. Neurons that output -1 are A, C_1 and C_2. According to Step 6, argument A, argument C_1 and argument C_2 are overruled in $\mathcal{N}$. Neurons that output 0 do not exist. According to Step 6, there is no defensible argument in $\mathcal{N}$.

These steps every time round are tabulated in Table 2.

3.5   Correspondence Theorem

In this subsection, we give a correspondence theorem and its inductive proof under the neural net computation introduced in this section. We also give a soundness theorem that the neural net computation provides a sound computation in the sense that it yields the same argument status as those by an argumentation network derived by Prakken and Vreeswijk's argumentation framework with the fixed point semantics.

In what follows, the phrase "argument A in $\mathcal{N}$" represents these three: "input neuron A_i, hidden neuron A_h and output neuron A_o in $\mathcal{N}$" together, and the

Table 2. Input and output table of the neural net computation in Fig. 4

		A	B	C_1	C_2	D_1	D_2
$\tau = 0$	input	1	1	1	1	1	1
	output	−1	1	0	0	1	1
$\tau = 1$	input	0	1	0	0	1	1
	output	1	1	−1	−1	1	1
$\tau = 2$	input	0	1	−1	−1	1	1
	output	−1	1	−1	−1	1	1
$\tau = 3$	input	0	1	−1	−1	1	1
	output	1	1	−1	−1	1	1
$\tau = 4$	input	0	1	0	0	1	1
	output	−1	1	−1	−1	1	1

phrase "acceptable argument A in $\mathcal{N}$" represents these three: "acceptable neuron A_i, acceptable neuron A_h and acceptable neuron A_o in $\mathcal{N}$" together. And similarly, the phrases "strictly defeated argument A in $\mathcal{N}$" represents these three: "strictly defeated neuron A_i, strictly defeated neuron A_h and strictly defeated neuron A_o in $\mathcal{N}$" together, and the phrases "undecided argument A in $\mathcal{N}$" represents these three: "overruled neuron A_i, overruled neuron A_h and overruled neuron A_o in $\mathcal{N}$" together.

Theorem 1 (Correspondence between the computation of neural net and the fixed point semantics)

- The set of acceptable arguments in $\mathcal{N}$ is identical with the set of F^0 in Definition 3 before getting outputs from $\mathcal{N}$ at $\tau = 0$.
- The set of acceptable arguments in $\mathcal{N}$ is identical with the set of F^i in Definition 3 after getting outputs from $\mathcal{N}$ at $\tau = 2(i - 1)$ (i is integer and $i \geq 1$).

We first prepare the following lemma that is convenient to shorten the proof. In what follows, "argument X attacks argument Y in $\mathcal{N}$" denotes "hidden neuron X_h gives a negative weight connection to output neuron Y_o".

Lemma 1 (Conditions of strictly defeated arguments and acceptable arguments in $\mathcal{N}$)

- If B is an argument which attacks an acceptable argument A in $\mathcal{N}$ after getting outputs at even τ ($\tau \geq 2$), then argument B is a strictly defeated argument in $\mathcal{N}$ after getting outputs at $\tau - 1$.
- If B is an argument which attack a strictly defeated argument A in $\mathcal{N}$ after getting outputs at odd τ ($\tau \geq 1$), then argument B is an acceptable argument in $\mathcal{N}$ after getting outputs at $\tau - 1$ or $\tau + 1$.

Proof of Lemma 1. Refer [9] for the proof.

Now we are in a position to prove the main theorem. We prove it inductively as follows.

Proof (Proof of Theorem 1).

- Before getting outputs at $\tau = 0$, a set of acceptable argument in $\mathcal{N}$ is $\emptyset$ since every neuron is an undecided neuron according to Definition 6. This set coincides with a argument set of $F^0 = \emptyset$ in $\mathcal{AN}$ of Definition 3.
- Assume that argument A in $\mathcal{N}$ is an acceptable argument after getting outputs at $\tau = 0$. At $\tau = 0$, the value 1 is given to every input neuron according to Definition 7. Thus, $U_{A_o} = W + n \cdot W = 1 - n$. Hence A_o must output 1 at $\tau = 0$, $n = 0$. It means A_o has no negative weight connection from other hidden neurons, that is, argument A is an unattacked argument in $\mathcal{N}$. So, after getting outputs at $\tau = 0$, the set of acceptable argument in $\mathcal{N}$ is the set of unattacked arguments in $\mathcal{N}$. It is obvious that a set of unattacked arguments in $\mathcal{N}$ is a set of unattacked arguments in $\mathcal{AN}$. Moreover, a set of unattacked arguments in $\mathcal{AN}$ is $F^1 = F(\emptyset)$. Hence, the set of acceptable argument in $\mathcal{N}$ after getting outputs at $\tau = 0$ coincides with F^1.
- Assume that the set of acceptable arguments in $\mathcal{N}$ after getting outputs at $\tau = 2(k-1)$ (k is an integer and $k \geq 1$) As coincides with the argument set of F^k in $\mathcal{AN}$. The set of acceptable arguments after getting outputs at $\tau = 2k$ in $\mathcal{N}$ As' is the sum of the following two sets:

  - the set of acceptable arguments that are undecided arguments before getting outputs at $\tau = 2k$ in $\mathcal{N}$ As''
  - the set of acceptable arguments which have been acceptable arguments after getting outputs $\tau = 2(k-1)$ in $\mathcal{N}$, that is As

Every argument in As'' after getting outputs at $\tau = 2k$ is attacked by some argument in the strictly defeated argument set Bs after getting outputs at $\tau = 2k - 1$ according to Lemma 1. And, every argument in Bs after getting outputs at $\tau = 2k - 1$ is attacked by some argument in the acceptable argumentation set As after getting outputs at $\tau = 2(k-1)$ according to Lemma 1. Every argument in As'' after getting outputs at $\tau = 2k$ is in F^{k+1} according to Definition 2 and 3. Hence, the set of acceptable arguments in $\mathcal{N}$ after getting outputs at $\tau = 2k$ coincides with F^{k+1}. □

Theorem 2 (Soundness of the neural net computation augmented for the fixpoint semantics).
Let $\mathcal{N}$ be the the neural net with the neural net computation augmented for the fixpoint semantics, and the argument status in $\mathcal{AN}$ be the one defined in Definition 4. Then, we have

- *A justified argument in $\mathcal{N}$ is a justified argument in $\mathcal{AN}$.*
- *An overruled argument in $\mathcal{N}$ is an overruled argument in $\mathcal{AN}$.*
- *A defensible argument in $\mathcal{N}$ is a defensible argument in $\mathcal{AN}$.*

Proof

- Assume argument A is a justified argument in $\mathcal{N}$. Then the output neuron A_o must output 1 in a stable state of $\mathcal{N}$ on the condition of Definition 10. Since

$U_{A_o} = 1 \cdot W + x \cdot W' = 1 - x = 1$, we know that $x = 0$. So, only acceptable neurons in the output layer can output 1 on the condition of Definition 10 and the acceptable argument A in $\mathcal{N}$ is a justified argument in $\mathcal{N}$. The set of acceptable arguments in $\mathcal{N}$ of a stable state coincides with the set of acceptable arguments in $\mathcal{AN}$ according to Theorem 1. Every acceptable argument in $\mathcal{AN}$ is a justified argument in $\mathcal{AN}$ according to Definition 3 and Definition 4. Consequently, a justified argument in $\mathcal{N}$ is a justified argument in $\mathcal{AN}$.

- Assume argument A is an overruled argument in $\mathcal{N}$. Then the output neuron A_o must output -1 in a stable state of $\mathcal{N}$ on the condition of Definition 10. $U_{A_o} = 0 \cdot W + x \cdot W' = -x \le -1$. Thus, we obtain $x \ge 1$ as a solution. It means argument A is attacked by acceptable arguments (justified arguments) in $\mathcal{N}$. It is obvious that argument A is attacked by justified arguments $\mathcal{AN}$. So, argument A is overruled in $\mathcal{AN}$ according to Definition 4. Consequently, an overruled argument in $\mathcal{N}$ is an overruled argument in $\mathcal{AN}$.

- Assume argument A is a defensible argument in $\mathcal{N}$. Then the output neuron A_o must output 0 in a stable state of $\mathcal{N}$ on the condition of Definition 10. It is obvious that argument A is not a justified argument and not an overruled argument in $\mathcal{N}$. Moreover it is obvious that argument A is also in $\mathcal{AN}$. So, argument A is defensible in $\mathcal{AN}$ according to Definition 4. Consequently, a defensible argument in $\mathcal{N}$ is an defensible argument in $\mathcal{AN}$. □

4   Can Argumentative Dialogues be Extracted from the Neural Net Argumentation?

In this section, we are interested in returning to symbolic argumentative dialogues from the neural net argumentation. The symbolic presentation of arguments would be much better for us since it makes the neural net argumentation process verbally understandable. The notorious criticism is that connectionism usually does not have explanatory reasoning capability. We would say our attempt here is one that can turn such criticism in the area of argumentative reasoning.

We already have the following theorem that suggests its possibility.

Theorem 3. *If an argument is prevailing in the neural net argumentation, then it is dialectically justified.*

Proof. This is easily observed by the two results: Theorem 2 and the completeness and soundness of Prakken and Vreeswijk's argumentation framework [3].

□

In what follows, we here give a more direct method of extracting an argumentative dialogue from the given neural net argumentation.

4.1   Extracting Dialogue Trees

Let an argumentation network be $\mathcal{AN}$. Let a neural network translated from $\mathcal{AN}$ by the neural argumentation algorithm be $\mathcal{N}$. The following extraction algorithm

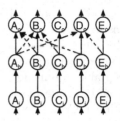

Fig. 5. An argumentation network

Fig. 6. The neural network translated from Fig. 5

add nodes and branches to a dialogue tree *d-tree*, referring to $\mathcal{N}$. Note that the initial *d-tree* is empty, i.e., it has no nodes and branches.

Step 1: Choose one output neuron A_o from $\mathcal{N}$. Then, add argument A to *d-tree* as the first proponent in a dialogue.[4] And let the 'focused neuron F_o' be the output neuron. Go to Step 2.
Step 2: Check if F_o has any negative connections from any hidden neurons or not.
  – If F_o has any negative connections, then go to Step 3.
  – If F_o has no negative connection, close the branch extension.[5]
Step 3: Let the hidden neurons giving the negative connections to F_o be X_hs. Check if every X_h is a parent node of F_o in *d-tree* or not.
  – If X_h is a parent node, change the connection $X \longrightarrow F$ to $X \longleftrightarrow F$ in *d-tree*.[6]
  – If X_h is not a parent node, add the argument X as a child of argument F to *d-tree*. Then the branch between X and F is $X \longrightarrow F$. Let the focused neuron F_o be X_o, and go Step 2.

4.2   An Illustrative Example

Example 2. As an illustrating example, let us consider the following argumentation network from which a dialogue tree is to be extracted: argument A attacks argument D and argument B, B attacks A, argument C attacks B, D attacks A, argument E attacks D. The argumentation network and neural network translated from it are depicted in Fig. 5 and Fig. 6 respectively.

We here assume that we are concerned with the argument A. Therefore, it is one that should be set to the root node of a dialogue tree to be constructed. According to Step 1, we take A_o in Fig. 6 from and add the argument A to *d-tree* as the root node (Fig. 7). Set A_o to the focused neuron. According to Step 2, we check if the focused neuron A_o has any negative connections. We know

---

[4] This node is the root of *d-tree*.
[5] Then argument F is a leaf in the *d-tree*.
[6] $X \longrightarrow F$ represents there exists an arrow directing from node X to node F. $X \longleftrightarrow F$ represents there exists a bidirectional arrow between node X and node F. It, actually, is an attack relation between argument X and argument F, which is an even cycle.

that it has two connections from Bh and D_h. According to Step 3, check if each B and D is a parent node of A in *d-tree*. Since neither B nor D is a parent node, add B and D to *d-tree* as the child nodes of A as in Fig. 8. The branches for those arguments then are $B \longrightarrow A$ and $D \longrightarrow A$ respectively. Next, B_o and D_o become the focused neuron and repeat the extraction steps for them. According to Step 2, we check if the focused neuron B_o has any negative connections. We know that it has two connections from A_h and C_h. According to Step 3, check if each A and C is a parent node of B in *d-tree*. Since A is the parent node of B, change the connection $B \longrightarrow A$ to $B \longleftrightarrow A$ as in Fig. 9. Since C is not the parent node, add C to *d-tree* as the child node of B as in Fig. 10. Then C_o becomes the focused neuron and repeat the extraction steps for it. According to Step 2, we check if the focused neuron C_o has any negative connections. Since C_o has no negative connection, do nothing for this branch. According to Step 2, we check if the focused neuron D_o has any negative connections. We know that it has two connections from Ah and Eh. According to Step 3, check if each A and E is a parent node of D in *d-tree*. Since A is the parent node of D, change the connection $D \longrightarrow A$ to $D \longleftrightarrow A$ as in Fig. 11. Since E is not the parent node, add E to *d-tree* as the child nodes of D as in Fig. 12. Then E_o becomes the focused neuron and repeat the extraction steps for it. According to Step 2, we check if the focused neuron E_o has any negative connections. Since E_o has no negative connection, do nothing for this branch. At this point, we have nothing to do any more for this *d-tree*, finishing extracting a dialogue tree.

From the extracted dialogue tree, we now can see that the argument A is dialectically justified from the perspective of the dialectical proof theory [3]. Of course, we can understand why it is justified through the dialogue process more easily than through its counterpart by the neural net computation.

Theorem 4 (Correctness of the extraction algorithm)

(1) For a justified argument in $\mathcal{N}$, the algorithm outputs a dialogue tree with height odd (called a winning dialogue tree).

(2) For an overruled argument in $\mathcal{N}$, the algorithm outputs a dialogue tree in which at least one node is attacked by a justified argument.

Proof. Refer to [9] for the proof.

5   Concluding Remark and Future Work

Neural net argumentation has a great potential for computing argumentation from the perspective of neural network computation. In particular, it enables us to hybridize symbolic argumentation with neural net one. The contributions of this paper are twofold. We have shown that

1. The neural argumentation algorithm can compute the fixpoint semantics for formal argumentation.
2. Argumentative dialogues can be extracted from the neural net argumentation.

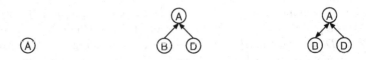

Fig. 7. Add argument A as the root node

Fig. 8. Add argument B and D as the child nodes of A

Fig. 9. Change a connection between A and B

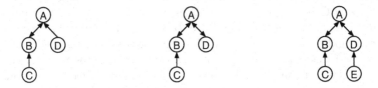

Fig. 10. Add argument C as child node of B

Fig. 11. Change a connection between A and D

Fig. 12. Add argument E as child node of D

The first result helps us understand what the neural net argumentation is doing from the semantical point of argumentation. As a matter of fact, we have been fascinated with such a beautiful correspondence between the neural net computation step and the fixpoint computation step. The significance of the second result is obvious since we wish to understand argument processes and results verbally. Overall, these results provide a significant mechanism to better integrate symbolic and neural net argumentation.

In this paper, we have obtained those results, paying much attention to Prakken and Vreeswijk's argumentation framework. This, however, is not a must. We could apply our results to other argumentation models as well since the symbolic argumentation networks are derived from the abstract notion of attack relations among arguments.

From the arrival point of the paper, we will further develop the syncretic relations of symbolic and neural net argumentation, in particular by employing our Logic of Multiple-valued Argumentation (LMA) for uncertain argumentation as a fledged value-based argumentation model [10]. We expect that other soft computing techniques such as fuzzy theory, genetic algorithm, rough set theory, etc. could have something to do with argumentation as well via considerations and results obtained in this paper. It is planned to incorporate the neural net argumentation based on the results of this paper in our symbolic argumentation system [11]. It would help to augment or enrich the dialectical proof theory of LMA.

Furthermore, we are going to explore its applicability to agent-oriented computing since neural nets and argumentation have close relationship with agents' capabilities such as environment-sensitivity and perceptibility. It is expected that the hybridization of symbolic and neural net argumentation could enhance those capabilities further in agent-oriented computing. We will deal with these issues separately in our future paper.

Acknowledgments. We are grateful to Dr. Artur d'Avila Garcez for giving us his comments on our initial results on the topics of this paper.

References

1. Makiguchi, W., Sawamura, H.: A hybrid argumentation of symbolic and neural net argumentation (part I). In: Proc. of Fourth International Workshop on Argumentation in Multi-Agent Systems, pp. 82–101 (2007)
2. Chesñevar, C.I., Maguitman, G., Loui, R.P.: Logical models of argument. ACM Computing Surveys 32, 337–383 (2000)
3. Prakken, H., Sartor, G.: Argument-based extended logic programming with defeasible priorities. J. of Applied Non-Classical Logics 7(1), 25–75 (1997)
4. Fodor, J.A., Pylyshyn, Z.W.: Connectionism and cognitive architecture. A critical analysis, Cognition 28(1-2), 3–71 (1988)
5. d'Avila Garcez, A.S., Gabbay, D.M., Lamb, L.C.: Value-based argumentation frameworks as neural-symbolic learning systems. Journal of Logic and Computation 15(6), 1041–1058 (2005)
6. Prakken, H., Vreeswijk, G.: Logics for defeasible argumentation. In: Gabbay, D., Guenthner, F. (eds.) Handbook of Philosophical Logic, vol. 4, pp. 219–318. Kluwer Academic, Dordrecht (2002)
7. Bench-Capon, T.J.M.: Persuasion in practical argument using value-based argumentation frameworks. Journal of Logic and Computation 13(3), 429–448 (2003)
8. Dung, P.M.: On the acceptability of arguments and its fundamental role in non-monotonic reasoning, logic programming and n-person games. Artificial Intelligence 77(2), 321–358 (1995)
9. Makiguchi, W.: A hybrid argumentation of symbolic and neural net argumentation. Graduation Thesis for Bachelor's degree, (in Japanese, 2007)
   http://www.cs.ie.niigata-u.ac.jp/~makiguti/HA_gt.pdf
10. Takahashi, T., Sawamura, H.: A logic of multiple-valued argumentation. In: AAMAS 2004, pp. 800–807. ACM, New York (2005)
11. Isogai, T., Fukumoto, T., Sawamura, H.: An integrated argumentation environment for arguing agents. In: 2006 IEEE / WIC / ACM International Conference on Web Intelligence(WI 2006), pp. 1077–1078. IEEE Computer Society, Los Alamitos (2006)

Author Index

Lecture Notes in Artificial Intelligence (LNAI)

Vol. 4737: B. Berendt, A. Hotho, D. Mladenic, G. Semeraro (Eds.), From Web to Social Web: Discovering and Deploying User and Content Profiles. XI, 161 pages. 2007.

Vol. 4733: R. Basili, M.T. Pazienza (Eds.), AI*IA 2007: Artificial Intelligence and Human-Oriented Computing. XVII, 858 pages. 2007.

Vol. 4724: K. Mellouli (Ed.), Symbolic and Quantitative Approaches to Reasoning with Uncertainty. XV, 914 pages. 2007.

Vol. 4722: C. Pelachaud, J.-C. Martin, E. André, G. Chollet, K. Karpouzis, D. Pelé (Eds.), Intelligent Virtual Agents. XV, 425 pages. 2007.

Vol. 4720: B. Konev, F. Wolter (Eds.), Frontiers of Combining Systems. X, 283 pages. 2007.

Vol. 4702: J.N. Kok, J. Koronacki, R. Lopez de Mantaras, S. Matwin, D. Mladenič, A. Skowron (Eds.), Knowledge Discovery in Databases: PKDD 2007. XXIV, 640 pages. 2007.

Vol. 4701: J.N. Kok, J. Koronacki, R. Lopez de Mantaras, S. Matwin, D. Mladenič, A. Skowron (Eds.), Machine Learning: ECML 2007. XXII, 809 pages. 2007.

Vol. 4696: H.-D. Burkhard, G. Lindemann, R. Verbrugge, L.Z. Varga (Eds.), Multi-Agent Systems and Applications V. XIII, 350 pages. 2007.

Vol. 4694: B. Apolloni, R.J. Howlett, L. Jain (Eds.), Knowledge-Based Intelligent Information and Engineering Systems, Part III. XXIX, 1126 pages. 2007.

Vol. 4693: B. Apolloni, R.J. Howlett, L. Jain (Eds.), Knowledge-Based Intelligent Information and Engineering Systems, Part II. XXXII, 1380 pages. 2007.

Vol. 4692: B. Apolloni, R.J. Howlett, L. Jain (Eds.), Knowledge-Based Intelligent Information and Engineering Systems, Part I. LV, 882 pages. 2007.

Vol. 4687: P. Petta, J.P. Müller, M. Klusch, M. Georgeff (Eds.), Multiagent System Technologies. X, 207 pages. 2007.

Vol. 4682: D.-S. Huang, L. Heutte, M. Loog (Eds.), Advanced Intelligent Computing Theories and Applications. XXVII, 1373 pages. 2007.

Vol. 4676: M. Klusch, K.V. Hindriks, M.P. Papazoglou, L. Sterling (Eds.), Cooperative Information Agents XI. XI, 361 pages. 2007.

Vol. 4667: J. Hertzberg, M. Beetz, R. Englert (Eds.), KI 2007: Advances in Artificial Intelligence. IX, 516 pages. 2007.

Vol. 4660: S. Džeroski, L. Todorovski (Eds.), Computational Discovery of Scientific Knowledge. X, 327 pages. 2007.

Vol. 4659: V. Mařík, V. Vyatkin, A.W. Colombo (Eds.), Holonic and Multi-Agent Systems for Manufacturing. VIII, 456 pages. 2007.

Vol. 4651: F. Azevedo, P. Barahona, F. Fages, F. Rossi (Eds.), Recent Advances in Constraints. VIII, 185 pages. 2007.

Vol. 4648: F. Almeida e Costa, L.M. Rocha, E. Costa, I. Harvey, A. Coutinho (Eds.), Advances in Artificial Life. XVIII, 1215 pages. 2007.

Vol. 4635: B. Kokinov, D.C. Richardson, T.R. Roth-Berghofer, L. Vieu (Eds.), Modeling and Using Context. XIV, 574 pages. 2007.

Vol. 4632: R. Alhajj, H. Gao, X. Li, J. Li, O.R. Zaïane (Eds.), Advanced Data Mining and Applications. XV, 634 pages. 2007.

Vol. 4629: V. Matoušek, P. Mautner (Eds.), Text, Speech and Dialogue. XVII, 663 pages. 2007.

Vol. 4626: R.O. Weber, M.M. Richter (Eds.), Case-Based Reasoning Research and Development. XIII, 534 pages. 2007.

Vol. 4617: V. Torra, Y. Narukawa, Y. Yoshida (Eds.), Modeling Decisions for Artificial Intelligence. XII, 502 pages. 2007.

Vol. 4612: I. Miguel, W. Ruml (Eds.), Abstraction, Reformulation, and Approximation. XI, 418 pages. 2007.

Vol. 4604: U. Priss, S. Polovina, R. Hill (Eds.), Conceptual Structures: Knowledge Architectures for Smart Applications. XII, 514 pages. 2007.

Vol. 4603: F. Pfenning (Ed.), Automated Deduction – CADE-21. XII, 522 pages. 2007.

Vol. 4597: P. Perner (Ed.), Advances in Data Mining. XI, 353 pages. 2007.

Vol. 4594: R. Bellazzi, A. Abu-Hanna, J. Hunter (Eds.), Artificial Intelligence in Medicine. XVI, 509 pages. 2007.

Vol. 4585: M. Kryszkiewicz, J.F. Peters, H. Rybinski, A. Skowron (Eds.), Rough Sets and Intelligent Systems Paradigms. XIX, 836 pages. 2007.

Vol. 4578: F. Masulli, S. Mitra, G. Pasi (Eds.), Applications of Fuzzy Sets Theory. XVIII, 693 pages. 2007.

Vol. 4573: M. Kauers, M. Kerber, R. Miner, W. Windsteiger (Eds.), Towards Mechanized Mathematical Assistants. XIII, 407 pages. 2007.

Vol. 4571: P. Perner (Ed.), Machine Learning and Data Mining in Pattern Recognition. XIV, 913 pages. 2007.

Vol. 4570: H.G. Okuno, M. Ali (Eds.), New Trends in Applied Artificial Intelligence. XXI, 1194 pages. 2007.

Vol. 4565: D.D. Schmorrow, L.M. Reeves (Eds.), Foundations of Augmented Cognition. XIX, 450 pages. 2007.

Vol. 4562: D. Harris (Ed.), Engineering Psychology and Cognitive Ergonomics. XXIII, 879 pages. 2007.

Vol. 4548: N. Olivetti (Ed.), Automated Reasoning with Analytic Tableaux and Related Methods. X, 245 pages. 2007.

Vol. 4539: N.H. Bshouty, C. Gentile (Eds.), Learning Theory. XII, 634 pages. 2007.

Vol. 4529: P. Melin, O. Castillo, L.T. Aguilar, J. Kacprzyk, W. Pedrycz (Eds.), Foundations of Fuzzy Logic and Soft Computing. XIX, 830 pages. 2007.

Vol. 4520: M.V. Butz, O. Sigaud, G. Pezzulo, G. Baldassarre (Eds.), Anticipatory Behavior in Adaptive Learning Systems. X, 379 pages. 2007.

Vol. 4511: C. Conati, K. McCoy, G. Paliouras (Eds.), User Modeling 2007. XVI, 487 pages. 2007.

Vol. 4509: Z. Kobti, D. Wu (Eds.), Advances in Artificial Intelligence. XII, 552 pages. 2007.

Index

Universitext

DiBenedetto, E.: Degenerate Parabolic Equations

Diener, F.; Diener, M.(Eds.): Nonstandard Analysis in Practice

Dimca, A.: Sheaves in Topology

Dimca, A.: Singularities and Topology of Hypersurfaces

DoCarmo, M. P.: Differential Forms and Applications

Duistermaat, J. J.; Kolk, J. A. C.: Lie Groups

Dumortier, F., Llibre, J., Artés, J. C.: Qualitative Theory of Planar Differential Systems

Dundas, B. I., Levine, M., Østvær, P. A., Röndigs, O., Voevodsky, V.: Motivic Homotopy Theory. Lectures at a Summer School in Nordfjordeid, Norway, August 2002

Edwards, R. E.: A Formal Background to Higher Mathematics Ia, and Ib

Edwards, R. E.: A Formal Background to Higher Mathematics IIa, and IIb

Emery, M.: Stochastic Calculus in Manifolds

Emmanouil, I.: Idempotent Matrices over Complex Group Algebras

Endler, O.: Valuation Theory

Engel, K.-J., Nagel, R.: A Short Course on Operator Semigroups

Erez, B.: Galois Modules in Arithmetic

Everest, G.; Ward, T.: Heights of Polynomials and Entropy in Algebraic Dynamics

Farenick, D. R.: Algebras of Linear Transformations

Foulds, L. R.: Graph Theory Applications

Franke, J.; Härdle, W.; Hafner, C. M.: Statistics of Financial Markets: An Introduction

Frauenthal, J. C.: Mathematical Modeling in Epidemiology

Freitag, E.; Busam, R.: Complex Analysis

Friedman, R.: Algebraic Surfaces and Holomorphic Vector Bundles

Fuks, D. B.; Rokhlin, V. A.: Beginner's Course in Topology

Fuhrmann, P. A.: A Polynomial Approach to Linear Algebra

Gallot, S.; Hulin, D.; Lafontaine, J.: Riemannian Geometry

Gardiner, C. F.: A First Course in Group Theory

Gårding, L.; Tambour, T.: Algebra for Computer Science

Gärtner B.; Matoušek J.: Understanding and Using Linear Programming

Godbillon, C.: Dynamical Systems on Surfaces

Godement, R.: Analysis I, and II

Godement, R.: Analysis II

Goldblatt, R.: Orthogonality and Spacetime Geometry

Gouvêa, F. Q.: p-Adic Numbers

Gross, M. et al.: Calabi-Yau Manifolds and Related Geometries

Gustafson, K. E.; Rao, D. K. M.: Numerical Range. The Field of Values of Linear Operators and Matrices

Gustafson, S. J.; Sigal, I. M.: Mathematical Concepts of Quantum Mechanics

Hahn, A. J.: Quadratic Algebras, Clifford Algebras, and Arithmetic Witt Groups

Hájek, P.; Havránek, T.: Mechanizing Hypothesis Formation

Heinonen, J.: Lectures on Analysis on Metric Spaces

Hlawka, E.; Schoißengeier, J.; Taschner, R.: Geometric and Analytic Number Theory

Holmgren, R. A.: A First Course in Discrete Dynamical Systems

Howe, R., Tan, E. Ch.: Non-Abelian Harmonic Analysis

Howes, N. R.: Modern Analysis and Topology

Hsieh, P.-F.; Sibuya, Y. (Eds.): Basic Theory of Ordinary Differential Equations

Humi, M., Miller, W.: Second Course in Ordinary Differential Equations for Scientists and Engineers

Hurwitz, A.; Kritikos, N.: Lectures on Number Theory

Huybrechts, D.: Complex Geometry: An Introduction

Isaev, A.: Introduction to Mathematical Methods in Bioinformatics

Istas, J.: Mathematical Modeling for the Life Sciences

Iversen, B.: Cohomology of Sheaves

Jacod, J.; Protter, P.: Probability Essentials

Jennings, G. A.: Modern Geometry with Applications

Jones, A.; Morris, S. A.; Pearson, K. R.: Abstract Algebra and Famous Inpossibilities

Jost, J.: Compact Riemann Surfaces

Jost, J.: Dynamical Systems. Examples of Complex Behaviour